INSIGHT GUIDE

SOUTHERN ITALY

Discovery CHANNEL

APA PUBLICATIONS
Part of the Langenscheidt Publishing Group

INSIGHT GUIDE

SOUTHERN ITALY

Editorial
Project Editor
Roger Williams
Managing Editor
Cathy Muscat
Editorial Director
Brian Bell

Distribution
UK & Ireland
GeoCenter International Ltd
The Viables Centre, Harrow Way
Basingstoke, Hants RG22 4BJ
Fax: (44) 1256-817988

United States
Langenscheidt Publishers, Inc.
46–35 54th Road, Maspeth, NY 11378
Fax: (1) 718 784-0640

Canada
Thomas Allen & Son Ltd
390 Steelcase Road East
Markham, Ontario L34 1G2
Fax: (1) 905 475 6747

Australia
Universal Press
1 Waterloo Road
Macquarie Park, NSW 2113
Fax: (61) 2 9888 9074

New Zealand
Hema Maps New Zealand Ltd (HNZ)
Unit D, 24 Ra ORA Drive
East Tamaki, Auckland
Fax: (64) 9 273 6479

Worldwide
**Apa Publications GmbH & Co.
Verlag KG (Singapore branch)**
38 Joo Koon Road, Singapore 628990
Tel: (65) 6865-1600. Fax: (65) 6861-6438

Printing
Insight Print Services (Pte) Ltd
38 Joo Koon Road, Singapore 628990
Tel: (65) 6865-1600. Fax: (65) 6861-6438

©2002 Apa Publications GmbH & Co.
Verlag KG (Singapore branch)
All Rights Reserved

First Edition 2001
Updated 2002

CONTACTING THE EDITORS
We would appreciate it if readers
would alert us to errors or out-
dated information by writing to:
**Insight Guides, P.O. Box 7910,
London SE1 1WE, England.
Fax: (44 20) 7403-0290.
insight@apaguide.demon.co.uk**

www.insightguides.com

ABOUT THIS BOOK

This guidebook combines the interests and enthusiasms of two of the world's best-known information providers: Insight Guides, whose titles have set the standard for visual travel guides since 1970, and Discovery Channel, the world's premier source of nonfiction television programming.

The editors of Insight Guides provide practical advice and general understanding about a destination's history, culture and people. Discovery Channel and its popular website, www.discovery.com, help millions of viewers explore their world from the comfort of their own home and also encourage them to explore it first-hand.

Insight Guide: Southern Italy is carefully structured to convey an understanding of the region and its culture as well as to guide readers through its many sights and activities:

◆ The **Features** section, indicated by a yellow bar at the top of each page, covers the history and culture of the country in a series of informative essays.

◆ The main **Places** section, indicated by a blue bar, is a complete guide to all the sights and areas worth visiting. Places of special interest are coordinated by number with the maps.

◆ The **Travel Tips** listings section, with an orange bar, provides a handy point of reference for facts on travel, hotels, shops, restaurants and more.

EXPLORE YOUR WORLD
Discovery
CHANNEL

The Volcanoes and Wild Places chapters are by **Carla Lionello**, who also wrote all but one of the mainland Places chapters. Lionello left her native Venice for Rome in 1989, where she has lived ever since, writing for guidebooks and food magazines and running culinary workshops. The chapter she missed out on was Apulia, written by **John Heseltine**, who looked at the region with a photographer's eye and contributed his pictures to the book. Insight Guides' regular writer on Italy, **Lisa Gerard-Sharp**, contributed the features on Pleasure Seekers, Movies, Music, Literature, Saints and Superstitions and the chapters on Sicily. Her help in shaping the book was invaluable.

Travel Tips are by **Jon Eldan**, who studied European history in his native California, then bought a one-way ticket to Europe in 1994, finally settling in Italy.

Many of the pictures are by American photographer **Bill Wassman**, a veteran contributor to the Insight Guide series. Other photographers whose work features include **Herb Hartmann** and **Gregory Wrona**.

Proofreading and indexing were undertaken by **Penny Phenix**.

The project editor was **Roger Williams**, who has lived and taught in Southern Italy. His novel, *Lunch With Elizabeth David*, is based on the life of Norman Douglas, the eccentric English travel writer often quoted in this book.

During the course of working on *Insight Guide: Southern Italy*, **Cathy Muscat**, the book's managing editor, made an unexpected discovery. One of her forebears had marched with Garibaldi's army, but deserted in Sicily and stowed away on ship to Malta.

The contributors

Nobody knows everything about a destination, and it is Insight Guides' policy to seek out expert writers, locally based whenever possible, who can write with wit and authority about their speciality. This book has assembled such a team.

The history and architecture chapters are by **Jonathan Keates**, whose interest in Italy has won applause, particularly for his book *Italian Journeys*. **Bruce Johnston**, award-winning Rome correspondent of London's *Daily Telegraph*, reveals the secrets of the daily life among Southern Italians, gives the inside story of the Mafia, and assesses the economics of the South. Food writer and broadcaster **Ursula Ferrigno** wrote the food chapter and wine expert **Jim Budd** wrote the chapter on wine.

Map Legend

— ·· —	International Boundary
— — —	Regional/Province Boundary
—•—	National Park/Reserve
— — —	Ferry Route
✈ ✈	Airport: International/Regional
🚌	Bus Station
❶	Tourist Information
✉	Post Office
✝ ✝	Church/Ruins
✝	Monastery
☾	Mosque
✡	Synagogue
🏰	Castle/Ruins
∴	Archaeological Site
∩	Cave
⌁	Statue/Monument
★	Place of Interest

The main places of interest in the Places section are coordinated by number with a full-colour map (e.g. ❶), and a symbol at the top of every right-hand page tells you where to find the map.

INSIGHT GUIDE
SOUTHERN ITALY

CONTENTS

Maps

Introduction

History

Features

Trulli houses in
Alberobello, Apulia

Travel Tips

Places

PASSIONS AND PALACES

The Mezzogiorno, the least known part of Italy,
combines timeless holiday favourites with a wild interior

The south of Italy is the most Latin region of Europe. This is the *Mezzogiorno*, the mid-day region, where beneath the high sun passions burn, voices rise, and the excitement of living is so uncontainable that it has to be expressed not just in words, but in gestures. Warm and extrovert, the people of the coast and cities are accustomed to tourists, as they have been accustomed to a variety of foreign rulers.

Pleasure seekers have been coming to *Campania felix*, the happy country, since the hey-days of Rome when the hedonistic highlights were, as now, to be found around the Bay of Naples and the islands of Capri, Ischia and Procida. They were only following in the steps of the Greeks who had earlier settled such communities as Sybaris in Calabria, where the behaviour of its inhabitants gave us the word "sybaritic", meaning a delight in excessive sensual pleasure.

Although this southern land has been enjoyed since the arrival of civilisation, its corners, its hill villages and off-beat towns are among the most remote in Europe. Travellers in parts of Basilicata, Apulia and Calabria today often find themselves fixed by the stares of people unused to seeing strangers. Ancient Greek still peppers dialects, an Albanian culture has survived intact after more than 400 years, and Sicily's southern flanks are tinged with Arabic. It is no surprise that in the year 2000 remote communities in Campania were selected for gene trials, for the families have lived for so long in one place that they have become a curiosity for science.

Life is not always easy. Crime is ever present, in particular in the shape of the Mafia and its sister organisations, and with it comes institutionalised corruption. Around the puffing volcanoes of Vesuvius and Etna and between seismic shudders, natural disasters are a further burden, to be heaped on the neglect and scorn frequently offered by the more prosperous north. But this harshness of life, which in the past century and a half drove many to emigrate, has kept the landscape raw and unmolested, and allowed wildlife to flourish and wolves to roam.

What keeps people healthy, however, as well as demonstrably happy, is undoubtedly a diet of fish and vegetables, pasta and olive oil, that produce such a sense of optimism and well being that wealthier nations can only struggle to emulate. The fact that the less well off have such a healthy diet is one of a number of contradictions that rule the south: friendly welcomes do not disguise endemic criminal practices; unemployment is high but signs of actual poverty are few; palatial buildings can be found in the poorest parts of towns; and the most hidebound male enclaves can vote for a woman mayor. ❑

PRECEDING PAGES: Belvedere of Infinity, Villa Cimbrone, Ravello; taking the air in Troina, Sicily's loftiest town, with Mt Etna behind; the old harbour of Lípari, Aeolian Islands; landscape in Sciacca, Sicily.
LEFT: Southern Italian woman of today.

Decisive Dates

PREHISTORY 5000–1000 BC

Earliest settlers include Samnites of Campania, Lucanians in Basilicata, Bruttians in Calabria, Darians in Apulia and Sicani and Siculi in Sicily. They trade with Minoans and Phoenicians.

ANCIENT GREECE AND ROME, TO AD 410

11th–8th centuries BC The beginnings of Magna Graecia (Great Greece). Foundation of Greek colonies in southern Italy, including the town of Parthenope, later Neapolis (Naples).

753 BC Foundation of Rome.
540 BC Pythagoras establishes philosophy school at Croton.
510 BC Croton's army, led by the legendary athlete Milo, destroys Sybaris.
6th–5th centuries BC Building of the temples at Paestum. Siracusa (Syracuse) becomes the greatest city in Europe.
326 BC Romans conquer Naples.
282 BC Pyrrhus of Epirus invades southern Italy and is defeated by Romans at Benevento in 275.
264 BC First Punic War (Rome against Carthage) begins.
216 BC Hannibal defeats Romans at Cannae.
212 BC Archimedes killed in siege of Siracusa.

c 280 BC Completion of Via Appia from Rome to Brindisi.
146 BC The Punic Wars end with destruction of Carthage by the Romans.
73 BC Revolt of Spartacus begins at Cumae.
65 BC The poet Horace born in Venosa.
43 BC Roman poet, Ovid (Publius Ovidius Naso) born at Sulmona.
26 BC Emperor Tiberius retires to Capri.
AD 79 Eruption of Vesuvius destroys Pompeii and Herculaneum.
324 Constantinople (Istanbul) founded as capital of the Roman Empire by Constantine, the first Christian Roman Emperor. Christianity becomes the dominant religion in southern Italy.
393 Roman Empire divided into Eastern (Rome) and Western (Constantinople) halves.
410 Sack of Rome by Alaric, King of the Goths, who dies two years later at Cosenza.

LONGOBARDS AND BYZANTIUM 6TH–10TH CENTURIES

535 Emperor Justinian brings all Italy within rule of Eastern Empire.
568 Longobards (Lombards), a Germanic tribe, start to overrun Italy. The *Mezzogiorno* is divided between Byzantine and Longobard rulers.
800 Pope declares Charlemagne the Holy Roman Emperor.
965 The entire island of Sicily falls under Arab domination after three centuries of attacks on coastal cities by Muslim raiders ("Saracens") from North Africa.

NORMANS 1042–1194

1042 William, son of Tancred of Hauteville (Normandy), becomes Count of Apulia.
1053 William's oldest son, Robert Guiscard, is Duke of Apulia and conquers all southern Italy.
1071 William's youngest son, Roger, takes Palermo and becomes The Great Count of Sicily.
1130 Roger II, son of Roger, is proclaimed King of Sicily after conquest of Naples and Amalfi.

HOHENSTAUFEN 1194–1268

1194 Fall of the Norman monarchy. Henry VI of Germany becomes King of Naples.
1197–1250 Emperor Frederick II, *Stupor Mundi*, brings good government and a cultural renaissance to his southern domains.

ANGEVIN DYNASTY 1266–1442

1266 After a power vacuum, Charles of Anjou becomes King of Sicily and Naples.

1268 Conradin, the rightful heir to the throne, is cruelly executed by Charles in Naples.

1309–43 Robert The Wise brings Giotto and Petrarch to Naples court.

HOUSE OF ARAGON 1282–1496

1282 Popular uprising on Easter Monday in Palermo (the Sicilian Vespers) brings Spanish House of Aragon.

1435 The Angevin kingdom of Naples passes to Alfonso of Aragon who seven years later reunites Naples and Sicily as King of Two Sicilies.

1453 Conquest of Constantinople by Turks ends Eastern Roman Empire.

1468 Albanians arrive after their country is overrun by Turks.

SPANISH VICEROYS 1503–1707

1503 Southern Italy becomes part of the Spanish Empire.

1647 Revolt of Masaniello against the Spanish government in Naples.

1669 Mount Etna erupts violently, destroying towns on the east coast.

1693 Earthquake in eastern Sicily.

HABSBURGS 1707–48

1713 Treaty of Utrecht awards the southern kingdom to Austria.

1737 Teatro San Carlo, Naples, begun.

BOURBONS 1748–1860

1748 Charles III of Bourbon is crowned King in Palermo and defeats the Austrians at Vietri.

1748 Excavations are begun at Pompeii and Herculaneum.

1759 Charles III dies and is succeeded by Ferdinand IV.

1790 Museo Nazionale in Naples founded with royal collection of pictures and antiquities.

1799 Revolution in Naples: "the Parthenopean Republic" is crushed by Lord Nelson and Cardinal Ruffo.

1805 The Neapolitan royal family flee to Sicily.

1808 Joachim Murat becomes King of Naples.

1816 Murat is shot in Calabria and Ferdinand is restored as Ferdinand I of The Two Sicilies.

PRECEDING PAGES: Neapolitan macaroni makers, 1880. **LEFT:** King Solomon in the 12th-century floor mosaic from the nave of the cathedral of Otranto, Apulia. **RIGHT:** *Vesuvius Erupting* from Sir William Hamilton's *Campi Phlegraeiae* (1779).

HOUSE OF SAVOY 1861–1944

1860 Giuseppe Garibaldi lands in Sicily with a force of 1,000, meeting up with the troops of Victor Emmanuel II of Savoy in Teano, Calabria. Francis II, grandson of Ferdinand I, is deposed. The south becomes part of the Kingdom of Italy under Victor Emmanuel II.

1870 Rome becomes the capital of Italy.

1908 Messina earthquake leaves 84,000 dead.

1915 Italy joins allies in World War I.

1922 Mussolini comes to power.

1940 Italy joins Germany in World War II.

1943 Allies land in Sicily and Salerno; Italy surrenders. Germans retreat from Naples.

THE REPUBLIC, FROM 1946

1957 Sicily granted regional autonomy. Under the Treaty of Rome Italy becomes one of the six founders of the Common Market (now the European Union).

1972 Bronze statues are discovered in the sea at Riace.

1980 Severe earthquake in Campania.

1992 Mount Etna erupts. Murder of anti-Mafia magistrate Giovanni Falcone.

1990s War in the former Yugoslavia drives Albanian refugees into Italy. Nato planes use local bases to bomb Kosovo.

2002 The Euro replaces the Lira as Italy's national currency. ❏

GREEKS AND ROMANS

The Greeks were the first to find a sybaritic lifestyle in these
fertile lands, but their prosperity soon attracted rivals

A few dolmens in Apulia are about the sum of the remnants of southern Italy's prehistoric inhabitants. When the colonising Greeks arrived, the east coast of the mainland was inhabited by Apulians and the central Apennines by Samnians. Campanians, Lucanians (in Basilicata) and Bruttians of the west coast spoke a common Oscan language. In Sicily the Elymni, Sicani and Siculi held sway.

The Greeks were the first to make a major cultural impact on the region. They had been driven westwards by a shortage of arable land and were seeking fresh markets to trade their metal goods. Soon after 750 BC, a series of settlements began to spring up along the bay of Naples, on the Calabrian coast and in the Gulf of Taranto. Neapolis, Rhegium and Siracusa expanded to become the regional capitals of Naples, Reggio Calabria and Syracuse, but there were equally important cities, such as Cumae, Sybaris and Metapontum, which would sink into insignificance or be abandoned.

Magna Graecia

The Greek colonists came from the cities in mainland Greece, Asia Minor and the islands of the Aegean, and they brought their religion, laws, ceremonies and customs. Temples, such as those at Paestum *(see page 106)*, were raised to a variety of deities. Theatres were built for the performance of tragedies by Aeschylus and Euripides, the one at Siracusa seating 15,000, and skilled painters decorated houses, tombs and public buildings with murals showing mythological scenes or glimpses of daily life.

Despite a shared cultural heritage and common language, the colonies were fiercely competitive, particularly over trade with the peoples of the north and the Carthaginians in North Africa. Their economy was based on an immensely profitable agriculture, centred on the production of wine and olive oil, and exports included earthenware, jewellery, weapons, textiles and the beautifully painted vases which characterise this Greek civilisation in the Italian south.

Later, the Romans designated this scatter of harbours and markets in Italy's heel and toe as Magna Graecia, "Great Greece", which had

become so prosperous by the 5th century BC that its cities were more affluent than their founding communities in Greece. In Calabria, Sybaris grew famously rich from fisheries, wool and livestock. Crowing cocks and noisy market traders were banned from the city limits, and the pampered citizens were known for their decadent habits of taking steam baths and dining in the company of their wives. Their skins, it was said, were so sensitive that contact with a rose petal could bring them out in blisters. The word "sybaritic" has come to mean a delight in excessive sensual pleasure.

At the same time, Syracuse (Siracusa) in Sicily became the largest city in all Europe.

LEFT: Greek warrior, found in the sea in Riace in 1973 and now in the Museo Nazionale, Reggio Calabria.
RIGHT: Tiberius, who retired to run the Roman Empire from his villa in Capri.

Wherever the Greeks travelled, they took their culture with them, and the cities of Magna Graecia nurtured rich traditions of philosophy, poetry and drama. Many distinguished writers and scientists came here as refugees from Greece. In 531 BC the mathematician, philosopher and teacher Pythagoras, from the island of Samos, arrived at Croton on the Tyrrhenian Sea, where he attracted an enthusiastic following of young disciples keen to investigate his ideas on science, music and the nature of the soul. During the 5th century the great poet Pindar, whose odes celebrated the winners of athletic championships and chariot races, visited

Carthage on the North African coast, founded by Queen Dido who led refugees here from the kingdom of the Phoenicians in present-day Lebanon. The Carthaginians established trading bases in Spain, overran western Sicily, and started to look longingly towards the Italian mainland where a new power was starting to make its influence felt.

By the middle of the 4th century BC the republican state of Rome had become feared among its immediate neighbours for its superbly trained army, a formidable fighting machine which had subdued the great strongholds of the Etruscans in the central regions of

the Calabrian town of Locri, praising it as a pioneer of good government, the first city in the Greek-speaking world, according to him, to have its own written code of laws.

How much the inhabitants of these towns appreciated beautiful things can be seen in the bronzes of Riace, found near Reggio Calabria in 1972. Superbly proportioned sculptures of bearded male nudes, they were probably the work of a talented 5th-century BC Athenian sculptor, such as Phidias or Polycleites, and may have been intended for a local temple.

Inevitably, the prosperity of Magna Graecia attracted the envy of states elsewhere in the Mediterranean. Among the most successful was

Lazio and Tuscany. When the Romans turned their attention to Magna Graecia, around 282 BC, several of its cities, led by the wealthy port of Tarentum (Taranto), turned for help to a powerful and charismatic leaders, Pyrrhus, ruler of the northern Greek kingdom of Epirus.

The original Pyrrhic victory

Brave, ambitious and skilful in battle, Pyrrhus had become a semi-mythical figure by the time the Tarentines sought his aid. A mere touch of his big toe was said to cure diseases of the spleen, while his whole body was rumoured to be untouchable by fire. He got off to a poor start, however, losing most of his expedition in a storm and arriving at Tarentum with a handful of cavalry and just two out of an original 20 elephants. The king then shocked the pleasure-loving citizens by closing all places of amusement, putting an end to drunken parties and conscripting every adult male capable of holding a sword or a spear. This businesslike approach reaped its rewards in several victories over the Roman armies, but Pyrrhus pushed his luck too far. His costly victories over the Romans brought him more losses than his enemy, which led to the

ISLAND OF PLENTY

"Sicily is the Republic's granary, the nurse at whose breast the Roman people is fed."
— CATO THE ELDER (234–149 BC)

trading power and began to cast an eye on fertile and prosperous Sicily. In 264 BC, mercenaries known as the Mamertines, who controlled the key Sicilian port of Messana (Messina), sought an alliance with Rome. This was a chance for the Romans to head off any possible Carthaginian incursion and the alliance provoked the first of the Punic Wars ("Punic" is from the Latin Punicus, meaning Phoenician or Carthaginian) which Romans won only after building a battle fleet to boost their sea power.

expression "Pyrrhic victory". In AD 275, he was defeated near Benevento, Campania, and he abandoned Magna Graecia to its new masters.

Having dealt with Pyrrhus, the Romans could concentrate on neutralising and ultimately annihilating the Carthaginians, who were by now their major commercial rivals in the western Mediterranean. Though the two peoples were nominally united by a series of friendship treaties begun in 509 BC, tension started to develop when Rome expanded as a

LEFT: painting from the Tomb of the Diver, Paestum, 475 BC. **ABOVE:** a mosaic from Pompeii showing a group of philosophers from the Athens Academy.

Defeated on the mainland and in Sicily, the Carthaginians retreated to the territories they controlled in Spain, where they determined to strike back at the Romans. Hannibal, son of vanquished general Hamilcar Barca, led Carthage into the Second Punic War (218–201 BC) His march from Spain across the Pyrenees and over the Alps into Italy with a vast army and elephants became the stuff of legend, and in 216 BC he inflicted a crushing defeat on the Roman army at Cannae, near the modern town of Canosa di Apulia. The Roman force of 100,000 was twice the size of Hannibal's, but the Carthaginians quickly routed the cavalry and then charged the infantry legions who were waiting in the rear for the signal to advance. The huge army scattered and its commander, Aemilius Paulus, was taken prisoner. Nothing now lay between Hannibal and the city of Rome, but instead of turning north towards this ultimate prize, he chose to march west into the fertile province of Campania, to take up winter quarters at Capua, near Naples. The Carthaginians were seduced by the city's opulence and good living, and the Romans were able to capture it after a prolonged siege.

Hannibal had failed to take Rome, and returned to Africa, where he was finally defeated by Publius Cornelius Scipio at the battle of Zama in 201 BC.

The Romans march in

The cities of Magna Graecia had seen Hannibal's arrival in southern Italy as their last chance to maintain independence from the Roman Empire. When Rome seized control of the region, after a third and final Punic War which resulted in Carthage's total destruction in 146 BC, the many Greek-speaking towns of Calabria, Apulia and Campania lost much of their importance. The new masters, absentee patricians, turned the countryside into ranch-style estates known as *latifundia*, run with slave labour, forcing peasants from the land and creating desolation through over-grazing. The

THE GREATEST SCIENTIST OF THE ANCIENT WORLD

The great Greek scientist Archimedes was the son of an astronomer from Syracuse (Siracusa), where he was born in 287 BC. Famously, if apocryphally, he jumped naked from a public bath and ran through the streets of the city shouting "*Eureka!*" (I've found it) after devising a way of measuring the volume of the crown of Hieron II of Syracuse, and thus determining that it was not made of real gold.

Archimedes was an intensely practical scientist and his theories and inventions are still in use today, notably the Archimedes screw, which raises underground water. He was such a master of the techniques of leverage that his maxim "Give me a place to stand and I will move the world"

became well known. Rising to a challenge and using a series of pulleys, he once apparently pulled a laden merchant ship across the sand using one hand. He was immensely useful to the king, and to Syracuse, especially in the defence of the city against the Romans, who had no doubt that they were up against a master of ingenuity.

Their siege began in 215 BC and lasted three years, largely through Archimedes' efforts. He devised catapults and cranes and huge lenses that deflected the sun and set fire to their ships. When the city succumbed, Archimedes was killed by a soldier who did not know who he was. The Romans had, understandably, wanted to take him alive.

slaves were often badly treated, and in 73 BC their discontents and those of the dispossessed small farmers found a spokesman in a former gladiator from Capua named Spartacus. Raising an army of more than 100,000, he swept north into central Italy, before turning back to devastate the southern province of Lucania (modern Basilicata).

Here he was finally defeated by Marcus Licinius Crassus, who crucified all surviving rebels, though the body of Spartacus, killed in the battle, was never found. Admired as much for his competent leadership and sense of fairness as for his personal courage, the rebel

Ancient Roman Florida, with luxury villas, seaside resorts and fashionable health spas developing both on the mainland and on the islands of Capri and Ischia. Capri was chosen by Tiberius for the site of an immense villa, where his orgies became the subject of lurid gossip among historians, while a beachside residence at Baiae near Naples was selected by the Emperor Nero as an ideal setting for the murder of his mother, the domineering Agrippina.

The south, during this early phase of empire, became a favourite haunt of Roman poets such as Virgil, Ovid and Horace, who were fond of its landscapes and keen to absorb the atmos-

leader became a symbol of proletarian revolt and the subject of one of the most successful of Hollywood's epics.

Once pacified, southern Italy became a tourist destination and an ideal spot for Roman holiday homes. The lush volcanic terrain of Campania, surrounding the ancient city of Neapolis, was particularly welcoming, and during the first century AD, in the reigns of the emperors Augustus and Tiberius, the whole area bordering the Bay of Naples became an

phere of Greek culture lingering from an earlier age. Virgil was buried at Naples in 19 BC, after dying at Brindisi of a fever caught while on a trip to Greece (though the monument traditionally shown to visitors as his tomb probably contains someone else's remains). Horace, who came from the Apulian town of Venosa, loved his native countryside and wrote affectionately of its streams, woods and mountains.

Ancient terrors

Southern Italy and its neighbouring islands of Sicily and Stromboli are the only area of the Mediterranean to contain active volcanoes, and these smoking mountains were contemplated

LEFT: Archimedes works out how to measure the gold in the king's crown (16th-century woodcut).
ABOVE: Pompeii painting, Museo Nazionale, Naples.

with awe and terror by the Greeks and Romans. Beliefs associated with them grew from ancient myths of imprisoned giants, who could raise storms and earthquakes. Among the Phlegraean Fields, a volcanic area around Puteoli (Pozzuoli), was the entrance to the Underworld, through an extinct crater named Avernus, from the Greek phrase "where no birds fly".

A real danger lay in the looming presence of Mount Vesuvius, dominating the skyline surrounding the Bay of Naples. Suspicions of a likely eruption, following an earthquake in AD 62, were discounted by the people of Pompeii, an ancient city lying in the volcano's shadow, who had spent large sums on refurbishing their temples, theatre and amphitheatre. The speed with which the disaster overtook them, on 24 August AD 79, was the result of a pyroclastic explosion, which suffocated many of those trying to escape the hail of volcanic debris and buried them under a 7-metre (23-ft) layer of ash and pumice stone. Further destruction awaited the neighbouring town of Herculaneum. It was engulfed in a torrent of boiling mud mixed with ashes and stones, which formed a hardened crust that obliterated the whole settled area even more thoroughly than at Pompeii. The ruins of both

THE DAY THE WHOLE WORLD PERISHED

A letter by Pliny the Younger (Gaius Plinius Secundus) to the historian Cornelius Tacitus recalls the catastrophic eruption of Vesuvius in AD 79. Staying with his uncle, the naturalist and scientist Pliny the Elder, he watched as a dense cloud covered the bay of Naples and the rain of ash started to fall. "Darkness came down, not the dark of a moonless night, but as though a lamp were extinguished in a shuttered room. You could hear the shrieks of women, the wailing of children and the cries of men." As the boy and his mother fled, the elder Pliny ordered a ship to be made ready and set off down the bay to try to rescue friends living closer to Vesuvius. "Ashes were already falling, followed by pumice and stones charred and cracked by the flames," wrote the young Pliny, but the rescuers came on shore and his uncle calmed everybody's fears by going to sleep in a nearby house, his snores resounding through the rattling hail of pumice.

When flames and a stink of sulphur warned of the approaching lava flow, he hurried back to the beach, but the fumes finally choked him to death. After 48 hours of total darkness, his body was recovered "looking more like somebody asleep than that of a dead man."

His young nephew recalled, "I believed the whole world was perishing with me and I along with it."

cities and their remarkable evidence of daily life and customs under the Roman Empire lay buried until excavations in the early 18th century began revealing this tragic yet always astonishing survival of an ancient civilisation at the height of its splendour *(see page 157)*.

The final break-up of the Roman Empire began after Emperor Constantine transferred the imperial capital from Rome to Byzantium in AD 330 and Germanic tribes began invading from the north. In 410 Rome was sacked by the Goths under Alaric. After a week of looting, they moved south through Campania, plundering Naples and other towns as they went.

Alaric looked forward to conquering Sicily and moving on to Africa, Rome's richest imperial province, but he died from malaria at the Calabrian town of Cosenza. At his extraordinary funeral, the Goths diverted the nearby River Busento in order to bury the king in its bed along with huge heaps of Roman treasure and art works. The river was then restored to its natural channel and the local slaves who had dug the grave were said to have been massacred to preserve its secret location.

Byzantium follows Rome

With the collapse of imperial government, stability and local law was often left to the Christian church and its embryo communities. For the next five centuries, the Italian south came under different spheres of political influence. The Eastern Roman Empire of Byzantium annexed parts of Calabria and Apulia, which were ruled by governors appointed from Constantinople. The towns of Otranto and Bari became flourishing Byzantine provincial capitals, graced with fine buildings and maintaining a vigorous trade with other Italian cities such as Pisa, Lucca and Genoa. Naples,w too, came under the Byzantine Empire and in due course was allowed to appoint its own Dux.

Northern Italy meantime fell under the control of the Germanic Longobards, who moved south and established at Benevento, Campania, an independent duchy which lasted 500 years.

LEFT: a wall painting in Pompeii from the Museo Nazionale Archeologico in Naples.
RIGHT: Islamic architecture from Palermo, Sicily.

APOPLECTIC POPE

Always hospitable, Neapolitans tolerated Muslim Saracen invaders, which so angered Pope John VIII he excommunicated the entire city.

Such conflicting influences turned the south into a racial and linguistic melting pot. Traces of Byzantine Greek can still be detected in the dialect of remote mountain villages, while blond hair, fair skin and blue eyes, in contrast to the characteristic southern swarthiness, is held to indicate descent from north European invaders.

In the early 8th century, a fresh ingredient was added to the brew when the Muslim armies which had swept into Sicily from North Africa pushed across the Straits of Messina and seized key fortresses and towns.

An Islamic culture hung on in various areas of the south until well into the 13th century. The Moorish style influenced agriculture, with the introduction of carob trees, prickly pears and citrus fruits, and brought a new sophistication to local decorative arts in ceramics and metalwork. It also profoundly affected the urban layout and lifestyle in southern towns. From a distance many still have the flat-roofed, whitewashed look of a Middle Eastern or North African *medina,* and the emphasis on cool shade among courtyards and alleyways, with houses placed close together, is a further indicator of this Saracen thread in the complex patchwork of local history. ❏

THE TWO KINGDOMS

From the arrival of the Normans to the rise of Napoleon, the crowns of
Sicily and Naples were passed among German, Spanish and French kings

During the 11th century a drastic overhaul took place of the existing structures of political power in southern Italy. A chance encounter in 1016 between a group of pilgrims to a shrine on Monte Gargano and a local Longobard warlord bent on raising a rebellion against the Byzantine imperial government, brought a band of Norman mercenaries into the south, whose military prowess made them unafraid of changing sides whenever it should suit them.

Over the next hundred years the Normans – relatives of those who conquered England in 1066 – succeeded in eliminating Byzantine rule in Apulia and Calabria as well as dislodging most, though not all, of their Islamic communities. The effect was to bind the whole area more closely to Catholic Christendom, breaking cultural and economic links with Constantinople and creating a powerful new state, which might become a useful ally or a dangerous enemy in the continuing political struggle for supremacy between the Papacy on the one hand and the Holy Roman Empire, founded by Charlemagne, king of the Francs, on the other.

A cosmopolitan court

Though the Norman kingdom eventually settled its capital in Sicily, at Palermo, the mainland provinces were of vital importance in the business of resisting the Papacy's territorial greed. Successive popes did not forget that in 1084 a mixed Norman and Saracen force had looted Rome before setting it on fire. Perhaps the most important feature of Norman rule, in terms of an enduring cultural influence on the south, was its monarchs' complete acceptance of a polyglot, multi-racial, multi-faith society. Kings such as Roger II (1130–54) reigned in the context of a court which included Muslim, Jewish and Greek Orthodox worshippers, and

the atmosphere was suitably cosmopolitan. Even the strongly Byzantine city of Bari had its character and traditions preserved rather than destroyed by the Normans.

A period of relative stability during the late 12th century was interrupted by the death in 1189 of William II, King of Sicily, and the

resulting struggle for power between his bastard cousin, Tancred of Lecce, and Henry VI, Holy Roman Emperor, who was married to William's aunt Constance. In 1194 Constance gave birth to Frederick, who became king of Sicily, and was crowned emperor as Frederick II in 1220. One of the most forceful personalities of his age, he combined the best qualities of his double inheritance, from Italianised Normans on his mother's side and German warriors on his father's. He was a poet, a scholar and a cosmopolitan in tastes and outlook, something of a Renaissance man long before the Renaissance, a shrewd diplomat and an energetic and successful leader of armies. Such a combination

LEFT: Frederick II (1194–1250) grants an Italian city a privilege, from an illuminated manuscript, *circa* 1300.
RIGHT: Roger II (1130–54) receives a petitioner in Palermo's Capella Palatina.

of qualities in a single man was calculated to alarm the rulers of neighbouring states, led by Pope Innocent III (1198–1216) who had done more than any of his predecessors to bolster the papacy's political power and influence. For most of his 30-year reign Frederick found himself in direct conflict with Innocent or his papal successor Gregory IX, and in 1241 a third pope, Innocent IV, excommunicated Frederick.

A rare benevolence

Whatever the feelings of his subjects as to the emperor's refusal to submit to papal authority, they admired him as a benevolent ruler, who brought to the Mezzogiorno one of the few periods of good government it was ever to know. In the so-called "Constitutions" he issued at Melfi in Basilicata in 1231, he made a serious attempt to codify the kingdom's laws, as well as to ensure fair and regular taxation, together with standardised weights and measures and an efficient customs service. By founding a university at Naples, Frederick aimed to develop a new class of properly trained civil servants to administer the everyday processes of government.

Unfortunately, the success of this experiment was undermined by a serious drain on Freder-

FREDERICK, THE WONDER OF THE WORLD

When not campaigning against power-hungry popes, German barons and rebellious Italian cities, or using diplomacy to reconcile crusaders and Muslims in the Middle East, Emperor Frederick II devoted himself to writing poetry and books on science and hunting.

Some of the earliest extant literature in the Italian language derives from his exotic court, peopled with Greeks, Arabs, Jews and even the occasional Englishman, surrounding him at his castles and palaces in such towns as Lucera, Trani, Foggia and Bari, or at the majestic octagonal Castel del Monte near Andria in Apulia, an image in stone of the harmony Frederick tried to bring to his empire in an age of bigotry and bloodshed. Frederick's own poems, their medieval Italian still easy to read nearly eight centuries later, used Arabic verse forms, made references to classical Greek myths and echoed the style of the aristocratic troubadours of France and Germany. Mostly about love, they were written for sheer amusement, but their elegance made them models for other poets, including Dante, who called Frederick "the father of Italian poetry". A keen bird watcher, he also wrote a definitive book on falconry.

Admired for his skills as warrior, law-maker, politician, architect, scientist and musician, the emperor was hailed as *Stupor Mundi* – "The Wonder of the World".

ick's finances as the constant military struggle with the popes continued. His sudden death in 1150 of a fever, near the Apulian town of Lucera, plunged southern Italy into confusion. While Frederick's legitimate heir Conrad succeeded as emperor, a bastard son Manfred was allotted the kingdom of Sicily and southern Italy, but when Conrad died four years later, Manfred found himself in direct conflict with the papal armies. Routing them easily enough, he concentrated on building up his power-base through alliances with different rulers.

As a rival candidate for the throne, the Pope chose Charles of Anjou, brother of the King of France, who gathered an army and advanced on the city of Benevento, where he defeated Manfred in 1266. Instead of exploiting his southern victory, however, Charles began developing a grandiose scheme for seizing the Byzantine Empire, an enterprise supported by a heavier taxation on the south than Frederick had ever imposed. The Greek emperor Michael Palaeologus, realising what was afoot, encouraged Manfred's daughter Constance and her husband the Spanish King Pedro of Aragon to seize the Sicilian throne by fair means or foul, and on Easter Monday 1282 a wholesale massacre of Charles's French troops in Palermo – the so-called Sicilian Vespers – sparked off a war which lasted 20 years. The upshot was the separation of the kingdom into two halves. While Sicily was awarded to the Aragonese, the Mezzogiorno was henceforth to be ruled by Charles's descendants, the Angevins.

SICILIAN VESPERS

The uprising supposedly began when a French captain grasped the bosom of a woman while searching the Easter procession. She fainted in the arms of her husband who cried out, "Death to the French!"

The Angevin kings

The solution may not have been perfect, but it ought at least to have guaranteed prosperity and stability to the whole war-torn region. As it happened, the Angevin kings, from their court at Naples, were keen to renew the cultural activities promoted by Emperor Frederick in the previous century, and the city attracted poets and artists from elsewhere in Italy, including Giovanni Boccaccio, author of the

Decameron, and the great Tuscan painter Giotto. The countryside, on the other hand, had suffered drastically from the effects of war, with much depopulation and a serious decline in agriculture. Areas once rich from growing wheat and barley were now turned over to pasture, and the feudal lords of the great estates into which most of the south was divided turned to plunder of herds and flocks, banditry and small-scale warfare with their neighbours in order to sustain their families and their

castles. The seeds had been planted of a social mentality which persists to this day throughout the Mezzogiorno, in which the rule of law, the sense of a common good and the idea of civic responsibility are far less important than clan loyalty, maintenance of status and a show of strength sufficient to intimidate enemies or competitors.

When the crowns of Naples and Sicily were reunited by the Aragonese monarch Alfonso the Magnanimous in 1442, he was forced to make a serious concession of rights and privileges to the feudal barons, with a consequent lightening of the tax burden on the aristocracy at the expense of the peasants. The revolts

LEFT: Frederick II and his falcon master, from his own book, *The Art of Hunting with Birds*, 1232.
RIGHT: the "Sicilian Vespers", an uprising in Palermo at Easter in 1242, divided the kingdom in two.

which followed throughout Calabria as a consequence were savagely repressed. Tightening their grip on both the countryside and the market towns of the south, the barons offered a significant threat to royal authority and in 1484 they felt sufficiently strong and united to declare open rebellion against the king.

Though they were temporarily crushed, an invasion of Italy 10 years later by King Charles VIII of France, leading a formidable army equipped with state-of-the-art weaponry, gave the signal for a further assault on the beleaguered Aragonese monarchy by its own nobles. In 1500 diplomatic attempts were made to

once more to the kingdom, known by now as "The Two Sicilies", a name it would bear until its dissolution in 1860.

A Spanish colony

To many observers it nevertheless became clear that the area was becoming little more than a colonial dependency of Spain, exploited for its agricultural produce, hardly benefiting from the wealth created by Spanish imperial expansion in South America and grossly overburdened with new taxes. Spanish culture meanwhile made a significant impact on all aspects of southern life. Naples was dominated by a Span-

divide the realm once more, this time between France and the newly united kingdom of Spain created from the marriage of Ferdinand of Aragon to Isabella of Castile.

Eventually Spain's sheer military might succeeded in clawing back Naples and southern Italy, and the coronation of Ferdinand and Isabella's son Charles V as Holy Roman Emperor in 1530 effectively sealed the Mezzogiorno's destiny for the next 200 years as a dominion of the Spanish crown. Charles was as forceful a personality on the 16th century scene as Frederick II had been in the 13th century, and what seemed at first to be a framework of good order and legality, brought peace

ish-speaking nobility and the use of the honorific "Don" as a title for men of influence quickly established itself, as did the custom of formally addressing others with the phrase "Your honour", together with verbs in the third person. This habit survives in modern Italian.

The Spanish viceroys of Naples saw it as their duty to impose the iron will of the monarch on a restless and potentially anarchic populace, yet at the same time they respected the local barons' determination to hang on to at least some of their ancient powers. The Holy Office, better known to us as the Inquisition, was never introduced into the mainland portion of the kingdom, despite its proven success as an instrument of government in Spain and Sicily. The nobles meanwhile were permitted to keep their elected assembly, which vetted the application of all fresh taxes. In an extensive rebuilding programme of cathedrals, monasteries and parish churches, the Church reaffirmed its wealth and importance, symbolised also in its considerable landholdings throughout the realm.

This combined authority of the crown, the nobility and the church fostered a smouldering resentment among ordinary citizens which

YOUR FEMALE HONOUR

Italians today address each other as "she" rather than "you", a legacy of the Spanish *merced,* a feminine word meaning honour.

conflict known as the Thirty Years' War, the need for fighting men, food to provision them and cash to pay them proved an intolerable drain on the south's resources.

Among other desperate stratagems for raising money, the viceroys resorted to selling feudal privileges and land rights, with accompanying titles of nobility, so that the Neapolitan aristocracy, its numbers already inflated, became the most numerous in any European state, the throng of princes, dukes, marquises, counts and barons running into hundreds.

grew more hostile as the Spanish monarchy entered a prolonged financial crisis towards the end of the 16th century.

Bandits and revolutionaries

Banditry now became a regular feature of southern life, sometimes involving whole villages and pitched battles. One viceroy condemned 18,000 people to death for this crime alone, while completely failing to stamp it out. As the early 1600s saw Spain and its satellites being drawn into the

LEFT: detail from the cloister of Santa Chiara, Naples.
ABOVE: the Aragonese fleet entering Naples' port in 1442, attributed to Francesco Rosselli (1445–1513).

Harassed by pressgangs and tax collectors, the people rose in revolt in the summer of 1647. Their leader was a young Neapolitan fisherman Tommaso Aniello, known as Masaniello, originally the spokesman of an infuriated crowd gathering to demonstrate against a new levy on fruit and vegetables. The rioters soon banded together under his championship, invoking the patronage of the Virgin Mary, and unrest spread quickly to other cities, fanned by foreign *agents provocateurs* and those with personal grudges against local overlords. The barons were slow to assemble an adequate counter-insurgency force, but meanwhile a group of Neapolitan nobles dispatched hired assassins to murder

Masaniello. It was more than a year before the revolt was successfully quashed. Masaniello's name by now resounded throughout Europe as a popular hero, and in later ages he became the subject of novels, operas and feature films.

Bourbon grandeur

The Treaty of Utrecht in 1714, ending the War of the Spanish Succession, awarded the Kingdom of the Two Sicilies to Austria, but in 1734 the state once more achieved full independence, with Charles of Bourbon, Duke of Parma, becoming the first king of its new ruling dynasty. Wealthy and ambitious, Charles, as

befitted a descendant of France's Sun King Louis XIV, had an exalted idea of his family's importance and laboured to create a suitably grandiose context at Naples for a Bourbon monarch and his court, building vast new palaces at Caserta and Capodimonte.

All the 18th century's enlightened despots were concerned to establish a reputation as reformers, and the king quickly gathered around him a series of capable administrators, devoted to overhauling the antiquated, inefficient and corrupt machinery of government inherited from the Spanish viceroys. Charles's reforms, spearheaded by zealous ministers such as Bernardo Tanucci, struck first at the power and wealth of the Church, and then attempted to remove several of the more offensive feudal privileges of the barons. Perhaps inevitably, such efforts at limiting aristocratic power had less success, and under Charles's son Ferdinand the whole impetus of reform ground to a halt.

Naples nevertheless became a lively and exciting city during the second half of the 18th century. Its intellectual life, more or less dead since the arrival of the Spaniards, revived as a result of greater press freedom, less interference by the Church and improved communications with other European cities.

Always fond of music, the Neapolitans had enthusiastically welcomed opera from Venice and Rome, and they now began developing their own special variety, a type of operatic comedy which introduced local dialect and familiar figures from everyday life. A whole group of talented southern composers concentrated on expanding the possibilities of this form, known to musicians as "*opera buffa*".

HORATIO NELSON, THE DEMON LOVER

It was on a visit to Naples in 1798, after defeating Napoleon's fleet at the battle of the Nile, that Nelson met and fell in love with the bewitching Emma Hamilton.

Her husband, Sir William, the English ambassador to Ferdinand I, was a wealthy connoisseur, internationally famous as an expert on Greek vases and as an enthusiastic amateur geologist. Emma was a Cheshire blacksmith's daughter, who had worked in a London brothel called The Temple of Health. She had been his nephew's mistress, and they married in 1791 when Sir William was 60 and she was 26. At Naples she gained favour with Queen Maria Carolina and was admired by foreign visitors for her "Attitudes", classi-

cal poses imitating Greek vase painting, in which she appeared as flimsily dressed as possible.

Hamilton seems to have encouraged Emma's passion for Nelson, and the King and Queen were delighted with the arrangement, especially when the British admiral helped them to suppress the 1799 "Parthenopean Republic". While her lover hanged the rebel leader, Prince Caracciolo, at the yard-arm of his flagship, Emma dealt harshly with petitions for mercy from wives of other revolutionaries. Accompanied by the Hamiltons, Nelson returned to a hero's welcome in London. For the Neapolitans, however, he and Emma became demonised as the agents of tyranny and reaction.

The best of them, such as Domenico Cimarosa and Giovanni Paisiello, were to influence such great international masters of operatic comedy as Mozart and Rossini.

Height of the Grand Tour

The area around Vesuvius also witnessed one of the most important events of 18th-century European culture in the gradual excavation of the buried Roman cities of Pompeii and Herculaneum, an enterprise begun by King Charles. Naples had established itself as one of the most important centres of the Grand Tour, the extended educational visit to Italy which

structure for the whole state. Unfortunately his son Ferdinand was a less intelligent monarch, fond of hunting and practical jokes, a king whose reactionary instincts were encouraged by his wife Maria Carolina of Austria, aided by her English lover Admiral Acton. Incensed by the execution in Paris of her sister Queen Marie Antoinette, she urged Ferdinand to join an alliance against the French, but when Napoleon's armies invaded Italy four years later the royal family fled to Sicily, along with their friends the English ambassador Sir William Hamilton and his wife Emma.

In 1799 revolutionaries in Naples proclaimed

became obligatory for young European aristocrats. Collecting antiques, particularly Greek and Roman statuary and vases, became a passion with visiting noblemen, and Neapolitans were able to make a profitable business out of selling curios and *objets d'art*.

The liberal tone of life in Bourbon Naples encouraged many people to hope that at the outbreak of the French Revolution in 1789, the reforms begun by King Charles would at length accommodate a more democratic political

LEFT: Masaniello, who led a popular revolt against the despotic Spanish monarchy in 1647.
ABOVE: a lithograph of the Teatro di San Carlo, 1840.

the so-called Parthenopean Republic (Parthenope was one of the city's ancient Greek names) led by high-minded intellectuals and freethinking aristocrats. Lasting only five months, it was finally overwhelmed by a combination of a Calabrian peasant army led by Cardinal Fabrizio Ruffo and the English fleet commanded by Lady Hamilton's lover, no less a figure than Lord Horatio Nelson. The terms of an honourable surrender were violated when Nelson, egged on by Lady Hamilton and Queen Maria Carolina, hanged the revolutionary leaders, and the massacres and reactionary repression which followed had a disastrous impact on the Bourbon monarchy's image throughout Europe. ❑

COMIZI DEL POPOLO

Il Popolo vuole
l'Italia una e indipend
con Vittorio Emanuele
Re Costituzionale
e suoi legittimi discender
Decreto 8 Ottobr

ONE NATION

With Unification, the "Two Sicilies" joined the rest of Italy.
But its history lingered in a culture too complex to be quickly assimilated

The rule of the restored Bourbons after the Parthenopean Republic's collapse was unsurprisingly short. On 14 June 1800 a French army under Napoleon Bonaparte won a decisive victory over the Austrians at Marengo in northern Italy, and soon afterwards a full-scale occupation of the Italian states by French troops began. The whole political map was now redrawn, with the north being transformed into the Kingdom of Italy, governed by a viceroy in Milan, Tuscany given to Napoleon's sister Elisa, and his brother Joseph made King of Naples. Afterwards sent to rule in Spain, Joseph was replaced by Joachim Murat, husband of the Emperor's sister Caroline.

Napoleonic rule

While the Bourbons had returned to Sicily, guarded by British warships, the Kingdom of Naples enjoyed what was probably the best government since the days of Emperor Frederick II. Under Napoleonic rule, new centralised bureaucracy and the wholesale abolition of feudal privileges brought with them an impartial administration, supported by the French Civil Code, which standardised legal procedure, introduced a fair taxation system and established adequate policing throughout the nation.

Unfortunately, this new regime, while sweeping away old abuses, did little to alter the social status quo, since the barons were still guaranteed ownership of their estates. Such fresh lands as became available were bought by the bourgeoisie who were created from the new ministerial class engaged in carrying out French reforms.

Napoleon was keen to encourage young Italians to join his armies, and for many this offered an excellent opportunity to improve their status and financial prospects while seeing something of the world during the Emperor's military campaigns. When Joachim Murat, as King of Naples, cut loose from his brother-in-law's empire in 1814, several Neapolitan army officers, familiar by now with other models of government, demanded a constitution in return for their support. Secret societies devoted to political reform, known as the Carbonari, had sprung up in various regiments, but Murat,

hitherto a wise and practical sovereign, preferred to repress them rather than capitalise on their potential support following Napoleon's defeat at Leipzig and exile to Elba. Austrian troops meanwhile closed in on the kingdom, defeating Murat's army at Tolentino in the Papal States in 1815. After fleeing to Corsica, he made a last desperate bid to regain his kingdom, landing in Calabria at the head of a small body of volunteers, but he was captured and executed by an Austrian firing squad.

Memories of Murat's reign and of his dream of unifying Italy under a single monarch lingered during the subsequent Bourbon restoration. The new Kingdom of the Two Sicilies

LEFT: results of the plebiscite to unify Italy are announced in Naples, 1860.
RIGHT: Garibaldi, hero of Italian unification.

brought together what had technically been two separate realms, with King Ferdinand IV becoming Ferdinand I at the head of his new state. During residence in Sicily he had granted the island a constitution, but once properly reinstated he abandoned his constitutional experiment, provoking anger among the new class of educated professionals. In July 1820 rioting broke out in the city of Nola and spread to other provinces, forcing the king to renew his former pledges. When rebel factions began quarrelling with each other, Ferdinand brought an Austrian force from the mainland, scattered the constitutionalists and restored the status quo.

To outsiders, the kingdom's apparent security, internal or external, scarcely concealed the poverty and lawlessness rife in much of the south beyond Naples and Campania. The restoration of the monarchy in 1815 had entailed the return of frontiers and customs barriers, with a resultant increase in smuggling of all kinds.

Owing partly to the unemployment caused by a depressed agriculture and the amalgamation of small farms into big ranch-style estates, banditry now resumed a greater significance in rural life than ever, and travellers ventured at their peril through the wilder reaches of Calabria, Apulia and the Abruzzi. The bandits

After Ferdinand's death in 1825, the Kingdom of the Two Sicilies slumbered in a climate of reaction and repression under the rule of his son Francis I and his grandson Ferdinand II. Neither was quite the fool or the ogre the rest of Europe liked to believe them to be, and many ordinary citizens were content with a despotic regime which ensured tranquillity and a semblance of order through press censorship, police informers and severe penalties for any activity remotely hinting at political dissent. Ferdinand II's remark that his realm was "safe between salt water and holy water" (referring to his fellow sovereign, the Pope) reflects a complacency echoed by many of his subjects.

themselves were often romanticised by local communities as Robin Hood figures protecting the poor against rich oppressors. One of them, known as Fra Diavolo, achieved international fame when in 1830 the French composer Daniel Auber made him the subject of an opera.

Italy united

Whatever the slowness of communications in 19th-century Italy, and despite the Bourbon government's suppression of any kind of political activism, the cause of Italian unity began gathering support among the professional class of doctors, lawyers and civil servants, as well as finding favour with a small number of liberal aristocrats and army officers. It was inevitable that even so conservative and backward a society as that of the Two Sicilies would feel the effects of growing unrest among other Italian states, as the movement towards unification, known to historians as the Risorgimento, shifted from theoretical to practical objectives.

In 1846 the ultra-reactionary Pope Gregory XIII died, and was succeeded by the comparatively young and apparently liberal Pius IX. Many anticipated a dawning of freedom and democracy, with the new pope as Italy's spiritual leader. The momentum of revolution was now unstoppable, and after demonstrations took place in Naples, full-scale revolution broke out in Sicily during February 1848. King Ferdinand, hastily granting a constitution as his father had done, waited on events. His new liberal ministers proved unequal to their task, and it was easy enough for the king to re-establish control by the age-old device of appealing to the *lazzaroni*, the Neapolitan mob of sailors, fisherfolk and beggars, whose support for the Bourbon regime could always be relied upon.

A haven for reactionaries

After mopping up whatever opposition remained, Ferdinand was able to present his kingdom as a haven for other sovereigns fleeing from their revolutionary subjects, such as Pope Pius IX and Grand Duke Leopold of Tuscany. Even the mildest political dissidents were now condemned to fester in jail, while the Church was persuaded to allow its priests to act as police informers and press censorship was tightened.

Such measures were no worse than those adopted in other European states at the time, but it was a visitor from Britain, a country which did not imprison its liberals and muzzle its newspapers, who turned Ferdinand and his kingdom into headline news. In 1851 the future Prime Minister William Ewart Gladstone, while staying in Naples, made enquiries into the repressive treatment of political prisoners and when he returned to London he published an indignant account of his findings. His pam-

---

A BRITISH VIEW

"Naples' Bourbon regime is the negation of God erected into a system of government."

– WILLIAM GLADSTONE, BRITISH PM

---

phlets drew attention to the corruption and injustice which had prevailed in southern Italy and Sicily since the monarchy's restoration. When and whether this same monarchy would fall was more doubtful. An attempt at an uprising in 1857, near Sapri on the Calabrian coast, was crushed by local peasants, but by the time Ferdinand II died in 1859, to be succeeded by his dim, unimaginative son Francis II, events were preparing to reshape Italy for ever. The war breaking out that year between France and Austria was

fought largely in northern Italy, resulting in the creation of an Italian monarchy under King Victor Emmanuel of Piedmont, which other states such as Tuscany and Modena, deposing their sovereign dukes, hastened to join.

Garibaldi's expedition

While southern Italy remained largely loyal to King Francis II, Sicily welcomed the 1860 expedition of the "liberator" Giuseppe Garibaldi and his "Mille" (Thousand) who freed the island from Bourbon rule. Garibaldi now pushed on into Calabria, his tiny force of 3,000 scattering the defenders of even such larger towns as Reggio. When he entered

---

LEFT: detail of an anonymous painting of an 1848 revolutionary, from Galleria Nazionale, Capodimonte.
RIGHT: Francis II, the last foreign regent of Naples.

Naples in triumph on 7 September, the Bourbon garrison turned out to salute him.

King Francis was still able to depend on the support of the large force he had mustered on the Volturno river, between Naples and Rome. He might have won the ensuing two-day battle with Garibaldi's troops, had he not insisted on taking full command of the army, deploying them in a complex pincer movement which broke down almost immediately. The king retreated to the fortress of Gaeta, and his young wife, Maria Adelaide, inspired the stronghold's defenders during a siege carried on for nearly a year, which gave the royal couple a kind of tragic dignity admired even among those most applauding the Bourbons' downfall.

Birth of the secret societies

The plebiscite by which the territory of the Two Sicilies signified its adherence to the new Kingdom of Italy was a democratic charade, rigged with the help of the Neapolitan secret society known as the Camorra. Like those of the Sicilian Mafia, the Camorra's origins are obscure, but during the late 19th century it emerged as a significant force in local politics, with a developing criminal arm whose influence grew more menacing as the city's urban problems

GARIBALDI'S MOST FAMOUS WAR WOUND

As the champion of liberty, admired for his courage, leadership and integrity, Giuseppe Garibaldi was a hero for most Italians, but not for Italy's first king, Victor Emmanuel, and his conservative ministers. Jealous of his success in Sicily and the south, and terrified lest his republicanism encouraged a revolt against the monarchy, they sought to exploit his potential as an icon of independence. The king encouraged him to invade the Papal States, but he soon worried that the enterprise would get out of control, and he sent an army into Calabria under General Cialdini to round up the invasion force and arrest Garibaldi. A battle on the slopes of the rugged Aspromonte mountain lasted 10 minutes, since Garibaldi's men had orders not to shoot at their fellow Italians. One of the only casualties was the hero himself, so badly wounded in the leg that it took 15 hours to get him down the mountain to the coast, where Cialdini had him hoisted aboard a gunboat. His foot had swollen so much that the bullet could not be located, and only after three months' examination by 23 surgeons from various countries was he saved from an amputation. Lying on an adjustable invalid bed sent to him by the wife of British Prime Minister Lord Palmerston, Garibaldi became more newsworthy than ever, while Aspromonte, the bandit-haunted Calabrian mountain, gained international fame.

increased. A similar organisation, the 'Ndrangheta, existed in Calabria, and this too gained in power, infiltrating all areas of regional government and economy.

As with the Mafia, both societies first evolved as a means of protecting the rural working class against oppression by feudal landlords and as an alternative to the injustices and incompetence of the Bourbon government. The new Italian kingdom, which lasted until 1946, did little to improve such matters throughout the south, and living standards in many small communities

IDEALLY SPEAKING

"We have created a nation. Now our task is to shape the people."
– GIUSEPPE GARIBALDI

restore order and legality to the south in the aftermath of a period of political unrest following Italy's entry into World War I in 1915.

The economy benefited from vigorous promotion of areas such as the Bay of Naples, the Costa Amalfitana and the islands of Capri and Ischia as tourist resorts, favoured by a vogue for sunbathing and the Mediterranean cruises which became popular with a new generation of holidaymakers.

Mussolini's obsessions, however, included the so-called "Battle for Wheat" designed to

remained at more or less the same level on the eve of World War II as they had been at the time of Garibaldi's expedition. For many villagers the only alternative to grinding poverty was emigration to the New World, taking with them the values of family cohesiveness and suspicion of the law which had always lain deeply ingrained in the life of the Mezzogiorno.

The advent of Fascism with Benito Mussolini's seizure of power as Italian Prime Minister in 1922 was hailed by many as a chance to

make Italy self-sufficient in food, and it was the Mezzogiorno which bore the brunt of Fascist agricultural reforms, with the clearance of valuable pastureland, olive groves and orchards to fulfil Il Duce's demands. Fascism could nevertheless count on widespread support from the politically conservative south, where Mussolini's pact with Hitler and his commitment of Italian forces to World War II was greeted with much enthusiasm.

In the weeks before the war, the exodus of foreigners from honeypots such as Capri was compensated for by an influx of Italians. The foreign minister, Count Ciano, packed off his children and his wife Edda, Mussolini's daugh-

LEFT: Garibaldi and his "Mille" (Thousand) land in Sicily to free the island from Bourbon rule.
ABOVE: swaggering anti-Camorra vigilantes, 1890.

ter, to Villa Ciano, their island retreat. The move was seen by many as an example to follow. War against Britain and France was declared in September and Italy invaded Greece. The Allies targetted ports and railheads in the south and the surprise air attack on Taranto in November is said to have so impressed the Japanese that they took the idea to Pearl Harbor.

After their success in Africa, the Allies chose Sicily as the landing stage for bringing the war against Hitler back to Europe. In 1943 the Americans landed on the island's west coast, the British and Canadians on the east coast. Troops had meantime landed in Taranto after bombardment by the British navy, and General Alexander later made Churchill a gift of the Union Jack hoisted there – the first Allied flag flown in Europe since Britain's withdrawal from France at Dunkirk.

On the morning of 8 September the German garrison on Capri awoke to see the horizon crowded with men-of-war, and soon the whole Bay of Salerno, all the shim-

ALLIED ATTACKS

"I am glad that Naples is having such severe nights. The breed will harden, the war will make of the Neapolitans a Nordic race."
– BENITO MUSSOLINI, July 1943

TASTE OF VICTORY

The people of Naples were starving by the time the Allies arrived. They had been banned from fishing in the mine-filled bay and the departing Germans were rumoured to have polluted their water supply. Many were reduced to eating barnacles and grass. But when the Allies arrived, they proved perfect hosts, laying on a banquet for the joint forces commander, General Mark Clark, in the splendid Renaissance Palazzo Cuomo. The main course was an ingenious creation: a steak of manatee, a seal from Naples' famous aquarium, cooked in a garlic sauce. It was all that was left. The other exhibits had long been consumed.

mering calm blue water to the south of the Sorrento peninsula, was crammed with ships and landing vessels. By the end of the afternoon Italian radio announced the country's unconditional surrender. The allied Fifth Army under the ambitious General Mark Clark began landing the following day when the German garrison withdrew from Capri. Three days later Rear Admiral Sir Anthony Morse settled himself into Villa Ciano as temporary governor of Capri.

Naples had suffered comparatively little bombardment prior to the Allied landing, but the Germans had blown up a number of key points in the city as they retreated, and the people were on the brink of starvation. For many Allied servicemen, Naples became a symbol of the resilience of the Italian south and its ancient civilisation across the centuries.

The postwar republic

Such resilience was to be tested in different ways during the late 20th century. The new Italian republic which came into being in 1946 merely succeeded in widening the already considerable gap which existed psychologically and economically between the Mezzogiorno and northern Italy.

The nation's substantially corrupt political system, supported by the US as a bastion

trafficking and illegal immigration, and a general sense that little, after all, had changed since the days of the barons and the Bourbons.

The break-up of Yugoslavia in the 1990s brought a fresh problem to the south. Refugees arrived by their thousands, and continue to do so. Kosovo Albanians came in waves, putting huge pressure on the Adriatic ports and the communities of Apulia. At the end of the decade the flow was not stemmed, and Kurds and Iraqis were also fetching up on the south Italian shores, as well as Kosovo Romanies who came in their thousands every day and, according to the president of the regional

against Communism during the Cold War, encouraged the creation in the south of a conservative fiefdom ruled by local bosses of the right-wing Christian Democrat party. A culture of cynicism and apathy was accompanied by the misuse of public funds on a grand scale, the failure to maintain an adequate infrastructure in either urban or rural areas, the spread of violent crime via the growing involvement of the Camorra and the 'Ndrangheta in drug-

LEFT: the 20th century began with emigration to America from the impoverished south.
ABOVE: it ended with conflict in Yugoslavia and the arrival of thousands of Albanian refugees.

council of Apulia, put the region "under siege". In attempts to ease the problem, refugees were flown to camps in Sicily, and it was no surprise to see press reports in early 2000 that money earmarked for refugee aid had ended up in the hands of the Mafia who were in collusion with their Albanian counterparts.

But the end of the Cold War also loosened America's grip on Italian politics during the 1990s and a genuinely representative system was allowed to develop, the attitude in many areas of the south became more optimistic, with signs that even such a deeply rooted resignation as that of the Mezzogiorno is ultimately capable of changing. ❑

PLEASURE SEEKERS

"It was all purple wine, all art and song, and nobody a grain the worse. It was
fireworks and conversation, civilisation and amenity" – Henry James

The normally taut prose of Henry James was tinged purple by a surfeit of sun and nostalgia in Sorrento when he wrote the above lines in 1881. The myth of Mediterranean plenty and the blazing vitality of southern life have caused many northern puritans to succumb to dreams of simplicity and flight. Other writers have been intoxicated by the romance of the south, from classical landscapes to the lost civilisation of Pompeii or the imperial palaces that once belonged to Nero, Caligula and Tiberius.

In his 1820 ode, *To Naples*, Percy Bysshe Shelley strikes a bitter-sweet tone, recording a "Metropolis of a ruined paradise / Long lost, late won, and yet but half regained!" In Pompeii some 20 years later, Frances Trollope, an inveterate traveller, evokes "the well-used curb-stone, against which the car almost fancies it can catch the grating of a Roman chariot wheel".

Romantic Grand Tourists

The 18th-century Grand Tourists simplified the south yet were deeply affected by it. Romantic visitors were concerned with experiencing the pathos, transience and futility of existence, a spirit which, in the Victorian era, became transmuted into restlessness and a longing for release from repressive northern climes.

Travel was imbued with lofty aspirations and couched in the language of self-denial. Frances Cobbe, criticised her fellow countrywomen for abandoning "the noble strife" of English life for "the lotus-eater life of the south". For repressed northerners, no idle malingering was acceptable, including travel for its own sake, particularly since morals were thought to decline as the climate improved.

The climate prompted northerners to follow the flock, migrating south in autumn and north in spring. The recommended cure for consumption was a spell in southern climes but, as

William Chambers noted in 1870, "Fashion, ennui and love of gaiety seem to send quite as many abroad as absolutely bad health." If the exodus to the south began as a whim of the artistic and cultural elite, social-climbers and pleasure-seekers soon followed. Even if the avowed reasons for travel were classical pil-

grimage and health, southern Italy became an escape from the sterile intellectualism of northern society.

Visitors steeped in classical lore had read Theocritus and Virgil and, uplifted by it all, they scoured Sicily and Campania, in thrall to the romance of ruins. In an atmosphere saturated with classical association, the southern landscape was invested with symbolic power. The biographer James Boswell indulged in the Grand Tour in the 1760s and he gushed over the classical associations of Naples: "Is it possible to conceive a richer scene than the finest bay diversified with islands and bordered by fields where Virgil's Muses charmed the

---

LEFT: visitors being shown Virgil's tomb, detail of a 19th-century painting, Neapolitan School.

RIGHT: cartoon of early tourists ascending Vesuvius.

creation, where the renowned of ancient Rome enjoyed the luxury of glorious retreat and the true flow of soul which they valued as much as triumphs?"

The classical ruins appealed to the Romantics' predilection for civilisations in decay. Faced with the panoply of classical culture, however, northerners experienced a sense of cultural inferiority. Norman Douglas, the connoisseur of southern culture, puts it in his inimitable way: "Most of us come to Italy too undiscerning, too reverent, in the pre-coital and pre-humorous stages... too stuffed with Renaissance ideals and Classical lore."

Unprotected Females in Sicily and Calabria, published in 1859, concluded that Calabria had no more than "a little peppering of danger to give romance".

But hers was not the general view. The Grand Tour usually went no further than Paestum, and lands beyond remained wild and apparently uncivilised well into the 20th century. Occasional intrepid travellers set off alone. In 1824 Craufurd Tait Ramage, tutor to the sons of the British Consul in Naples, went in search of southern Italy's "ancient remains and modern superstitions". For this purpose, he was "well furnished with capacious pockets, into which I

Violence, passion and daily life

The Grand Tour represented both an intense exposure to classical heritage and a cultural finishing school. Grand Tourists also went in search of exalted emotions, from moral edification to spiritual enlightenment. Another more secret purpose was to sense the violence of natural forces, sample southern passions and experience the intensity of everyday life. The risks posed by earthquakes, volcanic eruptions and the odd violent encounter with brigands simply added a frisson of excitement to travel.

Women travellers, in particular, enjoyed testing their increasing sense of independence by venturing south. The anonymous authoress of

have stuffed my maps and notebooks: nankeen trousers, a large-brimmed straw hat, white shoes and an umbrella, a most valuable article to protect me from the sun's rays."

A century later, Augustus Hare wrote in *Cities of Southern Italy*: "The vastness and ugliness of the districts to be traversed, the bareness and filth of the inns, the roughness of the natives, the torment of the mosquitoes, the terror of earthquakes, the insecurity of roads from brigands, and the far more serious risk of malaria or typhoid from the bad water, are natural causes which have hithertofor frightened strangers away from the south." To this he added one more item to be avoided, the *pizza napoletana*, which he described as "a horrible condiment made of dough baked with garlic, rancid bacon and strong cheese".

It was much safer to look at the classical remains in the shops and galleries around Naples. Priceless Roman statuary was appraised by foreign visitors with the acquisitive gaze of thrifty auctioneers. After a remorseless regime of galleries, churches and ancient ruins, Grand Tourists settled upon Neapolitan coral and cameos, Sicilian mosaics and alabaster replicas of Roman busts, returning home laden

INDISCRETIONS

"The wealthy English adulterers are the attraction of the place."

– J. H. NEWMAN, 1833

barren mountains, all thrown together in a most romantic confusion." And in his southern letters, the normally restrained Henry James was not above the "the gush and cant" he deplored in his fellow travellers: "I wish I could send you a patch of the blue sea that stretches away to Naples and Capri – a few square feet of the pale purple that covers the gentle-looking flanks of Vesuvius."

The 19th-century Anglo-American elite swiftly succumbed to the enchantments of winter in Naples, but the city had too much

with what Charles Dickens called "an infinite variety of lumber".

The picturesque nature of southern scenery, especially the Bay of Naples, was a distinct source of pleasure for Grand Tourists. The 18th-century Irish philosopher George Berkeley was entranced by Ischia, an island whose praises were sung by Homer and Virgil: "The island is an epitome of the whole earth containing within the compass of 18 miles a wonderful variety of hills, vales, ragged rocks, fruitful plains, and

---

LEFT: *Forum at Pompeii* by Lapira (19th century)
ABOVE: detail from *View of Naples from Capodimonte* by Lapira. Vesuvius is always in the picture.

character and self-confidence to become an archetypal anglophone colony. According to the contemporary Australian writer Peter Robb, "Naples gave the world ice cream, pizza, *opera buffa* and transvestism as an art form. Naples ravished Virgil, Boccaccio, Stendhal, shocked and disgusted de Sade, Ruskin and Sartre. Naples filled the paintings of the visitor Caravaggio and the operas of Mozart."

However, this picaresque city also had a well-deserved reputation for warmth and wickedness, enhancing its appeal as a canvas for foreign eccentricity, eroticism or elopement.

Goethe, at large in Italy in the 1780s, had his own private sexual agenda in the south but his

Italian Journeys contain tamer public pronouncements, including praise of Taormina as "a patch of paradise on earth". At the same time as the German poet was extolling the wonders of Sicily, his compatriots from the Prussian court came to paint picturesque, virtually photographic views.

From the 18th-century, pastiches of landscapes were custom-made for the collecting mania of the European aristocracy and appealed to such connoisseurs as the Englishman, William Beckford: "I viewed Vesuvius, rising distinct into the blue ether, with all that world of gardens and casinos which are scattered about the sea, just like a Greek temple, and light, light, light everywhere". This idyll was evoked in *The Story of San Michele*, published in 1929, which became an international bestseller.

The Vesuvius show

Landscape artists were drawn to the sublime spectacles of Vesuvius or Etna erupting, scenes which naturally appealed to the heightened sensibilities of the Romantics. The volcanoes provoked a mixture of awe and ghoulishness in earlier visitors. In the 1670 edition of *Voyage of Italy*, Richard Lassels records that the guide to Vesuvius "will show

its base". From admiration, it was but a small step to the acquisition of paintings and antiquities, complete with villa and views.

In Capri, the writer Maxim Gorki was at the heart of a Russian revolutionary set who played chess at the Caffè Morgano. A "School of Revolutionary Technique for the scientific preparation of propagandists of Russian Socialism" was set up in 1908 and Lenin paid a visit.

Axel Munthe, the Swedish writer and collector, incorporated the remains of a Roman villa into his eclectic Edwardian museum piece, stuffed with Etruscan and Roman statuary. His romantic vision for Villa San Michele was of a home "open to the sun, wind, and the voice of

you a channel in which from that spewing hill had run a filthy green matter mingled together of brimstone, alum, iron, water, saltpeter and sulphur". In the days of the Grand Tour, the ascent of Vesuvius was first made by mule, but later superseded by cable-car, until it was destroyed by the 1944 eruption, an event witnessed by an enthralled Norman Lewis. "The shape of the eruption that obliterated Pompeii reminded Pliny of a pine tree, and he probably stood here at Posillipo across the bay, where I was standing now, and where Nelson and Emma Hamilton stood to view the eruption of their day, and the shape was indeed like that of a many-branching tree".

Henry James witnessed "stricken Ischia", which was just recovering from the earthquake in 1883, but he preferred to focus on the romantic vision of the Bay of Naples: "Sorrento and Vesuvius were over against you; Naples furthest off, melted in the middle of the picture, into shimmering vagueness and innocence."

The discoveries and excavations at Pompeii and Herculaneum encouraged 18th-century foreign visitors to flock to the sites. With classical texts in hand, they sought out the most macabre tableaux to satisfy their morbid

> **TOURIST TRAP**
>
> "American and German tourists are popped systematically into the orifice of the Blue Grotto"
>
> – HENRY JAMES

instinctual humanity of the people. John Steinbeck, visiting Positano in 1953, idealised the natives as "Positano's greatest commodity – characters who have lived in America and come home again to bask in the moral, physical, political and sartorial freedoms which flourish in their birth town."

Harold Acton (1904–94), the Anglo-Italian writer and aesthete, was prone to celebrating southern manhood, including the *lazzaroni,* the street urchins of Naples: "They were children of nature, sturdy, excitable,

curiosity. Samuel Rogers, exploring Pompeii in 1815, felt "a strange and not unpleasing sadness", a sentiment shared by modern travellers. Evelyn Waugh, visiting Palermo's Cappuccini Catacombs in the 1950s, relished the surreal vision of the dead and the "delicious" perfume emanating from the desiccated corpses.

Apart from the classical sites and transcendent landscape, travellers were drawn to the

FAR LEFT: on Capri in 1908 Lenin plays chess with Bogdanov while Maxim Gorky looks on.
LEFT: Axel Munthe in his Villa San Michele, inspiration for his best-selling book. **ABOVE:** a Capri boy poses for the German artist C.W. Allers in 1890.

apparently cheerful and carefree, proliferating in primitive simplicity, sufficient unto the day, the passing minute walking and sporting on the seashore naked, with no more shame than Adam in his primal innocence, and thanks to the climate, content with little and sleeping under the stars most of the year."

A synonym for Sodom

But such idealised "primal innocence" was not a feature shared by predatory foreign visitors. Southern Italy has long been a place favourable to foreign and native vices, with all sexual proclivities catered for. On Capri, Tacitus delights in tales of the dissolute Roman emperor Tiberius (*circa* AD 70–140) who had a penchant for "secret orgies, or idle malevolent thoughts". Suetonius also speaks of the Emperor's "goatish" antics: "On retiring to Capri, he made himself a private sporting-house, where sexual extravagances were practised for his secret pleasure".

Describing early 20th-century Sicily, Harold Acton pronounced Taormina "a polite synonym for Sodom". The camp city, founded during a period of Greek decadence has, like Capri, long been a homosexual haunt. Otto Geleng, the 19th-century landscape artist, was

one of several German aesthetes who promoted Taormina to "the flower of European pederasty". Although married to a Sicilian, Geleng was a believer in the dictum of girls for procreation, boys for pleasure.

As well as participating in nightly orgies, his fellow reveller, Oscar Wilde, helped create kitsch photographic compositions, crowning the languorous peasant boy models with laurels or posing naked but for Pan's pipes.

Film-star appeal

In the 1940s Taormina was the glamorous haunt of such screen goddesses as Marlene Dietrich, Rita Hayworth and Joan Crawford, who danced until dawn at the parties of Gaylord Hauser, the Hollywood dietician to the stars. His credo was: "Taormina enchants, seduces, but above all rejuvenates". Over a period of 30 years, Hauser regularly rejuvenated Greta Garbo, the reclusive star, in his villa. (Although the prime secret of rejuvenation seemed to be seduction, a diet of lettuce and cultural pilgrimages were also part of the recipe for eternal youth.) It was after a lengthy stay on Taormina that Garbo decided to abandon cinematic stardom for seclusion.

Truman Capote and Tennessee Williams also indulged their wild-boy reputations in Taormina, before alcohol and drugs wreaked havoc with their writing. By comparison, D. H. Lawrence led a dull, sheltered life on the island, confining himself to writing *Lady Chatterley's Lover*, based on the sexual exploits of his wife Frieda with a Sicilian muleteer.

Peter Robb, a former Naples resident and the author of *Midnight in Sicily*, is briefly captivated by the pastoral idyll of the south: "For a nanosecond I thought I saw now an interior Sicily of poetry and sex, pipes and panic, light and shade that lingered in a few old poems". Then he realised that, like Theocritus, whose 3rd-century BC *Idylls* were ultimately exercises in nostalgia, he too had succumbed to escapist dreams of pastoral simplicity.

In reality, Sicily's Hellenistic golden age also witnessed great atrocities, as did the Sicilian Moorish heyday 1,300 years later. Yet these exiled Arabs, like their Greek predecessors, praised their adoptive homeland in nostalgic poetry, painting Sicily purple with the dreamlike patina of memory. Modern visitors to the south are equally prone to false-memory syndrome, whether on an archaeological "Trail of Tiberius" or on a package tour of "The Picturesque Amalfi Coast".

Since the south is a canvas for the projection of northern passions, it is primarily a playground for the soul and senses. Doubling as a realm of repose and a realm of the senses, it symbolises both innocence and experience, a sunlit holiday and a seductive haven. ❑

LEFT: *Palermo*, by Carl Friedrich Heinrich Werner, 1839.
RIGHT: *Fishermen Mending Nets in Capri* (detail), by Theodor Leopold, 1892.

THE SOUTHERN ITALIANS

A welcoming people with organised crime, a male society which elects women mayors... it's the contradictions that rule in the south

People who visit Southern Italy expecting to see Godfathers in dark glasses, or bare-footed street-urchins, swindlers, wailing widows dressed in black, and other stereotypes, may come away feeling short-changed. Such images of the south, while still evident to a degree, are now often clichés. Visitors can instead expect to see traipsing across a rather chaotic and reckless stage the entire human spectrum, often depicted in powerful primary colours.

Southern Italy is full of cultivated, educated, courageous, scrupulous and genuinely warm and welcoming people. But it is also home to no fewer than four organised crime associations, whose membership programme amounts to a satanic way of life, and which is based on silence and fear. Tourists will remark on the poverty, squalor and air of lawlessness. But they will also note the innumerable signs of wealth. And, as Charles Richards in his book *The New Italians* wryly observed, the urchins still exist in Naples – but now they have shoes.

The truth is that Southern Italy, like its cuisine, is a land of strong contrasts and contradictions. It is a riddle. Everything seems true – and also the contrary.

Dangerous but dapper

Greater Naples is a dangerous port and urban sprawl with one of the worst levels of juvenile crime in western Europe. But it is also the hub of a former kingdom, it has an aristocracy, and it is the port for the nearby charmed isle of Capri, which remains a popular haven for chic jet-setters. Naples, where innocent passers-by are accidentally killed or wounded by stray bullets fired by teenage Mafia hitmen high on cocaine, boasts Italy's finest tailors. Its manners are elegant, and there is a lively intellectual and theatre tradition. The city is home to the late great dramatist Eduardo De Filippo, the

PRECEDING PAGES: a wedding in Ravello; card players on the streets of Naples.
LEFT: a slow news day on the Amalfi coast.
RIGHT: ice cream seller in Sorrento.

legendary tenor Enrico Caruso, the San Carlo opera house, as well as to the Pizza Margherita. There is an unusually rich and old tradition of popular song, and an impressive local school of contemporary blues-inspired music.

Palermo is the Mafia capital; but it is also the anti-Mafia capital, where housewives defied

the Mafia by the symbolic mass-hanging from their windows and balconies of white sheets. There, the Mob-busting magistrates are protected by cool bodyguards, and have enjoyed the fame of minor pop stars. A centre of intellectual activity, Palermo has some top restaurants and contemporary art galleries, a major opera house (even if it took 23 years to restore), intellectual salons, and a host of small but inspired and dynamic publishing houses. Southern Italy has for years been a hothouse for cultural creativity, producing some of the country's finest authors.

Italy's highest and lowest achievements both stem from the south. Such contrasts and contradictions run deep through southern society where the politics are both progressive and reactionary. Local food is a celebration of sweet and sour experiences. In Palermo, Capri or Bari, you are as likely to be greeted by a cornucopia of culinary aromas wafting up from a kitchen as you are to be hit with the stench of foul drains. The ravages of 1960s Mafia building speculation in Palermo are still all too painfully evident, but appear side by side with the preserved palaces of a decayed nobility.

GHOST TOWN

In Naples, an entire new town was recently found to exist without planning permission.

Mingling among fine buildings and dramatically beautiful countryside, almost everywhere in the south the visitor will find houses in an often indescribably ugly, unfinished state, unrendered, and with steel cables poking up out of the concrete pillars, as if these were poised to have another floor added to them tomorrow. The reason is not only *abusivismo*, or illegal housing, which is a widespread phenomenon. Another explanation offered by locals – although it sounds a little too innocent – is that each floor is added for each new child in a family, as a way of looking after the individuals of a brood, by providing them with a nest-egg for when they get older. The truth, however, is that, as often as not, tomorrow never seems to come, meaning that many houses are in a permanent state of construction.

In the south, signs of religion and intellectuality abound, but are often juxtaposed with those of a cultural desert, and the fetid sub-culture of the criminal world. When Piero Aglieri, a fast-rising Sicilian Mafia boss, was flushed out of his lair on the edge of Palermo and arrested in 1997, police found a wealth of religious objects inside. There were indications that he had had private Mass celebrated in his hideout. A priest had become his confessor in hiding, and as a result briefly faced charges after Aglieri's arrest. As in the hideouts of several bosses of the Naples Camorra, copies of great works of literature were on the shelves, together with a much-used copy of the Bible.

Fear of emasculation

In the north, the well-to-do tend to take an active role in society. In the south, they will often have no part in it at all. They are two separate societies. In the south, men still rule the roost, and can often be insanely jealous of their wives, and harbour old-fashioned and potentially dangerous attitudes. Often these are a barrier to women's independence, and the tension between the two viewpoints is a common cause of violence and even tragedy in the home.

Stories of men shooting their wives and children and then themselves for a variety of domestic and personal reasons provide a staple diet for newspapers. The underlying message is often one of emasculation in the face of creeping social change.

But, by the same token, the seaside town of Cefalú, a short distance from Palermo, is virtually run by women, beginning with the mayor and the police chief, and including the unemployment office, education, and local entertainment industry. In San Giuseppe Jato – considered, along with the nearby town of Corleone, the historic centre of the Sicilian Mafia, and where the age-old code of silence, or *omerta*, continues to reign supreme – the local council is run by an inspired, left-wing woman mayor. But in another neighbouring town, Monreale, the local clergy has been investigated for rubbing shoulders with and even harbouring the *crème de la crème* of the Mafia.

The friendly and welcoming nature of the people of the south is a commonly overlooked trait. But it strongly contrasts with the frequent bloodletting of organised crime.

On the face of it, however, there may be little separating southerners from people living in any big city around the world. Stereotypical attitudes to sex, love and religion rarely now apply. Southern Italian children will now dress much the same as yours. And they will listen to more or less the same music, watch the same television shows, and suffer from many of the same problems and fears. Young people in the south, just as in the north, can now be seen kissing in the

The Mob is not what it was

While the Mafia has a ubiquitous presence, many locals treat it as if it didn't exist. This tendency to ignore the phenomenon is, however, truer of the areas of Campania, Apulia and Calabria, where the Mafia has a less pyramidal and hence, less obvious structure. But in Sicily, where the Mafia is more deeply embedded in the culture, and where the Mafia outrages of 1992–93 triggered a remarkable outcry, the phrase "anti-Mafia" is resonant in school classrooms and civic functions. At the same time, some people shake their heads, and lament at the way the the Mafia is "no longer what it

street, and in many other ways are much more modern than a newcomer might expect.

But here, too, there are the inevitable contrasts. People in Palermo, as in London or New York, will live together without being married. But at the same time, they will also be driven by a culture and a set of rules which seem totally ancient. In the South, the rich and poor still often have almost as much chance of blending together as they might be expected to do in India. And in small villages and towns, and the countryside, it is the old culture that remains dominant.

LEFT: tending an olive tree in late autumn.
ABOVE: hunters on Capri.

was". The old Mafia was full of honourable men. Now it kills children and women.

Still another contradiction is that despite the South's traditional poverty and joblessness – unemployment is roughly 25 percent, or twice the national average – extreme poverty is rarely evident on the scale expected. The reason is that parents tend to help their children in the south more than elsewhere. For this reason, it's hard to find a single, thirty-something person who doesn't live at home. Without overheads, the southern youth thus has an unexpectedly high buying power. This, and the sometimes superficial aspect of modern southern society, help to account for the high percentage of luxury cars driven by people whom we are told are out of work.

Reggio Calabria, ostensibly a dusty, rather broken town for a major city, is said to have the highest percentage of mobile phones in Italy. Many young people do in any case have some kind of work, but it is not declared, so that officially unemployment is high. Southern families substitute the State, making up for the lack of a job, money and accommodation. It is a means of survival and, like the

STATELESS

"One has the sensation that something is missing here… It is the State."

way of finding work in the South when technically there is none to be had, part of the philosophy which Neapolitans have developed into an art – *l'arte di arrangiarsi*, or the art of making do.

Continuing the southern tradition for education and intellectual creativity – much of Italian literature has its roots in the south – many young people get degrees compared to elsewhere in Italy, since there is more drive to get work. But the culture also has a tendency to lean towards the controversial, the detached, and the levantine.

One of the most noticeable things about Southern Italy is that there one has the sensa-

tion that something is missing. It is not always easy to pin down what it is. It is the State. Throughout the south, there is a glaring lack of landmarks of civilisation as we know it, which traditionally serve to soothe and allay the fears of the newcomer. Schools, police stations, traffic wardens, sports fields, libraries, pedestrian crossings, and many other institutional signs, are all in short supply in the South. Indications of social tissue are little evident.

Filling the void, there is sometimes an uneasy sense of emptiness that may feel oppressive to the unaccustomed outsider. It is easy to confuse this sensation with the presence, lurking in the shadows, of organised criminals, and to mistake everyone who is swarthy and wearing sunglasses as threatening.

The lack of an identifiable presence of the State provides the fertile soil upon which the Mafia most feeds, apart from unemployment. The Mafia is many things, but it is also the local response – run riot – to the State's weakness. In Catania, Naples, and elsewhere, the Mafia finds it easy to engage the services of unemployed young people, who are prepared to commit serious crimes – and even murder – for the price of a second-hand moped.

A life without stress

However, this lack of significant State activity often provides an alibi, and many young people who arguably could go north in search of work simply don't. Instead, they prefer to continue the unstressed lifestyle of a provincial existence, which, apart from friends and a favoured climate, offers little to a society.

For all its modern veneer, the south continues to give the impression, even to aware southerners, of a place where people prefer to take it easy, and to be helped, and to be waiting for a handout. There is little entrepreneurial spirit, although that is also changing. But is it changing enough? In Italy, there was heartening news early in the new millennium that the economy of the south was finally beginning to pick up. But the bad news was that the north-south economic divide in the country was widening as never before. ❏

LEFT: a countryman from Apulia.

A Woman from Reggio Calabria

Laura is in her mid-20s and comes from Reggio Calabria. She now works in Rome, where she can look back with some objectivity on her formative years in the provincial capital of the south.

Life in her home town was, she says, surprisingly pleasant, despite the dust, crime levels, lack of presence of the State, and the vertiginous unemployment figures, which show that almost two out of three young adults in the area is without work. In Reggio, a place that comes to life in summer, everyone seems to know each other, though the population is now approaching 2 million.

There are a number of film festivals and the night spots are bright. Even the fishermen's caves of the nearby town of Scilla are being turned into nightclubs, discos and fashionable cafés. Many families have two houses. Laura's family have three. Young adults living at home — Laura can think of no one who does not — once upon a time used to make love in their parents' cars. Now they do so in their summer houses. When Laura was in Reggio, she was hardly ever at home, although she tried to be there for lunch, or, better still, to have dinner if she was going to go out to a discotheque.

Like foreigners, she, too, says she would turn and stare if confronted by the spectacle of a black-clad woman carrying a bundle on her head — once an all too common sight in the South. Such sights can still be seen in the smaller villages, including Bova Marina and Bova Alta, where street signs continue to bear names in both Greek and Italian. Parts of Calabria are among the most remote in all of Italy but the women who carry on these traditions are mostly elderly, and thus such traditions seem unlikely to survive long into the 21st century. In the large towns, the process of modernisation has already set into the social fabric.

There was a time when Laura's grandmother spent all her mornings slaving over a hot stove. Now her mother, who is also a housewife, spends just 10 minutes doing the same thing. As a result of the influence of her children, she relies on pressure-cookers and microwaves to produce food more quickly, though she continues to pride herself on using fresh produce. The difference is

RIGHT: young women in the south. Those who go north may miss the comforts and support of home.

that it no longer comes from daily trips to the market, but rather from once- or twice-weekly visits to the supermarket.

Like many fellow Southern Italians who have gone north, Laura is highly motivated, which is why she has given up her easy life in order to get ahead on her own. In Rome, she misses the life that she had down South, where her doting mother saw to it that she never had to pay for a thing, or iron a stitch of her own clothing, let alone wash it.

Her mother still goes to church, but her father does not, while her father's brother is a Communist and an atheist. Laura does not go to church, but others in her age group still do, and on Sundays the

churches in and around Reggio continue to be full. Laura's father is a now retired after working all his life as a state employee. Her sister, however, is a high-powered economist, with a top job in the capital. Laura is herself a degree holder in political science, and she speaks both English and French.

Reggio now has a Serie A football team, a similarly well-rated basketball team, and also a volleyball team. All this brings people in from outside, and helps them to circulate more.

Southern men, Laura says, are more chivalrous, and southern people in general are warmer and more generous than people who are from the north. And never, ever, would anyone think of "going dutch" in a bar. ❑

A HANDY GUIDE TO LOCAL GESTURES

Rituals, recriminations and rackets are all signalled by gestures seen in everyday life, as are displays of affection and betrayal

Beggars rapping their chins constantly with their right hands is a sign for hunger; emptying an imaginary waistcoat pocket conveys to a market seller that he considers the price too dear; supporting an elbow with one hand, while making a limp-wristed movement with the other indicates a simpleton. Centuries of struggle have versed Southern Italians in the art of survival, so it is hardly surprising that many gestures are bound up in a subtly subversive system of respect and honour. The language is entirely democratic: coercive or ingratiating gestures are as likely to be made by market traders or *mafiosi*, black-clad widows or chic lawyers flashing gold accessories.

MOTHERS AND MANHOOD

Only in the South can the simple act of making coffee become charged with hidden pleas, taunts, and complicity, depending on accompanying looks and gestures. The hand-kissing of powerful men still exists, a legacy of *clientelismo*, an ingrained Bourbon culture of self-serving friendships and protection. Gestures concerned with gullibility and cunning are commonplace. Manhood and mothers are sacred, and a foolhardy gesture of abuse can result in a fight. Touching of testicles is the superstitious male response to any impending doom. A two-fingered salute refers to a cuckold, but the gesture has a broader meaning: the fingers pointing downwards invoke bad luck, while making this gesture at someone else brings them bad luck.

▷ **MAKE YOUR POINT**
"Do you see what I mean or have I got to spell it out for you?" In this conversational device fingers are tight together, stabbing the air, to make the point

△ **THAT'S LIFE**
"*La vita è così* – that's life – What do you expect? All politicians are thieves and liars." Hands are spread apart in a shrug of world-weary resignation.

▷ **MAFIA THREAT**
At a Sicilian Mafia trial, a *mafiosi* defendant warns the Supergrasses: "*Tieni la bocca chiusa*" – Keep your mouth shut or I'll cut your tongue out.

◁ **HANDS IN WAITING**
The parishioners do the the talking. While the priest listens, his hands remain silent, preparing their response.

MANNERS ON THE ROAD

◁ **QUESTION TIME**
"Che cavolo vuoi? – What on earth do you want? And what am I expected to do about the water shortage?" An open palm, raised and lowered, comes with the questions.

▷ **I TELL YOU THIS**
"So then my granddaughter decided to get married." Daily conversation, even for the most sedentary, requires the exertion of hand movements.

◁ **JUST KIDDING**
A *scugnizzo*, a street kid, cheekily displays the *cornuto*, an aggressive two-fingered salute and a symbol of sexual infidelity.

▷ **ON THE TOWN**
"*La vita è bella* – Life's great. Let's hit the town before my shades steam up." Urban life is intensely visual and lived out on the streets.

Hand signals, particularly rude ones, are an integral part of the southern Italian's vocabulary. Street signals, however, are there merely to be considered, and a queue at traffic lights may only encourage motorists and moped riders to mount the pavement. Streetwise kids, known as *muschilli*, "little flies", thanks to their moped skills, add to the chaos as they speed about their nefarious business.

Blaring horns serve to signal frustration or fury, appreciation or celebration, rather than to point out an illegal manoeuvre. If you're driving too slowly on a quiet country road, expect to be shaken by a blaring horn and a car right on your tail. Driving slowly is a sign of a lack of virility and prowess, just as the wearing of seatbelts may be considered a slur on the driver's skills. It marks the driver out as a timorous foreigner or northern Italian, equally worthy of derision.

MANY MAFIA

Each region has its organised crime, but the crackdown on Cosa Nostra has met with some success. However, other groups are taking its place

In Italy the word "mafia" can mean either the Sicilian organisation, which is sometimes known as Cosa Nostra (literally, "Our Thing"); or the other crime groups of the south – namely the Camorra of Naples; the unpronounceable and fearful sounding 'Ndrangheta of Calabria; or the newer upstart relative, Sacra Corona Unita, or Holy United Crown, of the Apulia region.

Yet, while the various mafias are distinguishable by their geographical origin, they are not by any means confined to them. All are represented elsewhere in Italy, largely by southerners who have emigrated north. Milan is a favourite colony, but other places that are becoming popular may come as more of a surprise – Tuscany, for example.

Meanwhile, some foreign crime organisations – particularly the Albanian mafia – have begun to operate on Italian soil, and are starting to share power with the indigenous organisations, even to the extent that they are acquiring a profile of their own.

A state of mind

But what the Mafia really is, most of all, is a state of mind. Its influence can be experienced throughout Italy – especially in the way that real or expected threats can still succeed in dissuading a person from going to the police – but it is prevalent in the south. Sicilians often surprise outsiders by freely admitting that people on their island "all have a little something of the Mafia" in them.

While hard to describe, such a state of mind can be unmistakable when expressed in everyday life. A few years ago, several journalists visited Corleone, the "capital" in the hills near Palermo of the dominant Corleone Mafia family, which inspired Mario Puzo in his book *The Godfather* to name his central character Don

LEFT: the wreckage of the bomb that killed Judge Paolo Borsellino in Palermo, 1992.
RIGHT: anti-Mafia protester after the assassination of Borsellino and another judge, Giovanni Falcone.

Vito Corleone. As the reporters, one of whom was an attractive blonde, strolled into a crowded bar filled with ancient men, the animated buzz of conversation died, and every eye became trained on the newcomers. After consuming their drinks, the visitors went to pay, only to be solemnly informed by a barman with

downcast eyes: "The bill's been settled." He did not say by whom. Nor did any of the dozens of staring people in the bar, in which a deadly silence reigned.

It would be unfair to label such an act as *mafioso*; and the likelihood that there was a member of the mob in the bar at the time was slim. But the key elements of the Mafia were all there: secrecy, silence, complicity if not conspiracy, and a dark sort of gallantry, where the subliminal message was about power. Imagine the same scene, but where the gesture is negative, or violent, and it is easy to understand how as a local citizen, you might find this hard to report to the police.

The main distinction between Cosa Nostra and the other mafias, which are dominated by it, is that the first is the only one that is a real organisation, with rules, even though these are now fast eroding.

While Sicily's Mafia is based on a pyramid of power, with a ruling commission, its cousin the Camorra is a more informal collection of families, and whose rules are much less cast in stone. The 'Ndrangheta is a stricter organisation than the Camorra, and horizontally arranged. It is more difficult for the police to penetrate than Cosa Nostra, since it is broken up into tiny, loosely strung together and appar-

degree. Ironically, however, as the State for years concentrated its efforts on the Mafia, its rougher cousin the 'Ndrangheta has profited and grown, to the extent that it now represents an arguably much bigger threat than even Cosa Nostra.

Evidence of an organisation

Until the 1990s, many people in Italy, including even some politicians, claimed that the Mafia did not exist as an organisation at all. By demonstrating how the members of the Commission took collegiate decisions, the late Tommaso Buscetta, the first important Mafioso to turn state's evidence, helped judges to estab-

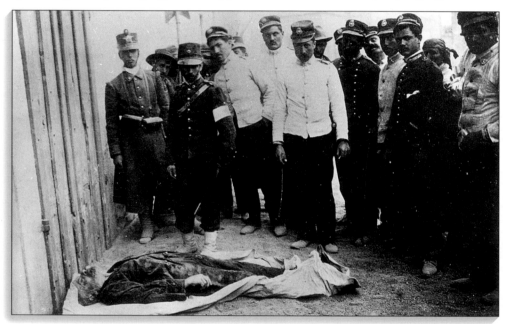

ently autonomous units, although bosses do meet from time to time for summits. This form of organisation, which the Sicilian Mafia used to have itself, is now being resorted to by Cosa Nostra, in its bid to survive in the wake of a crack-down by the State.

Nowadays the Mafia is a much reduced and more basic organisation. It has broken up into small groups that have gone to ground in an effort to avoid attention and detection.

Such changes mean that, out of fear of members turning state's evidence, bosses no longer discuss business in the presence of *mafiosi* of lesser rank – for example, their drivers. Total trust is now confined to relatives or friends of an equal

lish for the first time that the Mafia did exist as an organisation after all, in which individual decision-making members could be held to be jointly and severally liable for crimes they did not actually commit.

But while the old Mafia mentality has for long existed, its current expression as an indiscriminately violent organisation in Sicily is relatively new. To understand, one must delve into the so-called "industrial revolution" of Sicilian crime, meaning the postwar transition from an organisation that was once linked to the land, into one that got rich from drugs.

Until the mid 1970s, the Sicilian Mafia had been much as it always had been: a rough, rural, shadowy club. It is said to have had its roots in secret brotherhoods that were first pledged to honour, and to defend against corruption, foreign oppression, and feudal misdeeds typical of Bourbon misrule. Eventually becoming anti-government in nature, it was they who provided men, arms and money to Garibaldi and his Thousand. The sects were otherwise mainly connected to the land.

The old gangsters knew how to operate. In World War II, it was the Mafia that ensured that

BACK TO SCHOOL

Wary of electronic eavesdropping, Mafia communication now recalls the classroom: notes on scraps of paper known as *pizzini* are delivered only by trusted helpers.

tobacco smuggling based in Palermo developed into the trafficking of drugs, and the Mafia hardened its ties with Rome.

Ironically it was the bloody rise in Palermo of the Corleonesi – a family from the town of Corleone – in the late 1970s and early 1980s, which radically altered the face of the Mafia, turning it into a cold-blooded organisation bent on power and profit gained through the lucrative new heroin trade, which systematically began to wipe out its opponents.

the Allied troops were able to invade Sicily almost without a shot being fired, mainly through the good offices of the American gangster Lucky Luciano. He later stayed on in the old country, and introduced heroin refining to Naples, a change that would have a profound effect on both the organisation and Italy. Back in Sicily after the war, local Godfathers were thanked by the Allies for their work, by being appointed mayors of no fewer than 95 towns. But the island-based organisation remained rural until the mid-1970s, when

However, the Mafia at the peak of an earlier clan war in 1963 had already suffered a crisis for much the same reason, when Salvatore Greco, the then Godfather, unexpectedly stood down, dissolved the Commission or board of governors of the Mafia, and went abroad.

According to Tommaso Buscetta, what made Greco throw in the towel "was the realisation that the Mafia was abandoning its traditional principles, in order to transform itself into a criminal organisation."

The cause of the crisis was the fact that Luciano Liggio, a young peasant and "lieutenant" of the then boss of the Corleone clan, murdered a country doctor called Michele

LEFT: Camorra victim in the streets of Naples, 1890.
ABOVE: Mafia suspects arrive in court, Palermo.

Navarra in 1958 without referring the matter to the Commission. The murder opened the way for Liggio to mount an attack to gain supremacy of the port, market and city of Palermo. After Liggio's arrest in Milan in 1964, his two "lieutenants", Bernardo Provenzano and Salvatore "Toto" Riina, took up the reins of the family, which had yet to rise to supremacy within the Mafia. Soon after, Riina entered into a triumvirate with two other Godfathers, who suddenly were arrested.

In 1971, with the other two Godfathers in jail, and Liggio again in Palermo and on the run, the Corleonesi killed Pietro Scalgione, a

magistrate, and his driver. It was the first time in Italy that a magistrate had been killed, and Riina and Liggio were suspected of having personally taken part in the murder. The murder was meant as a punitive action for Scalgione who had just been responsible for sending a rival family of the Corleonesi to trial.

The Corleone war of Mafia supremacy followed Liggio's arrest in 1974. It is said to have left 1,000 dead and peaked in the 1980s with the murder of dozens of "illustrious corpses" of magistrates, police chiefs and local politicians. In 1992–93, the situation deteriorated along with the organisation, when it began to wage war on the Italian State.

"The cause of the well-being of most members of Cosa Nostra is simple," Stefano Bontate, an old-fashioned Godfather who died of unnatural causes, confided to Tommaso Buscetta. "The root of all the new wealth is trafficking in drugs. But it will be Cosa Nostra's downfall." Bontate told Buscetta, when the two were in jail, about how the organisation had substituted the smuggling of cigarettes, a former major source of income, with the production and sale of hard drugs.

The reason for dropping tobacco smuggling for that of heroin in 1978 was that there had just been an unprecedented state crackdown on the former. The first smuggler to change over was one Nuncio La Mattina, whose travels had enabled him to build up a large network for the provision of morphine. The smuggler had little trouble convincing the heads of Cosa Nostra. In a short time, a small group of people set up business to regularly furnish the families with morphine. Bosses, especially the younger and more entrepreneurial, then sold the heroin themselves, or used a network to export it. In the early 1980s, Sicily supplied a third of the entire US market.

"With the sale of drugs, all of the rules of behaviour of Cosa Nostra were re-opened for discussion." Fabrizio Calvi, an author of a key book on the inner workings of the Mafia, wrote: the division of labour changed, and for the first time, everyone in the Mafia could now deal in what and with whom they liked, even with people outside the organisation.

State's witnesses

Thanks to *pentiti*, or Mafiosi who have turned state's witness in trials and investigations, many of the key figures of the organisation have been jailed. The trend began in 1984 when Tommaso Buscetta revealed to investigators how the old families of Palermo had gone into drugs. A major roundup of criminals ensued, followed by a "maxi-trial" in Palermo in 1986, when almost 500 *mafiosi* were put in the dock.

The sentencing to life imprisonment of a number of people at the top of the organisation showed for the first time that the Mafia not only existed, but could be dealt a severe blow. The supreme court confirmation in 1991 of 19 life sentences rubber stamped this, but soon triggered a complex series of events that included the spectacular murder of the anti-Mafia magistrate Giovanni Falcone and Judge Paolo Borsellino, and the detonation of bombs in Florence, Rome and Milan, which appeared to have political as well as Mafia overtones. The overriding symbol of such collusion between Mafia and the State, although he was acquitted at the end of a huge, first trial in Palermo, was Giulio Andreotti, Italy's seven-times former prime minister and leading member of the once dominant – and Mafia-tainted – Christian Democrats.

> ### MAFIA EUPHEMISM
> *Bianca* means "white"; *lupara* is a shotgun used for hunting wolf. "Lupara bianca" is the name of the method resorted to when unwanted people are made to disappear.

The prime minister's lies

Judges in Palermo acquitted Andreotti in 1999 of collusion due to lack of evidence, but concluded that he had known some members of the Mafia, and that the key *pentiti* used by prosecutors to show that for years he had helped the Mafia in return for votes, was credible. In particular they said that Andreotti had lied when he told the court that he did not know the cousins Nino and Ignazio Salvo, powerful local tax collectors in Sicily and *mafiosi*.

The trying of Andreotti was popularly interpreted as the high-point of a revolution in Italy, since for decades he had stood for a corrupt system of power, in which Rome was seen to have handed over economic aid earmarked for the south to organised criminals, in return for the votes. However, a strong public reaction, which began with an outcry over the 1992 murder of the judges Falcone and Borsellino and a successive wave of Mafia violence outside Sicily, has now largely subsided.

The rush of *mafiosi*, many of whom were allegedly disgusted with the Falcone murder and the way the Mafia had become, to abandon the Mob and turn state's evidence, has now dangerously slowed, and the institution of "*pentiti*" has been undermined by a smear campaign conducted by the Mafia itself.

While it is tempting to draw the conclusion that the State's war against the Mafia has been lost – in the late 1990s, before dying of cancer,

a disillusioned Tommaso Buscetta deeply upset investigators by penning a book entitled *The Mafia has Won* – those in the front line insist that some key ground has been won in the State's battles. Above all, the mentality in Sicily, one Palermo police chief said, was no longer the same as pre-1992, when the Mafia was an accepted part of society.

One of the most curious and significant developments have been in Corleone itself. Once the home of the Mafia, the town now has an enlightened, Left-leaning

mayor. Properties confiscated from the Godfathers are being used for civic purposes, and the town has a new "Mafia Museum" and research centre (opened in 2000) dedicated to the study of organised crime.

Another tell-tale development can be seen in the recent study, which concluded that the Mafia was undergoing an "identity crisis". It found signs of anxiety, depression, disorientation and sexual and other disturbances being displayed by the members of Mafia families.

"The omnipotent hero is becoming fragile," the study concluded. "He is dying, being arrested, collaborating with the state, and becoming afraid." ❑

LEFT: Marlon Brando in *The Godfather*, a romanticised Hollywood movie about the Mafia, made in 1972.
RIGHT: magistrate Giovanni Falcone, assassinated in 1992 after successes against the Mafia.

THE ECONOMY

The precarious southern economy has some distinctive characteristics, such as
"Cathedrals in the Desert" and protection rackets

The economy of Italy's south must surely rank as one of the wonders of the modern world. Officially, an astonishing 23 or 24 percent of people in the area are unemployed, a figure that often peaks to levels of 50 percent or more among the young. Yet in 1997 the local GDP began to overtake the national average. At the same time, the north-south divide was said to be widening. Much of the explanation would appear to lie in the fact that the area's huge submerged economy has begun to take off. Why, it is difficult to say, but whatever the reason, such a fact can hardly be promising for the serious economist or politician; or, for that matter – in a part of the world dominated by the Mafia – to the forces of law and order.

If Italy's black economy can be held by the World Bank to account for 27 percent of the national economy, then imagine what it must represent in the south, where entire companies whose existence has never even been declared to the authorities – but which all the same are considered serious producers – abound. Even of the companies that toe the line by being registered, many still either evade tax, or dodge paying employees' contributions, or do both.

Just getting by

The South's black economy flourishes, especially in areas where people are given work to do at home and particularly in the province of Naples, which has a long tradition of handcrafted products, and where *arrangiarsi* ("getting by") is considered an art. The region is said to have as high a population density as Hong Kong, and the average earnings are the same as a standard state employee's in Milan, despite all the joblessness.

Local examples of such a contradictory well-being are in no way as isolated as one might think. Rather, they are representative of whole alternative systems of ways of doing business. In the greater Naples province, especially the

northeast, and in Calabria, there are not just a few examples, but whole networks, of such ways of commerce.

Examples of big but somehow illegal companies producing vast quantities of shoes, clothes or toys – in other words, products that do not require much cost to develop initially –

frequently thrive as a result of farming out work to people outside, a method that avoids tax and other contributions.

There are now whole areas of the south where bosses have been found to deal with producers or buyers in the north, and who establish a fixed standard of quality and price, as with any legitimate business.

One example would be the mediator for a man in the north, who goes to the south and buys 4 million pairs of shoes, especially where this trade flourishes, outside of Naples and near Salerno and Avellino. Each stage involved in the making of the shoes is contracted out, with costs well defined, even though the label may

LEFT: the industrial port of Salerno.
RIGHT: getting by – a street seller in Naples.

be unknown, or a fake of a noted fashion house in the north.

This applies to the whole province of Naples, where between a fifth and a third of the economy is thought to be submerged – hence, in part at least, the recent mad growth of the southern economy. A decision to include from 1997 the black economy when calculating the real growth of European countries, could not have been more apt than in the case of Italy's south.

By stark contrast, the signs of heavy industry in the lower half of Italy are desperately few. In Melfi, where Fiat makes its Punto cars, the impressively high-tech plant is ringed liked a

the south, as obscenely large amounts of money were indiscriminately poured in, often without any direction or apparent plan. The one exception is Melfi, which began at the start of the 1990s.

The "desert cathedral" of all time was surely Gioia Tauro, a huge port completed at the end of the 1970s with funding from the public Cassa del Mezzogiorno, but begun to be used as a container port only in the mid-1990s thanks to the enterprise of a Genoese privateer who hailed from the industrial transport sector. At the start of the 1980s, when the port was built and sitting doing nothing, the area was ear-

medieval fort with the factories and warehouses of the suppliers of the components.

In Gela, Sicily, a petrochemical complex refines the small percentage of oil that the island produces itself, and the vast quantities imported from abroad. Similar complexes exist in Taranto, in Apulia, and in the Campania region around Naples.

Cathedrals in the desert

The above are the scant results of the planning that went on in the 1960s, and are the "noble relations" of the "cathedrals in the desert", a perfect term used to describe white elephants of the kind which could once be found all over

marked as a coal-fuelled electrical plant; but the plan, which arguably would have destroyed the fertile Gioia Tauro plain with its thriving agriculture, was scrapped by an unexpectedly huge wave of local protest.

So Gioia Tauro remained the port-that-was-not-the-port that it was. Finally raised from the dead in 1994, it has now become the largest transhipment port in the Mediterranean, and after Rotterdam, the second largest in Europe.

Its new lease of life as a container port is ideal: the lack of any infrastructure around Gioia Tauro is of little importance, since the business it does merely comes and goes by ship. The local railway is pitifully poor – it has only one track. But who cares? The same applies to the Autostrada del Sole, the main motorway artery running down the boot of Italy, which while passing the port, is always hopelessly overcrowded. Built at the beginning of the 1960s to carry 20,000 cars, it now carries at least 50,000. But Gioia Tauro has little need of it. The downside of such splendid isolation is that the creeping tentacles of the Mafia, or 'Ndrangheta as the local organisation in Calabria is called, have managed to stretch out and quietly seize control of

> **FAMILY BUSINESS**
>
> Gioio Tauro, Europe's second largest port, has become a vital employer for every Mafia family in Calabria.

In his book *The New Italians*, Charles Richards, formerly the London *Independent*'s correspondent in Rome, told of how the coastal railway line that runs along the Ionian Sea from Reggio Calabria had never been electrified, as a result of a lack of funding. The book was first published in 1994. By the new millennium, the situation had not changed.

Faced with the argument that the line should be electrified, and a motorway built along the coast, southern economists will argue that, with all things considered, it would surely be better

many services connected to the port. As a result, Gioia Tauro has become a vital employer for almost every Mafia family in this part of Calabria.

However much its economy now begins to warm up, and no matter how many firms may be lured to the area with government offers of financial sweeteners, the glaring lack of infrastructure in the south will always seriously hamper its growth.

LEFT: Gioia Tauro, the largest trans-shipment port in the Mediterranean, is exploited by the 'Ndrangheta.
ABOVE: railway in Apulia. Road and rail networks remain underfunded.

to spend what little money there is on improving something vital to the economy that already exists, for example by widening the southern sections of the Autostrada del Sole.

During Italy's postwar boom years, funding was indiscriminately poured into the south, but the gravy train has since come to a halt. The lack of public investment is beginning to take its toll and strangle the south as much as it once fatally smothered what initiative it had. The sad truth is that while money once poured into the south in torrents, only to be wasted and line corrupt politicians' pockets, no one thought of providing aqueducts where they are badly needed. As a result, water continues to be rationed across the lower half of Italy as in times of war. Running businesses with such a sporadic supply is difficult.

Similarly, despite half a century of development policies, the "energy deficit" is so bad in some places in the south that it is almost impossible to run factories. Apart from having to spend large sums of money to transport raw materials from the north, and having to calculate the *pizzo*, or protection money to the Mafia into their costing (most firms find it advisable to pay up), producers in the south also have to

invest in "stabilisers" in order to cope with the fluctuating electricity levels. Not to mention black-outs, which in the south are a common occurrence.

Couch economy

From the start of the 1990s, however, an interesting transformation has been seen in different pockets of the south. At local level, traditions have been strengthened, often impressively, with the creation of *poli creativi*, literally, "creative poles," such as the "*polo divani*" – loosely translated, one might call it the "Sofa Valley" – of the Altamura-Matera area that straddles parts of Apulia and Basilicata.

> ### SOFA VALLEY
> Natuzzi, quoted on the New York Stock exchange, dominates the world's sofa business.

"Sofa Valley" is dominated by a company called Natuzzi, which not only dominates the settee business in the south, but also Italy and even the world. The company is the undisputed international leader in *divani*, or sofas. But in Altamura there are other international giants in the field. Near Naples, another "valley" now thriving is one that specialises in the manufacture of fibre optics.

An example may be taken from the Italian island of Sardinia, where there now exists one of the world's largest internet companies, the newly merged Tiscali-World On Line. The island, whose main industry used to be kidnapping, has now become a centre of the world service provider industry.

On the isle of Capri the main business has always been VIP tourism, fish, and the warbling of Santa Lucia by boatmen for tourists inside the Blue Grotto. But in 2000, Antonio D'Amato, the head of a refrigerated transport company with a branch in the south of England, emerged to become, against all the odds in northern-dominated Italy, the head of Confindustria, or local confederation of industry.

Pugilistic and aggressive in his approach, he views the south as containing the "hidden resource" able finally to unite Italy. In 2000, Enterprise Oil, a British company, drilled for oil in Basilicata and brought up amounts which, while comparatively modest on the OPEC scale, are impressive in a country which has few if any raw materials, apart from the incentive and innovative creativity of its people.

However, organised crime, which is a redistibutor rather a producer of resources, and which is rumoured to have disposed of its enemies in the cement pylons of motorways and others that prop up the "cathedrals in the desert", has developed its own answer to the *polo creativo*. It has achieved this by diversifying from kidnapping *(see right)* into the lucrative business of drug trafficking. In many southern towns, especially in Calabria and Campania, the visitor will see whole legions of young people hanging around, much of the time doing nothing, or working odd jobs only now and then. The image fits the reality, one would think, since almost one in three people, technically at least, is out of work.

But every so often, such a youth may take a

package to Milan by car, and when he returns home, he will be at the wheel of a much bigger car. He is today's answer to the "*casalinghe di Palermo*", the housewives of Palermo, who in the 1970s were flown as mules to New York with packets of heroin secreted all over them. In the US, they were treated like queens and put up in the best hotels, and on their return to Palermo were treated to a new kitchen by the local Mafia boss.

Yet another example of how the Mafia helps to buoy up the economy can be found in Caserta, near Naples, where the Camorra reigns. The transformation of the area from a

cial disposal centres, including in the north, have become prey to the practice of doctoring descriptions in order to make consignments appear harmless. Instead of being disposed of properly in accordance with the law – a costly procedure – shipments of toxic waste are transported down south and dumped into the holes.

The obvious ecological time-bomb aspect of such a foul practice in an area such as Naples province, which is where half of the entire population of the south resides, would never bother the organised criminal, or for that matter, the average southerner. For the civic sense which drives his society is dangerously backward. ❏

rural economy to one based on the production first of building materials, and then construction, meant that the holes that were dug in the area to extract the sand, could now be refilled with toxic waste.

Ecological time-bomb

Toxic waste is a new threat. Throughout Italy, new legislation demanding the proper treatment, disposal and labelling of such waste has begun to fuel a lucrative trade. As a result, spe-

LEFT: Pasquale Natuzzi, founder of the furniture giant.
ABOVE: fashion duo Domenico Dolce (right) and Stefano Gabbana found inspiration in Dolce's Sicilian roots.

A TOWN CALLED GETTY

One of the by-products of the local Mafia's once thriving kidnapping industry practised in the Aspromonte mountains of Calabria is a brash new town development called Via Borghetti. Sited in Bovalino, not far from Reggio Calabria, "Borghetti" is the local pronunciation for Paul Getty, heir to the Getty millions, who was kidnapped by locals in 1973. He was held in the area for six months and he lost part of one ear when the ransom failed to arrive as quickly as they had wanted. The $750,000 that was eventually handed over to obtain his release was said to have been used to develop the area (hence the name), although many dwellings still lack basic services.

MOVIES

Southern Italy is a self-conscious movie in the making. Intensely visual,
it is a backdrop of extremes, of exquisite morality and cold-blooded Mafia murder

Southern Italy has long been a source of inspiration for film-makers, with turbulent stories and settings presented on a plate. The dramatic landscape, melodramatic society and passionate people make the south a gift to directors, from Luchino Visconti and Francesco Rosi to foreigners such as Francis

Ford Coppola and Anthony Minghella.

Yet even within the south, locations are shamelessly transposed: "Film directors are magpies who plunder landscapes, corrupt geography, redraw maps, invent villages," Anthony Minghella admits to the liberties taken on *The Talented Mr Ripley*. His film was set in the Bay of Naples in that transitional time when postwar Italy meets the *dolce vita* boom of the 1950s. Yet while the island of Procida stars as itself, Naples opera house, Palermitan churches and the island of Ischia masquerade as cornerstones of other cities.

The sun-bleached image of Sicily is second-nature to cinema-goers as the land of *The God-*

father. The Mafia capital, Corleone, lends its jagged rocks and sullen populace to the trilogy. But, in recent years, Hollywood's infatuation with the glamour of gangsterland has been matched by the nostalgic, more whimsical appeal of such films as *Cinema Paradiso* and *Il Postino*. Yet, cinematically, the two poles of attraction remain Sicily and Naples, confirming their cultural superiority in the region.

Italian classics

There is an honourable tradition of memorable Italian films set in the south. Roberto Rossellini set part of *Paisa* (1946) in Naples, featuring the friendship between an American GI and a Neapolitan street kid. His unsentimental *Viaggio in Italia* (Italian Journey, 1953), shot entirely in Naples, features a distressed couple, with the city acting as a metaphor for an unhappy marriage. While the man discovers his weakness (infidelity on Capri), his wife, played by Ingrid Bergman, discovers her strength (meaning of life in the cemetery); the couple appropriately break-up in Pompeii.

The natural beauty of Sicily's Aeolian islands has always attracted film crews. Film buffs will recognise Panarea as the setting for Antonioni's *L'Avventura* while Rossellini's *Stromboli* (1950) is set on the most volcanic island of all. Stromboli sparked off the romance between Roberto Rossellini and his star, Ingrid Bergman, an affair as doomed as the brooding melodrama of the movie. In the film, Bergman's character goes into hysterics with each volcanic eruption while in real life the lunar landscape ruined her hairstyle and humour; volcanic dust was a passion killer.

More recently, the island of Lipari features in *Kaos* (1984), a Taviani brothers epic that conjured a Pirandellian universe of legends and lost loves. Equally distinctive is Nanni Moretti's charming and quirky *Caro Diario* (Dear Diary, 1994), shot on various offshore islands, including Salina, as was Michael Radford's Oscar-winning *Il Postino* (1994), a lyrical look at life in a delightful backwater.

The Neapolitan film industry has flourished since the 1900s, from the era of silent films to lightweight commercial successes and the halcyon days of Italian neo-realism. The strength of this realistic tradition survives in the work of contemporary Neapolitan directors, who manage to express the vibrancy of everyday life at the same time as facing up to the negative undercurrents in southern society.

Italian cinema has also been enriched by the presence of fine Neapolitan actors, from the expressive slapstick of Toto, Italy's Charlie Chaplin, to Sophia Loren. The two starred in De Sica's *Oro di Napoli* (The Gold of Naples, 1954), with Loren as a pizza-maker. Ten years later, De Sica also featured the celebrated seductress in *Marriage Italian Style*, based on the work of Eduardo de Filippo.

The Neapolitan director Francesco Rosi served his apprenticeship with De Sica in the heyday of Italian neo-realism and has made a career out of examining the underbelly of southern society. *La Sfida* (The Challenge, 1957), shot in the style of an American gangster movie, tackles the Camorra's corrupt control of the city markets while *Mani sulla Città* (Hands on the City, 1963) deals with dubious property speculation in the city.

The leading lights of contemporary Neapolitan film making are Mario Martone and Pappi Corsicato. Iconoclastic Corsicato is noted for his scorn and caustic humour in such films as *Libera* (1991) while Martone's *L'Amore Molesto* conveys the emotional charge of a city so much a law unto itself that it sways Neapolitans from leaving.

Magnet for directors

Sicily is not slow to respond to its rival's cinematic tradition. Maria Grazia Cucinotta starred in *Il Postino*, and in the James Bond action film, *The World is Not Enough*. The island has always acted as a magnet for renowned directors. Luchino Visconti, one of the masters of postwar Italian cinema, set several films on the island to great effect. His epic, *Il Gattopardo* (The Leopard, 1963) is worthy of di Lampedusa's novel of the same name. Giuseppe Tornatore is the best-known contemporary Sicilian

director, thanks to the Oscar-winning success of *Cinema Paradiso* (1990). This nostalgic slice of Sicilian history, which shows the arrival of the Talkies in a benighted backwater, was shot in the village of Palazzo Adriano, near Palermo. The autobiographical film celebrates Sicilian exuberance with a bitter-sweet humour that mocks the grinding poverty. In the United States, the film broke box-office records for a foreign film.

Tornatore chose Siracusa as a beguiling backdrop for *Malena* (2000), his spirited romance set in Fascist times. The film also depicts a dramatic re-enactment of the Allied Landing on Pachino's

beaches, the same location chosen by rival director Fabio Conversi for *C'era una Volta in Sicilia* (Once Upon a Time in Sicily, 2000), about the landing of Garibaldi's troops in Sicily.

There is no mistaking the most popular theme in the Sicilian film canon. Leonardo Sciascia's anti-Mafia fiction has long inspired directors, but the finest Mafia portrayal is, heretically, American: Coppola's *Godfather* trilogy, featuring Marlon Brando and Al Pacino. Inspired by the internecine Mafia wars in Castellammare during the 1950s, the infamous town of Corleone lent its name to the Godfather. Coppola, a visionary maverick, orchestrates Sicily in celluloid. ❑

LEFT: Sophia Loren, who famously grew up in Naples' slums and became the Neapolitans' favourite star.
RIGHT: *Cinema Paradiso*, a 1990 Oscar winner.

MUSIC

Naples' opera is world famous. It grew out of a strong
musical tradition which is still lively today

Music is a mainstay of southern life and the Neapolitans' natural forte. Henry James said: "Neapolitan song has been blown well about the world, and it is late in the day to arrive with a ravished ear for it." His judgment is unfair: melodramatic love songs, *bel canto* opera, dance music and urban blues

still sound fresh in this most southern of cities. Although the rest of the south is musically overshadowed by Naples, operatic Sicily responds with Scarlatti and Bellini, two of Italy's greatest composers.

The 18th century was the golden age of Neapolitan music thanks to Scarlatti and the creation of the superb San Carlo opera house in 1737. Samuel Sharp attended a performance there in 1763 and was struck by the noisiness of the audience during the music but their rapt attention to the dancing. He was informed: "The Neapolitans go to see, not to hear an opera." Exuberance aside, noisy Naples has one of Italy's most prestigious opera houses,

second only to La Scala in Milan. Alessandro Scarlatti (1660–1725), one of the greatest southern composers, was born in Sicily but founded the Neapolitan school of music. He was a master of *opera seria*, which was inspired by mythological or historical themes and characterised by recitatives, which advanced the plot, and arias, which crystallised emotions. Scarlatti can also be considered the father of *bel canto*, a lyrical style which stresses the melodic line and carries a great emotional charge.

As one of the liveliest courts in Europe, Naples was also the birthplace of *opera buffa*, a light-hearted response to *opera seria*, situation comedies dependent on drama and improvisation. One of the best known Neapolitan composers of *opera buffa* was Domenico Cimarosa (1749–1801), whose many operas included *Il Matrimonio Segreto* (The Secret Marriage). Naples also possessed conservatoires where the finest *castrati*, such as Farinelli, were trained in both male and female roles.

Romantic opera

While Sicily does not have a musical tradition to rival Naples or Milan, it has an operatic passion out of proportion to its achievements. Bellini (1801–35), born in Catania, personifies the enchanting art of *bel canto*, and is considered the founder of romantic opera. *Norma* is the best example of the genre, a *bel canto* masterpiece noted for its fine tone and ornamentation.

In spite of modest past musical accomplishments, Palermo has always felt entitled to expect an opera house worthy of any in Catania, Naples or Venice. The recently re-opened Teatro Massimo lives up to expectations, both an eclectic white elephant and a potent symbol of Sicily's cultural renaissance.

Not that southern achievements are restricted to opera. Neapolitan songs date back to the time of the troubadours and are characterised by their sweetness, melody, lyricism and poetic lilt. While the best-known songs tend to be 19th-century and are assured a place in the southern canon, the rest are still valued, particularly since the creation of the Compagnia di Canto Popolare folk society in the 1970s. If Neapolitan ballads are world famous, it is also thanks to opera stars such as Enrico Caruso, who did not restrict themselves to a classical repertoire. Today, Roberto Murolo is the greatest exponent of such traditional ballads as *O Sole Mio*, *Funiculì-Funiculà*, and *Torna a Surriento* (Return to Sorrento).

Southern musicians have a talent for improvisation and inspired borrowing, confirmed by the fact that many songs depend on a key-note similar to the traditional blue note in jazz. The Arab and African influences in the south have

recently, Avion Travel, a virtuoso Neapolitan band, won the San Remo song contest, Italy's musical showcase, with their mix of rock, chamber music and Mediterranean melodies.

At best, southern dance, like southern music, manages to be both accessible and elitist. The tarantella, a boisterous folk dance originating from Campania, is currently enjoying a revival, with squares in the historic centre of Naples welcoming nightly hordes of talented dancing fans. Accompanied by guitar and tambourines, the dancers weave and twirl around the musicians, often clicking castanets. The city produces percussion instruments that do not exist

also enriched the musical tradition so that while jazz and rock rhythms fail to work in standard Italian, they ring true in Neapolitan. Among the talented singer-songwriters from the south, Pino Daniele is known for his Neapolitan urban blues. Sicilian singers also graft southern songs and music on to blues, rap or classical music. The Palermitan Giovanni Sollima is one of the best-known contemporary Italian composers, who combines classical and cutting-edge sounds in the manner of Philip Glass. More

elsewhere, as well as characteristic flutes, mandolins and tambourines.

In the 1870s, Henry James enjoyed a musical evening in Sorrento, entertained by an impromptu quartet of barber, tailor, saddle-maker and carpenter who played the violin, guitar and flute high on a splendid Sorrento terrace. "And so the afternoon waned, the purple wine flowed, the golden light faded, and song and dance grew free." The romance of southern dance is at one with images of the sun and the wine-dark sea. But as night falls, the summer dancing is sure to give way to the love, longing and melancholy embodied by traditional Neapolitan songs. ❑

LEFT: Domenico Cimarosa, composer of *opera buffa*.
ABOVE: Neapolitan tarantella, in an 1840 lithograph. The dance is enjoying a revival.

LITERATURE

Neapolitan theatre is the most dynamic in the country,
while Sicilian writing has produced an impressive canon of work

Southern Italian literature is dominated by Sicilian genius in all genres, and by the theatricality of the Neapolitans. The richness of both traditions owes much to the cultural melting pot that is the south. Naples was founded by the Greeks, and it is not too fatuous to see a link between the citizens' ancient ori-

gins and a love of drama. The climate of tolerance and cosmopolitan culture in Naples has also enriched the city's literary life. Sicily might not claim the verbal virtuosity of Naples but it has an even more cosmopolitan literary canon, with Greek, Arab and mainstream European influences. Yet, whether politically committed or languidly sensuous, Sicilian writing has a distinctive spirit, and a powerful sense of identity rivalled only by the Neapolitan tradition.

Given the vivacity of the people and their passion for language and public performance, it is natural that the Neapolitan literary impulse finds its truest expression in the theatre. However, given the overlap between words and

music in the city, the theatrical output ranges from audience participation and sung fables to musicals and mime. The *sceneggiata*, for instance, is popular melodrama with musical elements, a traditional Neapolitan genre successfully revived in the 1970s.

Neapolitan showmanship is traced back to the 17th-century *commedia dell'arte* character of Pulcinella, which in turn inspired Mr Punch. This masked, white-robed figure falls between comedy and tragedy, and is often seen as a metaphor for Naples itself. Although a victim of unrequited love and cruel treatment by his master, Pulcinella survives thanks to his irrepressible spirit and native cunning.

The Neapolitan character

Eduardo De Filippo (1900–84), the city's greatest actor and dramatist, was born into a theatrical family, but was inspired both by Pulcinella and by Pirandello, with whom he worked in the 1930s. Although De Filippo's themes and settings are typically Neapolitan, the universal quality of his comic mockery transcends the narrow world of Christmas cribs and city dialect. His black comedy, *Filumena Marturano*, which deals with death and duty, strikes a chord with all Neapolitans. The plot revolves around the wish of an elderly courtesan for her lover to marry her, a ploy to prevent him from leaving for a younger rival. According to traditional Neapolitan logic, respect for death is paramount, if self-interested, since only the dead can pave the way for the living in the hereafter and, in the here and now, help loved ones to win the lottery, a local obsession.

"The theatre must be a picture which draws its life from reality, a reality which is at the same time prophetic," says one of De Filippo's characters – a view that could be the playwright's own credo. Yet De Filippo's realism and mockery is outweighed by his humanity and compassion, qualities singled out as truly Neapolitan by a lesser, much feted writer, Luciano De Crescenzo. As the city's best-known contemporary writer and media figure,

De Crescenzo goes on to offer an insight into the warped Neapolitan mind, with its familiar dicing with death: "And what about the orange light?" he asks an old man who spends his days at traffic lights waiting for accidents. "The orange? That doesn't mean anything. We keep it to brighten the place up."

The Sicilian spirit

Native writers have used Sicily as a rich seam, mined for raw material and welded into Italy's most vibrant literary tradition. Despite the diversity, the common thread is the elusive yet unmistakable Sicilian spirit. In particular, people from Agrigento are a mysterious breed, often called "*né carne né pesce*", neither fish nor fowl. Yet this curious province has produced exceptional Sicilian writers: Empedocles, the pre-Socratic philosopher; Pirandello, the Nobel prize winning playwright; and Sciascia, the political novelist. Di Lampedusa, the author of *The Leopard*, also had his ancestral estate here. All these writers were gifted mavericks who shared a bitter-sweet relationship with their homeland. Empedocles committed suicide on Etna while Pirandello was the master of split personalities. Sciascia called his land a "wicked step-mother" yet rarely left, while Lampedusa was a languorous Sicilian prince who still produced a posthumous masterpiece, the greatest Italian novel ever.

Pirandello (1867–1936) is Italy's greatest dramatist, a writer who unites petty, provincial Sicily with universal themes of identity and loss. Just outside Agrigento, in the hamlet of Caos, is Pirandello's birthplace. The irony was not wasted on the master of the absurd, who called himself a "son of chaos". As one of Italy's most versatile writers, Pirandello covered philosophy, novellas, drama and comedy. His work paints a bleak picture of Sicily as a volcanic, violent, bestial land, yet one also ridden with bourgeois convention, from pursed lips and stiff-back chairs to arranged marriages.

Whereas Pirandello was an innovator, Giuseppe Tomasi di Lampedusa (1896–1957) was a traditionalist, with a poetic style steeped in Sicilian culture, aristocratic decadence and oriental fatalism. He is famous for producing a

novel which E.M. Forster calls "one of the great lonely books". *Il Gattopardo* (The Leopard) is the work of a nostalgic prince who described the absurdity of progress and optimism ("Nowhere has truth so short a life as in Sicily"). The fictional prince revels in the "voluptuous torpor" of a "lovely, faithless land" that dooms all new initiatives, even love, which is "flames for a year, ashes for thirty". Behind the bustle of the story is the concept of life as the forge of memory: one lives in order to remember. Death is ever-present even in the midst of pleasure, and visible in Sicilian excess and sensuality.

Leonardo Sciascia (1921–89) represents the opposing, realistic strand in Sicilian literature, considering himself a free-thinker in an enslaved country. As one of many southern writers committed to social and political engagement, he denounced the abuses of power and the subterfuge at the heart of Italian politics. He tried to stir slumbering public opinion to protest against the abuse of power by the state or the Mafia. Di Lampedusa would have told the polemical novelist that he was wasting his breath: "Sleep is what Sicilians want." Yet, while both literary traditions are true of Sicily, in recent years Sciascia would have been more vindicated than his princely predecessor. ❑

LEFT: Pulcinella, a figure from the *commedia dell'arte*, is often seen as a metaphor for Naples.
RIGHT: a city book stall.

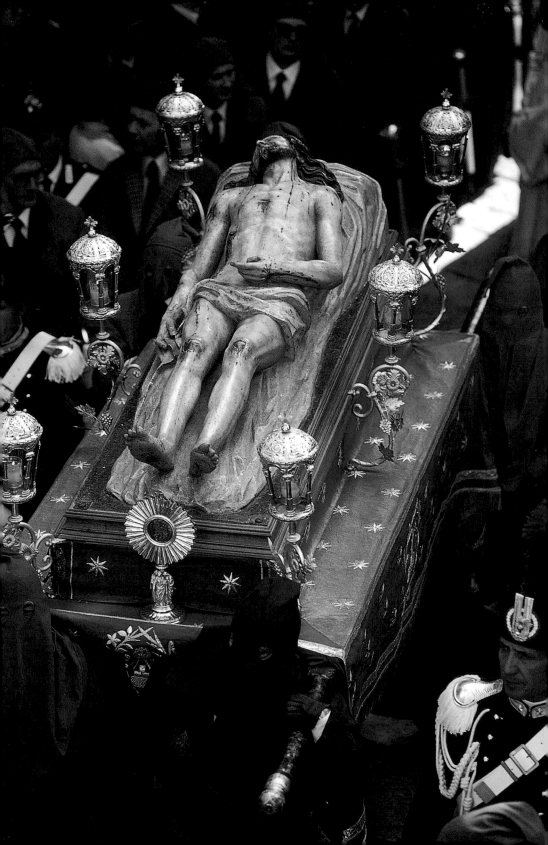

SAINTS AND SUPERSTITIONS

A deep belief in religion and strong superstition has created

a society of unusual customs and credos

While cast in the role of stereotypically sunny Italians, the southerners are deeply superstitious. "Under the purest of skies," wrote Goethe, "lie the most uncertain of souls." A deceptive serenity masks a fear engendered by the scourges of eruptions and earthquakes, epidemics and invasions, emigration and unemployment, crime and poverty.

In such a climate of uncertainty, it is hardly surprising if salvation is seen in terms of self-denial or self-preservation rather than self- fulfilment. Yet the spectacle of superstition, embracing miraculous apparitions and cabbalistic rituals, self-flagellation and paganistic festivals, only serves to deepen the southerners' genuine Catholic faith.

The south shelters a broad Church, instinctive and individualistic enough to ignore the Vatican's unease about unsanctioned practices, from the cabbala to the casting of spells, from ancestor worship to modern idolatry, or diabolical dancing and mortification of the flesh. In Sicily, for instance, the gory realism of the Easter re-enactments comes complete with penitential lashings. Even the *mafiosi* choose this moment to "make peace with God", or at least sign a short truce.

Charm offensive

Homes and cars are often adorned with amulets, dangling madonnas, and assorted charms while chapels are stuffed with bones and skulls, as well as the most impressive reliquaries in Christendom. Amid the grimacing statues and ghoulish skulls, there are enough pieces of the True Cross – many brought back through the crusader ports of Bari and Brindisi – to create a forest. In religion but not in business, people are happy to stretch their credulity, especially when traditional faith shifts to the far shores of the supernatural. These are the same rational citizens who visit charlatans as an insurance

LEFT: Good Friday procession in Molfetta, Apulia.
RIGHT: skull in Santa Maria delle Anime del Purgatorio, where a cult of the dead flourishes.

policy against the "evil eye". Southerners also remain fascinated by unsolved, and preferably blood-stained miracles, from the celebrated liquefaction of St Gennaro's blood to sundry Madonnas shedding red-tinted tears and even, such as in the case of the Madonna from Carinola, an abundance of milk.

In Naples, the blood of St Gennaro has liquefied, with a few telling exceptions, since 1389. Yet among the more convincing miracles, the so-called "Madonna detectives" have unmasked charlatans happy to produce valves of red liquid designed to be placed behind the relevant statue's eyes; triggered by a remote command, the statue then weeps blood. The Vatican does its best to play down such phenomena but to no avail: such "miracles" capture the public imagination.

San Biagio is the quarter famous in Naples for selling religious paraphernalia, from chalices and figurines to gilded saints and kitsch twinkling Madonnas. Esoteric perfumed candle shops include models that supposedly ward off evil spirits, as well as potions and remedies against the "evil eye", and personal talismans fashioned to your own requirements. But in typical double-edged Neapolitan tradition, there are also potions and manuals to guide dabblers in the occult through the intricacies of casting spells and curses. Southerners have a long tradition of casting spells. Remedies against the evils of the *jettatore*, or spellcaster, include touching a tiny horn of gold, silver or coral

> ### NUMBERS GAME
>
> In *La Smorfia*, a book of divination, numbers have different meanings: 19 represents both January and laughter; 17 simply means bad luck.

Armeno, the paraphernalia of the lottery is clearly visible, with wicker baskets ready for the magical numbers, and the lottery symbols written in both Neapolitan and standard Italian. *La Smorfia*, invented at about the same time as the lottery, is a mystical book of divination. In it, every dream is associated with a particular number, from 1 to 90, and used to predict the winning lottery numbers. The Church used to spur gamblers on by suggesting that all events were acts of divine providence, and disreputable clerics filled their coffers by confirming a link between divine grace and donations of specific sums of money.

(pictured on page 86). Folklore aside, southern cities still celebrate their patron saint's day with a fervour bordering on idolatry. To play a pall-bearer's role at a festival is considered one of the greatest honours in life.

Lottery and lucky numbers

Many southern Italians are slaves to the lottery, which has variously been seen as a way of rising above present circumstances, or as a chance to challenge fate and laugh in the face of the gods. Based on the Jewish cabbala, this Genoese import has been popular since the 16th century. In Naples, the numbers are drawn every Saturday. In atmospheric streets such as San Gregorio

Cults of life and death

Since it is considered impossible to win the jackpot without the intercession of the dead, the lottery encourages dealings with latter-day soothsayers, mediums in touch with spirits in the after-life. The Fontanella cemetery in Naples represents the overlap of the worlds of the living and the dead, and the place to consult the spirit world. Thousands of skulls and bones are lined up "ready for adoption" by people who have the time to devote to prayers for an anonymous, orphan soul. In return, and there is always a return according to local logic, the dead souls should watch over the living, helping them fulfil their dreams, and guiding them when it is time to "cross over to the other side".

The church of Santa Maria delle Anime del Purgatorio in Naples is a testament to the importance of the cult of death. The entrance is marked by three columns surmounted by a bronze skull, besides which are placed fresh carnations daily. This baroque church is built over an underground cemetery and ossuary where the skulls stacked in niches testify to the longevity of this curious cult. The church still belongs to an early 17th-century confraternity that was founded to collect alms to pay for Masses for the souls of the dead, thus speeding them on their way from purgatory to paradise. Although this practice of praying for trapped souls was officially banned by the church in 1967, the cult still survives, as do such macabre funerary motifs as the winged skull.

The wishes of the dying and care of the deceased are considered sacrosanct. All Saints Day, on 1 November, signals a bout of serious ancestor worship all over the south, with visits to the graves of loved ones on All Souls, *I Morti*, the Day of the Dead. After the tombs have been inspected and spruced up, special food such as *torroni dei morti* nougat is eaten. In the south, symbolic foods enliven the most sombre of occasions. Although this is a culture impregnated with death, the day is a festive occasion, with presents for children, and, in certain cases, propitiatory gifts to the gods. In Sicily, a rock-hard sugar doll, known as a *pupa*, is presented to the deceased before being ceremonially eaten by the living, in a cheerful form of cannibalism. The living soul symbolically

on walls communicate the news with the minimum of fuss, so pink or blue ribbons placed by a communal entrance indicate the sex of the latest arrival in the apartment block.

Greek beginnings

The south also represents the melding of different civilisations, each bringing its own set of superstitions and gods yet also displaying the essential vitality of southern culture. Fortune telling goes back to the time of the Greeks. At Cumae is the Antro della Sibilla, the sacred cave of the prophetess Sibyl, who was consulted by emperors and by Virgil, and foretold of the sack

takes on the spirit of the beloved, thereby assuming power over life and death.

Since southern Italians are also people of the here and now, the cult of the living is equally compelling. After a respectful nod to the deceased, a good Neapolitan takes the precaution of saying "*Salute a noi*", essentially a plea for a selfishly long and healthy life. The strength and immediacy of southern lives are clear in the confident public rituals regarding birth and death. Just as funeral notices pasted

LEFT: the casket containing the blood of San Gennaro, which liquefies three times a year.
ABOVE: services for the liquefication are well attended.

of Rome. Greek language and ritual were not generally suppressed in the south until the 12th century, and vestiges of it remain. Indeed the cult of the Madonna is seen by some to be descended from the cult of the great Greek goddesses such as Athena and Persephone.

In Sicily, the fertility cult is still celebrated in Enna, the site of the temple of Demeter, goddess of agriculture and fertility, and of her daughter Persephone's banishment to the Underworld. The origins of the tarantella, Naples' signature dance, supposedly date back to Greek times when the Three Graces created a seductive dance to entice Ulysses back after he had narrowly escaped falling under the spell of the song of the sirens, who lived in the siren lands, around the coast of Sorrento.

In the northeast of Sicily, the stretch of coast off Messina and Milazzo is awash with Greek-inspired myths: known as Mylae in classical times, Milazzo is the legendary site of Ulysses' shipwreck. Sailors north of Messina were wary of the twin demons of Charybdis, the whirlpool, and Scylla, the six-headed sea monster. It took an 18th-century scientist to demystify the whirlpools as the

> ### ALL YOU NEED IS LOVE
> "South Italians, famous for abstractions in philosophy, cannot endure them in religion. They only wish to love and be loved. The maxims of the Sermon on the Mount are incomprehensible to them"
> – NORMAN DOUGLAS, 1913

meeting of clashing currents. Marsala, set on Sicily's west coast, provides equally compelling classical allusions: by the shore of ancient Lilybaeum is a church built over a grotto to Sibilla Sicula, Apollo's prophetess. Her rock sanctuary is set over a sacred spring where, according to the cult of the sibyl, maidens drank her water and uttered incantations which the sibyl interpreted. This damp Delphic oracle still inspires devotion, from lovelorn girls to joyous citizens celebrating the Ferragosto festival.

Despite the grandeur of the Greek legacy, many southern myths and superstitions are far more ancient and atavistic. The central, most powerful piece of myth-making is connected with the life-threatening forces of Vesuvius and Etna, and the mountain gods who must be appeased at all costs. Adrano, set on the slopes of Etna, was the Greek city of Adranon, celebrated for its sanctuary to Adranus, the Siculi god of fire. Still today, during the bizarre August festival, a child dressed as an angel "flies" along a cord linking the old city powers: the castle, town hall and a statue of the god of fire himself. So far, Adranus has kept his city safe from fiery Etna.

The sense of appeasing the mountain gods survives in Zafferana Etnea, a hiking village and ski resort which found itself in the path of the 1992 volcanic eruption. Before abandoning his farmhouse to the volcano, Giuseppe Fichera, a local farmer, left bread, cheese and wine to satisfy "the tired and hungry mountain". Even gods of destruction need food and rest.

To present-day Sicilians, Etna is still an atavistic god. The city of Catania is a comfortable, commercial success yet feels distinctly uneasy living in Etna's shadow. In AD 253, Sant' Agata, the city's beloved patron saint, suffered martyrdom by being rolled in hot coals and having her breasts cut off. A February festival records her horrendous fate and she is tastelessly commemorated by breast-shaped jellies and cakes. Sant' Agata's statue or veil are still traditionally used to ward off impending lava flows, with mixed results.

Miracles and flying monks

Some miracle-working clerics have been seen to have power over volcanoes. Alfonso di Liguori, the 18th-century founder of the Redemptorist order, is said to have stifled Vesuvius and, like other saintly southerners, he also raised the dead. Miracle workers in the 19th-century included Fra Edidio of Taranto who brought back to life more than half a ton of eels (they are only sold live), and resurrected a butchered cow. In Calabria Francesco di Paulo raised 15 people from the dead while he was still only a boy.

Raising the dead was one miraculous power. Another saintly trait was flying, a particular 17th-century attribute. Most famous was Father Joseph, the Flying Monk of Copertino, who flew not just around his native Apulian town, but elsewhere in Italy, even appearing before an astonished Spanish Ambassador, a spectacle which apparently caused the Ambassador's wife to faint.

The miracles of these saints lived after them in the form of relics and images, which were used to repeat their supernatural feats.

Perhaps the most celebrated modern miracle worker, not yet quite a saint, though beatified in 1999, is Padre Pio di Pietralcina. He is one of more than 300, including St Francis of Assisi, who have claimed to have borne the stigmata – the wounds of Christ crucified *(see page 204).*

wants him." He called this process "a prolongation of the personality".

A great number of miracle workers in Apulia and Calabria have been made saints, and 10 popes came from the region. Reliquaries also abound. The 19th-century traveller Craufurd Tait Rammage wrote, "The quantity of holy relics in this part of the world is astonishing." He cites the monastery at Belforte as having a finger of Stephen (the first Christian martyr), a piece of the Holy Cross, the sepulchre in which Jesus was buried, and a fragment of the rod of Aaron, while the village of Soriano had a statue of St Dominic brought personally from Spain

Padro Pio's stigmata first appeared in 1918 while he was praying in the monastery at San Giovanni Rotondo on the Gargano peninsula. Like his flying predecessors, he had the ability to appear elsewhere: before the pope in Rome, and during World War II when his sky-borne image guided a lost American pilot to his base on the Italian coast.

Padre Pio believed that a person could be in two places at once. "One minute he is here," he said, "and the next moment he is where God

in 1530 by the Virgin Mary. Bari, on the other hand, claims to have the bones of St Nicholas, the original Father Christmas, which were brought here from Asia Minor and are now asked to work miracles among pilgrims.

The most famous pilgrimage site in the South is the shrine to the Archangel Michael on Monte Sant' Angelo. This crusader outpost was also the inspiration behind the creation of Mont Saint Michel in France. The spring water (now dried up) in his cave was undoubtedly once associated with dragon myths, as water is everywhere in the south, and it is not surprising that the dragon-slaying archangel should have found a home here. ❏

LEFT: lucky horns on sale, to protect against spellcasters known as *jettatori.*
ABOVE: Padre Pio on a balcony, San Giovanni Rotondo.

FESTIVALS AND THE PAGEANTS OF HISTORY

On land and sea, the south is cheered up with festivals for every season, celebrating local saints, glory days, wine harvests and the passing year

"There had been no bland evenings," wrote Henry James on a visit to Sorrento, "that, somewhere or other, on the hills or by the sea, the white glow and the red dust didn't rise to the dim stars. Dust, perspiration, illumination, conversation, plenty of fireworks, plenty of talk. That's all they want." The festivals that take place throughout the year all over southern Italy are a mix of pagan and Christian, historical, cultural, and agricultural. With music, costume and special food, they are all a matter of great local pride.

COSTUMES AND CARNIVAL

Food festivals are a feature of Salerno and, at Christmas, Naples. Pre-Lenten carnivals are held notably in Sciacca in Sicily, which is particularly rich with events. Easter sees the most activity in the streets, with hooded penitents from medieval fraternities and processions lasting up to 20 hours. Many towns celebrate their patron saints and Albanians hold their own festivals *(see page 258).* The past is re-enacted in a number of historical pageants, recalling days of former glory. In August the Saracen invasions are recalled in Positano, and Amalfi does not forget it was once a wealthy maritime republic. A palio at Orio, near Brindisi, puts on Swabian costume for the re-enactment of the wedding of Frederick II.

▷ **BUN FIGHT**
Festival bread, shaped like saints, is distributed in Agrigento on the first and second Sundays in June in honour of San Calogero, the town's patron saint.

▷ **FEBRUARY SONG**
Musicians from Sagra del Mandorlo in Fiore, Agrigento's celebration of almond blossom.

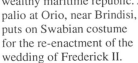

◁ ST NICHOLAS SETS SAIL
In May, the Bishop of Bari blesses the boat that will take the statue of St Nicholas, the town's patron saint, out to sea, accompanied by a flotilla of boats (far left).

△ MEDIEVAL FRATERNITY
One of the fraternities of St Nicholas in Bari, which date back to medieval times. The procession leads from cathedral where St Nicholas' relics are kept.

THE WARRIOR PUPPETS OF SICILY

Travelling puppet shows have provided entertainment in Sicily for centuries, telling tales of saints, bandits and heroes, but most commonly the Paladins, the knights of Charlemagne's court, and their battles against the Saracens. The Christians traditionally strut on the left of the stage, the turbanned, baggy-trousered Saracens on the right. The audience knows all the characters – the knights Orlando and Rinaldo, the beautiful Angelica and the traitor Gano di Magonza – who are as familiar as characters in a soap opera. Feelings run high, especially in the noisy battle scenes.

Almost life-size, the puppets are up to 1.5 metres (5 ft tall) and exquisitely attired (*the ones pictured above are on sale in Taormina*). A great puppeteer is judged by his skill in directing the battle, and by his sound effects, including commentary in an archaic dialect.

◁ AMALFI'S GLORY
The festival of Sant'Andrea in Amalfi in June celebrates the town's glorious past with costumes, fireworks and music.

▷ PALERMO'S PATRON
Santa Rosalia, the patron saint of Palermo is celebrated in the town's glittering festival of U Fistinu in July. The processions, fireworks and mayhem lasts six days.

◁ CARNIVAL CHARACTERS
Elaborate floats and figures in Sciacca, on the southeast coast of Sicily, make up one of the liveliest pre-Lent carnival parades in the south.

▷ VILLAGE FIGURES
Easter penitents in Montescagliosa, a hill village near Matera in Basilicata.

FOOD

Vegetables abound and there is pasta a-plenty, but each region retains its own distinctive cuisine

Southern Italy is so very different in character from both the northern and central regions of the country. It is truly a Mediterranean land dominated by the presence of the sea and specialising in hearty, spicy food – pasta, tomatoes, aubergines, fish, lamb and pork.

Campania is famous for Naples and its incomparable pizzas *(see page 96).* Calabria is a proud mountain area where life is simple and frugal, too, in parts. Basilicata, another mountainous region, is different – there the hunter tradition mingles with an Eastern influence to produce interesting dishes of lamb and pork. In Apulia, by way of contrast, vegetables and pasta predominate. Most of the great civilisations of the Mediterranean have left their mark on Sicily, the rich wheat basket of the Roman Empire, where pies were first made.

Campania

"The difference between the king and me is that the king eats as much spaghetti as he likes, while I eat as much as I've got." This old Neapolitan saying illustrates the unique character of Campanian cuisine: popular traditions and aristocratic traditions, having overcome ancient differences, find that they have a common bond in the higher ideal of pasta.

All Neapolitans are united in the name of macaroni and spaghetti and the phenomenon appears to be quite contagious. This simple and natural food has conquered the rest of the country and become the dominant feature of Italy's gastronomic culture. Without spaghetti and tomato sauce or macaroni and meat sauce (two of the specialities of this region), something very important is lacking and there is likely to be a feeling of unease and unhappiness.

This is not simply an old wives' tale or representation of a stereotype. It is part of a real need for an identity. Consequently a betrayal of, or offence against, spaghetti on the part of the cook is naturally not to be tolerated. A plate of inferior spaghetti, overcooked with an unsatisfactory sauce, causes frustration and disappointment and, like a character in a romantic serial, an Italian who suffers such an offence never forgets.

Calabria

A string of mountains between the Tyrrhenian and Ionian Seas, with only nine percent of its area low lying, where "the rivers are torrents, the mountain slopes subject to landslides, the forests destroyed" – this is a description of Calabria, the most southerly point of the Italian peninsula at the beginning of the 20th century. Travellers were struck by the violence of nature here, and by the theme of escape which seemed to dominate the character of the people.

When trade flourished in the Greek colonies of Croton and Sybaris, the Calabrians began leaving the mountains to move down to the sea. Subsequently they returned to the mountains to

LEFT: pasta making. The wheat fields of Sicily made the first macaroni, in classical times.
RIGHT: fish soup in Aci Trezza, Sicily.

escape the Saracen pirates, and when it became safe they went down once more to the sea and beyond in search of a better life. An isolated, patriarchal society held families together in the course of this displacement, so that each generation lived exactly the same way as the one before, even when it migrated abroad.

The only secure possession the people of Calabria could take with them and rely on in a foreign country was the dietary tradition of their ancestors. As soon as finances permitted, they re-created the lost atmosphere of their homeland around substantial quantities of *ragu* (beef larded with *pancetta* and cooked in wine with carrots, leeks, dried mushrooms, onions, tomatoes, nutmeg and cloves).

Calabrian cuisine is therefore a function of a collective memory, in which the dishes are evidence of time recaptured. How far back, for example, can we trace the taste of their cabbage soups or *pancotto* (broth, stale bread, garlic, bay leaves, celery and parsley) or mushroom soup or *lagane* (handmade *fettuccine* cooked in milk and sprinkled with *pecorino*, a hard cheese)? Each dish speaks of seasons' harvests and simple living on the edge of survival, where natural fruits of the earth and sea (snails, fish, game, figs, olives and almonds) were

BUFFALO CHEESE

In the terraced houses that line the winding streets of Naples, and in the farm kitchens of the rugged southern Italian countryside of Campania, with its fertile, volcanic soil, *mozzarella* has long been a staple part of the local diet. No one knows exactly how long the cheese has been made in the south of Italy but in AD 60 the Romans are recorded as making similar food, curdling fresh milk with rennet extracted from the stomach of a sheep or goat.

Legend also has it that the monks of San Lorenzo di Capua gave bread and *mozza* cheese to the hungry who came knocking on the convent door in the 3rd century. Eventually, the soft *mozza* cheese reputedly made by the monks became known as *mozzarella*. The word derives from the Italian verb *mozzare*, to cut off, the action of breaking the cheese curd into more manageable portions.

The transition of *mozzarella* made from sheep's milk to what is now considered the real thing made from the creamy milk of buffaloes came many centuries after the monks of San Lorenzo earned a reputation for their cheese. Indian water buffaloes, which roam wild in Southeast Asia, were introduced to southern Italy in the 16th century. They thrive in the mild dry climate, producing a rich, flavoursome milk from which the cheesemakers in the provincial capital, Naples, make *mozzarella di bufala*, buffalo *mozzarella*.

considered signs of the benevolence of the gods. Similarly, kid meat and cheeses recall the lives of the shepherds, while the many varieties of home-made pasta call to mind images of the family gathered around the table as the women of the household worked the dough.

The aubergine, too, the most used vegetable in this region, belongs to the same culinary world, whether it is cooked in vinegar and sugar or sautéed with garlic, stuffed or baked with cheese.

Basilicata

The region of Basilicata has two different names. Lucania is derived from the Lucanians, the earliest inhabitants of the area. The other is more recent, dating to the time of the Greek-Byzantine domination of the area; *basileus* is the Greek word for king, and the name Basili-cata meant a province of the Byzantine Empire. Thus the original pastoral-warrior civilisation was replaced by the sophisticated and decadent Eastern tradition – with note-worthy results in the kitchen.

On the one hand, there are some ancient recipes, typical of a primitive society of hunters, such as hare marinated in wine and flavoured with garlic and bay leaves, and par-tridge cooked with olives. On the other hand, there are flavour and taste combinations from the Near East that have come into general use in dishes such as *tagliolini*, made either with milk and saffron or with almond milk flavoured with cinnamon.

Another feature of Lucanian cuisine is that it has remained a private affair within the fam-ily or, at very most, the village. This is because the region is all hills and mountains, with iso-lated villages clinging to their tips. Poor com-munication in the past often meant that people could not leave the village even if they wished. Hence the traditions of the local cuisine have remained in the custody of household kitchens.

Two of the most popular dishes are boned lamb with celery, onions and rosemary and *gnumariddi,* lamb offal and sweetbreads cooked with garlic, onions and cheese. As in inland Apulia, lamb is the principal meat. Then there is pork, which is also made into sausages and hams of some repute, and for special occa-sions such as weddings, christenings and reli-gious ceremonies, chicken stuffed with *pecorino,* eggs and chicken livers.

The remainder of the diet consists mainly of vegetables, baked in the oven and eaten in vast quantities as a substitute for meat, which is too costly for family budgets. Aubergines and olives, anchovies and capers, potatoes baked with onions and *pecorino*, mixed dishes of vegetables including peppers, courgettes, broc-coli and tomatoes. Or else pasta, hard wheat *fusilli* with ricotta cheese and *strascinati* – tra-ditional pasta served with a sauce of chickpeas, green peas or lentils.

Apulia

Apulian cuisine is something of an anomaly in relation to the other regional cuisines. The pasta-meat-vegetable relationship here is, in fact, reversed; vegetables produced in vast quantities throughout the region come first and the other foods then follow. Peppers, aubergines, broccoli, spinach, artichokes, broad beans, tomatoes, peas and other produce unquestionably have the leading role in the Apulian diet with the other foods making up the entourage.

The tutelary deity linking the many-faceted vegetable world with the lesser world of the other foods is olive oil, more acidic and there-

LEFT: making *mozzarella* cheese in Potenza.
RIGHT: the fish market in Palermo.

fore stronger flavoured than the better known Tuscan oil. So what does one eat with the vegetables? Pasta first of all, in particular *orecchiette*. The women make these "little ears" of wheat-and-water dough following a ritual that goes back many hundreds of years.

Vegetables are also used in soups, notably the *maritata*, for which chicory, fennel, celery and *escarole* are boiled, layered alternately with *pecorino* and pepper and covered with broth; in *calzoni* and *panzerotti*, pastry rolls with various fillings that are baked in the oven or fried, or in the impressive pies made with kid meat, chicken, beef, potatoes, onions, courgettes,

tomatoes and cheese, which may be served as either first or second courses.

This cuisine has the same basic structure as that of Naples, with a baroque overlay; the dishes are complex, and preparation is lengthy and often done in several stages. The Apulians even go so far as to stuff figs, and fillings feature in all their traditional cakes and pastries for religious and agricultural festivals, including Christmas and Easter. The plentiful fish, molluscs and crustaceans of this region are known for their quality; the waters are largely pollution-free and teeming with life. Italy's major oyster beds are located here in Taranto, the oysters being brought into the harbour from the larger bay every season.

Even fish do not escape the pie pan, where they are alternated with layers of vegetables and flavourings from the Middle East. Cheeses – *mozzarella*, *scamorza*, *caciocavallo* and *pecorino* – are produced in large quantites inland, as is lamb which is cooked with garlic and herbs as it has been since ancient times.

Sicily

Sicily is a racial melting pot. Through the centuries, Norman, Islamic, Greek, Spanish and German cultures have left their mark and been distilled into a unique way of life. Over Sicilian cuisine float the fragrant aromas of aniseed, cloves, mint and cinnamon. It has been said that Sicily is a continent not an island, because there are elements in its geography and history that are unique and unrelated to the rest of Italy.

Located in the centre of the Mediterranean, Sicily has seen a succession of great civilisations: Greek, Carthaginian, Roman, Byzantine, Arab, Norman, French, Spanish and post-unification Italian. These civilisations accumulated one on top of the other, none of them actually disappearing, so that the economic, social and cultural structure of the island is the sum of all those that have preceded it over 2,000 years.

Its cooking is another aspect of this age-old baroque construction, composed of successive strata. The first and oldest is occupied by pasta; this is where wheat was first cultivated and made into flour, and where it was first mixed into the dough from which macaroni is made. Pastry making, known throughout the Mediterranean in Plato's time, was invented in Sicily. It was here that the seeds of the orange and lemon trees, pistachio nuts and dishes such as *cous-*

A ZEST FOR LEMONS

Whether as juice or grated zest, the lemon is utilised a thousand times a day. Covered with a vibrant peel, offering incomparable qualities, this "prince of fruits" was discovered on the slopes of the Himalayas and taken to Mesopotamia, the vast land between the Tigris and Euphrates. The Jewish people learned to cultivate the lemon during the famine of Babylon and then imported it into Palestine. When the Roman Empire extended into the East, lemons began to be grown in Sicily. Nevertheless, knowledge of the lemon did not spread to the rest of Italy until the 4th century, and did not reach France and Spain until the Middle Ages.

cous (tiny balls of semolina steamed with oil and then added to a rock fish broth) arrived from the Arab world. This is the birthplace of pasta with sardines, perhaps the most famous dish of the region. Recipes such as *caponata* from Spain and *stoccafisso* (salt cod) from Norway were elaborated here. The list could go on.

In simple terms, the cuisine of Sicily can be divided into "dinners for the rich and food for the poor" as the historian of Sicilian folklore, Giuseppe Pitrè, wrote at the beginning of the 20th century. From

CLASSIC DISHES

Siracusa was the gastronomic capital of the classical world, and here in the 5th century Mithaecus wrote *Lost Art of Cooking*, the first cookbook in the West.

all the island's specialities, *"fricasées, fricandea, ragouts* etc" and for desserts sorbets flavoured with peaches, figs and oranges.

The cooking typical of Sicily today is a combination of the eating traditions of the rich and the poor with additional differences imposed by the changing seasons. Sowing, threshing, the grape harvest, Christmas, Lent, Easter or the festivities of patron saints are ritually accompanied by gastronomic customs that have been handed down from father to son. On Christmas Eve, women

him we learn that the peasants lived mainly on bread: bread with onions, with broad beans, with olives, with cheese and, when they could afford it, with soup containing pasta or vegetables. To this basic diet, the fisherfolk added fish, mainly sardines, and tuna and swordfish for special occasions. And if worst came to worst, from August to December the entire island could count on prickly pears. The nobility, on the other hand, dined in a luxury that left foreign visitors open-mouthed; plates and cups of gold and silver, innumerable courses of

LEFT: lemons for sale in Amalfi.
ABOVE: lunch is a meal to be taken seriously.

still make *caponata* (so called because it is the traditional accompaniment to capon). On Sunday they still make pasta by hand; grape harvest time is still an occasion for eating roast peppers; and the return of the *paranze*, fishing boats, is celebrated with the wonderful taste of freshly caught sardines cooked on a spit. Sicilians continue to eat *cannoli* made with flakey pastry at Carnival time, meat pies at Easter; the saying "be frugal with salt because it hardens the brain and the heart" still goes, and the aroma of garlic, bay leaves, aniseed, mint, cinnamon and cloves still dominate Sicilian cooking. ❏
● *For a list of local dishes, see the Travel Tips section at the end of the book.*

The Perfect Pizza

Neapolitans lay claim to the birthplace of pizza. The author Elizabeth Romer describes the Neapolitan passion for pizza as a cult in Naples. It is an apt description, for in Naples mythology, passion and pizza entwine.

Naples was at its height in the 1780s, full of Bourbon wealth and spirit. Street vendors bought pizzas from small stands and roamed the city, selling slivers from a lidded metal box or a *tavolino*, a narrow board. The stands made pizza to order with simple, seasonal ingredients, including the newly

discovered tomato. It was at this time that *pizza marinara*, with its topping of tomatoes, garlic, oregano and olive oil, was born. A pizza delivered to King Ferdinando I and Queen Maria Carolina from Taverna de Cerriglio was said to be so well received that the king had a red-tiled pizza oven built at the Capodimonte Palace; another version of the story is that Maria Carolina, a Habsburg princess, would not allow pizza in the palace, so the king, tiring of going out for his favourite fare, built his own oven.

In 1830, Antica Pizzeria Port'Alba, the first *pizzeria*, opened in the heart of Naples. It quickly became a meeting place for the man in the street. For those who could afford it, there were pizzas topped with fish, shellfish and seafood, buffalo

mozzarella, cured meats and sometimes *cecinielli*, tiny white fish that are no more than larvae. The *Masturicola, a* popular pizza that no longer exists, was topped with lard, grated *pecorino* cheese and basil. Oregano and basil were the favoured herbs, as today. But because so many of the patrons were artists, students or workers living on shoestrings, the most common pizza was seasoned simply with oil and garlic.

The *pizzeria* developed a system for payment called *pizza a otto*; eat now, pay eight days later. The local joke became the question of whether pizza might be a man's last meal – if he died before he paid. Pizza was sold to passersby, along with deep-fried bits of dough studded with *prosciutto* ham, herbs or pieces of cheese and shaped into a variety of forms that were easy to carry and eat. These were originally made from odds and ends of dough but eventually evolved into a new form, fried pizza, which can still be found in some *pizzerie*.

Ask a Neapolitan what their favourite pizza is (*"Qual é la tua pizza preferita ?"*) and the chances are they will say, "La mia preferita é la pizza Margherita." As the story goes, the first classic pizza Margherita was made or at least named by Raffaele Esposito of the Pietro il Pizzaiolo *pizzeria*, now called Pizzeria Brandi. In 1889 Esposito was invited to the palace to create three pizzas for the visit of King Umberto and Queen Margherita of Savoy. The queen declared that her favourite was the patriotic one resembling the Italian flag with its colours of red (tomatoes), white (mozzarella) and green (basil). The pizza quickly became a Neapolitan classic and has been called *Pizza Margherita* after the queen to this day.

In the late 19th century, life was extremely hard for the Italian peasantry. By the end of the century, 5 million had made their way to America, 80 percent of them from the south. Their culture and their cuisine went with them. In pizza's migration, the crust has thinned and thickened, the shape has taken many forms and the toppings have stretched the culinary imagination. Few developed countries are without pizza and every culture has made its own stamp, from lotus-root-topped pizzas in Japan to pizza chain restaurants in Moscow.

In the 1950s and 1960s, as southern Italian families moved to the industrialised north seeking work, they brought with them their favourite food. Today the total sales of *pizzerie* exceed the sales of Fiat, the country's largest car manufacturer, and an estimated 7 million pizzas are produced every day. Local pizzas have become as accepted as the other indigenous foods of the area, incorporating regional ingredients and variations to provide a new tradition.

In Naples, it was only in the last two decades of the 20th century that the *pizzeria* evolved into a sit-down dining establishment. Now even some of the finest restaurants have a wood-burning oven to offer pizzas as a first course, while some *pizzerie* have begun to add other courses to their pizza menus. The colourful streets of Naples are still sprinkled with little stands selling pizzas by the slice, folded in half, a *libretto*, "like a book".

Neapolitans firmly believe that their original pizza is the best. And indeed it is. The water, flour, humidity and yeast combine to make excellent dough. Sunshine-ripened local tomatoes, which grow particularly well in rich volcanic ash, and delicious, dripping *mozzarella* cheese are impossible to beat.

In the mid-1990s a group of local *pizzaioli* or pizza-makers decided to create an organisation to defend the integrity of their product. *Associazione Vera Pizza Napoletana* has instituted courses and awards a diploma. Their logo is an image of the Neapolitan character Pulcinella, "Punch", holding a pizza paddle. Display of the emblem indicates that a *pizzeria* serves *vera pizza Napoletana,* a true Neapolitan pizza.

Their standards are based on the work of Carlo Mangoni, Professor of Physiology and Nutrition at the Second University of Naples. In alliance with the city of Naples, Professor Mangoni was asked to provide some research to establish the traditional ingredients and methods used to make a true Neapolitan pizza. The result was a 42-page document that outlined the historical roots of pizza, explored the traditional ingredients and the precise preparation and cooking process, and concluded with a detailed nutritional analysis.

This report was the first step in attempting to establish a DOC for pizza. The *Denominazione di Origine Controllata* (denomination of controlled origin) determines the geographic origin of specific foods and wines and outlines permitted ingredients and defines the production process.

The perfect pizza, DOC style, is based on three elements:
● First, the "crust", which is the simple combination of flour, water, salt and yeast. The Neapoli-

tans say that of all the components in their product, this makes it unique. The secret is in the overall rising time – at least six hours. Very little yeast is used for this slow rise and the result is a dough which is moist and very soft.
● Second, Neapolitan pizzas are scantily dressed. Crushed San Marzano tomatoes, slices of mozzarella, a few leaves of basil and a sprinkle of salt are added. All the ingredients used are raw, as the temperature of the pizza oven is high and the cooking time is quick. The final touch is a drizzle of oil from the *agliara*, dialect for the brass oil-can found on every pizza-maker's marble counter.
● Third, the oven: pizzas must be cooked in a

wood-burning oven. In a Naples *pizzeria*, the fire is almost never out. The oven stays warm with embers until the next kindling. ❑

Traditional DOC Pizza
Verace Pizza Napolitana Marinara Garnished with tomatoes, oil, oregano and garlic.
Verace Pizza Napolitana Margherita Garnished with tomatoes, oil, *mozzarella* and basil.
Verace Pizza Napoletana Margherita Classica Garnished with tomatoes, oil, *mozzarella*, basil and grated *Parmigiano-Reggiano*.
Verace Pizza Napolitana Margherita Extra Garnished with tomatoes, fresh cherry tomatoes, *mozzarella*, oil and basil.

LEFT: chef Silvio Martorano tosses the dough at the Gemma Pizzeria in Capri.
RIGHT: *pizzeria* in Naples, home of the ubiquitous dish.

WINE

Investors are increasingly interested in harnessing the bulk wine-producing regions and using local grape varieties to make top-class wines

Although Southern Italy has a proud wine tradition that dates back to the ancient Greeks, it has long been known for producing low quality, bulk wine. As in so many other aspects of Italian life, the famous wine names come from the north of the country. Marsala, the fortified wine from western Sicily, is the only Southern Italian wine that many people will know. Sadly, this is often because Marsala is widely used in cooking.

Since the beginning of the 1990s, however, this has begun to change and there are now many exciting developments. Local producers are increasingly turning from high-volume production to making quality wines, while investors both from other parts of Italy and the rest of the world are starting to take an interest in the south, especially in Apulia and Sicily.

Bulk wine production does, however, remain very important. Less than 5 percent of the wine produced in Southern Italy is bottled in the region rather than being sold off in bulk. Throughout Southern Italy only a small percentage of the vineyards are classified as Denominazione di Origine Controllata (DOC), the Italian version of the French *appellation contrôlée* system. There are a number of the best producers, especially in Sicily, who prefer to label their wines Indicazione Geografica Tipica (IGT), the Italian equivalent of the French *vins de pays* classification.

Local grape varieties are well adapted to the hot, dry conditions of Southern Italy *(see Grape Varieties, page 102)* and they produce many interesting wines which are welcome in a world of Chardonnay and Cabernet Sauvignon.

Campania

Campania includes Naples, Pompeii and the islands of Capri and Ischia. Of the 48,000 ha (120,000 acres) of vines planted only just over 1,000 are classified as DOC. The best wine is

LEFT: winemakers Giusto Occhipinti and Giambattista Cilia in their Sicilian vineyard.
RIGHT: wine from the Amalfi coast.

Taurasi, a red made chiefly from Aglianico. It is made in the hills near to the town of Avellino and is the South's first DOCG wine. DOCG is Italy's top wine classification and, so far, only 18 wines have this distinction. Taurasi develops complexity as it ages. The two leading companies are Feudi di San Gregorio and Mastro-

beradino. From Avellino also comes Fiano di Avellino, a white made from Fiano, possibly the best white variety of Southern Italy. Also from this area is another white, Greco di Tufo.

Basilicata

This is an area of long rolling hills and deep valleys. Basilicata is not obviously picturesque like much of Tuscany but it has an understated upland, rural charm. The vineyards are well inland and vines are planted up to around 600 metres (2,000 ft) above sea level. Because of the altitude the nights are cool even during the height of summer, which preserves the grapes' aromas and flavours. The region can suffer from violent summer storms. In June hailstones the size of golf balls can sometimes be seen cascading off tiled roofs as though they were bouncing along a fairway.

Aglianico del Vulture, is the only DOC of Basilicata. It has a long established reputation and has for many years been considered among the best red wines produced in Southern Italy. There are 1,200 hectares (3,000 acres) in the DOC centring on the small town of Rionero and the village of Barile. This wine is spicy and powerful and can be kept successfully for about 10 years. Paternoster is the best of the established producers.

Apulia

Along with Sicily, Apulia has been Italy's leading bulk wine-producing region. Now that the bulk wine market has declined and European Union subsidies are more tightly regulated, the region is turning more and more to producing less but of a higher quality.

Apulia is easily the largest wine producer of the mainland South, churning out around 800,000 million hectolitres a year. The vast majority of this is bulk wine, which still accounts for around 98 percent of the production. Only a small percentage is bottled as DOC. The main DOCs in northern Apulia are Castel

DOC WINES

Denominazione di Origine Controllata (DOC) denotes a delimited wine region, and the following are the DOC regions in Southern Italy.

Aglianico del Vulture, Basilicata. Potentially one of Italy's finest reds. Paternoster is the leading company.

Castel del Monte, Apulia. This northern Apulian appellation produces variable wines in all three colours. Rivera is the best producer.

Cirò, Calabria. The best red from Calabria and made from Gaglioppo. Leading producers: Librandi and San Francesco.

Marsala, Sicily. Fortified wine "invented" by a Liverpool wine merchant, John Woodhouse, in 1773. Much of the production is high volume, low quality at a cheap price. De Bartoli is the best producer; look out for his Vecchio Samperi, a VDT.

Salice Salento, Apulia. Red appellation close to Taranto with a growing reputation for powerful, easy drinking wines.

Taurasi, Campania. High-quality red made from Aglianico. Mastroberadino is the leading producer.

Vino di Tavola (VDT) is the day-to-day quaffing wine, like the ubiquitous Lacrima Cristi del Vesuvio, which comes from the vineyards in the area around Vesuvius.

Most Italians dining out will simply settle for a carafe of the local or house wine *(vino locale* or *vino della casa)*.

del Monte, Locotondo and San Severo. Castel del Monte comes in all three colours and is named after the imposing and geometrically intriguing octagonal Norman castle that dominates the northern Apulian plain, a rather featureless stony flatland sloping gradually towards the Adriatic.

There is a move towards making quality wines by reducing the yields and, as elsewhere in Italy, increasing the density of plantation. However, standards remain variable here. Rivera at Andria, a well established company, is the most dynamic and quality conscious in the area. The company was founded in 1950 by the

which is built around a steep, limestone ravine. Here an eponymous white DOC wine is made from Greco and Malvasia. Also in this part of Apulia is the co-operative of Locorotondo. DOC Locorotondo is solely for lemon- and lime-flavoured whites which can be made from Verdeca, Bianco d'Alessano and Fiano.

Wines from the hot Salento peninsula have a growing reputation, in particular the powerful Salice Salentino reds made from Negromaro and Malvasia Nera and also Copertino made from Negromaro. Around Manduria, Primitivo, which used to be used for blending, is now increasingly being bottled, giving big, juicy

de Corato family, who have long been bottling their wines. Their top red is the complex Il Falcone, which shows what can be achieved here. DOC San Severo comes from north of Foggia. All three colours are made and one of the leading producers is Alfonso di Sorda.

The land to the south and south east of Bari is more undulating and interesting. This is the area characterised by white huts called *trulli* centred around the town of Alberobello. Near the border with Basilicata is the town of Gravina,

opulent wines. Leading producers in southern Apulia include Francesco Candido, the co-operative of Copertino, Leone de Castris and Cosimo Taurino.

Calabria

Much of Calabria, the long toe of Italy, is too mountainous to be suitable for growing grapes and there are few areas suitable along its very long coastline where vineyards can be established before the mountains rise.

Cirò, produced on the Ionian Sea coast, is the best known wine of Calabria. A little white Cirò is made from Greco but most of the production is red from the Gaglioppo grape. From

LEFT: Apulian vineyard with *trulli* farm buildings.
ABOVE: vines thrive particularly well in the volcanic soil around Mount Etna.

a producer such as Librandi or San Francesco, Cirò is an attractive red that is probably best drunk within five or six years of the vintage. Greco di Bianco is a sweet wine made from semi-dried grapes from the town of Bianco in the deep south of Calabria. Across on the Ionian coast there are some interesting wines being made around Lamezia.

Sicily

Although blisteringly hot in July and August, Sicily has a number of natural advantages that makes it possible to make good quality wines. There are many hillside sites with thin, poor soils that, with the sun and low rainfall, make them ideal for growing vines. There are vineyards planted up to 900 metres (3,000 ft) above sea level. This moderates the heat of summer and means that the nights are cooler than on the plains. Both factors help to preserve grapes' aromas and flavours.

However, until recently Sicily concentrated on high-volume grape production for the bulk wine market. Much of the island's production was destined to be made into grape concentrate or sent for compulsory distillation. The emphasis is now gradually shifting towards making quality wines. The Duca de Salaparuta, a large modern winery just to the east of Palermo, is one example. Their Duca Enrico is one of Sicily's best reds. Other notable producers include Regaleali and Terre di Ginestra, both in the Palermo region. Sicily's most high profile foreign investor is the Australian company BRL Hardy, whose d'Istinto range is produced in their Calatrasi winery in Palermo.

Marsala is made at the extreme western end of Sicily. This fortified wine is made mainly from Catarratto, Grillo and Inzolia grape varieties. There are various grades of quality; the highest being Marsala Vergine or Solera. This is lightly fortified and has to be aged for at least five years. There is much indifferent Marsala made but it can occasionally be amongst the finest fortified wines of the world.

The island of Pantelleria, just off the Tunisian coast is known for its sweet Moscatos. Look out for Moscato Passito di Pantelleria. ❑

LEFT: vintage Marsala, Sicily's fortified wine.
RIGHT: the cellars of Carlo Pelleorino in Marsala.

GRAPE VARIETIES

Red

Aglianico: responsible for the two best reds of Southern Italy – Aglianico del Vulture (Basilicata) and Taurasi (Campania).

Gaglioppo: widely planted in Calabria. It is a long ripening variety and is not harvested until early October.

Magliocco: planted in Calabria and believed to be an ancient Roman variety.

Negromaro: most popular red variety of Puglia, producing powerful and deep coloured wines. It is most successful in Salice Salentino and Copertino.

Nero d'Avola: Sicilian variety, makes the island's best reds.

Primitivo: linked with Zinfandel of California, there remains a dispute whether Primitivo was taken over to the United States from Italy in the 19th century or whether Italian immigrants returning to Southern Italy imported Zinfandel which became known as Primitivo. Makes powerful, spicy wines in Puglia, especially at Manduria.

White

Fiano: perhaps Southern Italy's best white grape.

Greco: used to make successful whites in Basilicata and Calabria because it manages to keep sufficient acidity and aroma.

ARCHITECTURE

*The extraordinary diversity of architecture includes a blending
and extending of styles found nowhere else in Europe*

The earliest surviving buildings of any significance in Southern Italy belong to the period of Greek colonisation during the 5th and 6th centuries BC. These are the three remarkably well-preserved temples at Paestum, a city whose prosperity and importance under both Greeks and Romans are mirrored in the extent and variety of its ruins.

There were once many more temples, but the grandeur of those which remain, the so-called Basilica, originally dedicated to the goddess Hera, the Temple of Ceres, actually built as a shrine to Pallas Athene, and the imposing Temple of Neptune, bears witness to the sophistication of architecture in Magna Graecia generally, even if elsewhere the evidence for this is rather more fragmentary. In towns such as Taranto, Locri and Crotone, the sites of major Greek buildings are identifiable, but their actual stones were removed long ago, to be re-used in churches, castles and palaces, while the columns which formed a key element in classical architecture are often to be found in the nave of a cathedral, on either side of a doorway or built into the wall of a house.

Roman landmarks

The Romans, in occupying the southern cities after winning the Punic Wars, tended to respect the existing structures, enlarging the central *agora* or marketplace to create a colonnaded forum with adjacent law courts and baths. To the larger towns they also added amphitheatres, as at Capua (now Santa Maria Capua Vetere) which boasted the empire's second biggest after the Colosseum in Rome. Another characteristic feature of the Roman townscape which survives here and there is the triumphal arch, raised to celebrate the conquests of a reigning emperor and decorated with relief sculpture, inscriptions and busts. The grandest of these, essentially a fusion of the most elegant classical style with a

sequence of political propaganda statements in the form of inscriptions and friezes, is the Arch of Trajan at Benevento, built in the emperor's honour around the mid-2nd century AD.

Roman domestic building is best seen during a visit to Pompeii and Herculaneum *(see page 157)*, the cities preserved for centuries

under the crust of lava from Mount Vesuvius's catastrophic eruption in AD 79. The typical house of the period tended to concentrate on an inner atrium or courtyard surrounded by colonnades, with rooms leading off this, and an additional quadrangle, known as the *peristyle*, containing a garden and opening via a portico on to the street. Many of the Pompeiian houses reveal the highly developed lifestyle of ordinary people in the Roman Empire, with their frescoed rooms, heating systems and water supply created from catching rainwater in the *compluvium* or basin at the centre of the courtyard.

With the spread of Christianity throughout the empire, churches sprang up all over Southern

LEFT: building the cathedral in Otranto, from the 12th-century floor mosaic in the nave.
RIGHT: Valley of the Temples, Agrigento.

Italy, but only a few traces of such buildings from this period (2nd–5th centuries AD) remain, at Naples for instance, in the church of San Gennaro extra Moenia, with its nearby catacombs (underground chambers for Christian worship) and in the chapel of Santa Matrona at San Prisco near Capua.

A much stronger imprint on Christian architecture throughout the south was left by the Byzantine Empire, mostly in the form of small churches on a typically Greek plan, involving a central dome with four smaller domes clustered around it. The church of San Marco at Rossano, above the Gulf of Taranto, offers a good exam-

ple of late work in this style, while high up in the hills of southeastern Calabria, the Cattolica of Stilo is an almost perfect example of Byzantine architecture, with frescoes and re-utilised classical columns turned upside down to show Christianity's triumph over pagan superstition.

The Normans and Romanesque

The arrival of Robert Guiscard and his conquering Norman army during the 11th century brought with it the new style of architecture known to us as Romanesque, which had taken hold all over Europe, from France and Germany to the cities of Northern Italy. A typical

PAESTUM'S INFLUENCE ON WORLD ARCHITECTURE

The temples of Paestum represent some of the most influential buildings in the entire history of world architecture. Though travellers in the region had known about the ruins and the famous roses which had flourished here since the days of the Greeks, it was not until the mid-18th century that the site was "discovered" by connoisseurs living in Naples and Rome. Count Felice Gazzola, one of Charles III's ministers, encouraged foreign visitors to make the hazardous journey across the wild, malarial terrain surrounding the temples, and by 1787, when the German poet Goethe set out from Salerno to see them, a law had been passed to prevent coachmen overcharging such aesthetic

enthusiasts. Though Goethe was frightened by the blood-red eyes of the local buffaloes "which looked like hippopotamuses", his reaction on first seeing the temples was typical. "At first sight they excited nothing but stupefaction. I found myself in a world which was completely strange to me. Only by walking through them and around them can one attune one's life to theirs." Echoes of Paestum's magnificent Doric colonnades can be found everywhere, from Boston and Philadelphia, Paris and Moscow, to London's British Museum and the work of Scottish architects such as Glasgow's 19th-century genius "Greek" Thompson and Edinburgh's "Athenian" Stuart.

Romanesque church features an imposing portico, its columns resting on crouching lions and its bands of carving around the doorway adorned with figures from myth and folklore, as well as dragons and peacocks. Small, round-arched windows look down on a nave containing an ornate mosaic floor (as in Otranto Cathedral) from which steps rise to a presbytery and the high altar, with the bishop's throne behind it and an apse beyond. On either side of this part of the church are decorated pulpits *(ambones)* for the

NORMAN LEGACY

"I felt that I might have been walking on the Bayeaux tapestry."
– H.V. MORTON on Otranto cathedral's unique mosaic floor.

the relics of St Nicholas, recently looted from the Byzantine city of Myra in Asia Minor (Turkey). Sicily has the most splendid examples in the cathedral at Cefalú and the monastery of Monreale in Palermo.

In the late 12th century, the Romanesque style began to give way to Gothic, with its emphasis on greater height and volume in the overall design of large buildings, its more elaborate style of vaulting in the construction of church roofs and its fondness for decoration and ornament, in forms such as the

reading of the epistle and gospel at Mass, and below the whole structure runs a crypt, its columns intricately carved with religious scenes or fanciful ensembles of leaves and grotesque faces.

Examples of this style are found everywhere in the Mezzogiorno, from Canosa, Ruvo di Puglia and Bitonto to L'Aquila, Acerenza and Salerno, though the dominant model for them all was probably Bari's great, fortress-like church of San Nicola, begun in 1087 to house

LEFT: the Temple of Neptune, Paestum.
ABOVE: Monreale Cathedral, an apogee of the Sicilian mix of Arabic, Byzantine and Romanesque styles.

ogival arch, the rose window or the crocketed finial. Though we tend to associate Gothic more obviously with Europe north of the Alps, Southern Italy possesses several splendid examples of this type of architecture. The great abbey of Fossanova is among the most outstanding. Built by Cistercian monks in the late 12th century, in an idiom clearly deriving from their order's homeland in eastern France, its nave and aisles are separated by pointed arches resting on clustered columns, from which shafts rise towards a cross-vaulted ceiling.

In Naples, the strong French influence in a variety of Gothic buildings was due to the Angevin monarchs ruling the kingdom between

1268 and 1442. Many of the major churches, including the Duomo, San Lorenzo Maggiore, Santa Maria Incoronata and above all San Domenico, retain their medieval aspect, despite later monuments and decorative detail.

The city also has two important secular buildings dating from the period of Norman and Angevin domination, the Castel dell'Ovo, a fortress built by William I of Sicily in 1154 and the Castel Nuovo or Maschio Angioino, the chief fortress of Naples, begun in 1279.

SPAGNOLISMO

The Spanish aristocracy of Palermo delighted in *spagnolismo*, a love of ostentation, which was reflected in the Sicilian city's showy baroque architecture.

Frederick's classic Gothic

The most remarkable building to have survived from the turbulent Middle Ages in southern Italy is the Castel del Monte, near the Apulian town of Andria. Raised around 1240 by Emperor Frederick II on a barren hilltop, this octagonal structure combined the functions of a castle and a palace. Its most striking qualities, apart from the overall balance of its proportions, is the fusion of Gothic detail in vaults and windows with touches of Classicism, which seem to anticipate the Renaissance, especially in the entrance porch, whose angled pediment and flanking columns are probably ideas from Roman buildings surviving at the time.

Frederick's castle at Lucera in Apulia, is equally impressive, with walls a mile long that encircled his palace, treasury, mint, harems, zoo and, at one time, housed his 20,000-strong Saracen army.

From the Renaissance period (roughly 1400–1600) almost nothing of any real architectural significance exists in the Mezzogiorno to rival the outstanding achievements of northern and central Italy. There are several reasons for this. None of the southern towns enjoyed the same degree of independence and mercantile wealth as that of centres like Florence, Venice or Milan. The feudal nobility lacked the necessary public spirit to endow the building of churches, town halls or civic amenities such as loggias and fountains, and they showed little interest in planning handsome streets and squares to improve the appearance of the towns.

The Aragonese monarchy added minor embellishments to several cities during the 15th century, but the Spanish viceroys saw no reason to spend the kingdom's gradually diminishing resources on major architectural projects.

The most important examples of Renaissance building design in the Italian south are to be found in Naples. Though sculptors from Lombardy and Tuscany worked on the Triumphal Arch of Alfonso I, added in 1451 to the Maschio Angioino where the city council rules, the chief artists involved, Francesco Laurana and Domenico Gagini, were both firmly settled in Naples and helped to evolve a local sculptural style. The Arch is thoroughly representative of its period, displaying classical columns and entablature, allegorical figures in niches, carved relief panels and the figures of river gods in a pediment topped by a Corinthian column drum supporting the Archangel Michael dressed as a Roman warrior.

To the last years of the Renaissance belongs the Palazzo Reale, in Piazza del Plebiscito, the work of the Florentine architect Domenico Fontana, who began it in 1600, when it was hoped (in vain, as it turned out) that King Philip II of Spain would visit the city.

LEFT: Frederick's octagonal Castel Del Monte in Apulia, which anticipated the Renaissance.
RIGHT: Basilica Santa Croce in Lecce.

Catholicism and baroque

With the onset, during the late 16th century, of the Counter-Reformation, the Catholic Church's initiative towards recovering spiritual territory lost to Protestantism and other heretical beliefs, much effort was devoted to beautifying and sometimes wholly reconstructing churches throughout the kingdom, as well as building many new ones, often dedicated to newly canonised saints such as St Teresa and St Philip Neri, whose cults were energetically promoted. In the early decades of the 17th century the style we know as baroque, outwardly majestic and imposing, while its interiors were fanciful and heavily detailed in design, began to take hold throughout Europe.

Southern Italian Catholicism, fervent, ecstatic and embracing many elements of ancient paganism, took eagerly to this new architecture, more particularly because its exuberance ran counter to the rather more gloomy variety of religious devotion favoured by the ruling Spaniards, however scrupulous they were as practising Catholics.

Sometimes an entire town, not just in its churches and palaces, but in the decoration of ordinary houses and public buildings, might reflect this baroque enthusiasm, especially if

IL BAROCCO LECCESE

Lecce's baroque palaces and churches are among the most memorable of Southern Italy's unexpected visual delights. The development of a local architectural style during the late 16th century, making use of motifs derived from buildings further north, in Naples and Rome, was based on the availability of a fine honey-coloured sandstone, easily sculpted into ornamental forms for use in the creation of stately doorways and elaborate windows. The balcony also plays an important part in the impact of this "southern baroque". A dominant feature in town houses of the Mezzogiorno, it sometimes reminds us of Spain, whose cultural influence on the whole region was so strong.

The word "baroque" is of obscure origin and loosely applied. In Lecce, where the style lasted until the end of the 18th century, it involves a use of fantasy and improvisation in forms derived from classical architecture – the column, the pediment, the frieze, the volute – to create an effect of wilful exuberance in the individual profile and detailing of the various buildings, almost as if the architects, such as Giuseppe Zimbalo and Gabriele Riccardi, were deliberately stretching the established rules of decorum to breaking point. The Leccesi themselves will tell you that the architecture reflects Apulia's sturdily independent character in this refusal to observe convention.

the locality offered a suitably workable stone. This was especially true of certain towns in southern Apulia, notably Lecce *(see page 109)* and Martina Franca, where a brilliant species of vernacular baroque evolved during the mid-18th century, wholly altering the appearance of streets and squares with its grandeur, fantasy and elegance. The style spread to smaller neighbouring communities, and we can catch hints of it in the extravagant ornament of windows, doorways or balconies throughout the region.

Once the Bourbon monarchy had established itself, after 1734, the need was felt for additional royal palaces in Naples, to emphasise the

Flemish Van Wittel) presents by far the most expansive statement of the late baroque palatial style anywhere in Italy. The building would have been grander still, with a central dome and flanking pavilions, but King Charles's successors were uninterested in completing the project as originally planned in 1752.

Pompeii's legacy

The gradual shift in taste during the late 18th century towards a more austere interpretation of architecture's Greek and Roman heritage was much influenced by the rediscovery of Pompeii and Herculaneum which began taking

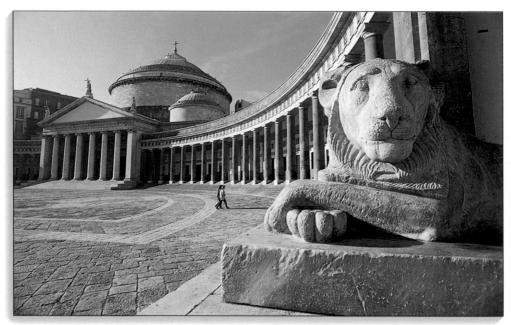

new king Charles III's status and to emulate his northern Italian fellow sovereign, the King of Savoy. Hence Charles built himself a summer hunting lodge, on a very grand scale despite its sober appearance, at Capodimonte (part of it now housing the Galleria Nazionale) with a park, a porcelain factory, an armoury and a sequence of handsome state apartments.

It was a second palace, at Caserta to the northeast of the city, which authenticated the Bourbons' significance among 18th-century rulers. Intended as a rural retreat in the unblushingly grandiose manner of Louis XIV's Versailles, Caserta, designed by the architect and painter Luigi Vanvitelli (an Italianised version of the

place at the same time. Architectural neoclassicism made comparatively little impression on the south, though a much admired example of the genre can be found in Pietro Bianchi's Neapolitan church of San Francesco di Paola (1817) based on the Pantheon in Rome, one of the most influential of ancient buildings in the inspirations it offered to European architects in the late 18th and early 19th centuries.

A significant new feature of Italian towns during the same period was the creation of theatres specifically designed to present performances of opera, the dominant musical form throughout Italy. These opera houses had an important social function as meeting places for the community, and during the occasional severe winter they had the added advantage of providing warmth in an age without adequate means of domestic heating. The traditional plan, involving a horseshoe auditorium arranged in tiers of boxes centred on a decorative proscenium arch, can be found in many southern cities from Salerno to Bari. Most distinguished among them is undoubtedly Naples' Teatro San Carlo, begun in 1737. Originally the back wall of this theatre could be removed to display a distant prospect of Mount

SOUND IDEA

When the San Carlo opera house was rebuilt after a fire in 1816, clay pitchers were inserted in the walls to improve the acoustics.

drained Pontine Marshes between Rome and Naples. Despite the discredited ideology which built them, their layout and architecture have been favourably reappraised in recent years. Industrialisation during the Fascist era did not improve the aspect of port cities such as Brindisi and Taranto, soon to be battered by repeated air attacks during World War II. After the war, little of any real distinction in the field of modern design was added to the average Southern Italian townscape. In recent decades exploitation by cowboy developers has

Vesuvius, which obliged with a minor eruption during the performance in 1827 of an opera entitled *The Last Days Of Pompeii*.

Mussolini's style

After Italy's complete unification in 1870, the major towns of the Mezzogiorno lost their walls and gates, while suburbs spread around their historic centres, where street-widening often resulted in the ruthless demolition of ancient buildings. Under Mussolini, new towns were founded at Sabaudia and Latina, in the recently-

LEFT: San Franciso di Paola, Naples, has classic grace.
ABOVE: modern departures in Vietri on the Amalfi coast.

helped to disfigure whole areas, especially in Calabria. Perhaps the best symbol of genuine architectural progress in the Mezzogiorno is the award of the contract for Salerno's new regional courts of justice to the cutting-edge British architect David Chipperfield, noted for his concern for the relationship between buildings and the environment.

Only a change in the prevailing southern culture of corruption in local government is likely to generate similar projects elsewhere, in an area which has always lacked the money and the initiative to create the kind of architectural contexts which lend beauty and grandeur to the cities and landscapes of northern Italy. ❑

VOLCANOES AND EARTHQUAKES

Ancient gods created them and tourists have flocked to see them.
The eruptions can be both spectacular and deadly, in this unquiet land

One could hardly imagine a more frightening natural event than an earthquake or volcanic eruption. And yet for thousands of years people have lived in the midst of areas prone to such disasters. The eruption of Vesuvius on 22 March 1944, moved the special correspondent for the *Manchester Guardian* to write: "These Italians show a truly remarkable indifference in the face of disaster. I had expected scenes of panic, frantic ladies, crazed family men. There was nothing of the kind. They gathered in groups to observe the slow sacrifice of the village."

Italy's danger zone for earthquakes and volcanic activity extends from the east coast of Sicily to the central–southern section of the Appennines, an area that includes the most densely populated portion of the peninsula: the string of towns at the foot of Mt Vesuvius, in Campania, which are home to more than 600,000 people, and the nearby city of Naples. For Italians living in the shadow of a volcano, the local monolith is an object of myth, affection and fear, an ever-present and long-silent reminder of the natural forces that have shaped the region's past and at any moment might alter its present.

Impotent science

Modern science has brought greater understanding of the causes of earthquakes, and organisation and technology can help to minimise their impact, using anti-seismic architecture, better and more efficient first-aid, and rapid reconstruction after the event. But experts still cannot tell us when or with what force the disaster will strike.

As inescapable as the threat of these natural disasters is, when they actually occur, they also tend to reveal some of the less appealing sides of the culture of Southern Italy: the corruption,

LEFT: lava flow from Mt Etna's last great eruption which lasted 473 days in 1991–93.
RIGHT: the Irpinia earthquake in Calabria in 1980 killed 6,000 and left 300,000 homeless.

bureaucratic morass and resigned fatalism of the South come into play and remain long after the lava flow and shaking have stopped. As always seems to be the case, it is the ordinary citizens who pay the price, many stuck for years and even decades in "temporary" shelters and prefabricated mobile homes. In the

scandalous aftermath of the earthquake that in 1968 hit the Valle del Belice, near Selinunte in Sicily, the 80,000 local residents lived in "emergency" housing for more than 20 years, as "interested" parties and Mafia contractors siphoned off government relief funds for reconstruction. The story of the earthquake which in 1980 shook the Irpinia area west of Naples is another notorious case of corruption and broken promises. After the earthquake, more than $30 billion earmarked for reconstruction never reached its destination.

Italy's enormous volcanic chain stretches, for the most part submerged, from Sicily to the Pontine Islands in Lazio along the western side of the peninsula. Most Italian volcanoes are long extinct; some have become lakes or were transformed into islands of charming beauty with post-volcanic activities such as the hot springs, geysers, pools of slightly radioactive mud and natural saunas of Ischia, Salina and Vulcano. Etna, Stromboli, and Vulcano (all in Sicily), as well as Naples' Vesuvius, are all active volcanoes, and major tourist attractions.

With a height of 3,323 metres (10,900 ft), a base of nearly 1,600 sq. km (618 sq. miles) and a perimeter of 150 km (93 miles), Mt Etna is the largest volcano in Europe. By contrast, Vesuvius (from the Latin *vesbius* meaning

"unextinguished"), only 1,277 metres (4,190 ft) high, is one of the smallest active volcanoes in the world. Vulcano and Stromboli, in the Aeolian islands, are constantly active, emitting modest quantities of vapours, ash, pumice and lava, creating a unique spectacle, especially at night. The Solfatara, in the Phlegraean Fields, is an example of a half-extinct volcano with whistling geysers.

Mythological meaning

Before being treated in a "scientific" way, volcanoes of the Mediterranean had a special place in classic mythology. For the Greeks, the Aeo-

VESUVIUS ENTERS THE WAR

The 1944 eruption of Vesuvius surprised the Allied force who had just landed on the Campania coast and occupied Naples. The eruption caused them more damage than a bombing raid by the German airforce could have done: an entire squadron of 88 B-25 bombers belonging to the American Air Force in a landing field near the town of Terzigno was quickly destroyed by the falling ash.

In *Naples 1944*, an extraordinarily vivid account of the time, an English Secret Service Official, Norman Lewis, wrote: "March 19: Today Vesuvius erupted. It was the most majestic and terrible spectacle I have ever seen... The smoke from the crater seemed a solid mass as it oozed

slowly in a spiral... the cloud must have been 30 or 40 thousand feet high and it expanded for many miles... Periodically the crater shot snakes of red flame into the sky that flashed like lightening."

The story continued with the description of San Sebastiano, a town reached by the lava that slowly flowed along the main road, while a crowd dressed in black prayed on their knees in front of the danger, clutching at sacred images, among them St Gennaro brought in directly from Naples for the occasion.

Nearly 15,000 inhabitants of San Sebastiano, Somma Vesuviana and Cercola were evacuated by the Allies.

lian islands in Sicily were the home of Aeolus, God of the winds, which he held in a grotto. According to legend, Aeolus forecast the weather by observing the vapours emerging from an active volcano (probably Stromboli); today it is known that the cloud formation over Stromboli is influenced by changes in atmospheric pressure.

ORIGINS OF LAVA

The word "lava", used to indicate the flow of magma on the earth's surface, originally comes from Neapolitan dialect.

Hephaestus, the Greek god of fire, kept his forge in the bowels of Etna, where he worked along with the Cyclops, giants whose single eye resembled a crater. The Roman God of Fire

lived around Vesuvius and Etna were not afraid to remain in their villages to combat the early effects of an eruption, sweeping the ashes from their roofs to avoid a collapse. The ancient inhabitants of the slopes of Etna, after protecting themselves from the heat by wearing wet sheepskins, used an iron stick to make holes in the surface of the still soft lava, so that a new lava flow was created underneath the surface, whose pressure would fracture the rocky crust; the liquid magma expanded and cooled, slowing its course and thus saving the

was Vulcan, whose home was on the Aeolian island of the same name – the mountains of fire which we call volcanoes were named after him in the late middle ages.

The common belief that a volcano is a sort of "pressure cooker" that can "explode from one moment to the next" could not be further from the truth. Unlike an earthquake, a volcanic eruption is a phenomenon that can be predicted well in advance, and the initial signs do not present a danger. The ancient peoples who once

LEFT: figures in a fiery landscape, Etna, 1992.
ABOVE: Etna's lava surrounds a farmer's property, but in the end it will enrich the soil.

houses and crops otherwise destined to be destroyed (this was the origin of the legend of Ulysses who pierced through Polyphemus-Etna's eye-crater with a spear).

Today, explosives are used on some volcanoes to alter the surface terrain in order to direct the flow of lava into an artificial canal in an effort to keep it away from inhabited centres, while on Vesuvius this kind of operation always failed because of the high viscosity of its lava. To attenuate the fury of Vesuvius, it was proposed that a colossal perimeter wall be built to deviate the hot clouds or to poke holes all around the volcano to release pressure, but these ideas were found to be impracticable.

Chronology of Disasters

In the past 600 years, Italy has suffered 340 ruinous earthquakes and was the scene of spectacular and terrifying volcanic eruptions, including, in the modern era, the formation of a volcano in the Phlegraean Fields.

● AD 62 An earthquake destroyed nearly half of the Roman town of Pompeii *(see page 157)*.

● AD 79 Vesuvius buried Pompeii, Herculaneum and Stabia.

● 1538 The youngest volcano in Europe, aptly called Monte Nuovo, was formed in the Phlegraean Fields on 29–30 September.

● 1614–24 The most prolonged eruption of ash. The cone of the volcano dropped 168 metres (550 ft) and the diameter of the crater doubled.

● 1651–53 Etna destroyed the town of Bronte.

● 1669 One of the most frightening eruptions of Etna brought lava above the city walls of Catania, burying parts of the city; 11 days later the lava reached the sea. The volume of the lava flow is estimated to have been greater than 900 million cubic metres and covered 35 sq. km (14 sq. miles) of cultivated terrain. The painter Giacinto Patania chronicled the event, and in the sacristy of the Duomo di Catania, a fresco shows the volcano during the eruption.

Terremoto Calabro-Siculo (28 Dicembre 1908)
Messina
La dogana distrutta

Etna in recorded history poured forth a volume of material estimated to be 1,000 million cubic metres over 21 sq. km (8 sq. miles).

● 1627 An earthquake in Gargano, Apulia, obliterated San Severo and a good part of the nearby towns, claiming nearly 5,000 victims.

● 1631 Vesuvius, long inactive and by then covered with green vegetation, re-awoke with the most violent eruption of the past 1,000 years. The early signs were the same that preceded the eruption that destroyed Pompeii: thunder-like rumbling, earthquakes and murky water in the wells. The damage was extensive: six towns buried by the lava and another nine by the mud; in Naples, roofs collapsed under 30 cm (12 in)

THE MESSINA QUAKE

At dawn on 28 December 1908, a sharp tremor struck the area of Messina and Reggio Calabria, followed by a violent tidal wave in the straits that divide the two cities. The boats and the military ships anchored in the port broke their moorings and smashed up against one another, and nothing remained of the beautiful ancient buildings and churches, nor of the famous Palazzata di Messina, the elegant row of 19th-century palaces that wound along the quay. The dead numbered 50,000, and funds were immediately raised among the expatriate community of Naples and Capri. Reconstruction began in 1911 with strict anti-seismic building codes.

● **1688** More than 1,500 were killed in an earthquake at Benevento, Campania.

● **1693** The earthquake of the Val di Noto, Sicily, on 11 January was the strongest in Italy's recorded history. The main jolt (there were more than 1,500) reached 7.7 on the Richter scale, or at least 20 times the power of the earthquake that destroyed Messina in 1908. About 50 villages in a 550-sq. km (212-sq. mile) area were brought to the ground, and nearly 90,000 died. The beautiful baroque town of Noto was rebuilt from scratch 8 km (5 miles) south of the collapsed Noto.

● **1794** For the third time after 1631 and 1737,

Annunziata and Boscotrecase; on 8 April, nearly a metre (3 ft) of slag and detritus fell on a church in San Giuseppe Vesuviano, crushing the roof and killing 105 people who had sought refuge inside.

● **1908** The Messina earthquake *(see page 116)*.

● **1928** Mt Etna buries the city of Mascali, killing two people.

● **1930** Irpinia earthquake: 1,500 killed.

● **1944** Vesuvius's latest eruption *(see page 114)*.

● **1968** An earthquake in the Valle del Belice, Sicily, killed 300 and left 80,000 homeless.

● **1980** The Irpinia earthquake, Campania: the towns of Sant'Angelo dei Lombardi, Bagnoli

the lava of Vesuvius penetrated the streets, houses and the churches of Torre del Greco, and after crossing the city plunged into the sea for another 400 metres (1,312 ft).

● **1783** Several earthquakes hit southern Calabria; nearly 30,000 were killed.

● **1857** Earthquakes in Vulture (Basilicata) and Avellino (Campania) claimed 12,500 lives.

● **1883** Earthquake in Casamicciola, on Ischia left 2,300 dead, among them many tourists.

● **1906** The lava of Vesuvius invaded Torre

LEFT: the earthquake in Messina in 1908.
ABOVE: the ruined town of Gibellina after an earthquake in the Valle del Bellice, Sicily, in 1968.

Irpino and Nusco still show traces of the catastrophe that killed 6,000, injured 10,000 and left 300,000 homeless.

● **1983** On 14 May the lava flow of Etna was about to hit the towns of Nicolosi, Belpasso and Regalna. For the first time explosives were used to modify the natural beds of the volcano and direct the lava into an artificial basin.

● **1991–93** This eruption lasted 473 days, and put forth more than 300 million cubic metres that destroyed streets and farmhouses, and reached the edge of the village of Zafferana Etnea.

● **1995-2002** Etna's four summit craters continue to produce activity, from mild rumblings to high lava fountain explosions. ❏

WILD PLACES

Spectacular, untamed landscapes in the protected areas of Calabria, Basilicata and Sicily can be explored along a network of hiking trails

Most of the southern Italian wilderness is found in protected areas, reserves and national parks. But these areas are not highly geared to tourism and visitors must often find their own way around. The wild parts of the south can be surprisingly green or predictably arid, with flora ranging from mountain evergreens to north African cacti and bushes. The protagonist along the coast and on the islands is the *macchia mediterranea*, scrubland of myrtle, mastic tree, rosemary, juniper, rock rose, broom, laurel, thyme and strawberry tree. Large populations of birds, including many predators, as well as rodents, foxes and wild boar live side by side with increasing numbers of endangered species such as roe deer, wolves and otter.

The best time to enjoy the natural spaces is in the spring and autumn, the two most colourful seasons. The winter brings other charms: wolves' paw-prints left on the snow which falls on the highest mountains of Calabria, Basilicata and Sicily, and the possibility of skiing. Calabria and Sicily have the most to offer in both variety and extension of protected areas. Basilicata and Campania follow, but the latter's most spectacular landscapes are not to be found in protected areas. Puglia's one great contribution is the Gargano Promontory.

The **Sentiero Italia** is a national trail running all through the Mezzogiorno, beginning in Montalto, in Calabria's Parco dell'Aspromonte. It runs along the spine of the Appenines, passing from valley to valley, with refuges at strategic points along the way where hikers can stay the night. The trail, sponsored by the Club Alpino Italiano (CAI), reaches Umbria and will ultimately go as far as Trieste. (For more information, contact Nuove Frontiere based in Reggio Calabria, tel and fax: 0965/898295.)

Many of the **islands**, although not protected, have preserved their wild nature both above

LEFT: the Peregrine falcon inhabits the upper reaches of the Pollino massif. **RIGHT:** roe deer roam in the wilder southwestern corner of Pollino national park.

and below the water. This is particularly evident on the island of Maréttimo off western Sicily, on Filicudi and Alicudi in the Aeolian Islands, on Pantelleria and on Ustica, which has the most spectacular diving in the Tyrrhenian Sea and is one of the most important marine reserves in the Mediterranean.

Campania

Campania is the most densely populated region in Italy, and its one protected area, the **Parco Nazionale del Cilento**, has little wilderness about it: expect a gorgeous piece of countryside covered with olive groves and wheat fields, with an endangered population of wolves and wild cats surviving in a few remote corners. Paradoxically, the chic island of **Capri** hosts some of the region's most impressive flora and fauna: beside the imported exotic agave, prickly pears and bougainvillea thrives the endemic and beautiful *macchia mediterranea*, which in the coves most protected from the wind leaves room for tiny forests of ilex. The southern coast between Punta Carena and Cala Ventroso and the area around the Arco Naturale are dotted with cluster-pines; the stretch of land between the Grotta Azzurra and Villa Jovis hosts the only palm which has spontaneously grown in Italy in the past 60 million years – the *Chamaerops humilis* – a remnant of the tropical climate that once reigned over the peninsula. The Faraglioni islands are home to the world's only blue common lizard, discovered in 1870 and named *Lacerta coerulea faraglionensis*. Perhaps the most curious of species in Campania is an extremely rare bulbous fern *(Woodwardia radicans)* found in the tiny nature

west part of the park. Their isolated position and the mountain culture of the 170,000 residents keep the park pristine. Various grandiose projects to build concrete "touristic" cities in the Pollino ended in 1993 with the official declaration of the Parco as a national park.

Botanists who first began by scientifically exploring the flora of the Pollino in the 19th century, were awe-struck by the enormous number of plants: *la macchia mediterranea* dominates the areas from the coast up to 800 metres (2,600 ft); the oak *(Quercus petraea)*, the Neapolitan alder *(Alnus cordata)*, turkey oak *(Quercus cerris)*, chestnut *(Castanea sativa)*, hornbeam

reserve of **Vallone delle Ferriere** in a wild corner of the Sorrentine Peninsula. Protected by international conventions, it has fronds reaching a length of 2 metres (6 ft).

Basilicata and Calabria

Italy's largest national park and the richest repository of wildlife in Southern Italy is the **Parco Nazionale del Pollino**, which is equally split between Basilicata and Calabria. It covers 196,000 hectares (750 sq miles) of mountainous territory in the provinces of Potenza and Cosenza. Its two main areas of interest are the **Pollino massif** in the centre and the wilder **Monti di Orsomarso** in the Calabrese south-

(Carpinus betulus), and the Lobel maple *(Acer lobelii)* thrive at elevations up to 1,100 metres (3,600 ft); splendid forests of beech trees *(Fagus sylvatica)* extend above 1,000 metres (3,300 ft), all but filtering out the daylight from the ground below, together with the white fir-tree *(Abies alba)* and black pine *(Pinus nigra)*.

But what renders the vegetation of the Pollino unique is the *pino loricato (Pinus leucodermis)*, which is only found here and in the Balkans. The emblem of the park, the *pino loricato* grows on the steeper and more rocky side of the Pollino massif and in the Orsomarso area where, at the foot of Mt Palanuda, the oldest specimens have reached a height of 40 metres (130 ft) and a width of a metre (3 ft). Sadly, the famous millenary *pino loricato* tree – the oldest living specimen – which stood at the Grande Porta del Pollino was burned down in 1993 by vandals who opposed the creation of the national park.

The tree takes its name from the unmistakable irregular pattern on its light grey bark, which reminded a local professor of the scales of the *lorica*, the scaled shield of the Roman legionaries. The highly resinous quality of the *pino loricato*'s fibres allows the trunk and branches to survive after the tree dies, becoming

ANNUAL TIDY UP

On the third weekend of September every year, hundreds of volunteers carry out a big clean-up campaign in Italy's national parks.

sought its prized skin, and by fishermen with whom it competed. The landscape of the park is extremely varied, ranging from the canyons dropping off the Argentino, Lao and Raganello rivers (navigable in the most dangerous sections with expert river guides) to the high plains and meadows, which after the snow melt are covered with a spectacular mantle of flowers – among which the bright pink peony *(Paeonia mascula)* and the yellow orchid *(Dachtylorhiza sambucina)* stand out, attracting some 2,000 different species of

a sort of arboreal monument of great beauty against the bare rocks.

Even though it is thought that, on average, the park hosts only 15 percent of the fauna it could potentially hold, the presence of certain species is a good ecological indicator of the park's general environmental well-being. In particular, the unpolluted rivers are full of the protected river shrimp *(Austropotamobius pallipes)* and the endangered otter *(Lutra lutra)*, which were nearly brought to extinction in the 20th century by pollution and poachers, who

insects. The steepest rocks make an ideal habitat for twelve species of predatory birds, including a few pairs of the majestic royal eagle *(Aquila chrysaetos)*, and the more common royal kite *(Milvus milvus)*, the astonishingly fast Peregrine falcon *(Falco peregrinus)*, which when it swoops down upon its prey reaches speeds of up to 300 kph (190 mph). Their diet consists mainly of serpents, lambs, hares and many species of rodents, but also includes wild cats, weasels, and skunks.

Mt Pollino (2,248 metres/7,375 ft) and Serra Dolcedorme (2,267 metres/7,438 ft), both in the Pollino massif, are the park's highest mountains: on a clear day, their peaks offer

LEFT AND ABOVE: wild cats and wolves are rare inhabitants of the southern forests.

views over the Ionian, Adriatic and Tyrrhenian seas – the only place in Italy you can see all three seas at once.

The wildest areas of the park are to be found in the Monti di Orsomarso, where the brown bear (*orso* in Italian) of the Apennines once roamed. The resident population of roe deer (*Capreolus capreolus*) is probably thankful for its disappearance. The shy Italian wolf (*Canis lupus italicus*) leaves its tracks in the snow and can be heard howling at the moon, but keeps its distance

> **BURNING ISSUE**
>
> Thousands of hectares of forest burn every summer; most fires are started deliberately by vandals or on behalf of companies specialising in reforestation.

from hunters, who continue to shoot wolves despite their protected status. In all of Calabria, only about a hundred of them survive. The government compensates farmers for livestock presumed to have been lost to the wolves but in reality the hens and sheep are killed by the 11,000 or more abandoned dogs that roam the park. Towards the more arid eastern border, a small species of vulture has been successfully reintroduced – the black-and-white *capovaccaio (Neophron percnopterus)*, known for its technique of breaking the bones of carcasses by bombarding them with stones from the sky.

There are two more national parks in Calabria. Parco Nazionale della Sila (13,000

hectares/50 sq. miles) and Parco Nazionale d' Aspro-monte (80,000 hectares/300 sq. miles) are 100 km (60 miles) apart and made up the former Parco Nazionale della Calabria. The rather small **Parco Nazionale della Sila** has a worthwhile nature trail near the Visitors' Centre at Cupone, which reconstructs the ancient environments and local skills, and contains a mini-zoo of local species, including roe deer, wild boar, deer and wolves. In the rest of the park, you might see foxes, badgers, weasels, skunks, dormice and black squirrels. At the Visitors' Centre, you can also pick up a map illustrating 10 easy itineraries that can all be done in less than a day. The landscape is characterised by gentle highlands and vast spaces, for the most part covered by forests of beech trees, with some poplar and maple. The dark-green *pino laricio* (the Calabrian variety of *Pinus nigra*) reaches a height of more than 50 metres (160 ft) in the Selva di Fallistro. Between December and February, there is good downhill and cross-country skiing (contact the tourist office in Camigliatello Silano for information).

The **Parco Nazionale d'Aspromonte** has the feel of a mountainous island, with granite reliefs nearly 2,000 metres (6,500 ft) high surrounded by the Tyrrhenian and Ionian Seas. On the rainy western side, the rocks are covered by lush woods of oak, chestnut, alder, maple, ash, hornbeam and (above 1,200 metres/3,900 ft) by *pino laricio*, beech and white fir; while on the drier eastern side, the rocks often appear bare. Rare animal species here include the wolf, wild cat and Bonelli eagle. More abundant are the royal owl, sparrow-hawk and buzzard; squirrels and other small rodents abound.

Many local associations organise unforgettable week-long excursions, providing camping equipment and donkeys, or mini-buses for difficult sections.

Apulia

Although all of Apulia's **Promontorio del Gargano** was made a national park in 1991, only a small part of it can be described as "wild": the **Foresta Umbra** in the interior, which extends for 11,000 hectares (42 sq miles) at an elevation of 700 metres (2,300 ft) above sea level. Its cool woods of oaks, pines and beeches hide a variety of wildlife (including the roe deer, re-introduced to the area), and a number of marked trails. The nearest tourist information office is in San Severo.

Sicily

The unique combination of vegetation and volcanic "sculpture" makes the 59,000-hectare (230-sq.-mile) **Parco dell'Etna** the most interesting of Sicily's protected areas. The fertile lowlands are cultivated with citrus, almonds and hazelnuts; juniper, ash and chestnut take over above 700 metres (2,300 ft), among which is the famous chestnut tree of Cento Cavalli, in Sant' Alfio. According to legend, the tree's 60-metre (200-ft) canopy gave shelter to Queen Joanna of Anjou and her escort of 100 knights. Further up, the forests of beech and *pino laricio* show the scars of the lava flows. This area is home to dormice, foxes, numerous birds and about 70 species of butterfly. Above 3,000 metres (9,800 ft), the landscape is composed of black rocks, ash and pumice stones.

More than 150 grottoes have been created by the gas produced when the water evaporated as it met the flowing lava. Among the most striking are the **Grotta del Gelo** (on the north-facing side, at 2,000 metres/6,600 ft), formed during the 1612 eruption, which has a small lake with a frozen and transparent bottom, under which the black lava rocks can be seen.

Nearby, along the road that leads from the village of Zafferana to the Sapienza refuge, is the 200-metre (660-ft) **Grotta Cassone** and the **Grotta dei Tre Livelli**, which can only be explored by experienced climbers.

The **Parco dei Nebrodi** extends over 85,000 hectares (330 sq. miles) of the Tyrrhenian coast between Capo d'Orlando and Santo Stefano di Camastra, and features a varied mountainous and coastal landscape. What renders it unique in Sicily are the humid zones: little lakes, marshes and streams between which sit the lakes of Biviere and Trearie, where a number of migratory birds overwinter. To the west is the 35,000-hectare (135-sq.-mile) **Parco delle Madonie**. With 200 million-year-old fossils, the rocks here are the oldest on the island. A good network of paths and gravel roads makes it easy to reach the

most remote corners. The Sicilian writer Giuseppe di Lampedusa described the area in *The Leopard* as "aridly undulating to the horizon in hillock after hillock… conceived apparently in a delirious moment of creation; a sea suddenly petrified at the instant when a change of wind had flung waves into a frenzy."

But the park also has patches of thick forest, mostly near the coast, and the suggestive evidence of a long-extinct culture. Shelters and tiny churches cut out of the rocks, imposing farming estates, hermitages and monasteries along the valleys – the Madonna dell'Olio sanctuary and the Annunziata church to name two. Others are

isolated in the mountains, most notably the San Guglielmo and San Cosimano hermitages, the Madonna dell'Alto sanctuary, and Gibilmanna abbey, a popular place of pilgrimage.

The **Ibleo high plains**, in the extreme southeast of Sicily, are made up of calceous rocks cut by spectacular river canyons (*cave*). Some are dry, others lush with vegetation. The most noted is the 14-km (9-mile), **cava d'Ispica**, perfumed with capers and herbs.

Finally, **Lo Zingaro**, a wonderful coastal reserve on the rocky northwest coast, is the most user-friendly of all Sicily's nature reserves. It can be reached by boat from the fishing village of Castellammare del Golfo (*see page 284*). ❑

LEFT: wild violets of the Aspromonte.
RIGHT: Red Valerian thrives on the volcanic slopes of Mt Etna.

PLACES

A detailed guide to the entire region, with main sites clearly cross-referenced by number to the maps

The four mainland provinces (Campania, Apulia, Basilicata and Calabria) and the nine provinces of Sicily *(see page 267)* of Southern Italy are set between four seas, which means a beach is never far away. Each coast has its distinct flavour. The Tyrrhenian side is the best known. It begins with the Bay of Naples, which curls round to the Sorrento peninsula so that Capri and the islands are never out of view. Then it takes the switchback corniche down the Amalfi Coast, one of the most dramatic and picturesque in Europe, to the Cilento Coast and Basilicata all the way to the tip of Calabria, where beaches and coves attract more visitors each year.

The opposite, Adriatic coast is a succession of ancient ports with bleached Norman churches and castles, which were nurtured by crusaders' zeal. This coast's high point is the Gargano Peninsula, the most dramatic event on Italy's entire east coast. Between the two, the Ionian sea makes a sandy sweep inside the instep of Italy's familiar "boot", changing its name to the Gulf of Taranto. Much of this stretch seems to have stagnated in time and remains largely neglected.

Outside of the main sights around Naples and in Sicily, don't expect to see much evidence of classical times; wars and earthquakes have taken their toll. The best museum is the Museo Archeologico Nazionale in Naples, which contains many treasures from Pompeii, Herculaneum and Paestum, but local museums, notably in the regional capitals of Bari and Reggio Calabria, have treasures, too. Naples, the capital of the south, is a great sea port and one of the most exciting cities in Europe, where a car is a liability, and a handbag needs to be clutched tightly.

Railways link the main cities and popular resorts, such as Gargano, but in the main the *Mezzogiorno* remains untamed by public transport. To make the most of it, you will need to go your own way. To seek out the Sassi, the cave dwellers of Matera in Basilicata, or the *trulli*, the strange circular houses in Apulia, or to explore the Gargano fully, or see the Albanians in festive mood, needs flexibility. Roads are not always straightforward. The Appenines, Italy's backbone, stretch all the way to the Aspromonte, the highlands on the tip of the toe, making inland roads twist and curve. But the rewards are a diverse and delightful countryside. In the quieter areas, don't expect full tourist facilities, even in the regions now designated national parks. These are not places for the package holidaymaker, but the curious traveller will find rich rewards. ❑

PRECEDING PAGES: viaducts carry the motorway through the rolling hills of Apulia; granite columns with Corinthian capitals (wrongly re-positioned in the 19th century) in the Greek Theatre in Taormina, Sicily; the atrium of Salerno cathedral, built with Corinthian columns taken from the nearby Greek settlement at Paestum. **LEFT:** overlooking the Cathedral of San Pantaleone in Ravello on the Amalfi coast.

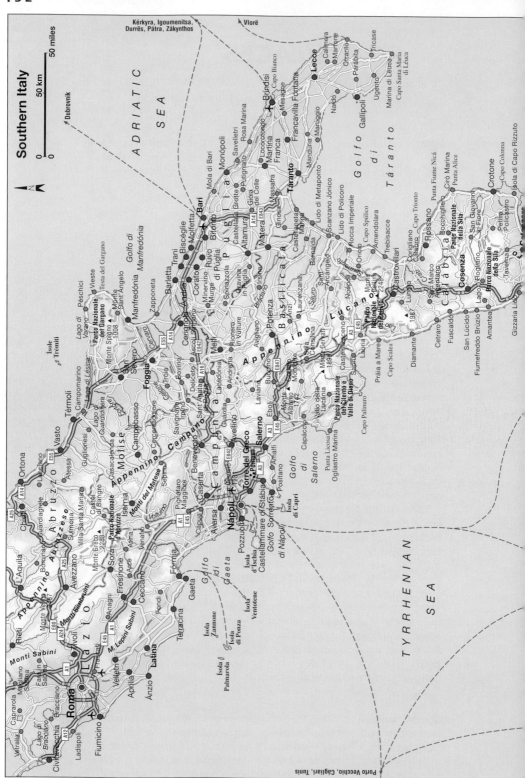

Southern Italy

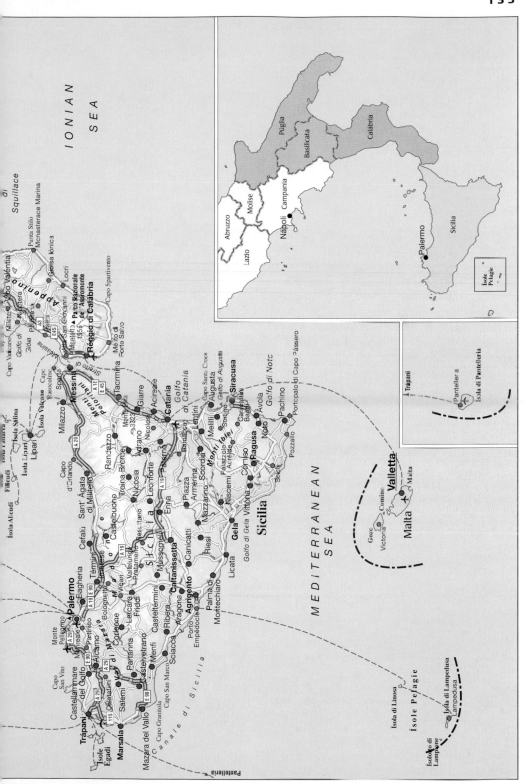

NAPLES

Italy's liveliest city is not to be missed. Whole-hearted enjoyment is to be had among its crowded streets and a cultural feast is waiting in its first-class museums

Map on page 136

●Naples

There has never been a lack of words to describe Naples. Unlike many other European cities, it provokes reaction in the most laconic of visitors. What's more, any random selection of quotes about the city and its inhabitants is likely to include admiration and detraction in equal measure. Heaven on earth, then, or the very crucible of hell? The writer Peter Nichols sums up this polarised response: "Neapolitans still reproduce what must be the nearest equivalent to life in classical times. Naples is one of the great tests. Some people hate it and some people love it."

Nichols' following remark, "I think that people who do not like Naples are afraid of something," clearly showing which side of the divide he is on, invites the instant retort, "No wonder!" in those he is talking about, for the image of modern-day Naples is one of progressive deterioration and rising criminality. But, in reality, this unfavourable image, fuelled by the national and international media, is as misleading as the romantic image which preceded it. Above all, Naples is a unique feast for the senses; here, every aspect of life, including survival itself, has been elevated to an art form. There is no better place to encounter this phenomenon than in the famous Spaccanapoli street.

Negotiating the city is not as fraught with danger as some people, including Neapolitans themselves, would have visitors believe. There are certain parts of the city which are effectively no-go neighbourhoods for tourists in the evenings (the slum areas of Forcella and Ponticelli, for example), but most of Naples is no more threatening than any other major city.

In the rush hour, when the traffic in the congested streets comes to its usual chaotic standstill, the best way to get around most of the city is to walk or, if need be, use public transport. The hills and the harbour and especially the castles and palaces, such as Castel dell'Ovo or Castel Sant' Elmo, provide reliable orientation in the maze of streets in the old part of the city.

Visitors should not be afraid to ask locals for help if they have lost their way. Locals have a reputation for friendliness and hospitality, and encounters with most Neapolitans are rewarding. The constant advice and warnings to safeguard cameras and money, to remove any valuable jewellery and to keep a firm grip on handbags and camera cases is well-meaning, if unnerving. Time and again, Neapolitans will offer to accompany you safely to your destination.

The Old Town

The first sight to confront most visitors to Naples is the noise and confusion of the city's main transport hub, **Piazza Garibaldi** ❶. Each day, hundreds of thousands of commuters converge here to catch their

LEFT: view over the city to the Bay.
BELOW: the best way of getting round town.

subway, train, bus or taxi. Don't let the fast-walking crowds, insistent street hawkers, zig-zagging scooters and cars discourage you – the notoriously bad Neapolitan traffic is at its worst right here. Be aware that this is prime pick-pocketing territory, so keep a firm hold on your belongings.

The narrow and quieter streets of the historical centre begin at the western end of Piazza Garibaldi. Conquerors of the past would enter the town through **Porta Capuana**, a sturdy Renaissance gate flanked by two mighty Aragonese towers. The open space in front of it, now used as a market place, was once the site for public punishments.

From here, the **Forcella** quarter spreads down to **Corso Umberto I** ❷. With a reputation for being the Camorra's main stronghold in central Naples, the area is swarming in sellers of black market cigarettes and fake brand-name sunglasses and watches. Via Forcella leads into one of the world's oldest urban streets, once the Roman *Decumanus Inferior* (main street running parallel to the longer axis in any planned Roman town), familiarly known as **Spaccanapoli** ❸. *Spacca* means "split", a reference to the way this long and straight street cuts right through the city. The street changes names as it progresses from east to west: Via Vicaria Vecchia, Via San Biagio dei Librai, Via Benedetto Croce, and Via Scura. This busy thoroughfare, dotted along its length with historic buildings, churches and squares, teems with life and atmosphere and is the real heart of the old town.

San Gennaro's Blood

Heading west, make a right turn into Spaccanapoli's main side street, Via Duomo, to pay homage to the patron saint of Naples, San Gennaro (the bishop of Benevento martyred at Pozzuoli's amphitheatre in AD 305). The **Duomo** ❹ contains the saint's holy relics – two phials of blood and the gold reliquary bust said to contain his skull – housed in the **Cappella del Tesoro**. San Gennaro's fame is due in no small measure to the miracle of the liquefying blood, celebrated in the cathedral twice a year (on the first Saturday of May and 19 September). During the mass, a reliquary

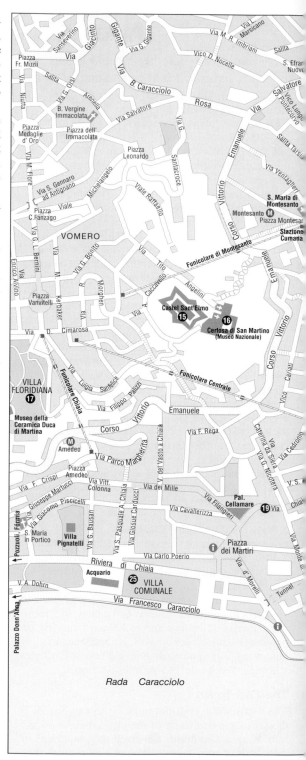

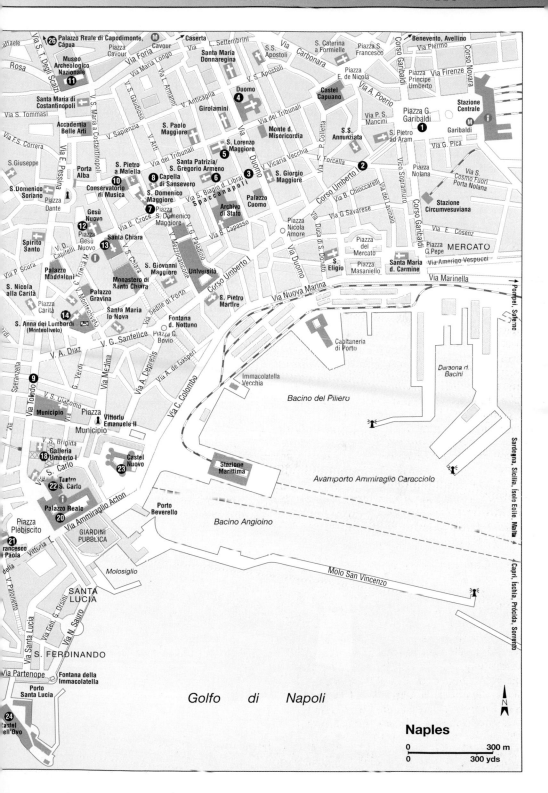

Naples

0 ——————— 300 m
0 ——————— 300 yds

containing the saint's blood is tipped to and fro in the midst of prayers, chants and an atmosphere rich with the hopes, tensions and fears of thousands of believers, willing the dried blood to liquefy. Amazingly, the blood does appear to liquefy on most occasions, and is cause for much celebration; the rare exceptions are considered to be a bad omen for the coming period. No scientist has ever been allowed to test the holy dark-red substance, but the last great eruption of Vesuvius (in 1944) and the earthquake which hit Irpinia northeast of Naples (in 1980) occurred in years that the blood refused to melt.

Of little interest in itself, the Duomo (begun in 1294, but with a neo-Gothic facade that dates to the early 20th century), encloses the oldest surviving structure in town, the church of **Santa Restituta**, built by Constantine in 324 with a fine baptistery (admission fee) and columns taken from the Temple of Apollo which stood on the site.

Dutiful daughters

Retrace your steps along Via Duomo as far as Via Tribunali. Turn right here and one block down across the road rises another Gothic church, **San Lorenzo Maggiore ❺**, with two large canvases by Calabrian Mattia Preti (*see page 262*) and many medieval sepulchres. Recent excavations have brought to light parts of the Roman *macellum* (food market) and a paleochristian basilica built on top of it (accessible from the cloister). Continue along **Via di San Gregorio Armeno** to the **Benedectine convent ❻** of the same name, which once served as a repository for the daughters of noble Neapolitan families who were forced to become nuns against their will to save on dowries. The quiet, exotic garden of the pretty **cloister** makes for a pleasant break.

Naples was founded in the 8th century BC by Greek settlers from nearby Cumae. They had already established a hilltop town known as Parthenope and as it prospered they built Neapolis (new city) to accommodate the growing population. The chequerboard pattern of streets around Spaccanapoli dates from this period.

BELOW: a *salumeria* selling groceries.

Back on Spaccanapoli

The Via San Biagio dei Librai leads to **Piazza San Domenico Maggiore ❼**. This attractive pedestrian square is marked by one of the many baroque *guglie* (wooden and stucco towers built for religious festivals, heavily decorated with *putti*, statues, garlands of flowers and fruit baskets, then carried through the streets for religious celebrations and royal parades) which Neapolitans erected as *ex-votoes* to the Madonna and various saints in gratitude for deliverance, in this case from the Black Plague of 1658. You can see other famous *guglie* on Piazza del Gesù (*guglia dell'Immacolata*) and next to the Duomo, on Piazzetta Riario Sforza (*guglia* of San Gennaro), but no other Italian town developed a taste for "petrifying" the otherwise temporary *guglie*. The church of San Domenico Maggiore, much altered since its completion in 1324 due to earthquakes, fires and damage inflicted during World War II, has some good examples of Renaissance sculpture and a copy of Caravaggio's *Flagellation* (now at Capodimonte).

Round the corner from here is the baroque **Cappella di Sansevero ❽** (Via Francesco de Sanctis; open July–Oct, Mon and Wed–Sat 10am–5pm, Sun 10am–1.30pm; Nov–June, Mon and Wed–Sat 10am–2pm, Sun 10am–1.30pm, Tues closed; entrance fee), not to be missed for the virtuoso monuments built for Prince Raimondo di Sangro (1749–71). Among them, Corradini's *Pudicizia* (Modesty), Queirolo's *Disinganno* (Disillusion) and Sammartino's masterpiece, the *Cristo Velato* (Veiled Christ) stand out.

Carved out of a single piece of marble, this statue of a recumbent Christ draped in a translucent veil is a remarkable feat of realism. Prince Raimondo was an alchemist and amateur scientist, who also dabbled in the occult. He used the chapel as his workshop. According to legend, the two gruesome mannequins in

Map on page 136

TIP

In Piazza San Domenico Maggiore, the long-established pastry-shop Scaturchio is one of the best in town for local favourites like *sfogliatelle ricce* and *cassate*; the *ministeriale* (chocolate with a creamy filling) is a house speciality.

BELOW: antique and bric-a-brac shop with local puppet figures.

the **crypt** were the result of one of his macabre experiments, in which he injected two slaves with a liquid to preserve their cardio-vascular systems. He was eventually excommunicated by the Pope for his dubious activities.

The most populous street in the world

Naples' grandest thoroughfare and main shopping area is **Via Toledo ❾**, which descends gently seaward from Piazza Dante to Piazza Plebiscito. Stendhal found it to be "the most populous and gayest street in the world". Officially re-named Via Roma at the birth of the Italian State, locally it is still referred to as Via Toledo. The energetic Spanish viceroy, Don Pedro di Toledo (1532–53) effected the most radical and ambitious urban redevelopment in the city's history, which included the construction of new streets, the doubling of the city's habitable space, and the enlargement of defensive structures. Always a bustling place, Via Toledo is at its peak of activity in the late afternoon when Neapolitans gather for their evening *passeggiata*.

Start your own walk along Via Toledo from Piazza Dante at the northern edge of the historical centre, best reached from Piazza San Domenico Maggiore through **Via San Pietro a Maiella**. This quiet street is flanked by shops specialising in musical instruments and sheet music catering to the students of the prestigious **Conservatorio di Musica ❿** (take a look at the cloister if open); more music shops can be found around the corner on Via San Sebastiano.

Piazza Dante is a departure point for buses going south to the Riviera di Chiaia and Mergellina; from here, you can also catch the No. 161 bus to **Capodimonte** *(see page 146).*

BELOW: a complex catacomb network lies beneath Naples' streets.

BENEATH THE CITY STREETS

Underneath the thronging, sun-baked city lies another, dark, cold and damp Naples, of which nobody knows the actual dimensions, although to date some 700 cavities have been catalogued. A trip beneath Naples passes through what was once the Greco-Roman Neapolis, to the catacombs, cemeteries and branches of the aqueduct, built during the reign of Emperor Augustus, that were used as shelters during World War II air raids.

The **cloister of San Lorenzo** *(see page 138)* is not the city's only gate to this underworld: other portals to Naples' past can be found at **Piazza San Gaetano 68** (Associazione Napoli Sotterranea, tel: 081-449821); on **Via Santa Teresella degli Spagnoli** (LAES, tel: 081-400256); and the **Cimitero delle Fontanelle** (church of Maria Santissima del Carmine). On Capodimonte you can visit the **Catacombe di San Gaudioso** (church of Santa Maria della Sanità; open Sun am only; tours at 9.45 and 11.45; entrance fee) which contain the remains of African bishop St Gaudiosus, who died in AD 452, and the larger **Catacombe di San Gennaro** (entrance from the street that skirts Madre del Buon Consiglio church, off Via Capodimonte; open daily; tours at 9.30, 10.15, 11 and 11.45am; entrance fee), with early Christian paintings.

Map
on page
136

Antiques and antiquities

North of Piazza Dante, on the opposite side of Piazza Bellini, is the attractive **Via Santa Maria a Costantinopoli**, lined with antique and bric-a-brac shops, which leads to the **Museo Archeologico Nazionale**  (open Sun–Mon and Wed–Fri 9am–7.30pm, Sat 9am–11pm, closed Tues; entrance fee) one of the world's largest and most interesting museums of Roman antiquity. The collection includes the Farnese sculptures and an exceptional display of everyday objects, frescoes, statues and mosaics from Pompeii, Herculaneum and Stabia. *(For further details of the museum, see pages 148–9).*

The point where Spaccanapoli crosses Via Toledo is a good place to stop and admire the long, narrow intersection. From here the Via dei Capitelli leads to Piazza del Gesú Nuovo. Passing the frilly **guglia dell'Immacolata**, built by the Jesuits but financed by "offerings" coerced from the public, you'll reach **Chiesa del Gesù Nuovo** ⑫. Lined with coloured marbles and gaudy frescoes by baroque painters Solimena and Ribera, the ornate church contrasts starkly with the austerity of **Santa Chiara** ⑬, opposite. In 1943, a bomb destroyed the spectacular 18th-century interior. Reconstruction efforts stripped away the baroque elements and restored the convent to its original French Gothic look.

The annexed **Chiostro delle Clarisse** (open Mon–Sat 9.30am–1pm and 2.30–5.30pm, Sun 9.30am–1pm; entrance fee) is one of Naples' true wonders. In 1742, the wife of the Bourbon King Charles, who frequently visited the nuns, decided to transform the lawn of the cloister into a refined garden. On the sides of the two avenues that today surround the garden, the ground level was elevated to allow a water pipe to pass beneath and a retaining wall was built. Dozens of built-in benches were placed on this wall, and between the benches, stand 72

A majolica figure in Santa Chiara's cloister.

BELOW:
the tiled cloister
in Santa Chiara.

Traffic cop – not the easiest of jobs to have in Naples.

BELOW: the sturdy medieval fortress of Castel Sant' Elmo.

octagonal pillars which support shady trellises of grape vines and wisteria. The walls, benches and pillars were completely covered with majolica tiles representing mythological images and scenes of daily life in the fields, and of fishermen and sailors. In 2000, the cloister emerged from a careful restoration project in which the medieval frescoes under the arcades were recovered and the garden replanted with the same species that were grown here in Bourbon times.

The notorious Spanish Quarter

Return to Via Toledo and cross to Via P. Scura, then turn into Via Pignasecca (second left) to visit Naples' most picturesque **food market** (open Mon–Sat mornings only). Via Pignasecca ends at the junction of Via Toledo, Piazza Carità and Piazza Monteoliveto; the latter leads to the church of **Sant'Anna dei Lombardi ⓮**. The interior is worth a look for its wealth of Renaissance sculpture, including the *Pietà* by Guido Mazzoni, a life-size group of eight figures with realistic facial expressions.

Continuing downhill along Via Toledo, the mesh of lanes and steep staircases which fan out to the right sprouted at the orders of Don Pedro di Toledo to house the Spanish garrison. Later, the neighbourhood was colonised by the poorest Neapolitan families who occupied even the dark and unsanitary ground-floor and basement slums known as the *bassi*, where, until not so long ago, through an open door or prison-like window you could glimpse *mamma* at the stove and *papà* mending his fishing nets. To a certain extent, the **Quartieri Spagnoli** still lives up to the romantic cliché of Neapolitan slums, where crumbling houses are held together by colourful washing lines, and *scugnizzi* (street urchins) run through the streets kicking a football or singing a song. But these days, thanks largely to infighting between rival factions of the Camorra, crime and degradation overshadow the picturesque.

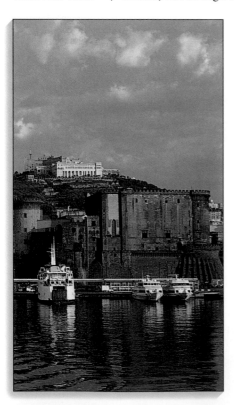

Funiculì Funiculà

The **Vomero** hill is worth a climb just for the fun of a ride on the funicular railway (from the bottom of Via Toledo) and the great view of the town below. But this modern neighbourhood also has some key landmarks, reminders of a more idyllic past, now turned into three of Naples' finest museums.

Start with **Castel Sant'Elmo ⓯** (open Tues–Sun 9am–2pm; entrance fee), a massive medieval fortress, built in the shape of star, with a commanding view of the Bay. Once used as a prison for political troublemakers, it is now a public exhibition space. Adjoining the fortress is the **Certosa di San Martino ⓰**, a bit older then the fortress but treated to an agreeable baroque re-styling that didn't cover the original Gothic ribs of the vault.

The old Carthusian monastery is now the site of the **Museo Nazionale di San Martino** (open Tues–Sun 8.30am–7.30pm, closed Mon; entrance fee) with 90 rooms of paintings, furniture, ceramics, model ships, coins and costumes illustrating the life and history of Naples. Highlights include the pharmacy, with antique glass jars from Murano; the outstanding pinacoteca of the **Quarto del Priore** (prior's apartment); and the well-kept gardens of the **Chiostro Grande** (great cloister). But the most charming section of the museum is the **Presepi Collection**, with a wealth of 18th- and 19th-century nativity scenes composed of statuettes, some the work of famous sculptors. The largest and most famous is the *Presepe Cuciniello*, made up of hundreds of little statues and objects.

A little to the west stands the neoclassical **Villa Floridiana** , originally a wedding present from Ferdinand I, King of the Two Sicilies, to his long-time lover, the Duchess of Floridia, who he married just after the death of the queen, by which time the two had already become grandparents. The villa houses the **Museo della Ceramica Duca di Martina** (open Tues–Sun 9am–2pm; closed Mon; entrance fee), filled with a splendid collection of majolica and porcelain of European, Eastern and Neapolitan manufacture, which deserves to be savoured slowly. If bowls and figurines are not your cup of tea, the unforgettable view of the Bay from the surrounding park is worth the detour.

Around Piazza Plebiscito

Towards the sea end of Via Toledo, opposite the funicular to Vomero, stands the majestic **Galleria Umberto I** , a good introduction to the "royal quarters" of the Piazza Plebiscito, even though the Bourbon dynasty had already succumbed to the newly born Italian State when the gallery was inaugurated in 1890. Although maintainance standards improved considerably in the 1990s, it's hard to imagine how grand the place must have looked at the turn of the 19th century when it was a meeting point of the Neapolitan intelligentsia and aristocracy. Today, the less-than-glamorous collection of shops do not do justice to the fine marble floor and cupola, a triumph of iron and glass nearly 60 metres (200 ft) high.

Map on page 136

TIP

No. 154 Via Chiaia is one of the last surviving roadside kiosks, or *acquafrescai*, where you can quench your thirst with a freshly squeezed *spremuta di limone* (lemonade).

BELOW: wedding pictures in the Galleria Umberto I.

CHRISTMAS CRIBS

In the first days of November, the streets between Piazza San Gaetano and Via San Biagio dei Librai become the most animated and crowded in the city. The stalls that surround the monastery of San Gregorio Armeno fuel the yearly craze for *presepi* (Christmas cribs) that overtakes Neapolitans. The seasonal marketplace offers the ingredients for do-it-yourself nativity scenes for all tastes and budgets. The creation of a nativity scene is seen as an art form and you can let your imagination run riot adding papier-mâché mountains, a fountain that spouts water, a miniature mill with power wheel. Neapolitan *presepi* are unique in Italy because Jesus, Mary, Joseph and the shepherds are often joined by singers, actors, politicians, football players and other contemporary characters. Popular local heroes include movie legend Totò, Pulcinella, Maradona, who played for Napoli in the 1980s, the mayor of Naples and Olympic swimmer Massimiliano Rosolino.

The fine work of Neapolitan craftsmanship and tradition can be observed all year round in nearby boutiques that specialise in figurines. One of Naples' best-known *presepe* artisans, Giuseppe Ferrigno (Via San Gregorio Armeno 10), turns out 18th-century style shepherds with terracotta faces, wearing robes cut from period fabrics.

Teatro San Carlo's opulent auditorium seats 3,000.

BELOW: timeless Caffè Gambrinus.

Naples' smartest shopping street, **Via Chiaia** , makes up for the loss. Wrily referred to as the only place in town where goods are genuine, even pizzas here come with an official stamp. Tucked away on Salita Sant'Anna, but clearly visible from Via Chiaia, is the old **Pizzeria Brandi**, credited with the invention of Pizza Margherita *(see page 96)*, and therefore an obvious mecca for pizza fans, but not even a tasty historical bite (offered in the form of a brochure) can fully redeem the flavour of what has become a benign tourist trap.

Piazza Plebiscito, recently liberated from its role as a chaotic car park, now looks grand and spacious. The piazza was laid out in 1602 as part of the hasty construction of the **Palazzo Reale** (open Sun–Tues and Thur–Fri 9am–8pm, Sat 9am–11pm, closed Wed; entrance fee), which the Spanish viceroy commissioned from Domenico Fontana in order to host Phillip II, who never came to town. With the exception of the eight portraits of monarchs which were added to the main facade in 1888 to symbolize the eight dynasties that ruled over the city, no king has ever inhabited the palace, which was occupied only by viceroys. The second floor museum is made up of 30 rooms, each richly decorated and furnished with period furniture and undistinguished paintings.

During his seven-year reign, Napoleon's brother-in-law Joachim Murat pulled down a convent to make space for the hemicircle of Doric columns pompously called the Foro Murat. At the centre of the colonnade stands the church of **San Francesco di Paola** , built between 1817 and 1846. It was commissioned by Ferdinand I, King of the Two Sicilies, to celebrate the end of his exile and Napoleonic rule, and the return of the Bourbon dynasty to power. Modelled on Rome's Pantheon, with a cupola 53 metres (174 ft) high and 34 metres (112 ft) in diameter, the church is a striking sight, especially when floodlit at night.

On the small Piazza Trento e Trieste is the inconspicuous facade of the **Teatro San Carlo** . Inaugurated on St Charles' day (4 November) 1737, when Naples was the the capital of music in Europe, it was Europe's largest opera house. The theatre quickly earned a reputation for the beauty of its six-tiered auditorium and the excellence of its productions; it is still noted for its perfect acoustics. Nearby is the historic **Caffè Gambrinus**, sleek with old mirrors and barmen dressed as if they were headed for the opening of the season next door.

From this piazzetta, it's a short walk to **Castel Nuovo** ㉓ (open Mon–Sat 9am–7pm, closed Sun; entrance fee) built in the late 13th century during Charles of Anjou's reign. The awesome, if incongruous **Triumphal Arch**, was added in 1467 to commemorate the entry of King Alfonso I of Aragon (later King of Naples and Sicily) into Naples. The ornate white arch stands in stark contrast to the bulky brown towers that support it on either side. Used as a royal residence until the construction of Palazzo Reale, today Castel Nuovo houses the meeting rooms of the City Council, a library and a **Museo Civico** with various paintings, sculptures and liturgical furnishings from suppressed churches and institutions.

Along the waterfront to Posillipo

The waterfront can be reached on foot from Piazza Plebiscito (or from il Vomero via the Funicolare Chiaia to Via Parco Margherita, then along Via dei Mille and Via Filangieri, passing a few attractive shops and some lovely Art Deco villas). Let the smell of the sea lead you to Borgo Marinari, the former fishermens' quarter, now full of sailing clubs and busy trattorias. A bridge connects Via Partenope with the formidable Swabian **Castel dell'Ovo** ㉔ (closed to the public) or "egg-castle", so named because, according to legend, it sits on an egg

In the 19th century, King Ferdinand I's pet crocodile, allegedly fed on a diet of unlucky prisoners, was embalmed and hung on the walls of the Castel Nuovo.

BELOW: French towers and Spanish arch, Castel Nuovo.

Map
on page
136

*Funicular railways
are one of the more
efficient forms of
transport in Naples.*

BELOW: elegant
facades by the sea.
RIGHT: sun seekers
and Castel dell'Ovo.

talisman which belonged to the Roman poet Virgil. The egg is inside a bottle and well-protected by an iron cage: should it break, Naples will fall.

Head west along pedestrianised Via Caracciolo, and while away some time in the **Villa Comunale gardens** ㉕. This is the place to come on Sunday afternoon if you want a taste of Neapolitan life. Families flock here after lunch in their Sunday best and stroll and chat under the shade of the palms while their children run around and beg for ice-creams. If you have your own kids in tow, visit Europe's oldest **Aquarium** (1872) (Acquario; open summer Tues–Sat 9am–6pm, Sun and hols 10am–6pm; winter Tues–Sat 9am–5pm, Sun and hols 9am–2pm; entrance fee).

Across the Riviera di Chiaia is the neoclassical **Villa Pignatelli** (open Tues–Sun 9am–2pm), once owned by the Rothschild family, which now houses a collection of porcelain and period furniture. Via Caracciolo ends in the Mergellina district, animated with crowds of fishermen supplying the local fish market. Piazza Sannazzaro is a popular nightspot, full of pizzerias and inexpensive restaurants *(for more about Neapolitan nightlife and suggested venues, see page 346)*.

Via Posillipo climbs from here to an intriguing building, the yellowish **Palazzo Donn'Anna**, built out of tufa rock in 1642. The view becomes spectacular once you reach the Parco della Rimembranza and Capo Posillipo.

Capodimonte

On the north side of the city, the Pompeiian red facade of the **Palazzo Reale di Capodimonte** ㉖ (open Tue–Sun 8.30am–5.30pm; entrance fee; accessible by bus from the Stazione Centrale on Piazza Garibaldi, Piazza Municipio, Piazza Dante and the Archaeological Museum) rises against the blue of the sky and the green of the fields, beyond which extend kilometres of thick forest that were once the hunting reserve of the Bourbon King Charles III. The construction of the palace began in 1738 in order to hold the **Farnese collection** of paintings that the king had inherited. The first rooms were ready just 20 years later, the last exactly 100 years after work had begun. In 1999, after six years of attentive restoration, Capodimonte was reopened in its entirety to the public. Over time many new works were added to the collection, most notably 300 works from the Galleria Napoletana, by local artists or artists who spent time in Naples, including Caravaggio, Mattia Preti and Simone Martini.

The museum's highlight remains the superb collection of 200 paintings by the most important Italian and Flemish painters – Masaccio, Botticelli, Bellini, Titian and Van Dyck, to name but a few – which the sharp eyes of the Farnese dynasty amassed over three centuries of avid collecting. The museum is too large to be seen exhaustively in one day, so try to focus on what interests you most: armour, tapestry, porcelain or painting. The magnificent **Salottino di Porcellana** is lined from top to bottom with Capodimonte porcelain tiles made in King Charles III's porcelain factory in 1757. It took two years and more than 3,000 pieces to decorate the walls and ceilings of the queen's parlour. Originally installed in the Royal Palace at Portici, the *salottino* was dismantled in 1866 and reassembled here. ❏

ART AND ANTIQUITIES OF THE ROMAN ERA

Naples' national museum ranks among the world's best, housing spectacular finds from Pompeii and Herculaneum, and the colossal Farnese sculptures

Originally a military barracks, then a university, the vast red *palazzo* north of Spaccanapoli was transformed into an archaeological museum under Bourbon rule. The rooms on the ground floor are devoted to the Farnese collection of statues that the Bourbon King Charles inherited through his mother from the powerful Farnese family. First-rate copies of older Greek masterpieces are mingled with original Roman creations. Over a varied crowd of heroes and warriors, Aphrodites and Athenas, towers the largest sculpture from antiquity ever found, the *Farnese Bull*, unearthed at the Baths of Caracalla in Rome. The rich collection of mosaics on the mezzanine floor comes from the floors, walls and courtyards of Pompeiian homes. One of the highlights here is the *Battle of Issus*, the remains of a war scene depicting Alexander the Great in his victorious battle against the Persian emperor, Darius (333 BC). Special permanent exhibits include the fine bronze figures from the Villa dei Papiri in Herculaneum (look out for the two athletes whose concentrated expression is almost disconcerting); the Egyptian collection, which contains a mummified crocodile; and the collection of carved precious stones, featuring the *Farnese Bowl*, a giant cameo with fine pink reliefs on a black field (c. 150 BC). A recent addition to the museum is a nearly complete fresco cycle detached from the Temple of Isis in Pompeii, with Egyptian landscapes and two episodes from the myth of Io.

▷ **BACCHIC CELEBRATIONS**
After centuries buried in ash, the freshness and colour of Pompeii's artworks are an amazing tribute to the craftsmanship of their ancient makers.

△ **MARBLE LEGEND**
Carved from a single block of marble, the huge *Farnese Bull* depicts the death of Dirce, tied to a bull by Antiope's sons for trying to murder their mother.

▽ **CLASSICAL GIANTS**
The Farnese collection of towering sculptures includes the famous statue of Hercules resting on his club (far end).

◁ **EMPERORS AND WARRIORS**
The noseless Emperor Augustus is one of many faces in a formidable line-up of Greek and Roman busts.

▷ **PAESTUM TREASURE**
Exquisite Greek vase portraying the nymphs in the Garden of Hesperides: one picks golden apples for Hercules while another distracts the serpent with offers of food.

POMPEIIAN EROTICA

After 200 years under lock and key, the museum's so-called "Gabinetto Segreto" (secret room) has recently reopened to the public. It contains erotic images which lift the lid on the racy ancient world. Romans had a taste for eroticism, and prostitution was a flourishing trade. Graphic sex was often depicted in the steam room, with scenes showing nymphs and satyrs disporting themselves, or an over-endowed Priapus simultaneously impaling several victims on his many-pronged member. Frescoes on view in Pompeii and Naples also depict the illicit love of Mars and the sexual antics of Jupiter, who disguised himself as a human to seduce women. Signs displaying male genitalia were considered symbols of good luck, as well as virility and fertility, and used to ward off evil spirits. In Pompeii, a sign of a penis outside a bakery might also indicate a plentiful supply of fresh loaves, while a goblet adorned with a salacious scene spelt promises of orgies to come.

△ MOSAIC SCENES
The delightful parade of cats and cockerels, still-lifes, coarse comic actors, brilliant 'aquarium' scenes, and more fills no less than 24 rooms.

▷ "SECOND-STYLE" FRESCO
Wall painting taken from a house in Pompeii depicting Perseus, son of Zeus, and Andromeda, who he rescued from a sea-monster.

△ BLUE VASE
Glass-cameo amphora from Pompeii, decorated with scenes celebrating the grape harvest.

▷ MOTHER NATURE
The many-breasted Artemis of Ephesus, made of alabaster and bronze, represents fertility.

AROUND THE VOLCANO

Map on page 152

Pompeii and Herculaneum attract nearly 3 million visitors a year;
Vesuvius, their slayer, is also a draw, as are the bubbling
Phlegraean Fields to the west of Naples

Naples is the best base from which to visit the Phlegrean Fields, Caserta and the hilly territory east of **Naples ❶**. Trains go practically everywhere in Campania and are generally more efficient in the densely populated areas around the city than travelling by bus or car on the crowded roads. Heading west from Naples, the suburbs continue along the scenic coastal drive to Posillipo, Pozzuoli, Bacoli and Cumae, which grew up in the Roman era. Swarms of poets, rhetoricians and a rich merchant class were drawn here by the salubrious climate and the beauty of the coast as well as by the springs, spas and an eerie volcanic landscape that fired many imaginations. The ancient Greeks, struck by the "boiling" terrain, named this stretch of land west of Naples the Phlegraean Fields (from the Greek *fleguròs* meaning fire).

Of the 20 or so extinct and long-dormant volcanoes that mark this area, many circular craters are still perfectly recognisable even though their characteristic cones have long been lost to the elements and the passing millennia, and the advancing Mediterranean has transformed some into lakes and ports. The landscape is made up of ample stretches of yellow and grey volcanic rock, sparse, low hills covered with dark green woods, and small lakes.

Fields of fire

Agnano Terme ❷ marks the start of an area of springs and spas. The drying out of the muddy Lago d'Agnano in 1870 brought some 70 thermal springs back to the surface. Today's Terme di Agnano are renowned for their restorative and curative powers. Further west the landscape becomes especially disquieting at the awesome crater of **Solfatara ❸** (open daily 7.30am–dusk; entrance fee), which in part inspired Dante's *Inferno*. The sulphurous springs were believed to be poisonous discharges from the wounds that the Titans received during their war against the Gods, and the eruptions were thought to have been the attempts by the Titans, buried alive by Jupiter, to break free. The mysterious crater has drawn curious visitors since Roman times. A strong sulphurous smell still pervades the area and as you walk towards the most active section of hissing steam jets (cordonned off), you can feel the heat rising from the ground which is hollow. Guides like to demonstrate this natural phenomenon by hurling a rock to the ground; it falls with a thud which resonates through the labyrinth of underground channels.

Further west is **Lago d'Averno ❹**, best seen at sunset, which was described by Virgil in the *Aeneid* as the entrance to the underworld. Its name derives from the Greek *àornos* meaning "without birds", presumably because no bird could survive the toxic vapours that emerged from the waters. Beyond the lake lies

LEFT: House of the Faun, Pompeii.
BELOW: sulphur spring, Solfatara.

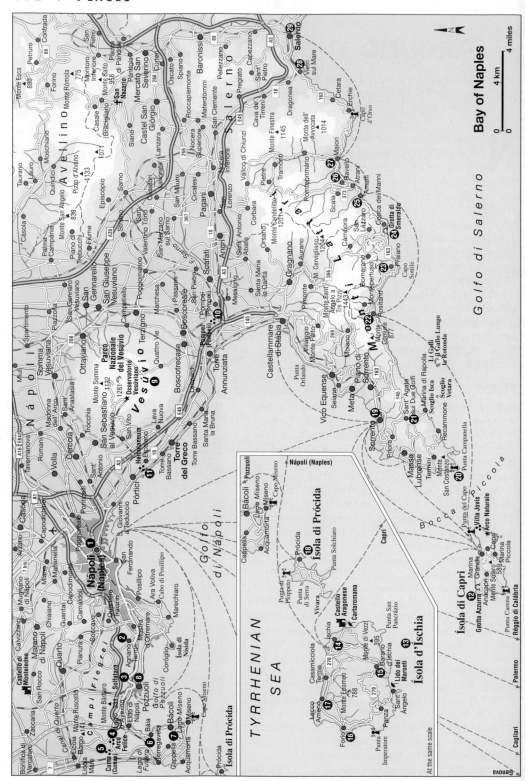

Bay of Naples

Europe's youngest volcano, the 130-metre (430-ft) **Monte Nuovo**, whose cone was created by the 1538 earthquake, well-worth the climb for the view of the Bay of Naples.

Map on page 152

The most famous sight in **Cumae ❺** is the Antro della Sibilla, a 130-metre (430-ft) corridor carved into the hill of the acropolis identified with the sacred cave of the Cumaean Sibyl, the same prophetess who in the *Aeneid* predicts the destiny of Rome, and who Michelangelo painted in the Sistine Chapel. The trapezoidal section of the gallery predates the foundation of Cumae; it is thought that it was used for storing goods and water. From here, the paved Via Sacra climbs to the scanty remains of the temples of Jupiter and Apollo, both transformed into Christian churches in the early middle ages, and a great view.

On the opposite coast, the imperial city of **Baia ❻** became a popular tourist destination, whose licentious habits were sharply described in Petronius' *Satyricon*. Capo Miseno served as an important military harbour. Unfortunately, most of the splendid villas and Roman buildings sank into the sea, lost to *bradisismo*, a phenomenon of rising and settling with respect to sea level, as a result of the pressure variations exercised by natural underground heat sources. Excavations at Baia include what remains of the baths and an imperial palace (open daily 9am–1 hour before sunset; entrance fee); local finds can be seen at the Museo Archeologico dei Campi Flegrei, housed in a 16th-century Spanish castle (open Tues–Sun, 9am–6pm; entrance fee). At **Bacoli ❼**, between Baia and Capo Miseno, is the striking Piscina Mirabile, a monumental underwater galleria-cistern carved from the volcanic rock (Via Creco 10; open daily 9am–1 hour before sunset; tip required). With a capacity of 12,000 cubic metres (2,650 gallons), this ancient reservoir supplied water for the Roman fleet anchored at Miseno. Made up of five naves and supported by 48 pilasters, the sunlight filtering through an aperture above, it looks more like a basilica than a giant cistern.

Sibyl's Cave, dedicated to the sibyl of Cumae who guided Aeneas through the underworld.

BELOW: Baia's 16th century castle.

For a while, Rome's main port was **Pozzuoli ❽**, which was originally known as Puteoli, from the Latin *putere* which means "to smell bad", which indeed it does due to the sulphurous vapours. This wealthy commercial town's modern claim to fame is as the birthplace of the actress Sophia Loren. It is also the home of Italy's airforce academy. The town has an exceptional, well-preserved amphitheatre, the 1st-century Anfiteatro Flavio (open daily 9am–1 hour before sunset; entrance fee), which was used to stage gladiatorial combats. It was the third largest theatre in Italy and could hold 30,000 spectators. Two of the three levels are still intact, and in the underground portions you can make out the changing rooms and how the scenery and beasts were transported to the arena level.

Up the fiery mountain

The most convenient places from which to take day trips to the area around Vesuvius and its victims, Pompeii and Herculaneum, are Sorrento and Naples (whose Museo Archeologico Nazionale holds an impressive collection of objects found during the excavations; *see pages 148–9*), which are well served by the local buses and trains; if you are travelling by car, they are within easy reach of the Amalfi Coast.

The unmistakeable profile of **Vesuvius** (Vesuvio) belongs to the Gulf of Naples much as the Golden Gate Bridge belongs to the San Francisco Bay. The stretch of sky between Naples and Pompeii is dominated by the smooth, dark cone of this mountain that immediately seems different from all others. Perhaps this is because of its imposing peak, strangely isolated and barren, rising above an otherwise flat and fertile landscape. Vesuvius imparts fear and unease even before it is identified for what it is: the only volcano still active on the European continent – an eruption today might endanger the lives of half a million people.

However, Vesuvius is among the most studied and closely monitored volcanoes in the world. The movement of magma, the chemical composition of the gas and water that flow from it, the micro-quakes and variations in the elevation of its base are constantly analysed with the sophisticated instrumentation of the *Osservatorio Vesuviano* (built in 1845, 600 metres/2000 ft up the west side of the volcano). It's virtually impossible that the *Osservatorio* would fail to forecast an eruption in time to evacuate the area, so you can safely climb to the top of the volcano. On a clear day, the view of the Bay, with Naples stretching to the right only 12 km (7½ miles) away, the islands of Procida, Ischia and Capri, and the fertile countryside below, is just too wonderful to be missed.

Vesuvius is a rare example of a pent-up volcano, made up of one cone inside another. The original cone, Monte Somma, once reached a height of 2,300 metres (7,544 ft). The eruption that destroyed Herculaneum and Pompeii in AD 79, opened a second crater within the Somma crater. This "new" crater, Vesuvius, is 1,281 metres (4,200 ft) tall, 200 metres (650 ft) deep, and has a 1,500-metre (4,900-ft) circumference. Its magma chamber that contains volcanic dust and rock fused at 2,000°C (3,600°F), reminds us of its vitality by the

BELOW: Vesuvius, seen from Naples' industrial port.

occasional belch of smoke and modest seismic activity. The highest point of the remains of the Monte Somma crater rises up to the north, beyond the deep semi-circular valley known as the *Atrio del Gigante*. This natural barrier around the 1,132-metre (3,714-ft) Punta del Nasone saved the villages north of the volcano during the eruption of 1631 (the most catastrophic after that which destroyed Pompeii). But on the south side of the mountain nearly 4,000 people were killed, and for days the smoke darkened the skies as far as Taranto.

The eruption of AD 79 occurred after a long period of dormancy and must have come as a complete surprise to the local population who no longer considered Vesuvius to be a volcano. The Pompeians were killed not so much by the lava but by the clouds of toxic gas, lapillus and various particulate matter that rolled over the city, incinerating everything in their path. Since then, Vesuvius has had another 18 violent eruptions. In 1794 the town of Torre del Greco was totally destroyed, but the latest eruption, which happened in 1944, did not cost a single life and the once familiar plume of black smoke disappeared (*see page 113*).

View from the top

The easiest and most comfortable ascent of Vesuvius is from the Herculaneum side of the mountain (if the weather is cloudy, rainy or very windy, call the Guide Vulcanologiche on 081-7775720 or 0337-942249 to find out whether access is open). If you are driving to the volcano, follow the signs for *l'Osservatorio Vesuviano* until you reach the car park where the road ends at a group of bars and souvenir shops. From here it's a pleasant, though somewhat slippery, half-hour walk to the crater. Alternatively, there is bus service from the excavations at Pompeii and Herculaneum to the car park and back (Trasporti

Map on page 152

TIP

The Circumvesuviana railway line runs regular services between Naples and Sorrento, stopping at both Pompeii and Herculaneum (*Ercolano*). It's a cheap, efficient and stress-free way to get around the bay.

BELOW:
looking down into Vesuvius' crater.

Vesuviani tel: 081-5365154, about six daily departures from Pompeii and Herculaneum in summer; three in winter; the trip lasts 1 hour 15 mins from Pompei, 50 mins from Herculaneum. There are also two daily departures to Vesuvius from Piazza Piedigrotta near the Mergellina train station in Naples).

A Golden mile of villas

The Italian poet Giacomo Leopardi (1798–1837) penned some of his most famous lyrics in the Villa delle Ginestre, one of a string of magnificent coastal villas built along the "golden mile" between Naples and Torre del Greco.

For a change of scene consider visiting the splendid **Ville Vesuviane**, built at the foot of Vesuvius in the 18th century. In 1738, the Bourbon King of Naples Charles III built the **Royal Palace of Portici** (now part of the Agriculture University in Naples; call 081-7754850 for a tour of the Botanical Gardens housed in the park of the palace), and the royal court soon followed suit, studding the stretch of coastline between Naples and Torre del Greco with 120 fabulous villas.

Surrounded by parks that descend toward the sea, and richly decorated with erotic and trompe l'oeil frescoes in imitation of the recently discovered "Pompeian style", these villas earned the road along which they were built the nickname **Miglio d'Oro** (Golden Mile). Having been for the most part abandoned, after World War II they were nearly demolished to make way for the urbanisation of the Gulf of Naples. Thanks to the *Ente Ville Vesuviane* a fundraising association set up by a group of locals in 1973, a number have been saved.

Villa Campolieto (Corso Resina 283, Ercolano; open Tues–Sun 10am–1pm; entrance free except when the villa houses special exhibits; tel: 081-7322134) and the neighbouring **Villa Ruggiero** (Via Alessandro Rossi; opening times and telephone number as for Villa Compolieto) have been magnificently restored, and the parks of Villa Favorita and of Villa delle Ginestre are expected to open regularly to the public in 2002–3.

BELOW: Via del Mercurio, looking towards the Forum.

Pompeii

The main sites in **Pompeii** (open Oct–Feb daily 8.30am–5pm; Mar–Sept daily 8.30am–7.30pm; last admission 1 hour before closure; entrance fee: a cumulative ticket includes admission to the excavations at Herculaneum and is valid for three days; tel: 081-5365154) can be covered quickly in about 2–3 hours, but since Pompeii is the kind of place that touches something deep inside many visitors, it's a good idea to get there early in case you fall a victim to its magic. The ideal times of year for a visit are early spring and early autumn. Pompeii can get quite hot in the summer, and the ruins offer very little shade, so try to arrive early in the morning and take a break around lunchtime; suffocating heat and sightseeing fatigue can easily spoil an otherwise highly rewarding day. While in winter you may find that you have all of Pompeii to yourself, custodians tend to keep the most interesting structures closed off; remember that a smile, a kind word and a tip in Italy go a long way. The entrance is a short walk from the Pompei Villa dei Misteri railway station on the Circumvesuviana Naples–Sorrento line. Trasporti Vesuviani buses also run from Pompeii to Herculaneum and Vesuvius.

Founded in the 7th century BC by the Osci, a local Italic population, Pompeii developed under Etruscan and Greek influence before the Samnites took control of Southern Italy in the 5th–3rd centuries BC. They in turn were defeated in 290 BC by the Romans, who granted Pompeii autonomy. The city grew into the biggest trading centre on the southern portion of the coast. It was made a Roman colony in 80 BC, following the so-called "social war" fought by a league of autonomous Italic towns seeking the same civil rights that Roman citizens enjoyed. In AD 62, Pompeii was severely damaged by an earthquake and reconstruction work was in full swing when the great eruption of Vesuvius buried the city 17 years later.

Pompeii's ruins were accidentally discovered during the construction of a canal in 1592, when remains of buildings with painted walls were found and documented, but at the time they were thought to have been from the ancient city of Stabia. Further excavations of the site didn't begin until 1748 and it was not until 1860 that the site was excavated scientifically and with a concern for adequate preservation of the discovered relics in the Museo Archeologico Nazionale. Until then, the goal of the excavations had been to recover relics for the Bourbon dynasty, and in the process, many buildings were gravely damaged and easily fell prey to art thieves.

Around the Forum

By AD 79, Pompeii had become a thoroughly Romanised town of some 20,000 inhabitants, which covered about 66 hectares (160 acres). The three to four-hour tour described below includes a selection of sights that should not be missed, but it is by no means exhaustive. Start from Porta Marina (near the main entrance), which leads into the **Foro** (Forum) with the ruins of the **Temple of Jupiter** silhouetted against Vesuvius and, just to the right, the **Macellum** (market hall): note the 12 short pilasters at the centre which supported a wooden shelter that covered a large circular fountain used for cleaning fish. Opposite stand the brick buildings which

Maps:
Area 152
Site 158

TIP

Exploring Pompeii is thirsty work, so it's a good idea to pick up a bottle of water from one of the many street vendors outside the station before entering.

BELOW: murals from the Casa dei Vettii

Pompeii

0 ——— 200 m
0 ——— 200 yds

N

Villa dei Misteri (Villa of the Mysteries) **F**

Villa di Diomede (Villa of Diomedes)

Via dei Sepolcri

Viale alla Villa dei Misteri

Via Consolare

Porta Ercolano

Casa d. Chirurgo (House of the Surgeon) **E**

Torre XII

Casa di Apollo (House of Apollo)

Torre XI

Torre X

Porta di Vesuvio

Casa di Sallustio (House of Sallust)

Vicolo d.

Casa d. Fauno (House of the Labirinto Labyrinth)

Casa d. Adonis (House of Adonis)

Via di Mercurio

Fullonica

Vico d.

Casa d. Nozze d'Argento

Casa degli A. Dorati (House of A. Dorati)

Casa d. Meleagro (House of Meleager)

V. del Vettii

Casa d. Vettii (House of the Vettii) **D**

Casa di Orfeo (House of Orpheus)

Via del Vesuvio

Casa de M. L. Frontone (House of M. L. Fronto)

Porta di Capua

Casa del Centenario

Casa dei Gladiatori (House of the Gladiators)

Via di Nola

Porta di Nola

Stazione Pompei Scavi

Poggiomarino

Porta di Sarno

Anfiteatro (Amphitheatre) **J**

Villa di Giulia Felice (Villa of Julia Felix)

Casa di Loreius Tiburtinus (House of Loreius Tiburtinus)

Grande Palestra (Great Palaestra) **I**

Casa di Venere (House of Marine Venus)

Via di Nocera

Via dell'Abbondanza

Casa di Trebio Valente (House of Trebius Valens)

Thermopolium

Officina di Verecundus

Fullonica Stephani

Casa del Menandro (House of the Menander) **H**

Casa d. Citarista (House of the Cithara Player)

Teatro Piccolo (Little Theatre)

Caserma d. Gladiatori (Gladiators' Barracks)

Stabia

Teatro Grande (Grand Theatre)

Via del Teatri

Casa di Giuseppe II

House of the Wild Boar

Via del Teatri

Viale ai Teatri

Parking

Porta di Stabia

Tempio d'Iside (Temple of Isis)

Casa di Epidio Rufo

Via Stabiana

Terme Sabiane (Stabian Thermal Baths)

Tempio di Vespasiano (Temple of Vespasian)

Lupanar Africani et Victoris **G**

Vicolo del Lupanare

Casa dell'Orso (House of the Bear)

Casa di Fortuna (House of Fortune)

Via degli Augustali

Augustali

Terme Centrali

Via d.

Edificio di Eumachia

Maecllum

Casa del Poeta Tragico (House of the Tragic Poet)

Tempio d. Fortuna Augusta (Temple of Fortune)

Foro (Forum) **A**

Uffici Pubblici (Public Offices)

Tempio di Giove (Temple of Jupiter)

Cafeteria

Terme d. Foro **B**

Casa di Pansa (House of Pansa)

Tempio di Apollo (Temple of Apollo)

Antiquarium

Basilica

Via della Marina

Porta Marina

Stazione Villa dei Misteri

Casa d. Fauno (House of the Faun) **C**

Boscoreale

Salerno

18

POMPEI

Necropoli

Porta di Nocera

Via Plinio

Castellamare di Stabia, Salerno

Sorrento

A3

18

A3

Napoli

Napoli

Napoli

Napoli

housed the **Public Offices**. Pompeians were politically active; although only men were allowed to vote, the entire population participated in the annual electoral campaigns of the two *duoviri iure dicundo* (magistrate-mayors), two *aediles* (assessors for construction, commerce, the games and the baths), as well as the election of the *ordo decurionum* (town council) held every five years.

On the east side of the Forum is the richly-decorated portal of the **Building of Eumachia**, a thriving wool factory named after its owner, Venus' priestess. After her death, the building became headquarters of the wool and textile guild: as you step inside, to the right is a small room with overlapping basins designed to collect the urine of passers-by, which was used in the wool blanching process.

On the west side of the Forum, beyond a locked gate protecting some archaeological material is a cubicle which served as a **Public Lavatory**: wooden and marble seats were located, without privacy, atop a canal that runs along three sides of the room. From here, cross Vico dei Soprastanti and, before heading north, take a look at the **Terme del Foro ❸**. These rather small-scale baths had all the features of larger Roman baths (dressing rooms, gym, and pools with cold, warm and hot water); the decor, now lost, would have included large round mirrors, glass ceilings, silver taps, mosaics, and precious marbles.

Plaster cast of one of the carbonised bodies found in Pompeii.

House of the Faun and House of the Vettii

Take Via della Fortuna to reach the **Casa del Fauno ❹** (House of the Faun) a luxury villa with four *triclinia* (dining rooms), one for each season of the year, two peristyles (porticos running along a central garden), and a small bath whose *calidarium* (hot water tub) made use of the heat produced by the oven in the adjacent kitchen. As in most of the villas, the gardens were planted with herbs,

BELOW: bath house with skylight.

THE FOUR STYLES OF POMPEII

The painted murals found in the buildings in Herculaneum and Pompeii have been divided into four styles that correspond with four distinct periods.

● The **First Style** (3rd century–80 BC), of Hellenistic origin, is the simplest and most sober. It is easily recognisable because of the absence of figurative subjects and the painting technique in glossy stucco. The predominant colours are dark red, black and yellow (see the House of the Faun).

● The **Second Style** (80 BC–Augustus), creates the illusion of "opening the walls of the house". Depth was added to the decorations through gradual use of perspective. The subjects are often inspired by theatrical backdrops with *trompe l'oeil* scenes of landscapes. There were also large paintings of mythical, heroic or religious subjects (an excellent example is the Villa dei Misteri).

● The **Third Style** (Augustus–AD 62) abandons the use of trompe l'oeil in architectonic elements which now appear stylized. Small panels with different subjects (*pinakes*) had an effect comparable to framed canvases. Beyond the miniature landscapes, there are portraits of daily life, still life, birds and exotic themes.

● The **Fourth Style** (Claudius –AD 79) is completely removed from reality, rendering the walls like opulent baroque tapestries, in which the ornamental motifs are crowded together and superimposed upon one another.

Cherubs stirring gold; detail from the Amorini fresco which decorates the Casa dei Vettii triclinium.

bushes and trees commonly grown in Pompeii, such as mint, camomile, oleander, grape vines, pomegranate and figs. The house is named after the statue of a dancing faun which adorned one of the two *atria* (inner courtyards), now replaced by a copy (the original is on display at the Museo Archeologico Nazionale, together with fragments of the impressive mosaic floors; *see page 141*).

At the junction of Vicolo di Mercurio and Vicolo dei Vettii stands the **Casa dei Vettii D**, famous for the outstanding paintings in the fourth style *(see box on page 159)*, which the Vettii, a family of parvenus who made a fortune in the wine trade, commissioned from the best local artists right after the earthquake of AD 62. The enigmatic fresco at the entrance (ask custodians if locked) portrays Priapus weighing his gigantic phallus on scales, and a sheep with the attributes of Mercury (the god of earning), both propitiatory images for wealth. The disproportionately large phallus was a venerated symbol put at the entrance of practically every home to ward off the evil eye.

House of the Surgeon to Villa of the Mysteries

Continue along Vicolo dei Vettii until you hit what's left of the city walls, and turn left to Porta Ercolano. Following the city walls a short way down Via Consolare you'll come to one of Pompeii's oldest houses, dating from the 4th century BC; it's called the **Casa del Chirurgo E** (House of the Surgeon) because 40 surgical instruments were found here, including forceps and pliers used to pull teeth (on display at the Museo Archeologico Nazionale). The ancient Romans used medicines based on herbs, spices, roots, honey, vinegar, olive oil and wine; prepared soothing balms from cooked cereals; disinfected wounds with a concoction of lime, baking soda and urine; ate snakes for good health and found that the raw

BELOW: Villa dei Misteri contains many frescoes.

Map on page 158

leaves of a Pompeian variety of cabbage eliminated the side effects of heavy eating and drinking. Not all the local pharmacists must have been trustworthy, though; in 81 BC a law was passed punishing those who sold dangerous medicines.

On the other side of Porta Ercolano is **Via dei Sepolcri**, lined with tombs, shops and suburban villas. Roman cemeteries were always located outside the city walls, usually built alongside important roadways, in this case the road to Herculaneum. Until the 1st century AD, the Romans cremated their dead and put the ashes in an urn together with a small coin to be used to pay Charon, the boatman who took the dead across the infernal river to the next world. The cult of the dead was widely observed, and special banquets at the burial place were organised for funerals and anniversaries. The funeral menu always included fava beans which served as a talisman against the evil spirits of the dead, a tradition that survives in all of Italy in the shape of the so-called *fave dei morti* (almond biscuits in the shape of fava beans made around 2 November, the Day of the Dead).

A pleasant walk further down the Via dei Sepolcri leads to one of Pompeii's highlights: the **Villa dei Misteri F**, which owes its fame and name to the extraordinary cycle of frescoes visible in the triclinium. The cycle, 17 metres (56 ft) long and 3 metres (10 ft) high, is the largest painting from antiquity ever found. The subject is derived from a 4th–3rd century BC Hellenistic theme, and its "mysterious" nature resides above all in the interpretation of the scenes. According to the most credited theory, they describe the initiation of a young woman, most likely a bride, to the Dionysian cult. Dinner was served in this room; the main meal of the day, it could last as long as seven hours and was often shared with friends. Jugglers, dancers, musicians and beautiful slaves often entertained the diners who ate while reclining on the triclinia.

Pompeii's Casa dei Vettii is decorated with rich murals of mythological scenes.

BELOW: Pompeii street scene.

Detail of the Neptune and Amphitrite mosaic that gives the house in Herculaneum its name.

BELOW:
a snapper snapped.

Bars and Brothels

Retrace your steps to the Forum to explore the so-called **Nuovi Scavi** (New Excavations), begun in 1911. The area stretches east for about 500 metres and is cut through by Pompeii's **Via dell'Abbondanza**, once a major thoroughfare lined with shops, houses and drinking spots. The taverns were the equivalent of modern Italian bars. Wine, sometimes served warm with spices, was preserved in large terracotta vases and kept cool in the circular cavities cut out of the marble countertops. Some shops had interior rooms and gardens.

Not far from the Forum, on Vicolo del Lupanare, you'll find the **Lupanar Africani et Victoris ⑤**, one of the city's official brothels (there were 24 others). Ten built-in beds were divided among the two floors; on the wall above the doorway of each room are frescoes depicting the "speciality" of the prostitute that worked there; the customers were in the habit of writing their comments on the house on the walls, as shown by the 120 examples of graffiti that are still visible today. Pompeiians apparently spoke freely about love and sex: prostitution and homosexuality were ordinary aspects of daily life without a stigma of shame. Up Via degli Augustali and to the right on Vico Storto is **Modestus' Bakery**, one of the city's 31 bakeries, complete with oven and grinding-mill, where 81 carbonised loaves were found.

Back on Via dell'Abbondanza, other impressive sights are the **Terme Stabiane**, the city's largest baths for men and women (damaged by the AD 62 earthquake and not yet restored in AD 79); the **Workshop of Verecundus** (No. 5–7) "maker of cloth, woollen garments and articles in felt"; opposite is the **Fullonica Stephani**, a laundry shop. Two blocks down the street is the **Thermopolium**, a snack stand which served hot food to take away. Popular items included: *mulsum*, a sort of onion omelette seasoned with wine; chick-pea soup; *moretum*, a flattened roll eaten hot; and pork patties stewed in grape must and *garum*, the famous Roman fermented fish sauce which the Roman poet Martial thought smelled like bad breath: "The breath of Papilo is so strong that it manages to transform the most intense aromas into *garum*." (Epigrams, VII, 94).

To the amphitheatre

Next, find your way to the **Casa del Menandro ⑪** (to the south on Vico Meridionale), a large house that belonged to a relative of Empress Poppea; and to the **Orto dei Fuggiaschi** with 13 plaster casts of the carbonised bodies of men, women (including one expecting a baby) and children (near Porta Nocera). To return to Via dell'Abbondanza, skirt the **Grande Palestra ⓘ** – a huge 141 by 107-metre (460 by 350-ft) square which housed a gym cum pool where Pompeian youth kept fit, practicing the famous Roman maxim: *mens sana in corpore sano* (a healthy body is a healthy mind) – and the world's oldest surviving **Amphitheatre ⓙ** (early 1st century BC), which seated over 20,000 spectators. It seems that the gladiator games were born locally and were originally celebrated in honour of the dead, as shown by the funeral paintings of the Osci as early as the 4th century BC. On Via dell'Abbondanza, make sure you see the **House of Octavius Quartio**, with the largest and most spectacular garden in town: its now empty T-shaped canal could flood the entire garden, imitating the floods of the Nile in order to provide a sacred setting for the nocturnal rituals of the sacerdotes of the Egyptian goddess Isis.

Herculaneum

At the foot of Vesuvius' western slopes are the excavations of **Herculaneum** (open Oct–Feb daily 8.30am–5pm; March–Sept daily 8.30am–7.30pm; last admission 90 mins before closure; entrance fee; a cumulative ticket valid for three days includes admission to Pompeii; tel: 081-7390963), destroyed in 79 AD not by a river of burning lava but by a monstrous avalanche of volcanic material which rolled down Vesuvius in the heavy rains that followed the eruption. The site was accidentally discovered by an Austrian well-digger in 1709 under 20 metres (65 ft) of petrified mud, which, having perfectly sealed the town beneath, effectively preserved the wood and household utensils that would otherwise have been lost over time. Systematic excavations didn't start until the 1920s, and have so far brought to light only half of the town, which might still yield sensational discoveries, especially considering that the first large group of carbonised bodies was found only in the early 1990s. Until then, it had been wrongly assumed that Herculaneum's population, unlike that of Pompeii, had managed to escape. The last set of excavations, in 1998, were centred on the famous **Villa dei Papiri**, named after the 1,800 carbonised papyrus scrolls found on the premises in the 18th century. Its artworks and artefacts fill several rooms of the Museo Archeologico in Naples.

As with Pompeii, Herculaneum can absorb your attention for the better part of a day, but a couple of hours are enough to see the highlights. The entrance is

The design of the John Paul Getty Museum in Malibu, California was modelled on Herculaneum's Villa dei Papiri, built by Julius Caesar's father-in-law.

Maps:
Area 152
Site 158

BELOW: Roman Herculaneum, with the modern town behind.

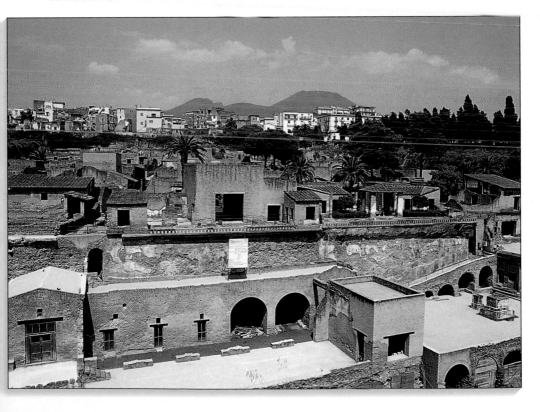

about a 10-minute walk downhill from Ercolano station, a stop on the Circumvesuviana Naples– Sorrento line. Trasporti Vesuviani buses also run from Herculaneum to Vesuvius and Pompeii *(see the Travel Tips section).*

Roman seaside resort

According to legend, the Greek settlement of Herakleia was founded by its patron deity Hercules. Like Pompeii, the town passed through periods of Oscan and Samnite domination before becoming a Roman colony in 89 BC. In the 1st century AD, Herculaneum, which lacked the commercial importance of Pompeii and was about half its size, was a town of some 5,000 residents and a favoured seaside resort of wealthy Romans. A few patricians owned the villas facing the Gulf of Naples, but most houses reflect the middle- and working-class status of their inhabitants, for the most part artisans, artists and fishermen. The city is laid out in the typical Roman grid pattern, with intersecting streets known as Decumani and Cardi. All the major sights are lined along the two central Cardi IV and V, which makes for a pleasant loop walk. Start from the Southern end of Cardo IV, at the **Casa dell'Atrio o Mosaico** (House of the Mosaic Atrium), one of the grandest Herculanean villas whose *atrium* (the inner courtyard which brought light to the surrounding rooms) still preserves its lovely black-and-white mosaic floor.

Across the street stands the **Casa a Graticcio**, a two-storey building with a balcony, named after the inexpensive wood-and-plaster construction technique used to build plebeian houses; you can climb upstairs via the restored inner staircase, which still retains some of the original steps. Next door is the **Casa del Tramezzo di Legno** (House of the Wooden Partition), another house on two floors, noteworthy for its almost intact facade and, inside, a wooden partition with hinges and

In contrast to the houses in Pompeii, where the roofs collapsed under the weight of the hailstorm of ash and pumice stone, Herculaneum's houses and their contents were preserved in the sea of mud which buried the town.

BELOW:
the Casa a Graticcio and Casa del Tramezzo di Legno.

lamp brackets, that closes the *tablinum* (tiny office) off the *atrium*. The corner shop at No. 10 displays a remarkably well-preserved wooden clothes press.

Cross the Decumanus Inferior to the fine **Terme del Foro**, decorated with mosaics depicting marine life which occupy the first block to the left. In the *calidarium* (hot chamber) of the men's baths, the partially collapsed vault reveals the heating pipes and smoke vents. The women's baths are intact.

Returning to the right side of Cardo IV, the **Casa Sannitica** (Samnite House), whose *atrium* features a graceful blind gallery and bronze spouts in the shape of animals, stands at the corner of the Decumanus Inferior. Two doors down is the **Casa del Mobilio Carbonizzato** (House of the Carbonised Furniture) and the **Casa di Nettuno ed Anfitrite** (House of the Neptune Mosaic), both haunted by the spirit of the owners, whose portraits greet you from the walls. On the ground floor of the second house, past the room stocked with *amphorae* that was once a **wine shop**, is a small courtyard paved with a beautiful mosaic of Neptune.

Turn right onto the Decumanus Maximus and the entrance of the **Casa del Bicentinario** (House of the Bicentenary), a patrician residence with smaller rooms upstairs, which may have been used by Christian servants or tenants, as the walls are scratched with crosses. The right side of Cardo V is flanked with more houses, while to the left, behind a row of shops with carbonised foods and metal utensils, stretches the large **Palestra** (gymnasium), with a cruciform pool like the one in Pompeii and a central bronze fountain in the shape of a snake. As you cross the Decumanus Inferior, note the corner cereal shop, with a striking marble counter. At the end of Cardo V, to the right, awaits the grandest of all Herculaneum's mansions, the two-storey **Casa dei Cervi** (House of the Deer), with remarkable frescoes and what must once have been a superb garden kissed by sea breezes. ❑

Map on page 152

TIP

As you walk downhill from the station to Herculaneum, you'll pass a tourist office on the right-hand side of the road where you can pick up a free map of the site.

BELOW: the exemplary House of the Mosaic Atrium

CAPRI, ISCHIA AND PROCIDA

Maps:
Area 152
Capri 168

Luxury, healthy waters, romantic scenery, tasty food, and sublime natural beauty make the islands of the Bay of Naples an international tourist destination

Naples

apri, Ischia and Procida all have fragrant hills, plunging views, shimmering coves, lush Mediterranean and sub-tropical vegetation, but there the similarity ends; each island has a very distinctive feel and charm. For this reason, if you are not pressed for time, you should visit them all. Don't make the mistake of going to Ischia thinking it's a sort of less expensive and relatively undiscovered Capri: the first Roman emperor knew what he was doing when he exchanged larger and more fertile Ischia for beautiful Capri. Some 2,000 years later, Capri is still well-worth the splurge. But do go to Ischia to enjoy the hills, well-run spas and hot water springs that you won't find on Capri. In laid-back Procida time seems to slow down. Here life is simple: expect lots of sunshine and blue water, genuine food and pleasant walks far from the madding crowd.

For centuries **Capri ⑫** has been a vacation spot for a rich and sophisticated international crowd, a fact that has in no small measure shaped the recent history of the island. Capri has more than its fair share of magnificent villas and prestigious residences, which give the landscape a sheen of glamour that will not be lost on the visitor. The "blue island" remains the undisputed queen of the Bay of Naples and one of the few places in Italy which has successfully balanced the protection of its natural beauty with the demands of a bustling tourist industry. Although Capri is known as a retreat for the jet-set, the island's hotels and restaurants aren't any more expensive than comparable establishments in Rome, Florence or Venice.

LEFT: heading for Procida.
BELOW: boatman in Marina Corricella.

Until the early years of the 20th century, Capri attracted mostly literary figures, artists and inveterate travellers, but little by little it became an island for everyone, rich and not-so-rich alike. In the peak season (July to August and weekends from June to early September), up to 6,000 day trippers come from Naples and the Amalfi Coast to join the 12,000 residents and some 3,000 hotel guests on the 10 sq. km (4 sq. mile) island. Between March and October non-residents are not allowed to bring cars to Capri on the ferry. But even at its fullest, Capri still offers some relatively intimate coves where you can pass the hottest hours of the day.

Island of goats

It's been said that Capri is Italy's claim to Eden, but to the ancient Greeks it was just another rocky island named Caprea, meaning "island of the goats" (in an ancient Italic language), "of the wild boars" (Greek), or "of the two cities" (Phoenician). Emperor Augustus was Capri's first fan: in AD 29 he traded Ischia to the Greek colony of Naples in exchange for it. He called it *Apragòpoli* (the city of the *dolce far niente*, literally "sweet doing nothing") and had several villas

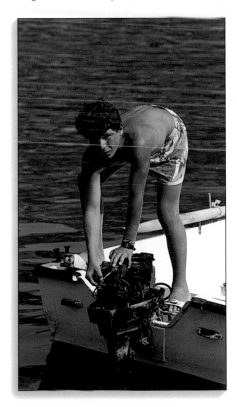

Views of Marina Piccola and the Faraglioni rocks can be seen from Punta Cannone just a 20-minute walk from Capri town.

built there, along with cisterns to collect water, and small temples dedicated to the cult of the Nymphs (Roman female deities who inhabited lakes, rivers, seas, woods and mountains) in the grottoes that surround the island, thereby making a sumptuous imperial park. But his successor, Tiberius, who ruled the Roman Empire from here for 10 years, left a greater mark.

Social centre

It is difficult to believe that such a popular island did not have a proper port until the **Marina Grande Ⓐ** was built in 1931. It's a short ride from here on the *funicolare* up to **Capri town Ⓑ**, one of the island's two social centres, known for its self-consciously chic ambiance. The hub of the town is the little square lined with outdoor cafés known as the Piazzetta.

A short walk from the Piazzetta along Via Vittorio Emanuele and Via Serena brings you in sight of Capri's medieval jewel, the **Certosa di San Giacomo Ⓒ** (open Mon–Fri 9am–1pm; Mon and Wed also 4–7pm; closed weekends; entrance fee), founded in 1374 by Count Giacomo Arcucci of Capri, the secretary to Queen Giovanna I d'Anjou, in gratitude for the birth of a son. Unlike the other monasteries built for the monks of the order of San Brunone di Colonia *(see page 255)*, no expense was spared. However, in the 16th century it was sacked several times by Saracen pirates, and in 1807 it was suppressed by Napoleon and fell into decline.

Partially restored in 1961, the Certosa di San Giacomo has been home to – in the words of its teachers – "the most beautiful high school in the world". The works of the visionary painter Karl Wilhelm Diefenbach, who lived on Capri from 1900 until his death in 1913, are on display in the refectory.

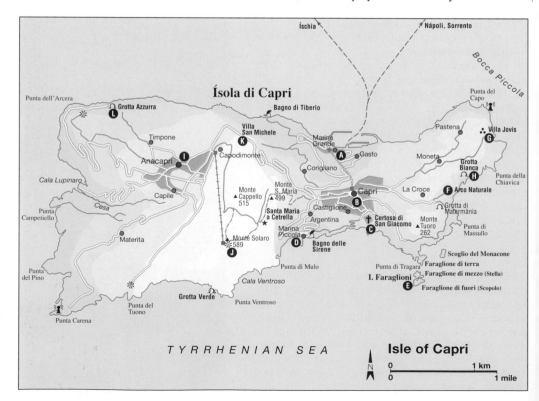

Scenic walks

Adjacent to La Certosa are the **Giardini di Augusto**, so named because they were laid out on the ruins of an ancient Roman settlement. These gardens are planted with a wide variety of trees and plants and enjoy an exceptional view. From here you can take a panoramic walk along the **Via Krupp**, that winds its way down to the sea with different views at every turn. It was financed in 1902 by the German magnate Friedrich A. Krupp to connect the Albergo Quisisana where he lived, with the **Marina Piccola ①**. Built in the 1950s in what was once a bay given over to fishing warehouses and landings, it is now home to the trendiest private beaches on Capri and more than a few seaside cafés. Marina Piccola is graced with a picture postcard view of the **Faraglioni ②**, four striking rocks jutting out from the sea (two of them more than 100 metres/330 ft tall), which the Italian Futurist poet Filippo Tommaso Marinetti likened to "an equestrian circus of galloping stones".

One of Capri's most rewarding excursions leads to the **Arco Naturale ③** (east of Capri town), a fabulous semi-circular opening in the rock which frames the blue-green Cala di Matermania glimmering below. From the Piazzetta take Via Vittorio Emanuele and continue along Via Camerelle until you reach the **Belvedere di Tragara** with fine views of the Faraglioni, Marina Piccola and Monte Solaro. Continuing east from here, just before the ascent towards the Arco Naturale you'll see the singular **house of the writer Curzio Malaparte**. Considered a masterpiece of Italian Rationalist architecture, it was designed in the 1930s by Adalberto Libera and Malaparte himself. Countless famous figures were guests at the villa, including Moravia, Togliatti, Cocteau and Camus. On the writer's death it was donated to the People's Republic of China. Later it became the headquarters of a cultural foundation. On occasion it is used for conferences and art exhibits, but normally it's not open to the public.

Beyond the Arco hides one of Capri's 67 grottoes, **Matermania**, consecrated in ancient times to the cult of Mater Magna, the goddess of the Earth. From here Via Matermania leads back to Capri town (1–2 hours).

The emperor's legacy

In AD 27, at the age of 68, Tiberius left Rome for the enchanting Capri, where for the next 10 years he governed the empire using a system of watch-towers that allowed him to communicate with the fleet stationed at Miseno, a coastal town east of Naples. One of Capri's highlights is what remains of Tiberius' favourite residence, **Villa Jovis ④** (open daily, 9am until 1 hour before sunset; entrance fee), 2 km (over a mile) from Capri town: follow directions marked on the tiles leading from the Piazzetta to Via Tiberio.

The grandiose multi-storey building spanned more than 5,800 sq. metres (63,000 sq. ft); the imperial apartments were built with panoramic terraces, there were apartments for dignitaries, splendid baths and an astronomical observatory. Just inside the excavation area is the **Salto di Tiberio**, a sheer cliff that plunges to the sea. According to legend, the emperor had his enemies and lovers of whom he had tired thrown off the precipice. This vantage point, some 300 metres

Map on page 168

TIP

Boat trips around Capri set off from the Marina Grande. The one-and-a-half hour trip around the rocky coast is a perfect introduction to the island.

BELOW: Marina Grande.

Grotta Meravigliosa, one of a series of dazzling grottoes only accessible by boat.

(1,000 ft) above the sea, offers a spectacular view across the Penisola Sorrentina. Below the villa is Capri's other famous grotto, the **Grotta Bianca** . Discovered by an English couple in 1901 in the Bay of Matermania, a vault-like ceiling covered in white stalactites earned it the nickname *Meravigliosa* (Wonderful).

Anacapri

Well-positioned for walks and excursions but relatively distant from the port, the island's other social centre, **Anacapri** ❶ has a more rustic atmosphere than its rival, and a stark moorish presence reflected in the whitewashed cube-shaped houses. It is set on the "highlands" at the foot of **Monte Solaro** ❶, the highest point on the island. The peak of Monte Solaro can be reached by chair lift from Piazza della Vittoria (coming back down on foot to Capri, the most beautiful path passes the hermitage of **Santa Maria a Cetrella**).

Of the eight churches scattered around the island, the one not to miss is the **Chiesa di San Michele Arcangelo** in Anacapri, which dates from 1719. Mother Serafina, a Carmelite nun, had made a pledge to the Archangel Michael that she would dedicate a sanctuary to him in exchange for a Christian victory over the Turks at the gates of Vienna. The highlight of the church on Piazza San Nicola is the extraordinary majolica floor, made from 2,500 *riggiole* (Neapolitan-style ceramic tiles) in warm pastel colours. The mosaics depict the Expulsion of Adam and Eve from Paradise.

BELOW: Villa San Michele, a doctor's dream home.

Villa San Michele

From Anacapri, take Via Orlandi to Via Axel Munthe and the **Villa San Michele** ❶ (open May–Sept daily 9am–6pm; Oct daily 9.30am–5pm; Nov–Feb

daily 10.30am–3.30pm; Mar daily 9.30am–4.30pm; Apr 9.30am–5.30pm; entrance fee; tel: 081-8371401), designed and built in the late 19th century by the Swedish doctor and writer Axel Munthe (1857–1949), where he lived between 1896–1910. The Villa was opened to the public in 1929, soon after the success of *The Story of San Michele (see page 170)*. Today it is owned by the Swedish government. The villa was designed to display Munthe's own art collection, and at the same time to highlight the beauty of the natural surroundings. "My house must be open to the sun, the wind and the voice of the sea," he wrote, "like a Greek temple and light, light everywhere!" Among the noteworthy objects on display are the Cosmatesque table, the marble bust of the Emperor Tiberius, the Medusa head and the Egyptian Sphinx. There is an extraordinary view of the Bay of Naples from the colonnade. In the beautiful garden is the *Olivetum*, a pavilion dedicated to the geology, flora and fauna of Capri.

From Villa San Michele you can reach Capri town by descending the so-called **Scala Fenicia** or Phoenician Stairway (actually a Greco-Roman construction). Until 1871 this stairway, made up of 882 steps, had been the only land connection between the low and high parts of the island.

Tiberius's cliff-hanging retreat on Capri is a miracle of Roman architecture.

Map on page 168

The Blue Grotto

In 1826, the Polish poet August Kopisch and the German painter Ernst Fries, together with two locals, "re-discovered" the **Grotta Azzurra** ❶ (Blue Grotto), and the cave soon became a major attraction for those on the Grand Tour. The cave had been known since the time of Tiberius, who had it made into a nympheum, but for centuries the locals avoided the grotto because they thought it to be inhabited by monsters and devils. The entrance to the Grotta Azzurra is

BELOW: Villa Jovis, Emperor Tiberius' residence.

TIP

The walk or mule-ride
to the top of Ischia's
extinct volcano,
Mt Epomeo (788m/
2,585 ft) is well worth
the effort. The path
starts from Fontana
and climbs to the
15th-century Eremo di
San Nicola, a
hermitage carved out
of the volcanic rock.
The views from the
top are breathtaking.

low and narrow so visitors enter in low-slung rowboats. Only one part can be visited (three other chambers are inaccessible): the so-called Duomo Azzurro (60 metres/197 ft long, 22 metres/72 ft wide, 14 metres/46 ft high), whose intense blue luminosity is due to the daylight that enters through an underwater aperture and reflects against the walls (the water absorbs the red). Boats to the Blue Grotto go from from Marina Grande, buses from Anacapri or you can walk there in an hour along the Via Grotta Azzurra. It is closed in bad weather.

Ischia

The extinct volcanos that form Ischia and Procida, together with Vesuvius and the Solfatara at Pozzuoli, are part of the so-called Phlegraean complex. Less than an hour's hydrofoil-ride from Capri, the two islands are separated by just a few kilometres. Nearly five times larger than Capri, **Ischia ⓭** is the largest of the islands in the Bay of Naples. The "Isola Verde" (Green Island) was already reputed in Roman times for its naturally occurring hot water baths and their curative powers, and for the fertile, volcanic soil which still yields some noteworthy white wine (Casa d'Ambra is one of the best-known producers). The countryside made up of pine woods, olive groves and vineyards, and the varied beaches and well-run spas of Ischia make it an ideal resort for families with children and the health-conscious. It is particularly popular with Germans.

Ischia has six small towns which are connected by a 35-km (22-mile) main road that circles the island. Buses are an efficient way to get around; alternatively, you can ride the pricey but charming three-wheeled open taxis or hire a scooter. The tour described below will take at least two full days; longer if you want to treat yourself to some time lounging in a spa or on a beach.

BELOW: drop off
the rocks, Ischia.

The island's main town is **Ischia** , with countless cafés, restaurants and nightspots. It is made up of **Ischia Porto** – the island's only harbour – built into the crater of an extinct volcano, and the historical centre of **Ischia**, named after the causeway that Alfonso I of Aragon had built in 1438 to connect Ischia to the picturesque little island known as the *scoglio* (rock). The highlight here is the **Castello Aragonese** (open daily 9:30am until sunset; entrance fee), built in 474 BC by the *siracusani*. In the 16th century it became the home of the noblewoman and poetess Vittoria Colonna, who turned it into a religious and cultural citadel: Michelangelo was a regular guest. The empty castle is especially worth visiting when it hosts the occasional concert or art exhibition. **Cartaromana**, to the south, is Ischia town's best beach.

The road continues south from Ischia town to **Barano d'Ischia** , an inland hamlet that makes a good starting point for excursions into the surrounding hills. From Barano, take the road that passes through Testaccio to the **Lido dei Maronti**, Ischia's best-known beach, its waters warmed by the hot springs of Olmitello, Nitruoli and Cava Scura (the latter, at 86°C/187°F, is the warmest on the island). If you intend to walk along the 2-km (1-mile) beach, be sure to take a pair of suitable shoes, as the underground streams can make the sand uncomfortably hot.

The lovely fishing village of **Sant'Angelo** (reached via the cart-road that leads from Maronti beach to Cava Scura) is perched on the southernmost tip of the island, with memorable views of the southern coast and Mt Epomeo in the background. Skip the unremarkable village of Serrara Fontana, and head straight for Ischia's wine capital **Panza**, a good departure point for walks to Ischia's most spectacular coastal panoramas. Beaches along the island's west coast are well-equipped with sun loungers, umbrellas and refreshment stalls.

Map page 152 Capri 168

Santa Maria del Soccorso, one of a dozen churches in Forio.

BELOW: Ischia Porto.

Forio  is the most populous town on the island, with a pretty historical centre and a dozen 17th- to 18th-century churches. Just outside the town at 35 Via Calise are the impressive gardens of **La Mortella** (open 9am–7pm Tues, Thur, Sat, and for Sun afternoon concerts; entrance fee), carved from an enormous volcanic rock quarry. They were designed by Russel Page, one of the great landscape architects of the 20th century, for the British composer William Walton and his wife, Lady Susana. The gardens host concerts on weekends between April and July, and September and October.

The next town is tiny **Lacco Ameno** ⑰, where the Greeks settled in the 8th century BC. Two archaeological museums display remains found in the local necropolis and shipwrecks just offshore: Museo Archeologico di Santa Restituta and the more impressive collection housed in the **Villa Arbusto** (10-minute walk out of town at 210 Corso Angelo Rizzoli; open Tues–Sun, Sept 16–May, 9am–noon, 3–7pm; June–Sept 15, 9am–1pm, 4–8pm; entrance fee). Emerging from the sea opposite Via Roma, is the town's emblem, a 10-metre (33 ft) tall block of yellowish volcanic rock called the **Fungo** (mushroom).

Less than 2 km (1 mile) down the road, is the popular spa town of **Casamicciola Terme**, where Henrik Ibsen began to write *Peer Gynt*.

Called Pithekoussai (island of the vases) in Greek, for centuries Ischia's economy was based on the production of terracotta, an art still practised in Casamicciola (at the Mennella factory, the oldest workshop on the island), as well as in Ischia Ponte, Barano and Forio.

Radioactive pools

Ischia's marvellous thermal baths were known to the Greeks and Romans, who found relief from arthritis in the pools of radioactive mud. However, the craze for the miraculous waters of Ischia only really took off in 1558 after a treatise by the Neapolitan doctor Giulio Jasolino, according to which the mineral waters of the island, "restore fertility to sterile women, heal men from exhaustion, comfort the stomach, melt kidney stones, restore the liver, heal scabs and excite the appetite." In those days even the less wealthy could benefit from thermal cures: in 1581 the bishop of Ischia, Fabio Polverini, had a hospice built for the diseased poor, and in 1604 some noble Neapolitans financed the Pio Monte della Misericordia at Casamicciola Terme, the first treatment centre for thermal and social cures free to the public. It was destroyed in an earthquake in the 19th century.

Different springs correspond to various benefits and Italians continue to consider spa treatments to have an important therapeutic role in the maintenance of good health. The 29 thermal baths, 67 *fumarole* (geysers) and 103 springs (ranging from 15°–86°C/ 59°–187°F) which rise to the surface all over the island and in the nearby waters, make Ischia Italy's foremost centre for thermal cures.

BELOW: taking the waters at Giardini Poseidon Terme.

Top Thermal Spas

The **Giardini Poseidon Terme** (2 km/1 mile south of Forio) has 21 thermal pools that are between 15°C and 40°C (59°–104°F), including three covered pools and one Olympic-sized pool, all surrounded by lush gardens. The **Negombo** botanical park features 12 pools (some filled with sea water), Turkish baths, a beauty centre, sun treatments with the added attraction of a season of classical, rock and jazz concerts (Lacco Ameno; open Apr 15–Oct 15 daily 9am–sunset;

Map on page 152

tel: 081-986152). The **Parco Termale Castiglione** at Casamicciola Terme (tel: 081-982551) has an extensive curative programme which includes mud-baths, hydromassages and other hydrotherapy treatments. The **Giardini Eden** in Ischia town has four thermal pools and is wonderfully located in the Bay of Cartomarana. In the beautiful Sant'Angelo area, the best establishments are the **Aphrodite-Apollon Mare** (tel: 081-999202) and the **Giardini Tropical** (081-999242), both offering panoramic views and surrounded by floral gardens.

Procida

Although closer to the mainland, tiny **Procida** ⓭ feels surprisingly remote. Inhabited by a small community of fishermen and farmers, it remains the most authentic of the islands of the Bay. The maritime spirit and unspoiled atmosphere of Procida were masterfully captured by Alberto Moravia's companion, the writer Elsa Morante in her great novel *L'Isola di Arturo*, published in 1957. What the island lacks in souvenir shops and tourist-related services, it more than makes up for in reasonably priced accommodation, and above all, a peaceful night is guaranteed. The only real town is also called Procida, but a number of tiny settlements animate the rest of the island with scenes of fishermen mending nets at the docks and tomato-laden donkeys plodding uphill. A bridge connects Procida with the tiny island of **Vivara**, a nature reserve.

A common element of settlements all over the island is the collective nature of daily life. This is also evidenced in the local architecture, where an apparently haphazard cascade of cube-shaped pastel coloured houses held together by stairways, terraces, balconies, arches and courtyards keeps families in inevitably close contact (a particularly good example of this is **Corricella**, which is a 15-minute walk south of the town of Procida).

Brightly painted porcelain, made in Ischia.

The construction of the defensive town of **Terra Murata** began in the 9th century in response to Saracen raids along the Italian coast, and was completed in the 16th century with the addition of the wall and **Palazzo-Fortezza d'Avalos**. In 1744, the Bourbons made it their hunting residence. Procida had become a royal hunting reserve, which on the one hand left the residents with certain fiscal benefits, but also meant that strict laws punished poachers with heavy fines and imprisonment, and prohibited the use of firearms and dogs or cats that would have posed a threat to the wild game population. Enforcement was so zealous that the mere presence of pheasant feathers in a home was enough to warrant torture. Palazzo d'Avalos was transformed into a prison in 1818; abandoned in 1988, the building is falling into ruin.

Although it is small (under 4 sq. km/1½ sq. miles), Procida offers a wide choice of beaches. West of the town of Procida are the beaches of **Sirulenza** and **Cannone**. In the opposite direction, near the cemetery, is the charming **Spiaggia del Pozzo Vecchio**.

Next comes the romantic **Spiaggetta degli Innamorati** (Lovers' Beach); you can sunbathe on the comfy volcanic rocks facing the islet of Vivara at **Santa Margherita Vecchia**. Finally, the **west coast** is lined with many long, sandy beaches colonised by camps of umbrellas. ❏

BELOW: Marina Corricella, Procida.

SORRENTO AND THE AMALFI COAST

A handful of historical towns adds a zest to the beauty of Italy's most spectacular coastline, creating a blend of art and nature which makes the Costiera Amalfitana world-famous

The Bay of Naples is closed from the south by the Penisola Sorrentina, a mountainous, tongue-like peninsula whose tip is only 8 km (5 miles) away from the island of Capri. The coast of Campania, which between Naples and Castellammare di Stabia appears rather industrialised and depressingly over-developed, becomes beautiful as it meets the reddish rocks of Sorrento. Beyond is the stunning Costiera Amalfitana at the southern part of the peninsula that faces the Golfo di Salerno.

Although Sorrento makes a good base from which to visit Naples, Pompeii, the islands and the Amalfi Coast, stopping in the prettier towns of the Costiera will add flavour to your trip. Among them, Positano and Amalfi offer the richest combination of lovely hotels, shops and vibrant nightlife, but prices here are steeper than elsewhere in the region. Sunbathing and swimming are not the only reasons to come here, and places such as Positano, Amalfi and Ravello are at their best in the spring and autumn. Plan on at least four days to take in the peninsula at a relaxed pace. There's a regular bus service between Sorrento and Salerno via the towns of the Costiera and during the tourist season, boat services operate between Sorrento and Positano.

LEFT: view of Sorrento.
BELOW: card players in front of the Sedile Dominova.

Sorrento

Presumed to be of Greek origin and much-loved by the Romans as a warm and beautiful summer retreat, **Sorrento ⑲** was "rediscovered" by foreign artists and tourists in the 18th century, and is today a first-rate tourist destination. The Venetian libertine Casanova, the writers Goethe, Ibsen (who finished *Peer Gynt* here), Byron, Scott, Dumas, Stendhal, Nietzsche and the composer Wagner were the tip of the iceberg of the rich and privileged who retired to what was once considered a sensually permissive town.

This is epitomized in the town's famous local anthem *Torna a Surriento* (Come back to Sorrento), in which a young lover was begged to return to "the land of love". Nearly a century after the song was written, Sorrento's orange and lemon groves, its seductive light and deep-blue sea, and the alcoholic euphoria engendered by *limoncello* (a sweet liquor made with Amalfi lemons) still work their magic.

There's very little sightseeing to do in Sorrento. Plan on a few lazy walks around town before resting on the benches of the **Villa Comunale's gardens** with an ice-cream cone as you discuss dinner plans and enjoy the views of Vesuvius and the Bay of Naples. The bulb-like dome emerging from the lush grounds of the gardens belongs to the bell-tower of the baroque

Apart from the inevitable tourist shops crammed with "typical" items, Sorrento has many a chic boutique where you can shop for stylish clothes, perfume and jewellery.

BELOW: coast and mountain backdrop near Sorrento.

church of **San Francesco**, whose medieval cloister, planted with vines and pink bougainvilleas, hosts a summer classical music series.

The old part of Sorrento centres on **Piazza Tasso**, named after the town's favourite son, the poet Torquato Tasso (1544–95), whose famous poem *La Gerusalemme Liberata*, modelled on Homer's *Iliad* and Virgil's *Aeneid*, is considered to be the best Italian example of a Renaissance epic. From here, Corso Italia leads to the **Duomo**, which features well-crafted choir stalls with typical *intarsi* (inlay work) by local masters, whose skills have been passed down to rather less refined artisans in the service of the souvenir industry.

On Via Cesareo is the **Sedile Dominova**, a peculiar Renaissance loggia with frescoes on the walls and a 17th-century majolica dome that served as a meeting place for the city's governors. Today, it is used as a kind of working man's club where Sorrentine men gather around baize tables to play cards, read newspapers and talk politics.

The **Museo Correale di Terranova** (open Wed–Mon 9am–2pm; closed Tues; entrance fee) is housed in the former villa of Conte Alfredo di Terranova. Its period furniture and decor conjures up the patrician ambiance of 18th-century Naples, topped with some good 19th-century paintings, a collection of clocks and majolica from Capodimonte, and some local archaeological finds.

Sorrento is built on a reddish tufa rock about 50 metres (160 ft) above the sea. Some of the best hotels are perched on the cliff edge with terraces looking out across the bay – the views are as captivating by day as by night. Many of the hotels have their own lifts that take you down to the sea and wooden sunbathing platforms. Sorrento's beaches are for the most part unremarkable. If you must feel the sand under your feet, try the narrow strips of beach of **Marina Piccola**

(right below the Villa Comunale, accessible via a stairway cut out from the rock) and **Marina Grande** (a 15-minute walk or short bus ride from Piazza Tasso); both beachfronts have modest entrance fees and umbrellas and beach loungers for hire. To find larger and cleaner beaches you need to head further west. If your explorations take you as far as the **Capo di Sorrento**, look out for a path on the right that descends to the sea, leading to the ruins of the Roman Villa of **Pollio Felix**.

If you're driving the most scenic way to approach the breathtaking stretch of road known locally as the "Costiera" (officially the SS163) is to go via **Punta Campanella ⓴**, following the unspoiled western coastline of the Penisola Sorrentina. Coming from Sorrento, instead of continuing on the SS145 towards Sant'Agata sui Due Golfi, follow the signs for Massa Lubrense and the picturesque village of **Termini**. From here, ask around for the "*sentiero che va alla Punta*"; a 45-minute walk along a panoramic path brings you to the Punta, which looks straight out to the island of Capri. It seems that a Greek temple dedicated to Athena once stood here, but the only remains visible today are those of the **Torre di Minerva**, built by the Angevins in the 14th century to watch for signs of Saracen pirates. The alarm was sounded with the little bell (*campanella*) in the tower, which gave the Punta its name.

From Termini, another path descends to **Marina di Rapolla**, with a small beach in front of which lie three small islands known as **Li Galli**. In the time of the Amalfi maritime republic, criminals were confined here while awaiting judgement. The Russian ballet dancer Rudolf Nureyev once lived on one of these islands, in a reconstructed Saracen tower.

The roller-coaster Costiera

The famous Amalfi coast road (SS163) begins at **Sant' Agata sui Due Golfi ㉑**, which commands gorgeous views of the Bays of Naples and Salerno. Inaugurated in 1853 by the Bourbon Ferdinand II, the tortuous and narrow road that hugs the Amalfi Coast was carved and drilled out of the cliffs and seaside hills. Facing south, the Costiera winds for 69 km (43 miles), almost entirely without guardrails. It's not an easy drive and can easily feel twice as long if you do it in one go. The best way to experience the Amalfi coast is to break up the journey with visits to the local towns and beaches. Keep in mind that in summer months the traffic can be heavy, especially at the weekends and at night, when the *pizza* and disco commuters between Salerno and Positano seem to think little of a few hours of bumper-to-bumper on the road. On the other hand, the road empties in the early afternoon while the locals break for lunch and a siesta.

Although SITA buses run hourly from Salerno to Sorrento and back (about one hour each way), a car allows for much more flexibility, night-time travel and quicker access to must-see Ravello (though there is a regular bus service up the hill from Amalfi). Perhaps because regular commuters grow tired of shuttling back and forth along "the most beautiful road in the world" four times a day on their own, this is one of the few areas in Italy that's friendly to hitch-hikers.

Map on page 152

TIP

The blue SITA buses that run between Sorrento and Amalfi can get very crowded with local commuters, so if you want to be sure of a seat with a view, avoid peak times and get to the bus stop at least 15 minutes before departure.

BELOW: Positano, a favourite of the *dolce vita* crowd.

The medieval cloister of San Francesco, one of Sorrento's hidden treasures.

Vertical town

The next town after Sant'Agata dei Due Golfi is **Positano** ㉒. The great notoriety of Positano began after World War II, when it became the favoured getaway of film stars and the *Dolce Vita* crowd. In 1953, a rapturous John Steinbeck wrote, "Positano bites deep. It is a dream that isn't quite real when you are there and becomes beckoningly real after you are gone." Positano's appeal did not lie in history or art but in what was especially clean water and worldly (but not crowded) ambiance.

As with Rome's Via Veneto, all that has long since faded. What remains from Positano's golden age are the expensive hotels, clothing and sandal boutiques with fast custom-made service, and a vague atmosphere of exclusivity. The town is at its best in late spring and September, when the crowds of day-trippers do not clog the narrow streets. Strange as it may seem, this summer resort becomes quite enchanting over Christmas and in the winter months, when lemon trees are heavy with bright fruit and almond trees are in bloom. Although the local beaches aren't particularly attractive (the water, though invitingly blue when seen from above, is actually murky when seen up close), a romantic stroll down the Spiaggia Grande (the main beach at the foot of the village) or to the Spiaggia del Fornillo (accessible via a short path that starts from above the hydrofoil pier) is a must, especially as the purple-red sunset casts its golden rays all over the beautiful, peaceful landscape.

The hamlet of **Praiano** ㉓ absorbs some of the tourist flow that doesn't make it into nearby Positano, offering a pretty beach squeezed between two cliffs, plus several coves nearby and a 16th-century church. The Costiera continues between steep precipices, including the spectacular gorge called **Vallone di Furore** (with

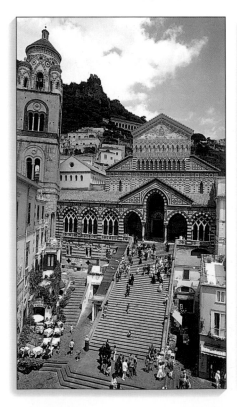

a tiny, intimate beach). Just past Conca dei Marini, there's a staircase (and an elevator) by a car park that leads down to the **Grotta di Smeraldo ㉔** (open daily 9am–4pm, weather permitting; entrance fee), a cavern that glows with a green light reflected from the water. It measures 24 metres (75 ft) high, 30 metres (90 ft) wide and 60 metres (180 ft) deep and columns of stalagmites and stalactites can be seen beneath the clear water. The grotto can also be visited by boat direct from Amalfi or Praiano.

The ancient republic of Amalfi

Amalfi ㉕ is the largest town on the Costiera. Its atmospheric hotels, many housed in what were once private villas and medieval convents, and choice of restaurants, *pasticcerie* and *gelaterie* – either in town or within easy reach – make it an excellent overnight stop.

Amalfi came to be feared as a maritime power as early as the 7th century, when Venice was little more than a confederation of islands still dependant on Byzantium; in 839 Amalfi won independence from the Duke of Naples and grew into a thriving republic. In its heyday, the city controlled the whole Costiera territory, its harbour serving as the main trading port in Southern Italy. Amalfi merchants established trading posts in Byzantium, Asia Minor and Africa. In the Holy Land, they founded the Hospital of St John of Jerusalem from which the Crusader Knights of St John developed. Their symbol, the Maltese cross, is still carved on Amalfi's street corners.

The stunning **Duomo di Sant'Andrea** was founded in the 11th century when the commercial fortunes of Amalfi were at their peak and the local population had grown to 80,000. The cathedral, which stands at the top of a long flight of

Map on page 152

Webster's brooding revenge drama, The Duchess of Malfi, *was based on the tragic life of Joanna of Aragon, the Duke of Amalfi's consort in the 15th century.*

BELOW: Piazza Duomo, Amalfi.

Ravello is a good place to buy Vietri ceramics.

BELOW: Vietri potter.

steps (a good spot in sticky weather to catch an evening breeze) was completely rebuilt in 1203 in the present Moorish-Norman style. The geometrical facade has an attractive pattern of black-and-white stones inlaid with horizontal stripes of vivid mosaics, with three tiers of interlacing arches. It is a faithful 19th-century copy of the original, which collapsed. The bronze doors were made in Constantinople in 1066. In the crypt are the holy remains of St Andrew the Apostle, a spoil from the sack of Constantinople during the Fourth Crusade, led by the Venetians in 1204. Like the miraculous liquefaction of San Gennaro's blood *(see pages 83 and 136)* in Naples, the cult of St Andrew attracts fanaticism among locals. The Manna of St Andrew, a mysterious oil, is said to seep from his bones. However, not even such a powerful relic was able to save Amalfi from decline. In the 12th century the Amalfitani suffered a Norman invasion and two sieges by their Pisan rivals. Then, in 1343, a storm nearly destroyed the city.

Attached to the Duomo is the **Chiostro del Paradiso** (open daily, 9am–1 hour before sunset; entrance fee), built in the 13th century as the burial place of Amalfi's prominent citizens, planted with palm-trees and evocative of a Mosque garden, ringed with white-washed pointed arches resting on double columns. The cloister is now a museum of sculptural and architectural fragments.

Inside the **Municipio** (open Mon–Fri 9am–1pm; entrance free), a sombre *palazzo*, the *Tavole Amalfitane*, the Latin book of maritime law that applied until 1570, is on display. Adjacent to Piazza Duomo is **Piazza Flavio Gioia**, named after the merchant-navigator traditionally credited with the invention of the compass in the 12th century; the exhibition space under the two tall aisles is all that survived of the republic's **arsenal** (open Mon–Sat, 9am–1pm; entrance free; longer opening hours and entrance fee when housing exhibits).

VIETRI'S CERAMICS

Displayed on street stalls, piled high in workshops, craft shops and tourist boutiques and glittering on the majolica cupola and bell tower of the Church of San Giovanni Battista, the famous ceramics of Vietri are omnipresent. Arab forms and techniques of ceramic production were introduced in the Middle Ages by the abbots of the Abbey at Cava de' Tirreni, although the vibrant colours and decorative styles you see today show no traces of the Arab influence. Vietri is also known for its nativity figures which were produced here after the Bourbon King, Charles III closed the factory at Capodimonte *(see page 146)*.

The **Museo della Ceramica Vietrese** (tel: 089-211835), 2 km (1 mile) from Vietri at Raito, has a collection of locally made ceramics from the 17th century to the present day, showing the technical and artistic influence of German ceramicists in the 1920s and 1930s.

The best selection of traditional items – plates, platters, vases and coffee services – can be found at the town's largest factory-shop, **Solimene** (7, Via Madonna degli Angeli). At **Carrera** you'll find the works of master ceramicist Ninuccio Carrera, (Corso Umberto I, 66), while **Pinto** is the best address for tiles (Corso Umberto I, 31).

The rest of Amalfi resembles the *medina* of a Muslim town, with narrow and twisting alleys leading more often than not to dead ends and private homes. If you take a walk to the Valle dei Mulini, you can still see a few water-operated paper mills. Although no longer functioning, they are a reminder of Amalfi's past as one of Italy's most important paper producing centres, where top-notch manufacturers turned rags and bits of old cloth into high-quality porous paper.

To learn more about this once-thriving trade, visit the small **Museo della Carta** (open Tues–Thur and weekends 9am–1pm, closed Mon and Fri; entrance fee). The Amatruda family, in business since the 15th century, still makes paper the traditional way and a good selection of their products can be found at Amalfi nelle Stampe Antiche, on Piazza Duomo, and at La Scuderia del Duca on Largo Cesario Console.

An inspiration for Wagner and Vidal

Just past Atrani, at the turn-off for Castiglione, the road to the left climbs up to **Ravello** ㉖, well worth the best part of a day. André Gide said that it was "closer to the sky than the seashore" and its romantic aspect has attracted writers down the ages. Boccaccio chose the town as the location for the bawdier stories in *The Decameron*, D. H. Lawrence worked on *Lady Chatterley's Lover* here and the American writer Gore Vidal has made Ravello his permanent home.

Built under Amalfi rule in the 9th century, Ravello's uncompromising location meant that it was often besieged but never conquered. With a population of about 30,000 and a thriving trade with the Near East, the town remained independent until 1813. The wealthy merchants imported the Moorish artefacts and architectural styles which remain one of Ravello's glories.

Map on page 152

LEFT: Ravello countryman.
BELOW: Arabic and Byzantine elements, Ravello Cathedral.

Map on page 152

TIP

If you are in Ravello during the concert season (June–July), make a point of going to one of the outdoor concerts at Villa Rufolo for the unforgettable experience of seeing an orchestra playing on a clifftop, with the sunset for a backdrop.

BELOW: Villa Cimbrone, Ravello. **RIGHT:** Cetara.

The **Duomo**, dedicated to St Pantaleone, is an 11th-century church. Its austere facade is emboldened by Romanesque bronze doors. Inside, the nave is supported by classical columns and adorned with marble busts. The exquisite Arabo-Byzantine pulpits are richly decorated: the smaller one (1131) has a mosaic depicting Jonah and the Whale; the larger one (1272) supported by six spiral columns, is also decorated with fine mosaics, showing dragons and birds held aloft by fierce lions. The crypt contains a small collection of medieval sculpture.

In the shadow of the cathedral stands **Villa Rufolo** (open May–Sept daily 9am–8pm; Oct–Apr daily 9am–6pm; entrance fee), an agglomeration of Norman-Saracen buildings begun in the 13th century by the wealthy Rudolfo dynasty. The corners of the tower are adorned with four statues depicting the seasons and the ruins are surrounded by lush, exotic gardens. Here Wagner found inspiration for the magic garden of Klingsor in *Parsifal*, his last opera in 1880.

Villa Cimbrone (open May–Sept daily 9am–8pm; Oct–Apr daily 9am–6pm; entrance fee), whose romantic gardens dotted with statues were laid out by an English aristocrat at the turn of the 19th century, has a breathtaking belvedere over the Golfo di Salerno. On a clear day the view stretches as far as Paestum.

There are lovely walks from Ravello to Fontantelle, Torca and the slopes of Monte Rotondo and San Costanzo.

Ravello to Salerno

Scala, the next village, has a Duomo with a fine Romanesque doorway and is the birthplace of Fra Gerardo Sasso, who founded the Knights of Malta in the 12th century. **Maiori ㉗**, surrounded by terraced vineyards, offers the Costiera's widest beach, and one of the most worthwhile around these parts. The basilica di **Santa Trofimena** in **Minori** contains the relics of the patron saint of Amalfi; at the edge of town are the ruins of a **Roman villa** (open daily 9am until 1 hour before sunset; admission free; tel: 089-852893) with mosaic floors and traces of frescoes. **Cetara** is a pretty fishing village with a fine 13th century bell tower and a reliable fish restaurant, Acquapazza (38 Corso Garibaldi, tel: 089-261606), which still prepares centuries-old, "poor" but very tasty dishes based on anchovies.

From **Vietri sul Mare ㉘**, famous for its pottery *(see box, page 182)*, you can take an inland trip to the **Abbazia di Trinità della Cava**, near Cava de' Tirreni, situated in a splendid position with a panoramic view. The church and monastery, rebuilt in baroque style in the 18th century, contrast with the 13th-century original and the Gothic Sala del Capitolo.

The Costiera finishes at **Salerno ㉙**, an unremarkable working-class town with a historic centre only half-heartedly restored after it was damaged by Allied bombing in 1943. Its claim to fame is as the capital of the Norman Empire in the 11th century. It also lays claim to the oldest medical school in Europe, supposedly founded by an Arab, a Jew, a Christian and a Turk. However, visitors who wish to savour the romance of the Amalfi coast should ignore Salerno and proceed to the Greek ruins at Paestum *(see page 193).* ❑

CAMPANIA

Campania's assets are not confined to the Bay of Naples and Amalfi Coast. Explore Capua and Caserta to the north, Paestum and the Cilento coast to the south and enjoy stunning scenery all around

Map on page 188

T he first four chapters in the Places section of this guide have been taken up with the most popular parts of Campania – the region around Naples, the island trio in the bay and the Sorrentine peninsula have some of the best known sites in Italy's south, but these are by no means the limit of Campania's attractions. To the north, the fertile Capuan plain has many sites of historic interest, most notably Caserta and Capua. Heading south beyond Salerno, towards Basilicata and Calabria, the Cilento coastline from the ancient site of Paestum is a long arc of cliffs, beaches and mini resorts that hug the mountains. The impoverished and neglected state of much of the Neapolitan hinterland cannot be ignored, but as you drive through dramatic mountain and coastal scenery, it's easy to understand why the Romans called this sun-soaked region *Campania Felix* – the Happy Land.

On the Capuan Plain

The old Roman town of Capua is today's **Santa Maria Capua Vetere ❶** (off the SS7b road from Naples, see below; not to be confused with Capua, which is a few miles further north). Capua is associated with two famous historical facts: it was in Capua that Hannibal's army wintered during the Second Punic War (216 BC) and fell prey to the town's notoriously licentious hospitality. It was here, too, that the rebellion of Roman slaves began, led by the gladiator Spartacus, immortalised on the silver screen by Kirk Douglas in Stanley Kubrick's Hollywood epic. All that's left of what was once Italy's largest city after Rome are the ruins of the monumental **amphitheatre**; the rest having been quarried away over the centuries. In addition, a remarkable **Mithraeum** (underground temple of the widespread Persian cult of the god Mithras) features some particularly well-preserved frescoes of Mithras killing a white bull.

One reason for stopping in **Capua ❷** is to see the **Museo Provinciale Campano** (open Tues–Sat 9am–1.30pm, Sun and public holidays 9am–1pm; entrance fee) for its collection of 200 *matres Matutae*, small dolls carved from volcanic rock in the form of women holding babies – the widest lap cradling twelve brothers and sisters. The dolls, dating from the 6th century BC to the 1st century AD, were found in the nearby temple of Matuta. They would have been offered up to the Italic goddess of maternity as a plea for fertility, or as *ex-votos*, after a smooth delivery. Capua's **cathedral** was founded in the 9th century, but only some of the columns and the bell tower survived World War II.

At the foot of Mt Tifata 4 km (2 miles) east of Capua, is the unmissable basilica of **Sant' Angelo in Formis ❸** (on the Napoli–Caserta train line), built in

LEFT: the "fable in Marble", Reggia di Caserta.
BELOW: schoolchildren in Capua.

1073 the nave walls are covered with frescoes depicting scenes from the Old and New Testament including *Judgement Day* (above the entrance), *Christ Pantocrator with the three Archangels* (in the apse) and a portrait of Desiderio, the abbot who founded the church. The unknown artists of these superb Byzantine-style frescoes gave an unusual warmth and realism to the figures.

Versailles' rival

From Sant'Angelo in Formis there's only one road that goes to **Caserta** ❹ (less than 10 km/6 miles away), home of Italy's grandest royal palace, the **Reggia di Caserta** (tel: 0823-321400; royal apartments and museum open: Tues–Sun 8.30am–7pm, closed Mon; entrance fee; park and English garden open: Apr–Sept, Tue–Sun 8.30am–1 hour before sunset; Oct–Mar, Tues–Sun 8.30am–3pm; closed Mon; entrance fee). Built by the Bourbon kings in an attempt to outdo the Palace at Versailles, the Reggia measures 247 metres by 184 metres (810 ft by 600 ft), has nearly 2,000 windows and 1,200 rooms over five

Campania

Map on page 188

floors connected by 34 stairways and four courtyards. Like Versailles, the palace is surrounded by an immense **park** (120 hectares/300 acres), which is particularly unusual for an Italian palace. Built on a gentle slope, the park is divided by a long and wide central avenue lined with spectacular waterfalls that collect in basins decorated with life-like sculpture groups representing Greek myths and divinities. Among them is the "fable in marble" of Diana and Actaeon: a series of marble "snapshots" showing Actaeon caught spying on the naked goddess and being turned into a stag. An aqueduct was built to bring water to the fountains from 50 km (30 miles) away.

Neither the Bourbon King Charles III, nor the director of the work, the Neapolitan architect Luigi Vanvitelli (1700–73), lived to see the 22-year project completed in 1774. Some 3,000 labourers – made up of prisoners and Muslims kidnapped from the coast of North Africa – were forced to work as slaves. The mammoth building was not universally praised. The English poet and traveller Henry Swinburne, who visited the palace at the time of its completion, thought the façade "gives too much the idea of a regular monastery… It's a pity that its enormous bulk drowns the minuter members of its architecture." The interior, he noted, was striking for "the vast dimensions of its apartments, the bold span of their ceilings, the excellence and beauty of the materials employed in building and decorating it, and the strength of the masonry."

The octagonal vestibule of the second floor leads to the **Palatine Chapel** and to the interminable sequence of royal apartments decorated with paintings and furniture from the late 18th/early 19th century. A salon in the Appartamento Vecchio features an unusual 18th-century *presepe* (nativity scene), with over 1,200 figures. The **Museo dell'Opera e del Territorio**, located in the

A few kilometres north of Maddaloni on the SS265 stands the Ponti della Valle, an impressive section of the aqueduct built by Luigi Vanvitelli in 1759 to bring water to the fountains of the Reggia di Caserta.

BELOW: magnificent formal garden of the Caserta palace,

The Arch of Trajan in Benevento celebrates the emperor's military victories.

BELOW: sports fans in Avellino.

basement, illustrates the history of the construction of the Reggia and contains a section devoted to daily life in the Bourbon court. Return to the ground floor and cross the second courtyard to reach the charming, horseshoe-shaped **Palatine Theatre**, which used the park as a natural backdrop for the staging of Ferdinando IV's favourite melodramas by Cimarosa and Paisiello. There's also an interesting **English garden** designed by the British botanist John Andrew Graefer for Queen Maria Carolina d'Austria, wife of Ferdinando IV. The first camelia in Europe bloomed here. For those who prefer sitting to strolling, a mini-bus makes a tour of the park.

The Bourbon kings were not only preoccupied with lavish living and promoting their image; they were also a dynasty of enlightened sovereigns who believed in progress and human rights, as evidenced by the utopian project of **San Leucio**, a working-class counterpart to the Reggia di Caserta. In 1785, Ferdinando IV set up a silk factory in the hamlet of San Leucio (follow signs; 2 km/1 mile from Caserta). The autonomous community of workers created a humane working environment and took pride in their profession, producing fine satins and brocades which became highly sought after in Europe. A special set of laws for the community guaranteed equal working conditions for men and women, education for their children and support for the old and sick. But this unique social experiment faded with the fall of the Sicilian Kingdoms in 1861 and the end of the Bourbons' protectionist regime. The factory went out of business due to high production costs and the construction of an entire city on this model was never realised. The factory and workers' quarters can be viewed from the outside only, but the beautiful shop **Tessuti Siola Alois** (8 Piazza Scuderia) sells hand-woven silk and hand-made braiding.

Northeast of Naples

Benevento **❺**, which lies 50 km (30 miles) east of Caserta, was a prosperous Roman town on the Via Appia, the consular road connecting Rome with Brindisi on the Adriatic coast, and one of Italy's most travelled roads. In 571, the city became the southern capital of the power-hungry Lombards and remained their stronghold until 1053, when the duchy passed to the papacy. Completely destroyed by an earthquake in 1688, Benevento suffered heavy damage in World War II. One exceptional monument survived: the 2nd-century Arch of Trajan, one of the finer and better preserved triumphal arches scattered throughout the former empire which were built to commemorate the reigns and military victories of the Roman emperors. The bas-reliefs on the side facing Benevento and Rome glorify Emperor Trajan "at home" (he is welcomed by consuls, offered a thunderbolt by Jupiter, and distributes gifts and benefits to the Roman people), while those on the side facing Brindisi and the overseas provinces celebrate Trajan's policies in the colonies (he is depicted recruiting troops and forming new colonies and being welcomed by river-gods).

The next stop is the **Santuario di Monte Vergine ❻**, 40 km (25 miles) south of Benevento (off the ss88 road; take the right-hand fork after Capriglia Irpina).

Founded in 1119 on what was once a sacred Roman site dedicated to the cults of Cybele and Diana, the mountain-top sanctuary preserves its original Gothic three-nave format, despite a 17th-century restructuring. Twice a year – at Whitsun and in early September – thousands of pilgrims wend their way uphill to the Montevergine Sanctuary, singing hymns as they go.

From the sanctuary, take the road to Avellino, then the ss400 to **Sant'Angelo dei Lombardi** ❼ (also reached by train from Avellino), one of the pretty hill towns in the Irpinia area that was shaken by the violent earthquake of 1980. Its restored historical centre is still pleasant to walk around, but the main attraction here is the 12th-century abbey of **San Guglielmo al Goleto**, 3 km (1 mile) out of town. Under restoration since the earthquake, the forlorn complex shows all the scars of neglect and past natural disasters, but these contribute to its romantic beauty. The entrance is through two arches which lead to two cloisters. To the left, there's a small structure made up of a lower Romanesque church and an upper Gothic church (reached via an external staircase); a third, larger church was added in the 18th century during a new period of vitality at the abbey. The tower on the right was built with the marble of a nearby Roman mausoleum in 1152.

Halfway between Avellino and Naples is another, more interesting religious complex: the paleochristian and medieval basilicas of **Cimitile** ❽ (third road to the right after Schiava on the ss7b road; also served by the Circumvesuviana train line Baiano–Napoli) originally constituted the pagan and early Christian burial place of nearby Nola. At sunset, the sight of the ruins – arcades, apses, columns, collapsed ceilings, mosaics, and fragments of frescoes – is enchanting.

Map
on page
188

TIP

The Piana del Lago Laceno (Plain of Lake Laceno), a vast green valley surrounded by mountains and dense forests, is ideal for hiking, biking and horse-trekking. Enquire at Avellino tourist office (Via Due Principati 5, Avellino; tel: 0825 74731).

BELOW: Morcone, a small-car town in Campania.

Certosa di San Lorenzo in Padula, the biggest monastery in the south.

BELOW: Palinuro on the Cilento coast.

The Cilento coast

The Campania coast from Naples to Salerno is covered in the "Sorrento and Amalfi Coast" chapter *(see page 177)*. After Salerno, the coast is flat and sandy as far as Agropoli which marks the beginning of the rocky Cilento coastline. The scenery along this stretch may not be a match for the Amalfi coast, but it has a wild beauty all of its own and remains relatively unspoilt. The Cilento coast is characterised by rugged cliffs opening here and there into small bays, some deserted, others belonging to the quiet resorts dotted along the road: Santa Maria di Castellabate, San Marco, Acciaroli, Pioppi, Marina di Casal Velino, Marina di Ascea, Marina di Pisciotta and Marina di Camerota are all reasonably equipped with a campsite or two and a few inexpensive hotels that mostly cater for Italians.

Capo Palinuro ⑨, the most beautiful corner of the Cilento coast deserves a special mention. According to legend, Aeneas's pilot, Palinurus, was shipwrecked here. The town makes a good base from which to explore the local beaches and two great archaeological sites: Paestum, on the Bay of Salerno just before Agropoli, and Velia, north of Palinuro between Marina di Casal Verino and Marina di Ascea *(see page 194)*. After Palinuro the coast curves back inwards, becoming the gulf of Policastro, and leads to the seaside village of Sapri, just before Campania's southern boundary.

Inland, the **Parco Nazionale del Cilento e Vallo di Diano** occupies most of the area bounded by the A3 motorway, and its remotest corners offer some uncrowded hiking routes, particularly around **Monte Cervati ⑩** (1,898 metres/6,227 ft) in the Vallo di Diano and on the **Alburni chain** that skirts the northern border of the park. East of Monti Alburni is the **Grotta di Pertosa ⑪** (if you're driving take the Pertosa exit on the A3; otherwise the Grotta can be reached by train on the Lagonegro-Battipaglia line, but you need to change at Polla; a 90 minute-journey from Battipaglia). The grotto follows an underground river and has some impressive stalactites. It can be explored by boat and on foot.

Carthusian monastery

About 30 km (20 miles) south of Pertosa, along the A3, is **Padula ⑫** and the **Certosa di San Lorenzo** (open daily, Apr–Oct 9am–7pm, Nov–Mar 9am–4.30pm; entrance fee) one of Italy's biggest monasteries. The basic structure was completed in the early 14th century, but over the following centuries it underwent many changes as baroque decorations were heaped onto the Gothic and Renaissance foundations. As with the monastery of San Lorenzo del Escorial near Madrid, its floorplan suggests the shape of the gridiron upon which St Lawrence was martyred.

The largest cloister, lined with monks' cells, is nearly the size of a football pitch. Another of the cloisters, built above the old cemetery, gives access to the kitchens, with original frescoes, furnishings and equipment. Built in a strategic position, the monastery retained a strong influence over the area until the early 19th century when it was suppressed. One of its most illustrious visitors was Emperor Charles V, who stopped off here in 1535 en route to Reggio Calabria. It is said that the monks prepared a special omelette for him using 1,000 eggs.

Paestum

In the 7th century BC, the Greeks of Sybaris *(see page 239)* founded a colony known as Poseidonia in honour of the sea-god Poseidon, which became one of the most flourishing commercial centres of the Mediterranean. After Sybaris fell to Crotone in 510 BC, the city absorbed the surviving Sybarites and all of their wealth. In the half-century that followed, three famous temples were built, later known as the temples of **Paestum ⓭** (excavations open daily 9am–1 hour before sunset; entrance fee; tel: 0828-811023), the Roman name for the city.

A rich and beautiful city, Paestum succumbed to malaria after the fall of Rome and was abandoned after Saracen incursions in the late 9th century. The ruins of Paestum, overgrown and submerged in swamplands, were rediscovered in the mid-18th century, during the construction of a road. Nothing remains of the town apart from some late-Roman additions such as the amphitheatre and pool, and the exceptionally well-preserved temples, which stand out in magnificent solitude on a grassy patch dotted by oleanders and rose bushes. The local travertine marble with which they were built in Doric style seems to glow from within with a warm, indefinable light that changes hues: mother-of-pearl under the fast-gathering grey clouds of an impending storm; a blinding ivory glitter at midday; a luscious orange glaze towards sunset.

The most important one, the **Tempio di Nettuno** (Temple of Neptune, in reality consecrated either to Hera or Zeus; the temples were misnamed by early archaeologists), dates back to 450 BC. Thought to have been inspired by Athens' Parthenon, it shows all the refinements of the Doric style. If you look closely, none of the columns are straight: the corner columns have slightly oval (rather than round) sections at the top and bottom; those on the longer sides curve

BELOW: Carthusian monastery of San Lorenzo, Padula.

Map on page 188

Acciaroli on the Cilento coast was one of Ernest Hemingway's favourite resorts.

inwards; while all the columns bulge outwards along the edges and taper in at the top. The miracle of this ancient construction is that when seen from a distance, all the columns seem straight and the temple perfectly proportioned. The roof is gone, but the 36 external columns are all in place, and the entablatures and pediments are for the most part intact. This gives an especially good sense of how this temple must have looked originally because, unlike the Parthenon and most other Greek buildings, the Temple of Neptune had no sculpted decorations on the outside. The English Romantic poet Shelley was struck by the harmonious blending of the man-made structure with its natural surroundings: "The effect of the jagged outline of the mountains through the groups of enormous columns on one side, and on the other the level horizon of the sea, is inexpressibly grand."

Near the Temple of Neptune is the so-called **Basilica**, in reality another temple to Hera, complete with all of its 50 columns and architraves (third quarter of the 6th century BC). Finally, further north is the **Tempio di Cerere** (Temple of Ceres), more accurately attributed to Athena and built sometime between the other two, which looks like a smaller version of the Temple of Neptune. Wraps are coming off after lengthy restoration work on the Temple of Neptune and Basilica.

Paestum's **Museo Archeologico** (open daily 9am–7pm, closed the 1st and 3rd Mon of the month; entrance fee, combined ticket available) holds some of Southern Italy's rarer objects, including the world's only example of Greek mural paintings, from 480 BC. Excavated from one of the necropoli just outside town after World War II, the four panels of the **Tomba del Tuffatore** (Tomb of the Diver) represent scenes of banquets, dancing, games and a young nude that with sensual elegance dives on to a trampoline (the dive is thought to symbolize the passage from life to the underworld).

BELOW:
Cilento beach.
RIGHT: Temple of
Neptune, Paestum.

Philosophical town

Southern Campania's other important archaeological site is **Velia ⑭**, one of the last Greek colonies to be founded on the Italian peninsula (mid-6th century BC). Originally, the Greek city of Elea stood on a promontory between two bays, a prime spot which allowed the port to flourish into a fishing and commercial centre of considerable wealth (by the 12th century the bays had completely silted up). Elea became a magnet for intellectuals and gave its name to the Eleatic school of philosophy. Among its most prominent philosophers were Parmenides (*circa* 515–440 BC), noted for his work *On Nature*, written in verse, and his disciple Zeno (born *circa* 490 BC), renowned for his sly paradoxes. The Eleatic school drew attention to the distinction between information based on the five senses and that based on pure reason, and caused a crisis in Greek philosophy.

Although Velia's ruins were discovered in 1883, excavations didn't start until the 1920s; compared to Paestum, little remains of the old town, which became a quarry for building material shortly after the fall of Rome. The thing to do here is to climb the beautiful paved street that leads from the agora (main square) to the **Porta Rosa**, a well-preserved arched gateway in the city walls whose discovery stripped the Romans of their title of "inventors of the arch".   ❑

APULIA

This region of wine, wheat, olives and curious trulli *houses hits a high spot in the Gargano peninsula. Neighbouring Albania and Greece have left their mark, as have Normans and Swabians*

Map on page 200

Apulia (Puglia in Italian) is the pointed heel of Italy's boot, running down the length of the Adriatic and forming an instep beside the Ionian Sea. This is one of Italy's largest provinces, and its architecture and landscape make it one of of the most diverse. It is a stepping-off point for the Adriatic and the east: crusaders embarked at Bari, the largest city, and the first great highway from Rome, the Via Appia, ends at Brindisi which remains the main ferry port for Greece 100 km (60 miles) away. Much of this ancient province is flat and fertile, providing an abundance of wheat, wine and olive oil. Here and there are the extraordinary, gaunt stones of the Norman and Swabian castles and churches, Romanesque outposts that the sun has bleached like old bones. The Normans knew the region through pilgrims who returned from the shrine of the Archangel Michael high above the Gargano peninsula, the most attractive stretch on what is the longest coastline of any Italian region.

The Greek colonists made the modern naval port of Taranto, on the Ionian coast, an important centre, and the Romans raided its molluscs to make their purple dyes. When Rome collapsed, the eastern, Byzantine Empire made Bari a regional power base. But Apulia's most persistent ghost is Frederick II (1220–50), Holy Roman Emperor and the last of the great medieval rulers *(see page 30)*. It is not hard to imagine his hawks hunting in the wide blue skies over his castles.

Unique architecture

Apulia's refreshingly complex cultural mix sometimes only just seems to fit into modern Italy. Its unique architecture ranges from beehive *trulli* houses to flamboyant Lecce baroque with a flavour of the east never far from sight. The broad cultural heritage combines with its southern climate, varied landscape and food to make up a region with strong, individual character, even compared to other regions of Southern Italy. Much of the countryside is sparsely populated, because many farmers live away from their land in "farming towns".

Be cautious, in the largest centres. In a land where people are friendly and welcoming, there is also, in cities such as Bari, a fearful reputation for crime. Don't be put off by the initial, ugly prospect of some towns: the most elegant centres disguise themselves on the outside with ill-designed blocks of flats, aberrations in the history of Italian design that in their unlandscaped and sometimes unfinished state, take on the appearance of a vandalised building site. It is nearly always worth persisting in an effort to reach the *centro storico*, the old town centre, which is often completely unspoilt and a magical world away from the suburbs.

PRECEDING PAGES: the upper Merge in early summer. **LEFT:** *trulli* houses. **BELOW:** Bari trooper.

Frederick II's many towered castle at Lucera, built in 1233.

The Tavoliere plain

Entering Apulia from the north you first come across the relatively featureless **Tavoliere** plain, an important agricultural area centred on **San Severo** surrounded by vines and the busy provincial capital of **Foggia ❶**. Lying at the centre of this important wheat-producing area, it was famous for its underground grain stores called *fovea*, from which the town may have taken its name. Frederick II's heart was kept in a casket here until it was lost in the earthquake of 1731 which destroyed most of the old town. As an important railway junction and air base, it also suffered from wartime bombing. Mainly a commercial centre, Foggia has a fine surviving cathedral, Santa Maria Icona Vetere. Built in 1172, its facade and crypt are all that remain of the original Romanesque building, and after the earthquake it was rebuilt in the baroque style.

Other baroque buildings, Chiesa delle Croci, Palazzo de Rosa and the Palazzo della Dogana are worth seeking out. The Museo Civico (open Mon, Wed, Fri, Sun 9am–1pm; Tues, Thur 9am–1pm, 5–7pm; entrance fee) contains artefacts from the pre-Greek Daunian period. Foggia's most famous son is Umberto Giardano (1867–1948), composer of *Andrea Chenier* and *Fedora*. The town's autumn opera festival is centred on the theatre named after him.

West of Foggia lies the ancient town of **Lucera ❷**. Once the principal town of this area, the importance of this settlement to the successive powers that controlled the region can still be seen in the architecture, particularly the massive castle, the finest among the many built in Apulia by Frederick II. Set on a 250-metre (820-ft) hillock, and enclosed by a kilometre-long wall with 24 towers, it has uninterrupted views of the surrounding landscape. The area inside is atmospheric, with a number of relics from the past. In 1233, Frederick,

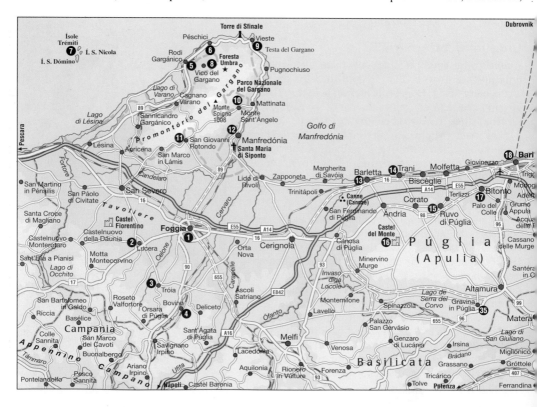

excommunicated by the pope, brought 20,000 Saracen troops here from Sicily to help in his wars with the rest of Italy and the town must have taken on a distinctly Arabic appearance. Charles of Anjou took the city following Frederick's death and the great mosque that the Saracens had built was replaced by a Gothic cathedral, making it the youngest and only Gothic church in Apulia. Its stone altar is thought to be the great banqueting table from Castel Florentino, where Frederick died in 1250; the castle ruins lie 14 km (9 miles) northwest. To the northeast of the town there is a Roman amphitheatre.

South of Lucera is **Troia ❸**, a small town with one of the region's most dramatic cathedrals, completed in 1125, in which classical and eastern influences are brought together in unique Apulian style. It has a magnificent rose window and a rich treasury. Just south of Troia lies **Bovino ❹**, less often visited but also with a grand cathedral from the same period. Among its many other historic buildings is a castle which became a ducal palace. A pleasant and unspoilt centre, Bovino is an attractive place to stay to make the most of this hilly and wooded part of Apulia which was once famous for its brigands.

Gargano Peninsula

Travelling east from the plains around Foggia, the landscape changes markedly as Apulia's highest hills signal the approach to the **Gargano Peninsula**, the most attractive piece of coastline on Italy's entire eastern seaboard. A private train, the Ferrovia del Gargano, serves the peninsula from San Severo, north of Foggia to Peschici, from where boats ferry visitors to Viesti and Manfredonia.

Contrasting with the flat landscape around Foggia, the Gargano's steep, wooded hills and winding coastal roads above white limestone cliffs offer sur-

Who can resist the appeal of a roadside advertisement?

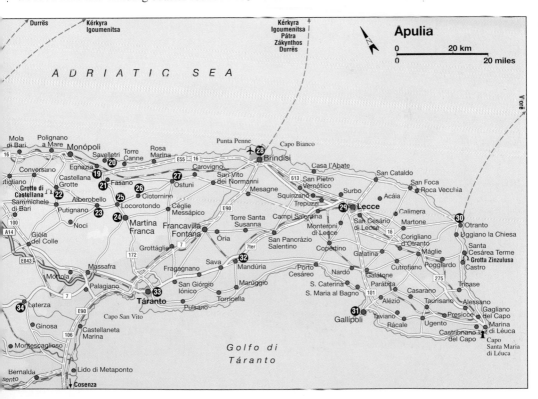

*The Gargano
Peninsula is
honeycombed with
caves and is a
favourite haunt of
speleologists.
Geologically part of
Dalmatia, it was
once an island.*

prises around every corner. The first place to experience the delights of the Gargano is in the fishing village of **Rodi Garganico ❺**, at the end of the ss89 from Foggia, which winds down the hillside past olive and carob trees to bring a first close look at the Adriatic's clear, turquoise waters. Below the town, built on bleached cliffs, is a neat harbourside where boats leave for the Tremiti Islands and seafood restaurants are inviting. This is a friendly town, unaffected by tourism. The old centre has a small maze of whitewashed houses and on warm evenings everyone turns out for the *passegiata*. On street corners locals sell cherries, nuts, oranges and lemons, or whatever else is in season, as well as wonderful bottled olives.

East of Rodi there are tempting stretches of beaches before the road winds up into the hills towards **Peschici ❻** perched high above the sea. Its relaxed, easy-going nature and its proximity to many excellent beaches have made the town a popular holiday centre and it has a number of hotels, restaurants and campsites, while the old centre of whitewashed narrow streets looks almost Greek.

Summer islands

Boats to the **Tremiti Islands ❼** leave from Peschici every morning, subject to the weather conditions and season, and tickets are on sale in the centre of town (boats or hydrofoils also go from Rodi and Manfredonia). With a full day to spare, a visit to these islands is a pleasant day out, but they are best avoided in August. About 30 km (19 miles) off the Gargano coast, this scantily populated archipelago attracts thousands of visitors a year, who go for the crystal-clear seas that lap the rocky shorelines or to cram on to the only beach, on San Domino. Those interested in the islands' history tend to head for San Nicola

BELOW: the coast at Rodi Garganico.

Map on page 200

to visit its monastery, which was founded in 1010 by Benedictines from Montecassino, or to the landmark Torre del Cavaliere del Crocefisso and the early church of Santa Maria a Mare.

While the coastline offers great attractions, no visit to the Gargano would be complete without a detour inland. From near Peschici it is a short drive to **Vico del Gargano** ❽, a delightful place where the *centro storico*, signposted as *Terra,* has large fortified walls and towers into which houses have been gradually incorporated over the centuries. Here herbs and tomatoes dry in the sun and working mules are tethered outside houses or kept in neighbouring houses that have become en-suite barns. There are some interesting early churches as well as the imposing Palazzo Bella (undergoing EU-funded restoration) and a compact Frederick II castle with a restaurant serving local specialities.

Further inland from Vico is the huge **Foresta Umbra**, last remnant of the primeval forest that once covered Apulia. On weekends and holidays the forest is full of Apulians enjoying elaborate family picnics under the shade of huge oaks and beeches, to the muffled sound of cowbells from the herds that wander the narrow roads through the woods. A circular tour leads to the coast at Peschici passing through Coppo dei Fossi.

From Peschici a pleasant stretch of coast road winds east through olive groves and fragrant pines, passing holiday and camping villages, often tucked away with their own private beaches. The coast has numerous strategic defensive towers such as the Torre di Sfinale, just before **Vieste** ❾. This attractive town has become the holiday capital of the Gargano and on Monday mornings it is further enlivened by an extensive market. The church dates from the 11th century and Frederick built a castle here. Down on the coast the Pizzomunno beach

The inland town of Vico del Gargano, on the way to Foresta Umbra.

BELOW: St Michael's sanctuary in Monte Sant' Angelo.

THE CULT OF ST MICHAEL

The cult of Michael the Archangel, captain of the heavenly host and scourge of the devil, was probably begun by the emperor Constantine in the Bosphorus in the 4th century. By the middle ages it had become one of the most prolific cults in Europe, and its most important source was Monte Sant' Angelo where the archangel put in several appearances. He first revealed himself in AD 490 to St Laurentius, archbishop of the now lost, great city of nearby Sipontum. At the end of this visit, he left behind his scarlet cloak and the instruction that the site should not be consecrated as he had already done so himself.

Thereafter it became one of the most important pilgrimage sites not only in Italy but in all Europe. In the 8th century St Aubert, a French monk, took a fragment of this cloak back to Brittany where he built the abbey of Mont-St-Michel. Known as the Warrior Angel, St Michael was adopted as protector by the invading Lombards, who built the sanctuary on Monte Sant' Angelo.

It soon became firmly fixed on the pilgrim and crusader routes to the Holy Land. Crusaders and many subsequent believers also adopted the image of St Michael as protective saintly warrior whose effigy, like his worldly manifestations, always appeared in high places.

Padre Pio

I mages and effigies of Padre Pio abound all over Italy but none more than in his native Apulia, where he was a priest until his death in 1968. He was born Francesco Forgione in Pietralcina north of Benevento to a farming family in 1887. As a child he was frail and at the age of 23 he was ordained as a Capuchin priest and sent to Foggia. Contemporaries describe him as extremely emotional and he is reported to have wept copiously during his long hours of prayer. After a brief period of duty as a medical orderly in Naples in World War I, he was discharged from the army due to pulmonary tuberculosis, and was sent to San Giovanni Rotondo where the mountain air was expected to improve his health.

On 17 September 1918, just after the community had finished celebrating the Feast of the Stigmata of St Francis, he went to meditate. The other monks heard a sudden cry and rushing to the choir found him uncon-

scious with blood flowing from wounds in the palms of his hands. When they took him to his cell they found that his feet were bleeding, too, just as Jesus' hands and feet bled when nailed to the cross. There was also an open wound in his side: Jesus' side was pierced by a Roman soldier to ensure that he was dead. The suffering that Padre Pio's wounds caused apparently gave him extreme pain and caused constant bleeding all his life. He nevertheless devoted himself to his faith and various miracles and acts of healing were attributed to him.

Pope Benedict XV said, "Padre Pio is one of those extraordinary men whom God sends on earth from time to time, to convert mankind". However, Pope Pius XI did not view the cult that grew up around the stigmatised priest so generously and restricted his active ministry. The suspension caused Padre Pio misery, but in 1933 he was reinstated although still prevented from preaching. His presence transformed San Giovanni Rotondo into a world famous pilgrimage centre. Many regarded him as a worker of miracles and for a large number of people he became known as a healer and even an embodiment of the living God, absolving sinners and guiding them on the path to redemption *(see Saints and Superstitions, page 83)*.

He conceived a major scheme to build a hospital city, and under his inspiration the Casa Sollievo della Sofferenza was built on his underlying principle that "Love is the first ingredient in the relief of suffering". In 1973, five years after his death, the Archbishop of Manfredonia initiated the proceedings towards Pio's beatification.

Since then, millions of faithful followers have visited the church where he worshipped for half a century. Padre Pio was beatified on 2 May, 1999 and many still look forward to his canonisation. Meanwhile, a project is currently under way to construct a vast modern church to accommodate the intense interest there is in Padre Pio. Money from America built Fiorello la Guardia Hospital, named after a mayor of New York, and foundations, institutes and websites bearing Padre Pio's name exist all over the world. ❑

LEFT: Padre Pio with the signs of the stigmata on his hands.

Map on page 200

begins beside an enormous pinnacle jutting out of the sea with its town perched above the white cliffs, and beyond it the quieter Scialmarino beach. To the south is the arch of San Felice, one of many arches and caves eroded in the steep, rugged limestone coastline.

From the pleasant, unpretentious town of Mattinata, a road leads inland and twists up 843 metres (2,765 ft) to **Monte Sant' Angelo ❿**, a town built on the cult of Archangel Michael who appeared inside a grotto *(see page 203)*. This became the **Santuario di San Michele** (open daily, Easter–Sept, 7.30am–7pm, Oct–Easter 7.30am–12.30pm, 2.30–5pm; entrance fee), a centre of devotion for pilgrims, crusaders and, today, visitors from all over the world. The Sanctuary, in the middle of the town's attractive old quarter, is approached through a large, richly decorated Gothic portico. Inside, 86 steps lead down to a pair of huge bronze doors made in Constantinople in 1076. These open to the interior, hewn out of solid rock and often packed with pilgrims. Inside there is an 11th-century bishops' throne and other precious works of art.

Souvenirs of Padre Pio in San Giovanni Rotondo.

Next door to the Sanctuary stands an unusual 13th-century octagonal bell tower and, below it, steps lead down to the Tomba di Rotari, long thought to be the tomb of an early Lombard ruler.

Still further inland, passing through a fertile landscape where shepherds tend their dark sheep, is **San Giovanni Rotondo ⓫**, birthplace of the famous miracle working Padre Pio *(see panel on facing page)*.

Back on the coast things start to get rather bleak towards **Manfredonia ⓬**, where a large refinery and other industrial complexes increase on entering the the poorly signposted town centre. Begun by Manfred, the illegitimate son of

BELOW: the beach and cliffs at Vieste.

Frederick II, the castle of this eponymous town was completed by Charles I of Anjou. Now well restored, it looks distinctly out of place among the blocks of flats that surround it. The National Museum (open 9am–1pm, 3–5pm, Tues–Sun; entrance fee) in the castle has stonework from the ancient Daunii.

Siponto, just to the south, was an important Daunian city which was developed by the Romans, and by medieval times it was the principal port of northern Apulia. Avoiding the Lido di Siponto, stay on the main road towards Bari and on the left you will find the delightful Romanesque church of Santa Maria di Siponto. Built in the 11th century on the site of a much earlier church, it has an eastern character and inside there are restored fragments of Byzantine mosaics. Its portal with lions is in the style of many other Apulian Romanesque churches of the 13th century.

On the last Sunday in July the "Disfida de Barletta" is re-enacted in the town. This fatal contest, which ended a siege in 1503, pitted 13 French against 13 Italians. The Italians won, as they have done in the re-enactment each year since.

Gargano to Bari

South of the Gargano, between **Lido di Rivoli** and **Margherita di Savoia**, the road passes first large areas of market gardens and then extensive salt pans which are a popular bird-watching haunt. At Margherita di Savoia are huge white hills of salt. Production of salt in this area is the most important in Italy and dates back to the third century BC. The coast road then approaches the large port city of **Barletta ⓭**, once a departure point for the crusades. The town centre's particular attraction is *The Colossus* in Corso Vittorio Emanuele. This 5-metre (16-ft) bronze statue, possibly of the 4th-century Emperor Valentinian, is supposed to be the largest surviving Roman bronze figure. Stolen from Constantinople by the Venetians in the 13th century, it was washed up on the shores nearby. Next to it stands the 13th-century Basilica of Santo Sepolcro,

BELOW: Apulian farmhouse.

Map on page 200

built in a mixture of styles, and an attractive Apulian-Romanesque Duomo. This was the seat of the Archbishop of Nazareth from 1291 to 1891 and an inscription over the left-hand doorway records the involvement of the crusading King Richard the Lionheart in the building. Watch out for your valuables in the streets of the old town at night.

Beyond Barletta, the olive trees and vineyards multiply and a short distance inland lies the site of the battle of Cannae, where Hannibal famously ambushed and defeated the Romans in 216 BC overcoming a force twice his size. **Canne di Batiglia** archaeological park (open 8.30am–7.30pm; entrance free) contains an array of ruined buildings and architectural fragments, some bearing Roman inscriptions, and some early painted ceramics.

Back on the coast road lies **Trani ⓮**, where the beautiful cathedral of San Nicola Pellegrino, with a pale stone facade and a tall, leaning campanile, occupies a striking position right next to the clear waters of the Adriatic. The Romanesque carvings around the doorway are particularly fine as are the bronze doors, from 1179, opening to the interior which includes one of the largest crypts in the world and the 7th-century crypt of St Leucius.

Inland, the cathedral at **Canosa di Puglia** contains a beautiful 12th-century bishop's throne supported by elephants. This string of cathedrals, some of the finest in Apulia, continues through this landscape of rolling hills called Le Murge.

At **Ruvo di Puglia ⓯** there is an excellent rose window and beautifully carved stone work around the door depicting griffins, lions and telamons. The Museo Archeologico Nazionale Jatta (open daily 8.30am–1.30pm, and 2.30–7.30pm Fri and Sat; entrance fee) in Piazza Bovio houses a large collection of classical vases for which the town was famous.

TIP

If you're visiting one of the large towns by car, it's a good idea to arrive at lunchtime. Shops, churches and museums may close until mid-afternoon, but parking spaces are easier to come by and you can explore the quiet backstreets before the working day resumes.

BELOW:
Trani cathedral.

TIP

Park in safe places and avoid leaving valuables in your car, especially in Molfetta, Barletta, Bari, Bitonto and Taranto. It is also wise to avoid showing off expensive cameras and jewellery or shouldering bags on the kerb side of the pavement where young lads on two wheels can get their hands on them.

Nearby **Terlizzi** is also an attractive town, which specialises in the cultivation of flowers and has some fine buildings. The doorway on the Rosario church, by Anseramo da Trani, was made for a cathedral that was destroyed.

Further west lies a building made famous through its appearance on the wine labels of the local robust red wine. The dramatic outline of **Castel del Monte** ⑯ (guided tours Apr–Sept, 9am–7pm; Oct–Mar, 9am–1pm) dominates the landscape of the lower Murge. Frederick II had a penchant for octagons and this angular building has 24-metre (80-ft) octagonal towers at each of its eight corners and eight rooms on each of its two storeys. It may have been built as a hunting lodge, but its purpose is far from clear. It has many architectural quirks, including a classical portal, and both academics and fantasists have attributed to the building mathematical, mystic and mysterious qualities.

Further along the Adriatic coast from Trani, **Molfetta** does not at first appear to be a promising place to visit, but it does have a nice old centre built around its important fishing port where the Duomo Vecchio is attractively situated by the sea. From here the road to Bari passes through almond and olive groves and the town of **Bitonto** ⑰, another place with a reputation for car theft and other crime, but also known for its superior olive oil as well as having one of the finest Romanesque cathedrals in the region. So it goes in Apulia. Its facade is harmonious, the arcaded south side supports an intricately carved gallery and inside there is a beautiful 13th-century pulpit at the entrance to the transept.

Bari: Apulia's pugnacious capital

BELOW: festival of St Nicholas, Bari.

Bari ⑱ is the principal town of Apulia, with a university and one of the most modern commercial centres in the south. During the September trade fair, *Fiera*

Map on page 200

del Levante, its many overpriced hotels fill with business visitors. The fishing fleet is still active, but little of its historic importance as a Byzantine maritime power remains in evidence. Its outskirts can seem forbidding and travellers are often warned by the locals to take care when visiting the narrow back streets of the Città Vecchia, the old centre, a maze of alleys in which to get lost (and to lose your valuables) on the promontory beside the port, from which ferries ply to Greece, Albania, Croatia and Turkey.

At the centre of the Città Vecchia is the 12th-century cathedral, but a more interesting church, Basilica di San Nicola, is just to the north. Never fully completed, it was one of the first Norman churches in the south. It has a finely carved doorway, stone altar canopy and a beautiful bishops' throne. The remains of St Nicholas, stolen from southern Turkey in 1087, lie in the crypt and are the source of pilgrimage for both Catholic and Orthodox Christians. Another huge **Frederick II castle** (open Tues–Sat, 9.30am–1pm, 3.30–7pm, Sun 9.30am–1pm; entrance fee) dominates the Città Vecchia. Surrounded by palm trees, it houses an interesting exhibition of church carvings from the region.

Bari also contains two important local museums: the Pinacoteca Provinciale, with artworks from the 11th to the 20th century, housed in the Pallazzo della Provincia on the Lungomare Mazaro Sauro, and the Museo Archeologico, directly inland behind the railway station in the Palazzo dell'Università, which has a good collection of ceramics and bronzes from the region (both open Mon–Sat 9.30am–1pm, 4–7pm, Sun 9.30am–1pm; entrance fee).

Greek vase from the Archaeological Museum in Bari.

South of Bari

The coast immediately to the east of Bari is not particularly attractive, but just inland is **Conversano**, a comfortable town on a hill overlooking the coast. Its fine baroque churches, cathedral, castle and Monastery of San Benedetto attest to its past importance. The attractions of the coastline resume at **Polignano a Mare**, a former Greek settlement in a spectacular clifftop position, which has a well-preserved old centre and a monastery dedicated to San Vito. Further on, **Monopoli** has an imposing baroque cathedral (open daily 8am–noon, 4–7pm; entrance fee) with a sacristy that exhibits objects of early religious art and Romanesque stone carving from the earlier church on the site.

Southeast from Monopoli, traffic becomes lighter and the surroundings less developed. At **Egnazia** ⓳ there is an important archaeological site of a former settlement of Roman and Messapian origin (open daily 8.30am–1.45pm, 2.30–7.30pm; entrance fee) and a well organised modern museum (open daily 8.30am–1.45pm, 2.15–7.30pm) standing next to the Necropolis. The main archaeological site close to the sea contains extensive remains of houses, two basilicas and a well preserved section of the Via Traina, a branch of the Via Appia that connected Benevento with Brindisi. It was built between 108 BC and AD 11 out of blocks of limestone on the route of the earlier Via Minucia along which Horace reputedly walked on his famous journey from Rome to Brindisi in 38 BC.

BELOW:
Bari's cathedral.

Beyond Egnazia is **Savelletri ㉚**, an enjoyable small fishing port and a tempting place to stay, with several waterside restaurants and a pleasant hotel. It is the value of fish rather than the tourist which is highly prized in this small town. Immaculately painted boats fish close to the shoreline and their catches go to dealers on the quayside and to the numerous local seafood restaurants.

Olives are harvested from trees that are several hundred years old.

Trulli and the Valle d'Itria

Some of the most interesting parts of central Apulia lie inland. **Fasano ㉑**, known mainly for its safari zoo, has an attractive centre and is a good base for touring the general area. It has elegant buildings and a large market that takes over the southeast side of town on Wednesday mornings. The landscape around Fasano is covered with olive trees, some several hundred years old. Another feature are the *masserie*, large fortified farmhouses which can be found in many parts of central Apulia. Further inland the road rises steeply to Selva where there is a panoramic view. West of Fasano are the **Grotte di Castellana ㉒** (open daily, Easter–Oct 9am–7.30pm; Nov–Easter 9am–4pm; entrance fee), some of the most spectacular limestone caves in Italy. It takes nearly two hours to take the guided tour exploring the 3 km (2 miles) of caves and tunnels containing spectacular stalagmites and stalactites .

The sight that attracts visitors to this part of Apulia more than any other, however, is the **Trulli** area south of Fasano. Here the landscape is covered with curious white-washed buildings with distinctive conical roofs *(see below)*. At **Alberobello ㉓**, *trulli* buildings are dramatically massed together, much to the delight of the numerous coachloads of tourists who arrive every day in summer to view the scene. In the surrounding landscape, smaller concentrations of *trulli*

BELOW:
trulli dwellers.

TRULLI SCRUMPTIOUS

Often topped with mysterious astrological or religious symbols, Apulia's *trulli* buildings are found nowhere else in Italy, or the world. The word has no known meaning and their origin is obscure: they may have been inspired by eastern structures. It has also been suggested that these buildings, dating from the mid-14th century, evolved to provide a rustic building that could be quickly erected or dismantled in order to avoid punitive taxes on permanent homes.

A *trullo* is made of limestone blocks collected from surrounding fields and placed together using the time-honoured technique of mortarless or drystone construction (although most inhabited ones have had mortar added in recent years). The conical roofs were built up using limestone slabs and inside the loft spaces provided storage for hay and the family's food stores. The roof space also draws off the heat, keeping the interior cool. The buildings are not large, and instead of constructing larger ones when more space is needed, other *trulli* are simply added on.

Although rural *trulli* can be found throughout the Itria Valley, their highest concentration is in Alberobello, where there are more than 1,500 still standing.

continue to provide functional homes and farm buildings, but in Alberobello they unashamedly offer themselves to tourists with open houses, rooftop panoramas, gift shops, restaurants or craft centres. In spite of this commercialism, it is still worth a visit, especially early in the morning or late in the day when there are fewer visitors. If you park in the Lago Martellotta, follow the steps up to Piazza del Popolo where the Belveder Trulli offers an excellent view over the wonderful concentration of *trulli* houses framed between palm trees.

Back down to the Lago, look for Via Monte Sant' Michele and walk up the hill among the *trulli* buildings, with endless winding alleys off it making it a delight to explore. At the top there is even a *trulli* church, the Chiesa a Trullos as well as houses advertising panoramas and invitations to see the interiors of everyday *trulli* homes. Not all of Alberobello is built in *trullo* style: the attractive town centre around the Piazza del Popolo is more conventional but it is a pleasant place to join in the evening *passegiata* or to eat out in one of the numerous restaurants. Here you can sample the local version of the regional ear-shaped pasta, *orecchiette.*

From Alberobello, the back road to Martina Franca is an attractive drive into Taranto Province. In spring the fields around the *trulli* are filled with poppies and other wild flowers, adding a rich carpet to the vines, olive and cherry trees. **Martina Franca** is one of Apulia's most attractive towns and offers an alluring combination of a slightly Moorish flavour, fine baroque architecture, attractive shops and restaurants (it is well known as a gastronomic centre) and an unhurried way of life. At its heart is Piazza Roma, entered through the Porta di Santo Stefano, or Arco di San Antonio, which was rebuilt in 1764 in baroque style. Beneath a group of palm trees there is a cool fountain in front of Palazzo

Map on page 200

TIP

Alberobello makes a good base: treat yourself to the Hotel dei Trulli where you can stay in a *trullo,* with your own patio in a garden setting with swimming pool. Tel: 080 432 3555.

BELOW: *trulli* in Alberobello.

*At Montalbano,
between Fasano and
Ostuni, is the Tavole
Palatine, the
Knights' Table, a
large dolmen
thought to be a
prehistoric tomb.*

Ducale making it a pleasant place to linger. A walk down Via Cavour, with its range of shops leads to the vast Basilica San Martino standing next to the clock tower on Piazza Plebiscito.

On the road north from Martina Franca there is a fine view across a cultivated landscape dotted with *trulli* buildings towards **Locorotondo** ㉕. Perched high up and surrounded by vineyards which produce a well-known *spumante* wine, Locorontondo is the other main town of the *trulli* area. It takes its name, "round place", from the fact that its streets spread from its centre like ripples in a pond. At the top of the town, opposite Porta Napoli, there is a leafy communal garden with an expansive vista of the *trulli* landscape. On the other side of the gate is a graceful baroque library with a clock tower.

Close by, in Via Morelli, is a wonderful arched doorway, and Piazza Fra Guiseppe Andria Rolleo in the middle of town is dominated by the huge baroque facade of the cathedral. Via Giannone passes whitewashed alleys and leads to steps down to Via Cavour and the elegant late Gothic church of Madonna della Grazie which has a simple facade and rose window.

The Salentine Peninsula

The attractive rocky coast at **Torre Canne** is popular for offshore fishing, but its pleasant beaches become crowded in summer. The road inland from here to **Cisternino** ㉖ crosses a pleasing landscape of olive trees and, in springtime, wild flowers. The town has attractive gardens with views over surrounding countryside. Nearby is the 13th-century Chiesa Matrice and Torre Civica. Passing through Porta Grenne, next to the tower, Via Basilioni follows a charming route passing a fine baroque balcony to reach Piazza Vittorio Emanuele at the

BELOW:
whitewashed
Ostuni.
RIGHT: sun-baked
Locorotondo.

Map on page 200

centre of the town. This is a pleasing and atmospheric place with narrow streets running off it, such as Via Regina Elena, where there are places to eat.

To the east is the charming, whitewashed hilltown of **Ostuni** ㉗ which is where the *trulli* area ends and the Salentine Peninsula begins. Its late 15th-century cathedral has a beautiful rose window and doorway as well as gracefully curved and richly carved cornicing. Distinctly Middle Eastern in style, Ostuni's narrow streets and alleyways are a delight to wander around, just to take in the exotic feel of the place.

From Ostuni to Brindisi, as the *trulli* buildings diminish, the towns become less interesting. **Carovigno** is shabby but has some interesting architectural features and despite unprepossessing outskirts, **San Vito dei Normanni** contains interesting rock churches, in particular San Biagio. Soon after midday, after working people have hastened home for lunch and a nap, all these towns fall silent except for the occasional clatter of dinner plates echoing from the windows shuttered against the heat.

From the second century BC, the Via Appia, the great highway from Rome of which virtually nothing can now be seen, entered **Brindisi** ㉘ passing the spot where the smart villa residences of Mesagne now stand. Southern Italy's busiest port was the end of the ancient Roman road and has been the point of embarcation for legionnaires, pilgrims, crusaders and traders on their way to the east. The 11th-century round church of San Giovanni el Sepolcro is a legacy of the Knights Templars. Beside it, the 15th-century Portico dei Cavalieri Templari leads to the provincial archaeological museum (Open Easter–Oct Mon–Fri 9am–1pm, 3–6.30pm, Sat–Sun and Nov–Easter 9am–1pm; entrance fee).

TIP

For a view of Brindisi, take a ferry across the harbour to the Monument to Italian Sailors, a piece of chunky Mussolini architecture built in 1933, where a lift rises 30 metres (150 ft) to its summit.

BELOW: Brindisi is the end of the road, where ferries set sail for Greece.

Now a busy naval port, Brindisi is the principal point of departure for people taking ferries to Albania and Greece and everywhere tickets are advertised. The attractive, lively sea front is a pleasant area for a wander but the famous single Roman column, one of two that for centuries marked the end of the Appian Way, has been taken away for lengthy restoration leaving only a rusty metal barrier and a graffiti-covered plinth to mark the historic spot.

Lecce's living baroque

Supporting figure on the facade of Santa Croce, Lecce.

Most people stay at Brindisi only if they are taking a ferry, but to the southeast along the SS613 motorway is a town where many find reason to tarry. **Lecce** ㉙ is one of the most important baroque cities in Italy *(see page 109)*. At odds with the surrounding countryside, the sophisticated main centre of the Salentine peninsula is crammed with fine architecture. Around every corner there is a beautiful doorway or balcony but even these are little preparation for the riot of incredible detail carved into the soft golden stone of Santa Croce, Lecce's celebrated church. Begun in 1549 by the local architect Gabriele Riccardi, it has a well preserved baroque facade with intricately designed balconies, arches, columns and friezes alive with carved figures, flowers and animals. Next door stands the imposing 17th-century Palazzo dei Celestini.

The centre of Lecce is compact and it is a short walk to Piazza Sant'Oronzo which is dominated by the missing column from Brindisi's Via Appia, now surmounted by the carved figure of Sant' Oronzo, the Bishop of Lecce martyred in the 1st century. Below this lies the Roman amphitheatre. From here, Via Vittorio

BELOW: Basilica Santa Croce, Lecce.

Emanuele leads past Sant'Irene, which has a finely detailed baroque interior, to the beautiful Piazza del Duomo. The Duomo as it stands was designed by Giuseppe Zimbalo and completed in 1570, and its entrance is framed on either side by the stone figures standing on balconies. Next to it is the graceful Palazzo Vescovile adding to the Piazza del Duomo's beautiful architectural array. A short way down Via Guiseppe Palmieri opposite, is the small Piazza Salconieri and the 16th-century Palazzo Balsamo with a wonderful balcony supported by four figures on either side. There is a wide choice of places to eat and drink and, with many other churches to see, such as Gesù and Santa Chiara, and other fine buildings, a visit is not to be hurried.

Outside Lecce is **Acaia**, a quiet and attractive fortified town entered through a handsome Renaissance gateway. From Acaia, the pleasant drive to the coast arrives at **San Cataldo**, a small seaside resort with a good sandy beach. Further along the coastal route is the popular fishing spot of **Rocca Vecchia** and the crumbled remains of its ancient Messapian site beside clear blue waters. There are several dolmen scattered around this area.

The mosaics of Otranto

Close enough to Albania to be able to glimpse its distant coastline on clear days, **Otranto** ㉚, Greek Hydruntum, is Italy's closest port to Greece and Turkey, and it prospered in the heydays of Byzantium and, from 1070, under the Normans. But after the fall of Byzantium in 1480, the town was sacked by a joint Turkish

Map on page 200

and Venetian fleet and the Christians slaughtered by Turks. Last to be slain, it is said, was the Turkish executioner, who had a last-minute conversion after seeing how steadfastly his victims stuck by their faith. Ten years later the Aragonese erected the defensive castle. Nowadays the old town has quiet winding back-streets and an attractive waterfront. It is easy to park near here to walk under the massive fortified Porta Alfonsina and up to the cathedral. Behind its graceful facade, the church reveals a splendid mosaic floor, recently restored and one of the finest in Italy. This extraordinary tapestry in stone, designed around 1165 by a priest named Pantaleone, depicts the months of the year, historical figures and legends, and a host of animals, all centred around a huge tree of life in whose branches are entwined images of a range of biblical and mythical subjects. A chapel in the south transept has the bones of the inhabitants killed by the Turks.

After Otranto a small coast road continues along the scenic, rugged coastline all the way down to Finibus Terrae (Land's End), taking in some attractive places and viewpoints on the way. At **Santa Cesarea Terme** there are popular spas and a pleasant resort facing a distant view of Albania. South of here a sign points to a short steep road down to the **Grotta Zinzulusa** (open daily, 10am–6pm; entrance fee), seaside caves reached by a footpath leading to the rocky inlet. **Castro** is a pleasant town with a castle and attractive marina. There follows a stretch of winding, unspoilt coastline dotted with cacti, palms and olive trees as far as the southern tip. Many might feel a sense of disappointment arriving at **Santa Maria Finibus Terrae** and the lighthouse next to the church marking the most southeasterly tip of Italy. The mournful Masses broadcast on the church's outdoor loudspeakers, the lighthouse surrounded by wire fences, and the car park often crammed with coaches do not encourage the visitor to

"When the story was finished, I looked on the map of the Kingdom of Naples for a well-sounding name, and that of Otranto was very sonorous".

– HORACE WALPOLE
ON THE WORLD'S FIRST
GOTHIC THRILLER, *THE
CASTLE OF OTRANTO* (1765)

BELOW: Finibus Terrae, land's end.

linger. The great Apulian aqueduct ends here, and below lies the more cheerful **Marina di Leuca** where boat excursions can be made to Grotta di Diavolo.

The Ionian coast and the Gulf of Taranto

There is more than one Gallipoli. The name comes from the Greek kalli polis, *which means "beautiful city".*

Rounding the tip of Apulia, there is little to hold the traveller's interest until reaching **Gallipoli** ㉛. Built on a small island, this attractive, fortified town typifies the history of Apulia. Greek in origin, it was subdued by the Romans in 265 BC and then occupied by Saracens, Normans and Spanish. The town outgrew its island site and spilled over to the mainland where it has lately developed a busy, unattractive urban sprawl which can be off-putting. But the old town, reached by a bridge, remains lively and full of character and its harbour is still a busy fishing port. The most famous landmark lies on the mainland just on the left before you approach the old town. This is the beautiful Fontana Ellenista which bears witness to the Greek history of the town.

Up the coast from here are new resorts, such as **Santa Maria al Bagno**, **Santa Caterina** and **Porto Cesareo**. Once a quiet fishing village, Porto Cesareo still has a pleasant harbour, but it is now more connected with the busy summer holiday business and taking advantage of its clear blue waters and good beaches of white sand.

Many of the towns inland are worth visiting. **Galatina** has a Greek flavour and its 14th-century Franciscan church of Santa Caterina d'Alessandria is a legacy of its former wealth. The town is at the centre of an important tobacco and vine growing area. Further east, **Corigliano d'Otranto** has a fine 16th-century castle with a superb gateway and a richly decorated balcony. **Nardo** is a particularly attractive old town with an untouristy air. At its heart is the Piazza

BELOW: fishermen in Gallipoli.

Antonio centred on the Immacolata Spire Sedile and an unusual Fontana di Torro. Here is another detailed cathedral facade, and the arcaded Piazza Mercato is a pleasant place to stroll. Further north, **Copertino** is a town dominated by its huge castle with a Rennaissance portal carved in Lecce stone. It is was also the birthplace, in 1603, of Joseph, the flying monk *(see page 86)*.

Grottaglie is a town with numerous limestone grottoes but its main activity is pottery which is immediately evident: thousands of terracotta pots are set out to dry in the sun. Ceramics and terracotta have been made here for hundreds of years, though its glazed wares are most notable, including copies of ancient Greek vases, huge plates and pots.

Sava is an attractive agricultural town. At the centre of a wine producing area, it has whitewashed houses, a tufa castle and a medieval bell tower. **Manduria** ②, known for its strong local wine, Primitivo di Manduria, is mainly visited for its caves and many miss the attractive town centre. Parking by the clock tower at the end of Via Ferdinando Donno, there is a short walk to the superb early 18th-century Palazzo Corcioli Giannuzzi where a fine portal leads into a compact courtyard surrounded by a magnificent balcony. There is also a fine Romanesque cathedral with 16th-century lions guarding the doorway. On the edge of town lies the Zona Archeologica with remains of the old city walls and a necropolis. Nearby is the Fonte di Plinio, a well Pliny noted in his *Natural History*, which had a water level that remained constant.

At **Francavilla Fontana** the ornate Palazzo Imperiali is one of several baroque buildings worth visiting. Once the main town of the ancient Messappians, **Oria** was an important stopping point on the Appian Way. It has some fine buildings and shows signs of its early Jewish settlement around the Porta Ebrei.

Map
on page
200

 TIP

Grottaglie pottery is famous all over Italy. In the town where it is made, it can be bought far more cheaply.

BELOW: crabs and swordfish in Gallipoli's market.

Map on page 200

Although Taranto was famous for its school of Pythagoran philosophy and as the birthplace of Aistoxenes, who first notated Western music, the Tarrentines liked their leisure. According to Strabo, they had more holidays than workdays in the year.

BELOW: pottery in Grottaglia.
RIGHT: cathedral in Martina Franca.

Major port and oyster centre

On the approach to **Taranto** ❸ the sea grows a little murky, but people still have an appetite for the oysters that are cultivated in the shallow waters around this ancient city, which the Spartans founded as Taras in 708 BC. From the east, the city reveals large-scale industry, an unhealthy smell, heavy traffic and sickly-looking trees. With the Mare Piccolo on the inland side and the Mare Grande sheltered from the sea, Taranto consists of three separate parts, all surrounded by water. The busy modern district in the southeast is connected by a swing bridge to the historic centre, sited on a small island. This, in turn, is connected by bridge to the northern part of the city where steel works and dockyards, Italy's second largest, preside. A main road crosses the Mare Piccolo, bypassing the town completely, which some may wish to do in order to avoid the modern sprawl and the old town's reputation for pickpockets and car crime. Half way across the lagoon, this road passes Parca Remembranza where the oyster beds and fishing boats, naval docks and the city can be viewed at a distance.

A stop in the city is rewarded by a cathedral with a baroque chapel, a lively fish market and a colourful Old Quarter. The **Museo Nazionale** (open daily 9am–1.30pm; entrance fee) in Corso Umberto I on the southern mainland, recalls Taranto's importance as a centre of Magna Graecia. Its huge collection, of mainly Greek terracotta and sculpture, and Roman sculpture and mosaics, is second only to the the Museo Archeologico Nazionale in Naples. The most popular exhibits are in the Sala degli Ori, which has a fine collection of gold jewellery from the Magna Graecia period.

Northwest of Taranto, the road heads towards Matera in Basilicata *(see page 227)*, which was once part of Apulia. On the way to this town of caves are

many subterranean places. Despite its busy, poorly signed, unprepossessing outskirts, **Massafra** has extensive rock-hewn churches made by Greek monks from Asia Minor scattered around its ravine setting. Some are hard to find and it requires persistence to locate the person looking after the keys. Its neighbouring town, **Mottola**, has cave frescoes notably in the Chiesa di San Nicola.

Laterza ❹, near the Basilicata border, is built in a spectacular canyon-like setting and contains numerous cave dwellings, some of which date back to 2000 BC. There are reputed to be 180 churches carved into the rock, some with Byzantine frescoes. It is not easy to explore these successfully without a guide, but the ravine is an inspiring place to walk and attracts much wildlife, including several types of hawk. This landscape of deep ravines extends all the way to Matera, 10 km (6 miles) to the west. North of this Apulian canyon country is **Altamura** which owes its existence to Frederick II. It has a fine cathedral and its old town is a pleasant place to wander.

In a similar way, **Gravina in Puglia** ❺, noted for its breed of horses, has a maze of interesting narrow back streets in the old walled town. There are baroque Palazzi and the church of Madonna delle Grazie which has a fine facade. More cave dwellings as well as one of the largest underground churches in Apulia, San Michele dei Grotti, can be found here. ❏

BASILICATA

Between forests, sandy coves, castles, excavations and rock-hewn churches, there's plenty to explore in this region entirely off the beaten track

Map on page 224

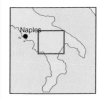

Regarded by many as the most economically undeveloped, culturally backward regions in Italy, Basilicata lacks the long coastlines of its neighbours Apulia and Calabria, both of which are seen as summer getaways. There are, however, two *bona fide* tourist destinations in Basilicata: the chic seaside resort of Maratea, on the Tyrrhenian coast, and the Sassi di Matera, a striking complex of cave-homes in the centre of Matera, but only geography-oriented Italians would be able to locate them in Basilicata on the first try. Even the well-known Parco Nazionale del Pollino, which is evenly split between Calabria and Basilicata, more often than not is associated only with Calabria.

Perhaps part of Basilicata's unfortunate image is due to the lingering effect of *Christ Stopped at Eboli* – a superb, widely read documentary novel by Italian writer, painter, doctor and political activist Carlo Levi, who was condemned by the fascist regime in 1935 to live in the isolated mountainous centre of Basilicata *(see page 232)*. The title alone, which refers to a popular local saying, speaks volumes about the extremely difficult life of Basilicata's stagnant peasant culture at a time when much of the rest of Italy was feeling the effects of modernisation and industrialisation. The phrase suggests that south of Eboli (about 30 km/19 miles from Salerno), the people were not Christians, but instead lived as animals. The peasants' daily struggle for survival and sustenance was such that they felt forgotten and abandoned even by God.

PRECEDING PAGES: Matera, cave town. **LEFT:** Rivello, a typical hill town. **BELOW:** content in Lagonegro.

But all this is part of a past that the region is quickly leaving behind. Emigration is no longer the only way to escape misery; successful small industry, supported by special European Union funds for developing areas, are finally bringing Basilicata out of a long economic slumber, transforming its once strictly agrarian and backward economy; and its tourist sector is slowly expanding.

Take to the road

Like Apulia and Calabria, Basilicata is a region best seen by driving through, stopping when necessary, rather than basing yourself in a town. Hotels are inexpensive and, unless you are going to the beaches in July and August, reservations are not necessary. A full tour of the region will require six or seven days. For those travelling without a car, **Potenza** makes a good base from which to take day trips by train to **Melfi** and **Venosa**, the historical towns of the Vulture area.

The short stretches of the Ionian and Tyrrhenian coasts are also served by the Ferrovie dello Stato (FS), while Matera is on the Ferrovie Calabro-Lucane, and is connected by train to Apulia, but only by bus to Potenza. To explore central and southern Basilicata, a car is strongly advisable.

The castle at Melfi drips with history and houses a museum.

Closer in spirit, history and landscape to Calabria than any other region, Basilicata is also dominated by a backbone of mountains which descend through dramatic foothills to the sea, but its mere 75 km (47 miles) of coastline is not enough to give the region the same island-like atmosphere found in Calabria.

The Vulture and the castles of Frederick II

A relatively small area around **Melfi** ❶, on the SS93 between Foggia and Potenza, offers the best mix of natural landscapes and historic places in the region. It is easily explored by car or public transport. Melfi itself is a small, unprepossessing town. Frederick Barbarossa, grandfather of Frederick II, used to hunt in this area and he spent a good deal of time in the Norman castles of Melfi and Lagopesole. It was in the rooms of the Castello di Melfi, an imposing square-shaped fortress defended by a double perimeter wall and eight polygonal towers, that Pope Urban II launched the First Crusade in 1089. Thirty years earlier the Norman conqueror Robert Guiscard was here crowned Duke of

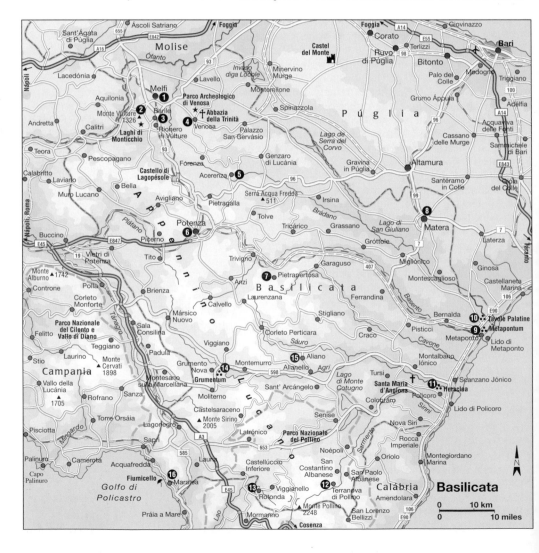

Apulia and Calabria. The castle became the Swabian Hauhenstaffen's first stronghold in Italy and in 1231 Barbarossa announced the *Constitutiones Augustales*, the first laws that regulated feudal rights. The castle is now home to the **Museo Nazionale del Melfese** (open daily 9am–8pm; entrance fee), which displays Roman and pre-Roman archaeological finds, Byzantine jewellery and Swabian ceramics. The highlight is the 2nd-century AD, salmon-pink sarcophagus of Rapolla, with fine reliefs of Greek gods and heroes. The region around Melfi is dominated by the **Vulture massif**. At 650 metres (2,130 ft) above sea level, its two lakes, the **Laghi di Monticchio ❷**, occupy the craters of a volcanic cone. A cableway between Lago Grande (big lake) and Lago Piccolo (small lake) rises to Monte Vulture (1,326 metres/4,350 ft); another splendid view is from the Norman **Abbazia di San Michele** (heavily restored in the 19th century), set on the wooded slopes of the Lago Piccolo crater. From here the panoramic SS167 descends to Potenza.

A few miles south of Melfi on SS167, lies **Barile ❸**, a humble mountain town of Albanian origins *(see page 258)*, famous for its Easter *Processione dei Misteri*. On the afternoon of Good Friday, hundreds of people in costume pour through the streets, including 33 small children dressed in black to symbolise the age of Christ when he was crucified. Three children in white represent the three Marys. The character of an eccentric gypsy woman goes around town glittering with Arbëreshe gold loaned to her by the local women.

Roman Venusia

Less than an hour away from Melfi, **Venosa ❹**, successor of the flourishing Roman city of Venusia, remained important until modern times because of its strategic position above the surrounding territory. For centuries it was a centre of learning and it was fought over by the powerful families of the region. Frederick II's son Manfred was born here, as was the Latin poet Quintus Oratium Flaccus (65–8 BC), who, according to legend, lived in Vico Orazio, where remains of a Roman structure known as the Casa di Orazio are located (not open to the public, but visible from behind the gate). In 1443, Venosa came under Pirro del Balzo (the city was part of his wife's dowry), who enriched it with monuments.

To erect the Castello, which today houses the Museo Archeologico (open Wed–Mon 9am–8pm, Tues 2am–8pm; entrance fee), Pirro had the original cathedral demolished and rebuilt on Piazza del Municipio. Via Frusci leads out of the town centre to one of the most interesting areas in Basilicata: the **Parco Archeologico di Venosa**.

The park is centred around the unfinished Abbazia della Trinità, but also includes Roman and paleo-Christian remains, Jewish and Christian catacombs, a thermal complex and the amphitheatre that seated 10,000 spectators. The abbey (open May–Sept Wed– Mon 9am–7pm, Tues 2–5pm; Oct–Apr shorter afternoon hours; entrance free) is one of the most intriguing buildings in Southern Italy. It is made up of the so-called *chiesa vecchia* (the old Norman church), and the topless *chiesa nuova*, a huge basilica (70 metres by 48 metres/

Map on page 224

TIP

Just 2 km (1 mile) from Melfi, toward Rapolla, is the rock-hewn church of Santa Margherita, with a remarkable 12th-century fresco. If you plan to visit, call the Melfi Pro-Loco on 0972-23975 to make sure that the church will be open

BELOW: the Archaeological Park in Venosa.

230 by 157 ft) planned by the Benedictines in 1135 but never completed. Built of stones from an earlier pagan temple on the site, the abbey is a treasure trove of inscriptions, sarcophagi and frescoes emerging from a small grove of olive trees.

On the way to Potenza from Venosa you can take the ss169 at San Nicola to Pietragalla, from where a tortuous road leads to **Acerenza ❺**, a pretty town with a remarkable Romanesque-Gothic cathedral, built in 1280 by French architects for a French bishop for what was then the capital of Basilicata. West of Acerenza, on the road from Melfi to Potenza, is the attractive rose-coloured **Castello di Lagopesole** (open Jun–Sept daily 9am–1pm, 4–7pm; Oct–May daily 9am–1pm, 3–5pm; entrance fee), another of Frederick Barbarossa's residences. It hosts temporary exhibitions and is rented out for weddings, conferences and special events.

Potenza and the Appenine Dolomites

The Byzantine-style icon of the Virgin in the church of San Francesco in **Potenza ❻**, known locally as the *Madonna del Terremoto* (Madonna of the Earthquake), has had plenty of opportunity to protect the city. Basilicata's capital has suffered more than its fair share of earthquakes, even for a southern town on seismic grounds. The last tremor hit in 1980, and reconstruction has not exactly been miraculous. Built on a spur of rock between two valleys, the historic centre of Potenza looks down on modern suburbs scattered at its feet.

With the exception of the Museo Archeologico Provinciale (Via Ciccotti; open Tues–Sun 9am–1pm, Tues, Thur, Sat also 4–7; entrance fee), which is a 25-minute walk downhill from the centre (or take bus No 3, 5 or 6), and several good-looking churches clustered along Via Pretoria, there is little worth seeing. The

TIP

Potenza and Matera are the only towns fully geared for the traveller in Basilicata. In Matera try the evocative Hotel Sassi in the middle of the Sasso Barisano. Tel: 0835 331 009.

BELOW: Tricorico, a typical hilltop town.

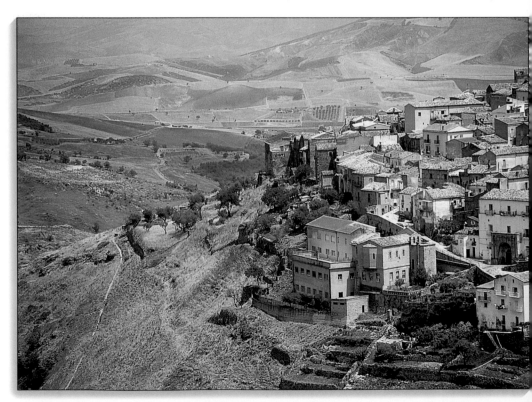

street takes on a pleasant atmosphere during the evening *passeggiata*, however, which somehow makes up for the relative lack of vintage architecture. The menu of the Antica Osteria Marconi, on Viale Marconi 233 (tel: 0971-56900) has a long list of hard-to-find traditional soups and home-made pasta dishes.

South from Potenza stretches the **Appennino Lucano**, which along the Basento river assumes a surprisingly "dolomitic" look, with bare, pointed rocks sculpted into bizarre forms by the elements. From this vantage point, the most famous tourist attraction is **Pietrapertosa** ❼ (southeast of Potenza, off the ss407), named after the *pietra forata*, or drilled stone): a town 1,088 metres (3,570 ft) above sea level surrounded by spires that look like objects and animals, and dominated by an unusual fortress entirely carved out of the mountain.

City of caves

Matera ❽ is known as the "City of the Sassi", the cave-like habitations cut into the steep rock of the ravine upon which Matera rests. What appear from a distance to be mere holes in the stones are windows and doorways, terraces, alleys and even churches. Once the dominion of the farmers and shepherds of Matera, the Sassi have been recognised by UNESCO as a world cultural heritage site and are currently undergoing restoration and repopulation. The finest example of "cave-architecture" in the Mediterranean, the Sassi have become the region's main tourist attraction *(see next page)*.

Located in a part of the country that has been inhabited since prehistoric times, as evidenced by the numerous relics found in the excellent Museo Ridola *(see page 229)*, Matera has Greek and Roman ruins of only modest importance. Repeatedly invaded by barbarians, Byzantines and Saracens, between the 9th

Map on page 224

Oil was struck in Basilicata in Val d'Agri in the late 1980s, and until at least 2025 is expected to provide for 10 percent of domestic consumption.

BELOW: the town of drilled stone, Pietrapertosa.

Sassi Cave Homes

The Sassi (stones) of Matera are the most complete and complex troglodyte dwellings in the Mediterranean. These cave dwellings, which date from Paleolithic times, line the steep slope of the ravine above the Torrente Gravina upon which Matera is built. Divided into two distinct quarters, the better off Sasso Barisano faces northwest, the more impoverished Sasso Caveoso faces northeast. (Caves on the north side of the ravine, once inhabited, were never populated in the same way.)

It is a city within the city, built over the centuries according to the custom of living in grottoes that was once common in the vast surrounding region known as the Murgia. Simple occupation of numerous natural grottoes led to their being enlarged by excavation and enclosed with exterior walls.

Until the beginning of the 20th century, the Sassi cave dwellings were not without a certain intrinsic functionality in harmony with the needs of their residents. An ingenious system of tiny canals regulated the flow of rainwater and sewage. The small hanging gardens and orchards stained the grey volcanic rock of the ravines green, and numerous little underground churches of noteworthy architecture, conferred a sense of decorum and dignity to this part of town.

But this was completely lost in the period between the two world wars when overcrowding and the decay of the common urban structures cut into the general living conditions. An increase in population meant that grottoes originally used as stalls and storage rooms became occupied, and unhealthy caves were inhabited by entire families with hens and pigs, without running water or indoor plumbing.

In 1950, the Sassi were declared a "national embarrassment". Of the 2,997 dwellings, 1,641 lacked fresh air and light. As a result of special legislation in 1952 to restore the Sassi to a habitable condition, some 15,000 residents were able to leave these house-caves and relocate to other parts of town.

From that point, the ancient cavernous borgo, which measures 300,000 sq. metres (3.3 million sq. ft), has slowly come back to life. No longer considered an emblem of sub-human social conditions, the Sassi are now recognised as an important part of Italy's cultural heritage, an unusual habitat worth preserving, and in 1993 they were added to the UNESCO list of World Heritage Sites. The walls that for reasons of security blocked access to much of the area, have for the most part been removed, and many of the cave dwellings have already been rebuilt and repopulated. The area is slowly being transformed into a museum neighbourhood. Before long, visitors will probably be able to book a room in the Pensione Caveosa or have lunch in the Trattoria Flintstones.

It is easy to become lost in the warren of streets in the Sassi areas, even with a map. There is no shortage of locals who will offer to be your guide, but a better bet may be to contact the tour service at Piazza Vittoria 42 (tel: 0835 334 633). ❏

LEFT: the Sassi area of Matera, once a home for the impoverished, is now being renovated.

Map on page 224

and 10th century, the city was destroyed and rebuilt three times in 130 years. Originally part of Apulia, it was annexed by Basilicata in 1663, and served as its capital city until 1806, when that function passed to Potenza.

The great legacy of the Byzantine civilisation in Basilicata is the so-called *chiese rupestri*, or little rock-hewn churches carved out of the tufa like a kind of surface level catacomb, with built-in altars, pilasters, domes and frescoes in the style of Greek icons dating from the 9th to the 15th centuries. In the area around Matera there are more than 150 *chiese rupestri*, of which 48 are in the Sassi. Santa Barbara, Santa Maria de Idris, Santa Lucia alle Malve, San Nicola dei Greci, the Madonna delle Virtù, the Convicinio di Sant'Antonio and Santa Maria della Valle are the most important and best preserved. The best way to see them is with a guide, because of the difficulty in finding them and because of access (the guides often have keys to the unguarded churches).

Most of the historic centre of Matera winds through the area of the Sassi *(see opposite)*. From Piazza San Pietro Caveoso, with the eponymous church (rebuilt in the 17th century), Via Buozzi leads to the 17th-century **Palazzo Lanfranchi** (call ahead to visit tel: 0835-310137 or 310171; open Mon, Wed, Fri 9am–1pm; Tues, Thur 1–6.30pm; entrance free), which houses the Pinacoteca d'Errico – a collection of Italian paintings from the 13th to 18th century – and the more interesting Centro Carlo Levi, with impressive canvases immortalising the places and people in his novel *Christ Stopped at Eboli*.

The **Museo Ridola** (open daily 9am–7pm; entrance fee), on Via Ridola, is a step above the usual local, dusty archaeological museum for its first-class display of relics from Paleolithic to Roman times found in local excavations; further along the street stands the baroque Chiesa del Purgatorio, dedicated to the

Frescoes of the Apostles in Santa Maria de Idris.

BELOW: the altar of Santa Maria de Idris cave church.

TIP

After the rocky, dry environment of the Sassi, the natural reserve of the Lago di San Giuliano is ideal for a picnic and a nap in the shade. If you need a longer break, stay the night at the Agriturismo San Giuliano, a 15-minute walk from the reserve, at Migliònico about 12 km (8 miles) south of Matera (tel and fax: 0835-559183).

BELOW: the Sasso above Torrente Gavina, Matera.

medieval cult of the Holy Souls of Purgatory, with a curvaceous facade and some gruesome Halloween-like decorations carved in the tufa of the main doorway to remind the faithful that death awaits us all.

At the junction with Via del Corso is the 17th-century Chiesa di San Francesco, with a polyptych by Bartolomeo Vivarini behind the main altar. Piazza del Sedile features a handsome 16th-century palace, seat of the local conservatoire, and leads into Via Duomo and the cathedral, begun in the 1230s in the Apulian Romanesque style. On the great rose window on the facade rest small statues of the Archangel Michael and of two fancily dressed noblemen together with the bizarre figure of a man wearing a short gown: a thoughtful homage to the multitude of artisans who worked on the cathedral. The church is dedicated to Matera's patron saint, the Madonna della Bruna, visible in the Byzantine-style fresco above the first altar to the left.

Christian and pagan rites

The Sagra della Madonna della Bruna, celebrated on 2 July, is the region's most important festival in honour of the Virgin. The curious name of this Madonna, venerated for at least 1,000 years, might derive from Mt Hebron in Judea, where Mary went to find Elizabeth to tell her that she was with child. The name might also allude to the dark colour of the skin of the Byzantine Madonnas, or to the ancient propitiary rites for the agricultural season, in which "bruna" perhaps signified "terra". The celebration, officially established by Pope Urban VI in 1380, retains many pagan traits. The triumphal float requires up to five months of preparation, in which the friezes and panels in painted and gilded wood, which feature views of the Sassi or church facades,

Map on page 224

as well as the *papier-mâché* statues representing a different biblical episode every year, must also be built anew. Late in the morning, the 18th-century statue of the Madonna is accompanied by a procession of shepherds to the town's Piccianello neighbourhood. At sunset the statue is placed on the triumphal carriage, pulled by eight mules harnessed with coloured, festive straps and escorted by horsemen with showy uniforms, who bring it back to the cathedral. The carriage is then attacked by the townspeople, who dismember it to grab the pieces in an atmosphere typical of pagan country festivals. A band plays as loud as it can and bursts of fireworks reflect against the Sassi.

The evening *passeggiata* takes place along Via del Corso, Via Roma and Via San Biagio; its focal point is the Piazza Vittorio Veneto, which gets cleared of traffic for the occasion. For a fairly priced dinner or pizza, a good restaurant to go to is the Il Terazzino sui Sassi (Vico San Giuseppe 7, tel: 0835-332503) with a memorable view of the Sasso Barisano by night.

Classical sites on the Ionian coast

In Basilicata, the ruins of classical antiquity are concentrated in three areas: in Metaponto and Policoro, both on the Ionian Coast, and at Grumentum, inland toward the border with Campania.

About 3 km (2 miles) from Lido di Metaponto and its well-equipped beaches are the remains of the Greek colony of **Metapontum** ❾. The Zona Archeologica begins at the junction of the ss106 with the road to modern Metaponto. There are few *in situ* remains, but this is the only ancient Mediterranean colony for which archaeologists have completely identified the entire urban layout, including the surrounding agricultural terrain. The first batch of ruins includes the

The name Basilicata, comes from basilikòs, the Byzantine administrator who governed here before the Normans arrived in the 11th century. The region is also known as Lucania, from the Lucani, who lived here in the 5th century BC.

BELOW: the beach at Metaponto.

The 5th-century BC acropolis of Heraclea at Policoro

remains of a theatre (built on landfill) and traces of the foundations of four temples. More evocative are the so-called **Tavole Palatine** (open daily 9am until 1 hour before sunset; entrance free; tel: 0835-745327), the 15 standing columns of the Doric Temple of Hera from the 6th century BC, situated north of modern Metaponto just before the SS106 crosses the Bradano river.

The **Museo Archeologico Nazionale** (Via Laverana, about 2 km/1 mile from the Zona Archeologica towards Metaponto, open Tues–Sun 9am–8pm, Mon 2–8pm; entrance fee) has a display of the statuary and ceramics found in the area, but the most interesting items are housed in the Museo Archeologico di Potenza *(see page 226)*.

Like Metaponto, **Policoro** is a new town with not much to detain a visitor except a dip in the sea. Excavations are still in progress at the **Parco Archeologico di Policoro** (open daily 8am until 1 hour before sunset; entrance free), which so far has revealed the acropolis of **Heraclea** , founded by the rulers of Taranto in the 5th century BC on the site of older Siris, one of the richest colonies in Magna Graecia which was destroyed by its rival cities in 540 BC. The first-rate Museo della Siritide (open Wed–Mon 8am–8pm, Tues 2–8pm; entrance fee) contains remains found in the valley between the Agri and Sinni rivers, as well as more local finds.

National park with Albanian enclaves

BELOW:
a more prosperous,
modern Eboli.

In the southern part of the region is the **Parco Nazionale del Pollino**. When compared with the Calabrian portion, the Basilicata side of the Pollino massif looks rather tame, yet it is no less rich in wildlife and splendid natural scenes *(see Wild Places, page 119)*. On the eastern side of the park is **Terranova di**

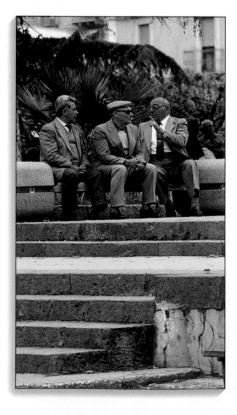

CARLO LEVI AND EBOLI

Eboli is a modern town with not much to detain the visitor today, but its name is known throughout Italy and beyond through the phenomenal success of *Christ Stopped at Eboli* by Carlo Levi. Born to Jewish parents in Turin in 1902, Levi studied medicine and set up an antifascist organisation, Giustizia e Libertà (Justice and Liberty). These activities led him to be exiled to Basilicata in 1935–6 in the villages of Grassano and Aliano (the house in Aliano where he lived is now a museum, *see page 234*).

He continued to practise as a doctor, in what he found to be a superstitious, poverty stricken society. From 1939 to 1941 he lived in France, but he returned to Italy and, while hiding from the retreating Nazis, wrote *Christ Stopped at Eboli*, his account of his time in Basilicata, recording with particular vividness the cave dwellers of Matera who came out of their dark holes to beg not for money, but for quinine for their malaria. The book was an immediate success when it was published in 1945, and it has never been out of print.

Levi was also an accomplished painter, exhibiting at the Venice Biennale from 1954. He continued to be politically active, as a journalist and politician, and was a member of the Italian senate from 1963 until his death in 1975.

Pollino ⑫, where wooden handicrafts are still produced by local artisans: here you can buy pretty kitchen tools, walking sticks and various souvenirs, all made by hand. The restaurant Luna Rossa, on Via Marconi 18 (tel: 0973-93254) offers some of the best "Pollino fare" such as *ferrazzuoli, rascatielli, tapparelle* (local pasta dressed with breadcrumbs and raisins, wild herbs, mushrooms), goat's cheese, lamb, kid and chestnuts.

Latronico, just beyond the western confines of the park, about 10 km (6 miles) away from the A3 and off ss653, is famous for its alabaster workshops; **Sant' Arcangelo**, a few miles above the northern edge of the park, off ss598, is renowned for its wrought-iron workshops.

The "capital" of the Parco Nazionale del Pollino is **Rotonda** ⑬, close to the Calabrian border and easily accessible from both the A3 and ss19. It makes an excellent starting point to explore the park further.

The ss653 cuts across the park and puts most of the towns within easy reach. Among them, **San Costantino Albanese** and **San Paolo Albanese** (both located in the southeast of Basilicata) have been home to Albanian communities since the mid-16th century. Though not very numerous, the Arbëreshe *(see page 258)* in Basilicata rival their Calabrian cousins for the tenacity with which they maintain their language and ancient traditions, which are publicly displayed above all during their religious celebrations. In San Paolo Albanese, the festival of San Rocco is celebrated on 16 August with a procession led by the *gregna*, a trophy of wheat sheaves carried on the shoulders of four men. In San Costantino Albanese, a series of *nuzazith* (costumed *papier-mâché* puppets) are set ablaze on the second Sunday in May during the course of celebrations of the Madonna della Stella.

Map on page 224

TIP

After working up an appetite climbing the slopes of Serra Dolcedorme *(see page 243)*, treat yourself to the hearty mushroom and wild game dishes of the restaurant Da Peppe, at Rotonda on Corso Garibaldi 13. Tel: 0973-661251.

BELOW: Piano Ruggio in Pollino National Park.

Map on page 224

Classical and literary tour

Grumentum ⓯ (excavations open daily 9am–1 hour before sunset; entrance free; Museo dell'Alta Val d'Agri open Tues–Sun 9am–8pm, Mon 2–8pm; entrance free), near the modern town of Grumento Nova, was a flourishing Roman town. You can see the ruins of its 1st-century BC amphitheatre, where crowds were entertained for some 600 years, and visit the Grande Casa dei Mosaici (3,600 sq. metres/38,750 sq. ft on two floors), which features parts of mosaic floors and several wells which were once filled with snow and used as refrigerators. The Siri Bronzes, which were dug up here in 1823, are in the British Museum.

From the Val d'Agri, at the junction with Alianello, the road climbs north to **Aliano** ⓯, the place where Carlo Levi was exiled, which served as the basis for the Gagliano of *Christ Stopped at Eboli*. Contact the *comune* for information about the **Parco Letterario Carlo Levi Tour**, which covers most of the places described in the novel (tel and fax: 0835-972154), although Aliano and its surroundings are easily explored on your own, book-in-hand, as little has changed since 1945. The author's personal items are on display at the **Museo Carlo Levi** (open Mon–Sat 10am–noon, 5–7pm, Sun 10am–noon).

The brief Tyrrhenian shore

Basilicata's small slice of the high and rocky Tyrrhenian coast between the extensive shores of Calabria and Campania's Cilento coast is a mere 30 km (19 miles) long. Characterised by lush vegetation and a splendid sea, the coastline is riddled with gorges, hidden grottoes and coves. It is best explored from **Maratea** ⓰, where the railway from Rome arrives at the coast on its way down to Reggio Calabria. The so-called "city of the 44 churches" looks out onto the blue Gulf of Policastro and these days more Italians come here to swim and be seen than to pray. Promoted by tour operators as a posh seaside resort with a well-equipped tourist port which brings worldliness and sophistication to the natural beauties of the area, the town reveals little of its past as a Greek colony. The acropolis rose from the rock that looms above the modern city, more or less where the huge white marble statue of Christ, with arms outstretched, now stands.

Start your visit from the busy *piazzetta* (Piazza Buraglia), taking Via Cavour to reach the Piazzale di Santa Maria Maggiore. From here, Via Santicelli climbs to the old *borgo*, where the pretty little streets and steps wind, leading to many noteworthy churches. The oldest of all is tiny San Vito, which dates from the 10th–11th centuries. At the very top of the rock, stands the Santuario di San Biagio, built on the site of what was the temple to Minerva. There's a wide choice of accommodation in Maratea, but the most atmospheric hotel of all is the Locanda delle Donne Monache, housed in an 18th-century former convent *(see the Travel Tips section)*.

North of Maratea is the wide beach of **Fiumicello**, situated next to the rocks of Punta Santa Venere. Nearby **Acquafredda** is reputed to be an excellent place for fishing. ❑

BELOW: Maratea shopkeeper. **RIGHT:** the beach at Maratea.

CALABRIA

Map on page 240

When Rome was still a village of shepherds, Pythagoras was teaching philosophy here. But today, behind miles of shoreline, Calabria conceals some of the remotest spots in Italy

Naples

The toe of Italy's boot, the region of Calabria separates the Ionian Sea from the Tyrrhenian Sea and reaches out to Sicily across the Strait of Messina. For thousands of years its history has been defined by the peoples who have migrated through and settled upon this narrow passage between the eastern and western Mediterranean. In spite of its 780 km (485 miles) of coastline – fully one-fifth of the Italian peninsula – and blue waters rich with fish, Calabria is essentially a sparsely developed mountainous region. Thick forests, lakes, impetuous torrents and unspoiled landscapes rarely found in the heart of tame Old Europe set Calabria apart from the rest of Italy.

It was not always so. In the 7th century BC, throngs of colonists from nearby Greece landed along the narrow coastal plains of the region, and established some of the most powerful cities of the pre-Roman world: Rhegion (Reggio Calabria), which participated in the Peloponnesian War as an ally of Athens against Sparta; Lokroi Epizephyrioi (Locri Epizefiri), the first Greek city to adopt a written legal code, in 664 BC; Sybaris (Sibari), so opulent and refined that it gave birth to the word "sybaritic"; and Kroton (Crotone), site of the most important medical school in the Western world. But don't come to Calabria in search of ruins; its grounds have not yet been excavated seriously, and archaeology – like so many other aspects of the region – remains relatively underdeveloped. The archaeological parks at Locri Epizefiri, Roccelletta di Borgia and Capo Colonna (all along the Ionian coast) feature the thin remains *in situ* that have so far been brought to light. Museums in Reggio Calabria, Crotone and Sibari are well-stocked with everyday objects, statues, and perhaps the most typical example of the culture of Magna Graecia: the *pinakes*, or terracotta *ex votos*, offered in churches in fulfilment of a vow.

PRECEDING PAGES: medieval Gerace. **LEFT:** Tropea, flower of the Violet Coast. **BELOW:** Crotone, on the Ionian shore.

Refuge in the hills

As the Greeks faded from the scene, so did their great cities. The Romans saw Calabria as the answer to their desperate need for wood during the rapid expansion of the Republic. Their relentless deforestation of the region resulted in severe hydro-geological damage, which altered not only the terrain, but also the culture and way of life. Once-navigable rivers were transformed into spectacular torrents, the *fiumare,* which during periods of drought invest the southern landscape with a primitive, lunar-like allure. Soon after the fall of the Roman Empire, the coastal plains turned to malarial swampland, forcing the local population to take refuge in the inland hills.

For centuries thereafter, the coast was associated with disease, as well as the threat of invasion. No traditional Calabrian dish involves the use of fresh fish.

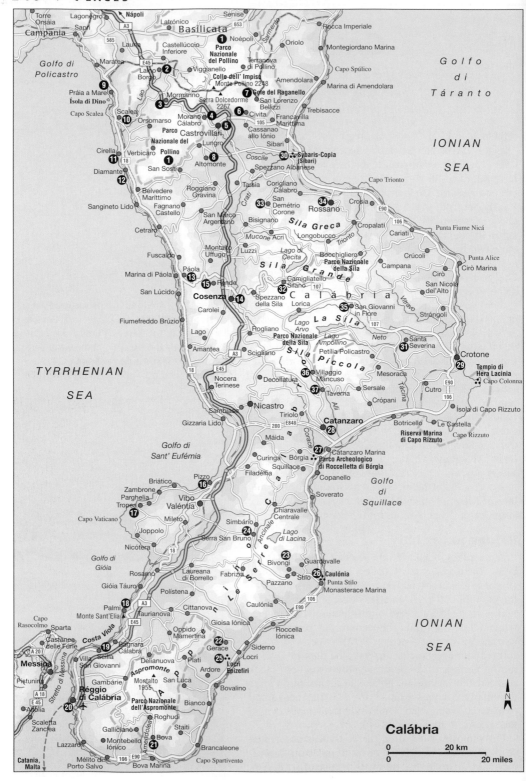

Calábria

Furthermore, when the Reform Act of 1950 forced the great landholders of the region to cede some land to the labourers, they kept for themselves what they considered the "good" land – that of the interior. Although the land reclamation had rendered the coastal areas habitable, in their collective myopia coastal lands remained "bad".

Great coastal resorts, fine national parks

Today Calabria offers some of the best seaside resorts in Italy. The Tyrrhenian coast was the first to be developed. The first boom came in the 1970s with resort towns such as Praia a Mare, Scalea, Pizzo and, above all, Tropea, nick-named "the Capri of Calabria", which for its restaurants, vibrant nightlife and location makes the best base from which to explore this area. In the 1990s, development shifted to the Ionian Coast, which south from Catanzaro is today rife with *marine,* tiny seaside wards of towns perched on the coastal highlands. In the summer months, the towns along the Gulf of Squillace are home to the region's wildest nightclubs. Accommodation here ranges from secluded bun-galows to *agriturismi* and comfortable, family-run hotels; staying in Crotone might be worth the extra 30-minute trip to the nearest clean beaches if you pre-fer a larger town with more shops and cultural activity.

In spite of this, the authentic Calabria is still found by climbing a fair distance from the sea to ancient towns packed on steep slopes, rising above the remains of castles which themselves seem to grow from the rocky hills. Of striking rus-tic beauty, these small towns have a bare architectural style suited to this earth-quake-prone region, and are the best Calabria has to offer. With the exception of Cosenza, part of whose historic centre has survived four earthquakes in the past 200 years, and some bits of Catanzaro and Crotone, the major cities of the region are unremark-able, unattractive modern agglomerations.

What it lacks in human development, Calabria more than makes up for in natural splendour. Three National Parks – the Pollino in the north, the Sila in the centre and the Aspromonte in the south – lie between the cliffs of the Tyrrhenian Sea and the unspoiled beaches of the Ionian Coast. All of them offer great trails and walks, and with some notice you can hire English-speaking guides. In the Pollino you can overnight in almost any of its 56 towns, but Civita and Castrovillari offer the added bonus of super restaurants. In the Sila, Camigliatello Silano's inexpensive hotels or the self-catering cottages of Villaggio Mancuso are both good options. The Aspromonte is scattered with good qual-ity *agriturismi* and its informal, reliable hospitality system called *ospitalità diffusa* (rooms inside private farms and country houses, *see Travel Tips for details*) will help you make contact with the locals and their traditions. In fact, the entire region has the feel of an enormous living museum of pastoral culture.

The surprising diversity of microclimates and land-scapes in Calabria gives the rhythm of a visit here a sort of cinematographic quality. From the height of the Isthmus of Catanzaro, which is the narrowest point (35 km/22 miles) of the Italian peninsula, you can pass from the Ionian to the Tyrrhenian coasts in mere

Map on page 240

Calabria was the Roman name for what is today the Salento (the southernmost part of Apulia, at the heel of the boot). In the 7th century, the Byzantines applied the same name to the region on the western side of the peninsula.

BELOW: in a Calabrian garden.

Face at the doorway: in many inland towns visitors are scarce.

BELOW: Pollino National Park.

minutes. From May to September, in a single day you can swim in limpid waters, rest in the mountains under the cool freshness of ancient pines and beech, and perhaps visit a Byzantine church, a tiny ethnographic museum, or stroll along the disquieting narrow streets of tiny abandoned towns. In winter, the peaks of the Sila and Aspromonte are covered in snow and the touristic towns of Camigliatello Silano and Gambarie host a healthy traffic of local skiers.

The approach by road

The FS (Italian railways) trains connect the coastal towns and main cities, but a car is necessary to appreciate the region. Coming from the north by car, the best way to enter Calabria is to cross the Pollino range. The splendid Autostrada del Sole (A3) then bends south and passes through Cosenza on its way to Reggio Calabria. Alternatively, it is possible to take the coastal highways (*statali costiere*), but this should be avoided in July and August when local beach traffic is heavy. Whichever way you manage to get to Cosenza, remember that the city is practically unnavigable during peak traffic hours (8am–10am, 6pm–9pm).

If there is no time for long stops along the northern part of the region's Tyrrhenian coast, a good alternative for a visit to Calabria is to leave the Autostrada at Pizzo, where a beautiful coastal tract begins along the ss522, taking in Tropea and Capo Vaticano. From Nicòtera, it is possible to continue along the coast by taking the ss18 that passes through Rosarno, or else rejoin the Autostrada, which continues south to Reggio Calabria. The Ionian Coast is served by the ss106. The Calabrian landscape is so compelling that there are few roads not worth a drive, but with the exception of freeway A3, plan on slow, careful driving along narrow and twisting mountain roads. Chains might be

required in the winter months. Note that there are no toll roads in Calabria. A complete tour of the region will take at least two weeks. Room reservations are necessary in high season: July to August at seaside resorts and in national parks; Easter week in national parks and December to February at ski resorts.

Map on page 240

The Olympus of the Appenines

In the north of Calabria rises the **Pollino massif**, named after the abundance of *pollentes herbae* (medicinal and magical herbs) that ancient peoples collected there. The area has been part of the **Parco Nazionale del Pollino ❶** since its creation in 1993 *(see Wild Places, page 119)*. The park, has 172,000 people spread among 56 towns and villages, stretches for 1,960 sq. km (760 sq. miles) between Calabria and Basilicata, and has a multitude of nature itineraries. Unless you are accompanied by a guide *(see Travel Tips)*, a good map is essential.

From Colle dell'Impisu, to the north of Morano Calabro, it is easy to reach the **Piani del Pollino** (Pollino Plains), a stupendous alpine meadow with a small lake at 1,780 metres (5,840 ft) above sea level, in a two-hour round trip. **Mount Pollino** is a five-hour round trip and an eight-hour trip encompasses the massif's highest peak, **Serra Dolcedorme** (2,267 metres/7,438 ft), whose name and shape suggest the body of a sleeping woman. The touching landscape of the Pollino moved the English travel writer Norman Douglas (1868–1952) to write in *Old Calabria*: "Silhouetted against the sky in the morning light, these stupendous mountains seem to melt into a fog of amethyst at sunset. A vision of peace."

A famous highlight of the park is the population of elegant, tall *pini loricati*, a native species of fir, that thrives on the **Grande Porta del Pollino** mountain pass and has been adopted as the emblem of the park. To reach the Grande

TIP

Enquire at one of the newly opened visitor centres in the Pollino National Park about the so-called "Literary Park": a trail between Cosenza and Crotone that takes in the places described by Norman Douglas in his novel *Old Calabria*.

BELOW: landscape near Delianuova, Aspromonte.

*Castrovillari hides
one of the tastiest
attractions in Italy:
the Locanda di Alìa,
where traditional
Mediterranean food
is prepared with a
flair. Try the ravioli
filled with goat
cheese and herbs in a
wild anise sauce, the
carne 'ncartarata
(pork meat in a
piquant honey sauce)
and the liquorice
mousse. There are
also rooms to let in
the adjoining inn (see
Travel Tips for
details).*

BELOW:
a red rose in Pizzo.

Porta del Pollino, drive to the Pianoro di Acqua Tremula from San Severino Lucano (15 km/10 miles) or Terranova di Pollino (10 km/6 miles); the trail to the Grande Porta (a four-hour round trip) begins 400 metres (1,300 ft) south of the Pianoro.

The best time of year on the Pollino is between mid-May and mid-June, when wildflowers – daisies, violets, crocuses, peonies, orchids, and many more – cover the high plains, and the jagged peaks still show a touch of snow.

Towns and villages of the park

From Basilicata, the first town along the A3 is **Laìno Borgo** ❷, famous for the Good Friday *Giudaica*, an ancient interpretation of the Passion by locals in costume. Laìno is a good base from which to explore the valley of the Lao river, where rafting and canoe trips are possible.

The medieval town of **Mormanno** ❸ 10 km (6 miles) further south, is a favourite overnight stop for climbers heading to the top of the Pollino and the Orsomarso mountains. It is also a good place to stop for a stroll through the narrow streets on a quick and easy excursion in the heart of the Pollino massif: from Mormanno take the carriage road to the SS19 Campo Tenese exit, and then climb to the Ruggiu plain. Park near the de Gasperi refuge and follow the path to the right for 25 minutes to reach the Belvedere.

The SS19 leads down to **Morano Calabro** ❹, a town draped across the mountaintops. Morano was severely hit by emigration in the 1950s, and now has the typical feel of an "old persons' town" with dozens of elderly men clustered out on the *piazzas* every day. Its wildlife museum, Centro "Il Nibbio" (Vico II Annunziata 11; open June–Sept: daily till 8.30pm; closed 1–4pm; Oct–May: daily till 6pm; closed 1–3pm; entrance fee; tel: 0981-30745, 0347-0687418) should not be missed; dioramas of the fauna and flora of the Pollino and other areas of Calabria include dried plants and a variety of stuffed animals (deer, wolf, porcupine, badger and several dozen birds). Guided tours of the exhibits in English are available on request. The museum entrance looks out on to the Sibari plain; on clear days the view extends all the way to the sea.

If you have time, you can visit Morano's many churches as well as a small Museo di Civiltà Contadina which has displays of utensils, objects and popular costumes from the local farm culture. Situated next to the Comune (Town Hall), it has irregular opening hours and is closed at weekends.

Laid-back **Castrovillari** ❺ is the most populous town in the Pollino area. Its busy shopping street, Strada del Mercato, is flanked by fruit and vegetable stalls and various shops, including the Galleria d'Arte Il Coscile, which sells contemporary Calabrian artwork, and a bookstore specialising in Italian books and maps about the region. In Piazza del Comune, sandwiched between two dilapidated noble palaces in Neapolitan baroque style, is a tiny museum (entrance through the door to the left of the tourist office; open Mon–Fri 9am-1pm; entrance free) dedicated to Andrea Alfano (1879–1967), Castrovillari's favourite son, a talented painter with an Impressionist style.

Map on page 240

Founded by Albanian refugees in the 1470s in one of the most beautiful valleys of the Pollino, **Civita** ❻ (off the SS105, 30 minutes from Castrovillari in the direction of Francavilla Marittima), is a town of old narrow streets that have changed little over the centuries. The Church of Santa Maria Assunta has an unusual iconostasi sculpted in walnut and olive wood.

Also worth visiting are the **Museo Etnico Arbëresh** (usually open Mon–Fri 9–noon, but call ahead on 0981-73043; donations welcome) with a small exhibit of Albanian artisanal work and a sort of tourist office, and the famous **Gole del Raganello** ❼, one of the most spectacular canyons in Italy. Various paths wind their way through it, ranging from easy walks among the broom and wild oleander to serious cave explorations to try with an expert guide.

At the southern edge of the park and a tortuous drive south from **Castrovillari** on the SS105, **Altomonte** ❽ has in the past 10 years emerged as Calabria's "city of art". The residents of this ancient *borgo* (little village) rebelled against degradation and restored its medieval streets, churches and historic palaces, and even raised the funds to build an amphitheatre that hosts the Festival Mediterraneo dei Due Mari (Mediterranean Festival of Two Seas) every year in July and August. In the wake of the more famous Festival of Two Worlds at Spoleto in Umbria, Altomonte's international event draws tourists interested in concerts and plays focused on Mediterranean culture and traditions, and makes the most of the town's beautiful natural setting and its architectural finery, with vases of coloured flowers appended to the ancient stone walls that surround it.

Don't miss the Church of Santa Maria della Consolazione (1380), the only surviving example of Gothic-Angevin style in Calabria. Beyond the gate to the left of the facade, a belvedere winds around the church; to the right is an

TIP

To reserve a guided tour of the Gole del Raganello contact the bar-restaurant Il Pino Loricato in San Lorenzo Bellizzi, where they also have a list of rooms for rent (tel: 0981-493151).

BELOW:
Altomonte, the region's "City of Art".

entrance to the Domenican Convent (1440), which today holds the small but interesting collection of the **Museo Civico** (open Mon–Sat 9am–noon, 4–7pm; entrance fee). Among the artwork from the 14th and 15th centuries is a painting by Simone Martini and the intriguing *Madonna delle Pere*, an unattributed work in which an unattractive baby Jesus is portrayed reading a book, showing that wisdom cannot be distracted by beauty. If you wish to stay the night in Altomonte, the Castello di Altomonte, in a Norman castle, is one of Calabria's nicest period hotels (*see Travel Tips for details*).

The Beaches of the Tyrrhenian Sea

The 240-km (150-mile) Tyrrhenian coast is marked by emerald water, rocks studded with cedars, hills covered with fig trees and olive groves, stretches of golden sands, and a few remnants of Greek and Arabic towns. Down here, concrete has not taken over – at least not yet. Driving along the coastal road, especially from September to May, it is easy to be hypnotised by the infinite range of blue and green tones that give form to this uncontaminated landscape.

The first stop along the SS18, which runs parallel to the Parco Nazionale del Pollino for about 50 km (31 miles), is **Praia a Mare** ❾. Boats can be rented from its large beach to explore the caves and grottos of the wild, tiny **Isola di Dino**. Soon after the road passes **Scalea** ❿, a picturesque town hanging on the steps of rock, hence its name (from *scale*, meaning stairs), where you can stop for lunch and a stroll along the promenade.

Next comes **Cirella** ⓫, where the calcified ruins of the old city are clustered on a hill near the sea, the Isola di Cirella, another uninhabited islet, and a 4-km (2½-mile) beach. Finally, you can spend the night in **Diamante** ⓬, a pretty

TIP

The gelateria Pierino, on Diamante's Lungomare, makes wonderful hot chilli ice cream.

BELOW:
market near the sea at Diamante.

Map on page 240

coastal resort with good restaurants. Diamante is known for its murals depicting scenes of Calabrian life, and for being headquarters of the Accademia del Peperoncino (Academy of the Hot Chilli, on Via Amendola 3), which preaches the virtues of Calabria's most popular spice through publications (in Italian), national summits, "hot" summer camps and *peperoncino* tastings.

About 30 km (19 miles) south of Diamante on the SS18 is medieval **Paola** ⓭, named after one of Italy's most revered and solicited saints, the miracle-worker San Francesco da Paola, founder of the austere mendicant order of the Minims, who was born here in 1416. The Sanctuary that bears his name has a harmonious Renaissance-baroque facade, and is a stop on the pilgrimage route, despite its isolated location in the gorge of the Isca torrent. A route of his miracles begins beside the basilica. To the north, just outside town, is the little, underground Chiesa di Sotterra which pre-dates the 10th century and has some of the oldest Byzantine frescoes in Calabria. But you might just want to relax on the beach that skirts Paola's modern expansion, **Marina di Paola**, before you take SS107 east to Rende and Cosenza.

Cosenza, without the lightness of being

Saved from earthquakes but shaken by an intense flow of immigration, busy and sultry **Cosenza** ⓮ can be quite a shock to the visitor accustomed to the relaxed rhythms and the breeze of the rest of the region. Yet, as far as major cities go, Cosenza's historical centre is Calabria's best. Called the "Milan of Calabria", the city has developed excessively toward the northeast, where suffocating traffic and a constant building boom attracted the mountain dwellers of the Sila, who came down to live and work, and even those who once lived in the historic

TIP

The Lavorazione Artigianale Fichi Secchi of Ciccotti Maria Carmela prepares delicious dried figs (a Calabrian speciality), either plain or stuffed with nuts or dipped in chocolate and honey.
(Via Rupa 15, Paola, tel: 0982-583255.)

BELOW:
San Domenico, Cosenza.

Legend has it that Alaric the Goth, who died of fever in Cosenza in 410, had his tomb built at the confluence of the rivers Crati and Busento, where he was buried with the treasures from the Sack of Rome.

centre, which today seems a ghost town. Surrounded by seven hills, perhaps it was not by chance that the Bruzi (the Italic tribes that in the 4th–3rd century BC assumed control of what had been the Greek colonies) chose it as their capital city. The Roman occupation of the city was followed by a long period of decay and barbarian invasions, which ended with the expulsion of the Saracens in 986. Under the Angevins, the Aragonese, the Normans and the Spaniards, Cosenza saw a cultural and economic rebirth that for centuries made it among the most urbane and lively cities in Southern Italy.

In spite of its university, which draws thousands of young students from the province's hinterlands, Cosenza seems rather grim. The proverbial hospitality and "lightness of being" of the south have inexplicably died out; you might find it harder to snatch a smile or a kind response here than elsewhere in Calabria. Don't plan on sleeping in Cosenza, as the city's few decent hotels are expensive, ugly and away from the historical centre.

Half a day is all you need to visit the historic centre which, unusually for a Calabrian city, remains for the most part intact. There are a couple of worthy restaurants and the handsome Caffè Renzelli, founded in the 19th century with period decor and memorabilia left by Italian *heroes del Risorgimento* (Piazza Parrasio 17). From Piazza Campanella, where the baroque church of San Domenico rises, Corso Telesio makes its way uphill towards the 12th-century Duomo. Consecrated by Frederick II in 1222, it contains a 4th-century Roman sarcophagus, inside which the Emperor's eldest son, Henry, was put after his suicide, and the Gothic sepulchre of Isabella of Aragon (died 1270). Contact the Soprintendenza to see two splendid Byzantine works: a gold and enamel reliquary containing a fragment of the Holy Cross, and the icon of the Madonna del

BELOW: Briatico on the Violet coast.

Pilerio, protector of the city, which for security reasons are no longer kept inside the Duomo (Piazza Valdesi 13, tel: 0984-75904, fax: 0984-74987; entrance free).

Take Via del Seggio to reach the **Monastery of San Francesco d'Assisi**, founded in 1217 but partially reconstructed in later centuries. On beautiful Piazza XV Marzo are the neoclassical Teatro Rendano, famous for its opera season, and the Accademia Cosentina, founded in 1514 as a centre of human-ist culture and today used as a conference centre. From the piazza, climb up to the formidable **Norman Castle** (open daily 8am–8pm; entrance free), of which remain only the perimeter walls and the ruins of several back rooms.

On the way to Cosenza from Paola is **Rende ⓑ**, a pretty hill town worth a detour for its great views and a visit to the interesting Museo Civico (open daily July–Sept 9am–noon, 4–10pm; Oct–June 9am–1pm, 4–7pm; entrance free), dedicated to ethnic minorities and emigration.

The Violet Coast

Another fascinating stretch of coastline lies south of Cosenza, winding from **Pizzo** to **Palmi**, between the Gulf of Sant'Eufemia and the Gulf of Gioia, where the jagged Promontory del Poro reaches into the sea. Here smooth lava and pointed granite crags alternate with intimate coves and narrow stretches of beach. The vegetation consists of agave, prickly pears and, inland, centuries-old olive trees and gigantic ferns. The promontory's most attractive beaches, all sandy and safe for children, are at Zambrone, Parghelia, Tropea, Joppolo and Nicotera. Between Tropea and Joppolo is **Capo Vaticano**, one of the most enchanting and unspoiled corners of the region, despite the several campsites which have sprung up near the most spacious beaches. At Palmi begins the

Map on page 240

On the Costa Viola, even the onions turn purple: the sweet onions grown here are renowned throughout Italy. Don't miss a chance to try a salad of "cipolle di Tropea" (Tropea onions) tossed together (raw) with ripe tomatoes, fresh hot chilli peppers, oregano and olive oil.

BELOW: deserted beach at Pizzo.

Fisherman at Scilla, a village that seems to belong to Sicily.

splendid **Costa Viola** (so-called because of the beautiful purple hues of the sea at sunset), which snakes further south toward the Strait of Messina. This Tyrrhenian itinerary is made more vivacious by the lovely towns that have sprung up around the local fishing economy, which transform themselves into busy summer resorts and offer inexpensive seafood meals along the way. Tropea is definitely the most chic place to spend the night. Two other good options are Pizzo and Scilla, where there is a youth hostel. Between Pizzo and Scilla there are dozens of well-equipped campsites.

Stop at **Pizzo** ⑯ for a *tartufo* (chocolate and hazelnut ice-cream filled with caramel), a walk through town and a visit to the bizarre Chiesetta di Piedigrotta (open daily 9am–1pm, 2.30–7.30pm; entrance free), carved out of the volcanic rock and decorated with statues sculpted out of the rocks; among the religious sculptures are the figures of John Kennedy and Fidel Castro.

The historic centre of **Tropea** ⑰, which faces the sea from a sandy cliff partially transformed into houses, is ideal for an overnight stay. It has numerous restaurants, pizzerias and ice-cream shops, and irresistible white beaches. Make sure you climb to the **Church of the Madonna dell'Isola** (open daily 8am–7pm; donations welcome) on the cliff facing the Belvedere, and its magical Mediterranean Garden.

The big attraction of **Palmi** ⑱ is the Museo Civico di Etnografia e Folklore (open Mon–Fri, 8.30am–1.30pm, 3.30–5.30pm; entrance fee), the best of its kind in all of Italy. The museum is dedicated to agricultural and maritime life, to popular art and music, to magic and religion. The collection contains more than 3,000 items, including beautifully carved distaffs given to maids as love tokens, giant *papier-mâché* dolls, wooden cake- and bread-moulds and

BELOW:
Piazza cafe, Tropea.
RIGHT: Pizzo
shopping street.

implements to catch swordfish. The earthquake of 1908 destroyed the historic centre of Palmi, so after visiting the museum you might head for the Lido di Palmi, a roomy cove with fine sand.

The Costa Viola ends at **Scilla** ⑲, a charming fishing town whose spirit, dialect and traditions make it feel more Sicilian than Calabrian. The view of the Straits of Messina at sunset is stunning and the locals are pleased because the much-discussed plan to build a bridge across the Straits will finally come to fruition. Take a stroll down to Chianalea, and explore the unusual but picturesque fisherman's neighbourhood. Here the houses are built right by the water's edge, just as they are in Venice, and each one has two main doors – one to the sea and one to the street.

Seminara (about 5 km/3 miles inland off the SS18 at Monte Sant'Elìa) is famous for 'babbalutu' (multicoloured bottles in human shapes) and other ceramic objects that protect against the evil eye.

The regional capital

Reggio Calabria ⑳, with a population of more than 180,000, is the regional capital. It lies at the end of the motorway and is the main gateway to Sicily, only a 30-minute ferry trip away. Completely flattened by the terrible earthquake of 1908, Reggio, as the Italians call it, was rebuilt in the form of a modern urban grid, with spacious rectangular streets and tree-lined squares. Many rundown areas make Reggio little more than a transit harbour, but the famous Bronzi di Riace, the Greek bronzes which rank among the most important marine archaeological finds ever made (*see below*), are reason enough to make a stop.

These are found in the **Museo Archeologico Nazionale** (open 9am–8pm, closed the 1st and 3rd Mon of the month; entrance fee), which holds numerous prehistoric objects – among them the mould of a famous engraving of a figure of a bull, from the Grotta del Romito on the western Pollino, and a rich collection of

BELOW: pride of the Reggio museum.

THE RIACE MIRACLE

On 16 August 1972, a young man on holiday from Rome noticed a bronze arm emerge from the Riace Marina at exactly the same spot where the locals immersed the reliquary of the venerated Saints Cosma and Damiano to bring on rain. For the faithful, there was no doubt that this was a prodigious apparition of the two miraculous martyrs. The two Bronzes "of Riace" brought great fame to the Ionian coastal town. They were sent to Reggio for eight years of meticulous restoration and were not put on display until 1980, in Florence. The exhibition was a phenomenal success and the following year the Italian President, Sandro Pertini, had the bronzes publicly exhibited at the Quirinal Palace in Rome after which they returned to the Museo Nazionale di Reggio di Calabria.

These glorious, virile, 2-metre (7ft 7in) warriors even inspired a Milanese publisher to create a pornographic comic strip called *Sukia*.

During the first months of going on show in Reggio, many visitors tried to "feel" the statues and lifted babies to touch them, too. The atmosphere was similar to that of a Southern Italian religious festival, in which according to the pagan-influenced popular Catholicism of the South, young children participate in divinity through touch.

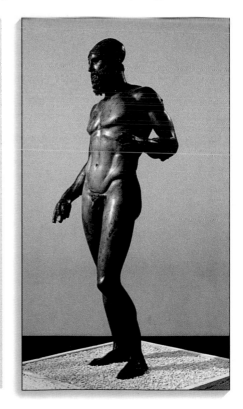

Interior of the Cattedrale dell'Assunta, Gerace.

BELOW: Gerace Cathedral, the largest in Calabria.

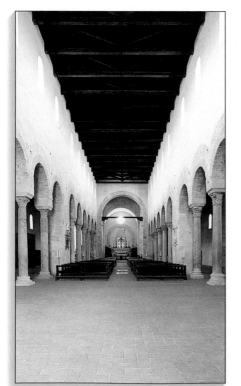

the art of Magna Graecia. Highlights include the *Cavaliere sostenuto da una sfinge* from the Marafioti Temple at Locri (5th century BC), a good example of the prevalence of terracotta in even large-scale Greek sculpture, and the marble group of the *Dioscuri* from an Ionic temple at Locri (5th to 4th century BC).

The Bronzi di Riace are kept in an anti-seismic room downstairs. The two warriors have still not been identified, but their solemn, well-formed figures – the ideal way to represent divinity in Greek culture – qualifies them as one of the great heroic representations of all time. Some important stylistic differences between the two statues suggest that they were made 20 years apart and were not part of the same sculpture group. The warrior who smiles and has his muscles contracted, known as *Statue A*, is dated to 460–450 BC; the warrior missing an eye *(Statue B)*, for its flexion at the thorax, appears to have been influenced by the works of Polyclites, and is therefore dated to 434–430 BC. The symmetry that renders them a "couple" is in reality the result of a restoration of the arms of *Statue B*, which was made long after the statue was sculpted, presumably by a Roman-era antiquarian. On the same floor is the *Testa del "filosofo"* (Head of a Philosopher), a *bona fide* portrait of old age in bronze. The work is difficult to date, because the portrait is a type of representation that remains far outside of Greek conception of figurative art.

The Romanesque Duomo has been restored and the walls and two towers of the 15th-century Angevin castle still look down on the city. Reggio's flora is another attraction. A sub-tropical microclimate allows a vigorous and spectacular growth of exotic plants in the city, in particular in the gardens of the **Villa Comunale** and on the internal side of the **Lungomare Matteotti**, which offers a splendid nighttime view of the Strait.

The Aspromonte

"The Aspromonte deserves its name," writes Norman Douglas with a reference to the Italian word *aspro* (sour, tough, rough) and a mountain that is difficult to live on, hard to cross, and given to natural disasters. Even today, those who live in this wild, isolated area between Reggio Calabria and Bova Marina, speak a dialect that traces back to the Greek colonists who settled here more than 2,000 years ago. *Grecanico,* full of guttural stops and more like the language of Homer and Plato than modern Greek, is incomprehensible to other Calabrians.

Frequent mudslides and floods, and the absence of electric power and basic services have made many of the *borghi* here uninhabitable, turning them into ghost towns and off-the-beaten-track tourist attractions, half-buried by vegetation that in springtime erupts in colours and scents.

In spite of the arid climate, under the dry Aspromonte flow the *fiumare*, subterranean veins of water that serve as the region's principle water source, feeding extensive coniferous forests and chestnut and beech woods, as well as the local Calabrians and their fields. The torrents that flow above ground in the spring dry up and leave white trails the rest of the year, until the first rains bring the return of the *fiumare* torrents, which tear down the earth and vegetation in their path. The largest is the silvery *fiumara* Amendolea, which crosses olive groves, vineyards and orchards of citrus, fruit and almonds. Hanging off the high walls of sandstone rocks that define its course, two towns capture the traveller's eye: **Gallicianò**, a genuine centre of Hellenistic art and traditions; and a few miles further up the Amendolea, the breathtaking, disquieting **Roghudi**, a sort of Calabrian Machu Pichu tormented by frequent mudslides (it is advisable to check road conditions before your trip).

More than 800 metres (2,600 ft) above sea level shines a little gem of the Aspromonte: **Bova ㉑** (follow the signs to Bova after passing Bova Marina on the SS106), the cultural capital of the towns in the area. In August, it hosts the most important ethnic music festival in the Mediterranean, the Paleariza, with a programme of events which include the display and sale of artisanal products and local gastronomic items, and various hiking activities.

To the northeast, nestled between the Aspromonte and the Serre, the well-preserved medieval town of **Gerace ㉒** (on the scenic SS111) throngs with tourists who come to see the Cattedrale dell'Assunta, the largest church in Calabria: 76 metres long and 26 metres wide (250 by 85 ft), with two majestic apses, a Byzantine crypt and three naves lined by 20 columns, some brought from ancient temples at Locri. The warm tones of the church facade are particularly striking at sunset. Consecrated in 1045, the Norman basilica has undergone several restorations and withstood earthquakes. "Had Gerace been in the north of Italy," said the travel writer H.V. Morton, "it would have been known to everybody and be as famous as San Gimignano." To fully appreciate the city's name, which comes from the Greek for sparrowhawk, climb to the ruins of the Norman castle with a gorgeous view of the Locride and the Ionian Sea.

Map on page 240

TIP

Contact Ugo Sergi, owner of the *agriturismo* Il Bergamotto, for information about donkey trekking in Aspromonte (tel and fax: 0965-727213).

BELOW: wild flowers in the Aspromonte.

TIP

The Marmarico
Waterfalls can be
reached on foot,
climbing from the
fiumara Stilaro coming
from Stilo towards
Bivongi along the
Sentiero del Brigante.
Alternatively, Vincenzo
Murace offers guided
tours of the falls and
San Giovanni Therestis
from Bivongi.
(Tel: 0347-1822574,
0964-731450.)

BELOW: 9th-century
Cattolico di Stilo.
RIGHT: San Giovanni
Theristis, Bivongi.

Sparviero (sparrowhawk in Italian) is also the name of the lovely trattoria on Via Luigi Cadorna 3 (tel: 0964-356826), where you can sample home-made pickles in olive oil, fresh pasta dishes, soups and *pesce stocco* (stock fish).

The Serre

Less charismatic than the Aspromonte, less alpine than the Pollino and the Sila, the **Serre** are two low mountain chains with extensive forests of fir, beech and alder in whose shade grow numerous kinds of wild mushrooms. A way into the Serre is via Stilo on the SS110, set at the foot of Mount Consolino.

Just outside the town is the **Cattolica di Stilo**, a minuscule 9th-century jewel that retains traces of frescoes. According to legend, the four Greek columns from nearby Kaulonia on which the vault rests were carried here by young maidens through divine intervention. The Corinthian capitals that came with the columns were turned upside down and used as pedestals to symbolise the triumph of Christianity over paganism.

Above Stilo is the hamlet of **Bivongi** ㉓, famous for a strong, sweet table wine and a good place from which to visit all the sights in the Serre, which takes a full day. To appreciate the lush woods of this part of Calabria, start with a gentle climb to the **Marmarico waterfalls**, at 90 metres (295 ft), the second highest in Italy; less than an hour away from the falls and only a couple of miles from Bivongi, the landscape and air temperature change abruptly: a sun-stricken terrain with an ocean of wild flowers in springtime, but no vegetation growing the rest of the year, surrounds the small 11th-century Byzantine-Norman **basilica of San Giovanni Theristis** (open 16 Sept–June: weekends and holidays 10am–noon, 3–5pm; July–15 Sept, daily 5pm–sunset; entrance fee).

Map on page 240

Situated on an isolated hill not unlike the Greek region of Mount Athos, where the monks who live here today originally came from, the little church was abandoned in the 17th century and then used as a shelter for shepherds and as a stall. It was rediscovered in 1912 and finally restored in 1994.

From the same period as San Giovanni Therestis, but very different for its humid, subterranean atmosphere, is the church of Santa Maria di Monte Stella in **Pazzano**, which lies just to the west of Bivongi on the ss110. This impressive grotto-sanctuary carved in the rock is about 10 metres (33 ft) beneath ground level.

Take the ss110 back toward Pazzano for a more in-depth visit to the Serre. In the summer this is a particularly pleasant drive under tunnels of shady fir-trees. Right in the middle of the Serre, at 800 metres (2,600 ft) above sea level, rises **Serra San Bruno ㉔**, whose origins are connected to the construction of the majestic **Certosa** in 1094. It was built by Bruno of Cologne (1030–1110), founder of the monastic order that built the first Carthusian monastery in France, near Grenoble at Chartreuse, a name that was subsequently corrupted into English as Charterhouse, and into Italian as Certosa. From the outside the Certosa di Serra San Bruno looks much like the French palace at Versailles. It certainly looks more like a small, fortified city than a church, but a Certosa is actually a cloistered convent where, according to St Bruno, "repose is united with work, and activity is without agitation or disturbance."

In 1994, the Museo della Certosa (open May–Oct: daily 9am–1pm, 3–8pm; Nov–Apr 9.30am–1pm, 3.30–6pm, closed Mon; entrance fee) was opened. With an attractive didactic display, the museum introduces the visitor to the secrets and regulations of the monastic life inside the Certosa.

The locals have a weakness for the meat of the "ghiro", a protected species of dormouse that is illegally trapped and sold at an extraordinary price.

BELOW: necropolis of white goods.

Classical sites along the Ionian shore

In the second half of the 7th century BC the Greek colonists of Locri founded Hipponion near what is today Vibo Valentia. Vibo is a modern city with a small historic centre and a worthwhile Museo Archeologico in the Norman-Swabian castle (open daily 9am–7pm; entrance fee). Just outside town, near the cemetery, are the ruins of the Greek perimeter walls.

Dense with seaside towns but in other parts deserted for long stretches, the ss106 that runs parallel to the Ionian Coast is a particularly relaxing drive. There are a number of classical sites en route, but few remains are visible.

One of the most prosperous colonies of Magna Graecia, **Locri Epizefiri** ㉕ (Lokroi Epizephyrioi) (open daily 9am–7.30pm; closed 1st and 3rd Mon of the month; shorter afternoon hours in winter; entrance fee; tel: 0964-390023) had 40,000 inhabitants. Founded in the late 8th century BC, it was surrounded by 7.5 km (5 miles) of walls, still partly visible, and built on a rigid city plan. The entrance to the excavations is through the Antiquarium in Contrada Marasà, which contains several remains found in the area, though the most important pieces have been transferred to the Museo Nazionale in Reggio. Of the four large temples, only a few fragments remain of the columns and capitals, while in the natural slope of the hill the profile of the theatre is visible.

Caulónia ㉖ (Kaulonia), about 50 km (30 miles) north of Locri, was an Achean colony that reached its maximum splendour in the 6th century BC. Remains by the beach near Punta Stilo include the foundation of a large Doric temple dedicated to Apollo, and ample stretches of the perimeter walls. Another 45 km (30 miles) further up, beyond the trendy coastal resorts of **Soverato** and **Copanello**, there is the entrance to the **Parco Archeologico di Roccelletta di Borgia** ㉗ (open daily 8am until 1 hour before sunset; entrance free) on the road to Borgia just after the junction with the ss106.

Skylletion once rose here, which according to some literary sources was founded by Ulysses, when he was shipwrecked on his return from the Trojan Wars. More likely the city was founded as a sub-colony of Kroton. In any case, the only wall structure excavated so far belongs to the Roman Scolacium, of which parts of the Forum and the theatre are visible. Inside the park are the imposing ruins of the Norman basilica of Santa Maria della Roccella; and the first electric olive oil mill in Calabria, which belonged to the old proprietors of Villa Mazza that today holds the Antiquarium.

From here, you have the option of continuing along the coast to Crotone or heading for the Sila right away. In the second case, you pass through **Catanzaro** ㉘, a windy hill city founded in the 10th century by the Byzantines. Earthquakes, war damage and building speculation have left the town pretty devoid of character. If you do make it there, the *passeggiata* takes place along the shopping area of Corso Mazzini, and there are several surviving baroque churches to visit (dell'Immacolata, del Rosario, dell'Osservanza). The most worthwhile site is the Villa Comunale, Catanzaro's public gardens planted on the edge of the ravine upon which the city rests. The fresh air and the 360-degree view of the Golfo di Squillace and of the Sila Piccola are impressive.

If you continue to Crotone, just before Capo Rizzuto, on a picturesque little island connected to the mainland by a narrow strip of land, rises **Le Castella**, one of nearly 150 Norman and Aragonese fortifications built along the Calabrian coast to confront the danger of the ferocious Turkish invasions. The restau-

BELOW: horses near Catanzaro.

rant Da Annibale (Via Annibale 3, Le Castella, tel: 0962-795428) is highly recommended, with a short but straight-from-the-fish-market menu and a delicious *pecorino* cheese (often served as dessert) made by a local producer.

Map on page 240

Old Greek base

The coastline from Soverato to Le Castella brims with fine hotels. **Crotone ㉙** was Kroton in the time of Pythagoras when it was the most important city in Europe. Nothing of the ancient city survives but a column of the temple of Hera Lacinia at Capo Colonna, a few remains in the Museo Archeologico (open daily 9am–7.30pm; closed 1st and 3rd Mon of the month; entrance fee), and the "KR" on the licence plates of the cars of the region ("CR", "CT" and "CN" had already been given to Cremona, Catania and Cuneo). The Spanish castle now stands on the site of the acropolis, but Kroton's "suburbs" stretched out to the sea. If it were possible to excavate under the nearby Montedison industrial complex, archaeologists believe that a large part of the Greek town would be brought to light.

Laid-back, modern Crotone is an agreeable place to base yourself if you are planning to spend some days on the surrounding beaches. It has a busy fishing port, and plans to improve and enlarge the marina are under way. Every May, Crotone hosts the Festival dell'Aurora, a schedule of concerts, conferences, and theatrical pieces focused on themes of Pythagoras and Magna Graecia.

The tourist office in Crotone has information about visiting the **Riserva Marina di Capo Rizzuto**, the largest marine reserve in Europe, which extends between Torre Brasolo and Capo Donato.

The richest and oldest Achean colony in Italy, **Sibari ㉚** (Sybaris) (Via Casoni near Sibari's lakes; open daily 9am–7.30pm; entrance fee; excavations open

A true Calabrese breakfast, typical of Reggio and the Ionian coast up to Crotone, features several round brioches soaked in a glass of iced almond milk.

BELOW: twisting over the hills near Catanzaro.

The Albanians

Of the many ethnic groups that live in Italy, the nearly 106,000 Arbëreshe (pronounced are-*bre*-shay) make up one of the most numerous: 52 communities are spread between the regions of Le Marche and Sicily, two-thirds of which are concentrated in the Calabrian provinces of Cosenza and Catanzaro. Their presence on the Italian peninsula dates from the Ottoman invasion of Arbëria (modern Albania) in the 15th century. Entire communities relocated to Southern Italy where the climate, mountainous terrain and abbeys of Byzantine rites resembled the land they had left behind.

The first significant settlements were in Apulia and date from 1461–2, when the ruling Aragonese rewarded the Albanian national hero Giorgio Castriota Skanderbeg with feudal land for the victories he led over the Angevins. Local leaders gave the Arbëreshe land that was untenable or had been devastated by war or natural disasters in exchange

for a share of their production. The isolated position of these feudal lands and the prohibition against building cities or fortresses guaranteed that these communities could not join together and pose a threat.

The fragmented population was held together by their Arbëreshe traditions, which have been tenaciously preserved, above all in the Pollino-Alto Ionian area. Of the adult population, 85 percent currently speak a language that descends from modern Albanian, and the first Arbëreshe grammar book has recently been published. In Calabria, many religious communities belong to the Eparchia (the Byzantine equivalent of a diocese) of Lungro, where an Eastern Orthodox liturgy was instituted in 1919 by Pope Benedict XV for Italo-Albanians.

A particularly interesting aspect of the Arbëreshe culture is the costume. The vibrant clothes worn by the women at weddings and on festive occasions have been compared to multicoloured mosaics. They are all hand-made in a variety of styles that vary according to location, economic and social circumstances. The most elaborate are made up of at least 20 pieces, and are striking for the regal form of the pleated or frilled gowns, for the striking colour combinations, for the starched lacework, and for the richness of embroidery, shot through with threads of gold.

The best time to appreciate them is during the *Vallje*, a folk dance through the streets of Civita performed on the Tuesday after Easter, which commemorates a victory against the Turks. Combining a complex choreography with improvised movements, the dancers imprison a member of the public, ideally a *lëtir* (Italian), who symbolically pays his own ransom at the bar while improvised expressions of praise and thanks are sung to him.

Costumes can also be seen during Easter week in the strongest centres of Albanian tradition (Civita, Lungro, Firmo, Acquaformosa, Eianina, Spezzano Albanese, Santa Caterina Albanese, San Demetrio Corone, San Cosmo Albanese, and Santa Sofia d'Epiro). Another occasion on which to witness the Arbëreshe spirit is the festival of Sant'Atanasio at Santa Sofia d' Epiro, on the first Sunday in May. ❑

LEFT: elaborate costumes are essential in maintaining the Arbëreshe tradition.

daily 9am until 1 hour before sunset; entrance free; tel: 0981-79391) was founded in 737 BC, and reached the height of its power in 530 BC. According to the historian Strabone, its dominion extended as far as the Tyrrhenian coast and included 25 cities. Sybaris was destroyed by its rival city Kroton in 510 BC, when even the course of the Crati river was diverted in order to flood any buildings still standing. A second Greek city, Thourioi, replaced by the Roman capital Copia, was built near the archaic Sybaris, and the excavations in the Parco del Cavallo brought to light the Roman phase. The Museo Archeologico Nazionale della Sibaritide features remains found all over the area.

Signs in both Italian and Albanian.

Looking down on the Neto Valley

Inland from Crotone is the *borgo* of **Santa Severina** ㉛, which was always fought over because of its strategic clifftop position, dominating the entire Neto valley. The town has a long history, having been founded by the Greeks; ruled by the Romans, Byzantines, and then taken by the Arabs in 840; liberated by the Venetians, reconquered by the Byzantines and then taken by the Normans; made a metropolis and archdiocese under the Angevins and Aragonese. All of this is written in the foundations, walls and bastions of the formidable Castello, named after Robert Guiscard, thought to have been built after 1073 on the remains of a Byzantine fortress, which itself had been built upon the ancient city's acropolis.

Re-opened to the public in 1998 after five years of thorough restoration, the enormous castello (10,000 sq. metres/108,000 sq. ft) has a museum of the history of Santa Severina. Across the piazza is an extremely well-presented Museo Diocesano. In addition to a free guided tour of the museum, descriptive panels explain everything one might want to know about liturgical vases and pastoral

BELOW: festival in an Albanian town.

letters (tickets are sold at the castle). The 13th-century cathedral is indefinitely closed for restoration, but the Byzantine baptistery is open. Note the design of Piazza del Campo, redone in the 1970s by Anselmi and Patanè, a rare example of a historic piazza restored with modern touches.

The Sila

The famous carpets with Oriental motifs made in the Sila by Albanians and Armenians can be found in Longobucco and San Giovanni in Fiore, respectively. At Tiriolo, the most beautiful multi-coloured pezzare (mats made from fabric remnants) in Calabria are produced.

Since the times of Ancient Greece, the Sila have been the most important of the mountains in Calabria. Norman Douglas described the Sila with words that exude respect: "The venerable, granite-like high plain had already risen when the proud Appenines still slept on the muddy ocean bed."

More like a huge plateau than a mountain range, the area – whose name is close to the Latin *silva* (thick wood) – was once covered with uninterrupted forests. Subdivided into the **Sila Grande**, **Sila Greca** to the north (in the province of Cosenza) and the **Sila Piccola** to the south (Catanzaro), they currently include about 13,000 hectares (32,125 acres, roughly 10 percent of the high plain) of the **Parco Nazionale della Sila**, but there are plans to expand the protected area six-fold. From a naturalist's point of view, the best place to be is the Sila Grande; the Sila Piccola and the Sila Greca offer several artistic itineraries. Known as the "robust green heart of the Mediterranean" for its pine forests that alternate with extensive prairies, pastures, lakes and cultivated valleys, this corner of the deep south is surprisingly suggestive of parts of Northern Europe, especially in winter.

BELOW: grazing the green Sila.

Despite its proximity to the sea and comparitively low elevation – which at its highest reaches 1,928 metres (6,325 ft) but averages around 1,000 metres (3,300 ft) – the Sila range enjoys an alpine climate, and offers cross-country

skiers Scandinavian-style trails that pass through thick forests and wide open plains. Bars that double as souvenir shops are usually well-stocked with guide books and maps of the park's trails, but the best tourist information office is at **Camigliatello Silano** ㉜ (30 km/19 miles east of Cosenza on the SS107).

Visitors "discovered" the Sila in the 1910s, which makes it Calabria's pioneer in the tourism industry. Although there is no lack of places to stay, reservations are necessary from November to February and in July and August. Each season brings a gift to the Sila: an explosion of wild flowers in spring; refreshing, cool breezes in summer; a riot of coloured leaves and wild mushrooms in autumn; snow and potatoes in winter. Since the 8th century, populations that follow the Greek-Byzantine rite have settled on the northern slope of the high plain, which is known as the **Sila Greca**.

Albanian town

The isolated **San Demetrio Corone** ㉝ is one of the oldest and most important Albanian towns in Italy, and well worth a detour from Sibari (about 40 minutes, this being the less tortuous inland road) for its Chiesa di Sant'Adriano and Collegio Italo-Albanese, a boarding school for secondary students which in the 19th century had an important role in the Calabrian cultural scene.

Today it is a junior high school, but it is still possible to visit the refectory and the sleeping quarters. Sant'Adriano is the rare example of an 11th- to 12th-century church that, notwithstanding heavy restoration work on the outside, has much of its interior intact. The marvellous Norman mosaic pavement represents geometric figures of serpents, birds and large felines; also worth noting are the frescoes of saints and the Virgin Mary from the second half of the 12th century.

Map on page 240

TIP

For horseback excursions in the Sila, contact the Club Trekking Val Calamo (Località San Zaccheria, Acrì, north of Camigliatello Silano).
Tel: 0984-941287 or 0984-401253.

BELOW: poppies in the Sila Grande.

Map
on page
240

*Calabria holds the
Italian title for the
region in which the
most Porcini
mushrooms are
collected. They grow
in the forests of the
Sila and of the Serre,
along with more than
3,000 other varieties
of mushroom.*

BELOW:
park rangers.
RIGHT: Sila's
Lake Ampollino.

Byzantine centre

Rossano 34, toward the Ionian Coast on the SS177 (best reached from the coastal road SS106) was one of the main Byzantine centres in the region. It retains precious examples of the numerous Byzantine-Norman churches in the area, above all the Abbazia del Patirion. Built at the beginning of the 12th century with a panoramic view, it features three apses decorated with yellow, black and orange stone, in accordance with Armenian-Syrian decorative schemes, and a floor mosaic with animal figures. The tiny church (*chiesetta*) of San Marco is perched at the top of town, while in the narrow alleyways behind the cathedral stands the Chiesetta della Panaghia (of the Holy Saint, or the Madonna) with remains of Byzantine frescoes. The cathedral, built in the Angevin period, is dedicated to Santa Maria Acheropita (the name refers to the 7th- or 8th-century fresco on a pilaster in the central nave supposedly painted by a non-human hand).

The city's name is associated with the famous ***Codex Purpureus Rossanensis***, one of the most ancient and beautiful Greek illuminated manuscripts of the Gospels, made up of 188 sheets of incredibly thin purplish parchment, with splendid full-page illustrations. It is thought to have been made in Palestine in the 6th century and brought to Calabria the following century and is displayed in the Museo Diocesano d'Arte Sacra, inside the Palazzo Arcivescovile (open daily 10am–1pm, 4–7pm; entrance fee).

The last of the primeval forest

The **Sila Grande** extends to the centre of the high plains and includes **San Giovanni in Fiore 35**, the Sila's biggest town, the tourist centres of **Camigliatello Silano** and **Lorica**, with ski runs at **Monte Curcio** and **Monte Botte Donato**, and

artificial lakes at **Ampollino**, **Arvo** and **Cecita**. The last 56 trees of the primeval forest of *pino larico* are near Camigliatello Silano in the **Riserva di Fallistro.** Called the "Giants of the Sila", the oldest among the pines are more than 2 metres (6 ft) in diameter and reach more than 40 metres (130 ft) in height. One of the most scenic roads is the **Strada delle Vette**, which goes from the Lago di Cecita to Monte Scuro, Monte Botte Donato (at 1,928 metres/6,325 ft the highest peak) and the Lago di Lorica. The best trail (9km/5 miles) – No 4 on the park's map – begins in the vicinity of Fossiata at the 5 km mark of the SS282 (direction Bocchigliero), east of the Lago di Cecita, near a picnic area.

To the south is the **Sila Piccola** where you'll find **Villaggio Mancuso 36**, one of the first purpose-built tourist villages in Italy. Founded in 1929, it still fills up with crowds of Italian visitors who prefer its self-catering, pretty wooden cottages among the trees to the fancier hotels at Racise, Ciricilla and Trepido (minor resorts located along the SS179). The baroque painter Mattia Preti (1613–99), known as Cavalier Calabrese, was born in the town of **Taverna 37** (on the SS109B between Catanzaro and Villaggio Mancuso). Although he lived elsewhere, Preti left a few dozen paintings to the town: the best are hung in the church of San Domenico, but there are others in the churches of San Martino and Santa Barbara, as well as the Museo Civico (open daily 8am–1pm; entrance fee). ❏

SICILY

Across the Straits of Messina lies an island that invented pasta,
embraced Moorish culture and had the original Volcano

To Goethe, Sicily was unique, "clear, authentic and complete".
Modern Sicily has its share of scruffy, one-horse towns, inscrutable
hill-top villages and industrial sprawl. As a touchstone, Tomasi
di Lampedusa's vision of his homeland is more perceptive: "a landscape which knows no mean between sensuous sag and hellish drought;
which is never petty, never ordinary, never relaxed."

Sicilian scenery is gruff but seldom graceless. The granary of the
ancient world contains citrus groves, pastureland and vineyards as
well as endless wheatfields. Trapani's weird lagoons and salt pans
seemingly float in the unrelenting heat. Away from the accessible
coast, an intriguing volcanic hinterland unfolds in mountains, gorges
and the scars of abandoned sulphur mines. Like a dragon in its lair,
Etna's smoking breath threatens vineyards and lava-stone castles.

Still, first impressions are safer. After breakfasting in Taormina,
Cardinal Newman found it "the nearest thing to paradise". To most
tourists, Taormina is still the acceptable face of Sicily, a place of
undiluted pleasure where culture shock is absent.

Outside this cosmopolitan pocket, the adventure begins. Sicily is
not what it seems. The markets and inlaid street patterns of Mazara
del Vallo and Sciacca would not be out of place in Morocco. The
perfect medieval town of Erice is a shrine to pagan goddesses, Astarte
and Venus. In Sicily, all periods are petrified for posterity. The jewel
box of Palermo's Cappella Palatina is a fusion of Arab and Christian.
The Arab west of the island is overladen with Spanish finery while
the Greek east is truest to the pure Classical spirit.

Despite a patina of neglect, Sicily's architectural riches gleam.
The island of Mozia retains its Phoenician port and sacrificial burial
grounds. Built to "intimidate the gods or scare human beings", the
Greek temples of Agrigento, Segesta and Selinunte are a divine
reflection of Magna Graecia. The Romans may not have matched
these lovely sites but left the vivid mosaics of Piazza Armerina as an
imprint of a sated but sophisticated culture.

Cefalù and Monreale cathedrals are a tribute to Byzantine craftsmanship, Arab imagery and Norman scale. Elsewhere, Moorish
palaces, Swabian castles and domed churches are interpretations of
this inspired Sicilian hybrid. Baroque, the island's last great gasp,
explodes in the theatrical fireworks of Noto and Catania. As the cultural capital of the ancient world, Siracusa presides over Greek ruins
and Christian catacombs with a luminous grace all its own. Palermo,
its psychic opposite, radiates sultry splendour. ❑

PRECEDING PAGE: the ferry from Sicily crossing the Straits of Messina
approaching Reggio di Calabria.
LEFT: soaking up the sun in Terrasini.

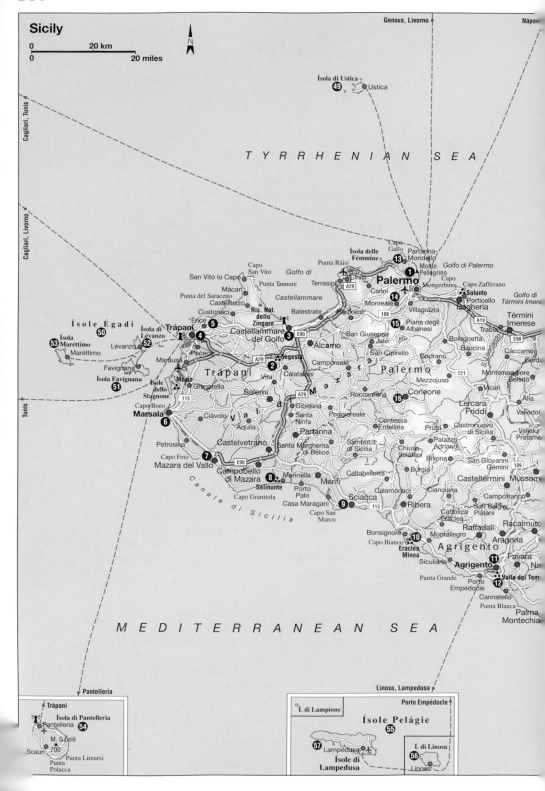

Sicily

0   20 km
0   20 miles

PALERMO

*Palermo's history is like the persimmon: exotic, ripe, decadent,
and extremely difficult to peel. It's a question of scooping
out the fruit and savouring the sensation*

Map
on page
272

Palermo is both an essay in chaos and a sensuous spice box of a city.
Domenico Dolce, one half of the Dolce & Gabbana design duo, is passionate about the spirit of his home town: "Don't go with an itinerary, go
with an open heart." This is sound advice for a city that represents an assault on
the senses rather than a sweet seduction. Sicily's capital is a synthesis of bomb-
sites and beauty, with sumptuous Arab-Norman and baroque splendour interspersed with an intriguing Moorish muddle.

If Palermo is sweet, it is the cloying oriental sweetness of a Sicilian dessert,
and if it is sour, it is with sorrow at the rape perpetrated on the city by ignorant
political administrators and corrupt speculators. It is sentiments such as these
that provoked Gesualdo Bufalino, the Sicilian novelist, to describe his homeland
as a place of "light and lamentation".

A Phoenician colony existed from the 8th century BC but not a stone of Punic
Palermo remains, nor its original name. The Greeks called the city *Panormos*
(all-haven) for its harbours stretching along a bay known as the Conca d'Oro
(the golden shell) because of its glittering citrus groves. As a Roman province,
Palermo has revealed scant Classical remains compared with its cultured east-
coast rivals. Under Byzantine rule, the city developed its principal poles of
power: a Byzantine church on the site of the future
cathedral; and the Palazzo dei Normanni, the palatial
home of the city rulers, later the royal palace and currently the seat of the Regional Government.

LEFT: olive stall in
Vucciria market.
BELOW: Palermo
panorama.

However, it was only with the Arab colonisation
that Palermo prospered and came into its own. The
city was home to Jewish and Lombard merchants,
Greek craftsmen and builders, Turkish and Syrian artisans, Persian artists, Berber and Negro slaves. It was
the most multiracial population in Europe, and out of
such diversity was born the complex city culture that
knows many masters. The medieval city welcomed
300 mosques and was ringed by pleasure palaces such
as La Ziza, and on the outskirts were palms, vineyards, citrus groves, silk farms and rice paddies. Arab-
Norman rule coincided with Palermo's golden age,
one of expansion, enlightenment, prosperity and cultural riches. Citizens acquired a love for Arab ornamentation and excess that has never left them.

Decay and renewal

Under Spanish rule, the Arab-Norman city was
remodelled along grand arteries but, behind the
baroque facades, today's historic centre is a maze of
Moorish alleys, confirming the city's deeper affini-
ties. In 1943, Allied bombs destroyed the port and
much of the centre, leaving it with gaping holes half-
filled with crumbling *palazzi*. The Mafia stepped into

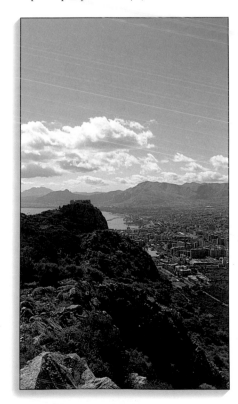

Racy rider: a motor scooter with class.

the void, later accepting funds from the European Union to rebuild the devastated city. Instead, corrupt politicians in league with *mafiosi* contractors siphoned off the funds for their own illicit ends. One key culprit was Salvo Lima, the political power-broker for the Mafia in Rome. When he was gunned down in Palermo in 1992, the balance of power shifted. Following the Mafia murders of the high-profile public prosecutors Falcone and Borsellino, Palermitans experienced a rare wave of revulsion that provoked citizens to public protest.

After a period of political instability, a new feeling of hope began to permeate the air in 1993 when local boy, Leoluca Orlando, became the anti-corruption city mayor. Still more significant is the burgeoning sense of civic responsibility, especially among the young. This has been formalised into the creation of countless voluntary associations in which disadvantaged, unemployed or underemployed citizens successfully manage churches, theatres or cultural centres. Most churches are now run by associations whose members act as unpaid guides. Orlando also saw it as his mission to beautify the city, from planting

Map on page 272

palms to restoring palaces. The gentrification of Palermo is a long way off but restoration is underway, with long-abandoned baroque palaces converted into museums. Increased civic pride has also led to greater public safety and given a boost to the notoriously low-key Palermitan nightlife, with more bars in the historic centre staying open in the evening.

Palermo is an incredible jumble of periods and styles. No map does justice to the city's confusion. Given that the Spanish grid system is subverted by Moorish blind alleys, squalid bomb sites and rampant urbanisation on the outskirts, it is surprising that the city is so legible.

On the junction of Via Maqueda and **Corso Vittorio Emanuele**, the pollution-blackened crossroads of **Quattro Canti** divides Palermo into rival quarters, each with its own centre. Every quarter reveals a picturesque clutter of decaying mansions, raucous markets and sombre baroque churches with luminous interiors. However, the Kasr represents the public face of historic Palermo. This off-centre heart of the city is the great Arab-Norman nucleus, and contains both the city seats of power, temporal and spiritual.

The Castle and Cathedral quarter

Named after the Arabic for castle, the **Kasr quarter** contains the cathedral and the royal palace, once the upper castle. Access to the major public monuments is along the time-blackened **Corso V. Emanuele** ❶, the main thoroughfare through the historic centre. Known as the Cassaro, this former Phoenician road was remodelled in 1500 and graced by grandiose city gates at either end. Under the Spanish, the street also acquired a series of patrician palaces which line the route to the cathedral, and are gradually being restored.

The **Cattedrale** ❷ (open daily 7am–7pm) is a Sicilian hybrid: mentally erase the cathedral's incongruous dome and focus on the tawny stone, sculpted doorway and crenellated Moorish decoration of the façade. A lovely Catalan-Gothic portico opens onto a peppermint and grey interior, a cool neoclassical shell and the wanly neutered setting for the **royal Norman tombs**. Borne by crouching lions, the tombs are made of rare pink porphyry and sculpted by Arab masters, the only craftsmen who knew the technique in Norman times. Behind the Duomo emerges the striking geometric design of the Arab-Norman apses, with black-and-white inlays.

Palazzo dei Normanni ❸ (open Mon–Fri and Sat 9am–noon; entrance fee) stands on Piazza Ind2pendenza, at the landward end of the Cassaro. Now the seat of the Sicilian Parliament, this eclectic royal palace has been the Sicilian centre of power since Byzantine times. An 18th-century carriage drive leads to the Arab-Norman palace that once rivalled Cairo and Cordoba. The cube-shaped palace has walled gardens overgrown with royal orchids, papyrus, hanging banyan trees, *ficus belgamine* and kapoks. The African kapoks store water in barrel-like trunks and are a favourite with monkeys, a reminder that the Arab emirs bred an exotic menagerie here. The most precious trees are the *cicas*, dwarf palms whose leaves take 50 years to grow.

Parco d'Orleans (open 9am–1pm, 3–5pm), the lush gardens behind the Palazzo dei Normanni, belong to the Sicilian President but a sign specifies that only adults accompanied by children can enter. Shrewd ragamuffins offer their services as "borrowed" kids for the duration of the walk.

BELOW: balcony scene.

Leading off a loggia is the **Cappella Palatina** (open weekdays 9–11.45am, 3–4.45pm; entrance fee*)*, the royal chapel designed by Roger II in 1130 and representing the fusion of Byzantine, Arab, Norman and Sicilian civilisations. This jewel of Arab-Norman art is Palermo's greatest sight. The gold mosaics recall the Crusades when Palermo was a port of departure for the Holy Land. In the penumbra, the mystic **Byzantine mosaics** slowly emerge. Christ Pantocrator occupies the cupola, surrounded by archangels and saints. On the walls are sumptuous Biblical scenes framed by Islamic decorative devices with the texture of tapestry. Individual masterpieces include the delicate marble paschal candlestick, Corinthian capitals and an inlaid Cosmati marble pulpit. The gold and porphyry throne occupies a dais below a mosaic pointedly entrusting the Norman kings with the Holy Law. The ceiling is unique in a Christian church, a composition of ineffable Oriental splendour. The Normans asked Arab craftsmen to portray paradise and they maliciously obliged with naked maidens, which the Normans prudishly clothed and crowned with haloes. Still, the roof remains a paradise of the senses, where Persian octagonal stars meet Arabian stalactites.

On the floor above is the (rarely open) gilded **Parliamentary Chamber** (1350) and **Royal Apartments**, which reflect the taste of past viceroys. From the balconies stretch views of the Conca d'Oro, the scenic shell surrounded by lemon groves, the port and hills. The finest Moorish rooms depict a profane vision of paradise; the **Sala dei Venti** is open to the winds; and the naturalistic **Sala di Re Ruggero** is frescoed with hunting scenes.

Nearby, just beyond the palm-ringed Piazza della Vittoria, stands the romantic red-domed **San Giovanni degli Eremiti** ❹ (open Mon–Sat, 9am–6.30pm, Sun morning only). Now the symbol of Palermo, this Byzantine basilica was

TIP

Motobeeps, covered versions of a motorbike-taxi, take visitors quickly, safely and cheaply around the city (freephone: 091-800 445445). Drivers also have basic training as guides.

BELOW:
Palermo Cathedral.

converted into a Benedictine abbey and a mosque. Byzantine foundations cede to Arab squinches, filigree windows and Norman cloisters overgrown with jasmine. The shape of the early mosque is still visible, as are stiff frescoes and Muslim arches. The tiny garden is the most enchanting feature, a riot of acanthus and mimosa, crab apple and pomegranate.

South of the Corso Vittorio Emanuele and nudging Via Maqueda is the ramshackle **Albergheria** quarter, once inhabited by Norman court officials and rich Pisan merchants. Approached along **Via Albergheria ❺**, the area is either a squalid slum or an evocation of the old hugger-mugger of backstreet life. Although tottering houses propped up by rotten planks are home to illegal immigrants, a dynamic sense of community prevails over scenes of urban decay. An excellent community tour (Albergheria Viaggi, tel: 091-218344), led by young volunteers, shows visitors the underside of the area, from a visit to a carob factory to a workshop specialising in painting carts. A visit often ends with the sampling of street snacks in **Ballarò market ❻**, centred on Piazza Carmine, the noisy haunt of artisans and students, housewives and bootleggers. Currently Palermo's liveliest market, Ballarò is authentic and sprawling, with the hurly-burly of exotic food outlets clashing with the second-hand clothes stalls by **Casa Professa ❼** (open daily, 7.30–11.30am), also known as Il Gesù. The baroque marble interior of this cloistered Jesuitical church teems with tritons and cherubs.

Around the Quattro Canti

From Casa Professa, the quaint Via Ponticello leads to Via Maqueda and **Piazza Pretoria ❽**, another showpiece. This baroque square is where the city puts on its best public face. It was once nicknamed Piazza Vergogna (Square of Shame)

Map
on page
272

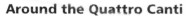

TIP

Unless your hotel has a car park, avoid using a car in Palermo – it will only be a handicap and there will be no redress if it disappears. One of the few fairly safe places to leave a car is with an attendant in a peaked cap in Piazza Marina or Piazza Bellini.

BELOW: the basilica of Giovanni degli Eremiti.

A cast of heroes in the traditional puppet theatre.

BELOW: Foro Italico during the feast of Santa Rosalia.

after its saucy nude statues cavorting in the fountain. Amid uproar, this scandalous Mannerist fountain was brought here from Florence. The vast circular basin is peopled by tritons, nymphs and river gods. Reputedly, the local nuns chopped off the noses of the nude gods but stopped short of castration. Adjoining the square is the **Palazzo delle Aquile** (open daily, 9am–8pm), the mayor's over-restored Gothic city hall, and the towering presence of **San Giuseppe Teatini** (open Mon–Fri, 8am–noon, 6–8pm), a theatrically baroque church.

On the adjoining Piazza Bellini stand two delightful domed Arab-Norman churches. **La Martorana** ❾ (open Mon–Sat, 9.30am–1pm, 3.30–7pm; Sun 9.30am–1pm) was founded in 1143 by George of Antioch, King Roger's Syrian emir and admiral. Although raised in the Orthodox faith, the emir planned La Martorana as a mosque. To complicate matters, he chose Greek Byzantine craftsmen to make the splendid mosaics. The space interweaves Byzantine and Muslim iconography: the Pantocrator is present but so is the figure "8", the Arabic number of perfection. The church featured as a backdrop in the film *The Talented Mr Ripley*, which was partly shot in Sicily. Next-door, the triple-domed church of **San Cataldo** ❿ (open Mon–Fri, 9am–3.30pm, Sat–Sun 9am–1pm) is one of the last sacred buildings built in the Arab-Norman style. The Oriental impression is confirmed by the brooding Syrian interior. If at first this exquisite space seems sparse, it is only as a reaction to the gilded La Martorana.

There is no escape from the **Quattro Canti** ⓫, the notional centre of old Palermo. Known as "*il teatro*" (the city theatre), it offers a cross-section of Palermitan baroque, Arab-Norman splendour and medieval muddle. Behind their forbidding Spanish facades, the four concave-shaped screens of the city conceal chaotic districts, of which La Kalsa is the most subject to restoration.

Seawards to La Kalsa quarter

Stretching seawards from Via Maqueda to Foro Italica and the sea is **La Kalsa**, a partly restored quarter with fine museums, austere Catalan-Gothic *palazzi* and vibrant streetlife. Meaning "pure" or "chosen" in Arabic, La Kalsa is no longer ironic given that Mother Teresa's mission settled off the bomb-struck **Piazza Magione** ⓬. Wealthy Palermitans were horrified at being lectured by an Albanian nun, even one incarnating sainthood. Her message was that since Palermo was as poor as the Third World, charity should begin at home. The message seems to have struck a chord since the area is now being regenerated, resulting in a greater sense of safety, not to mention the cheerful materialism heralded by new bars and scaffolding-clad palaces close to the gentrified Piazza Marina. Moorish filigree windows and blind arcading announce the ancestry of **La Magione**, an imposing Cistercian church with a plain Arab-Norman interior.

Seawards, in the honeycomb heart of the Kalsa, awaits **Lo Spasimo** ⓭ (open daily, 8am–midnight), an open-air cultural entertainment complex set in an atmospheric Catalan-Gothic monastery. Concerts are held in the cloisters and the roofless church, which, given a sultry night and swaying palms, creates a romantic, Moorish atmosphere. With the recent restoration, not only was this early 16th-century monastery rescued from decay, but one of the most deprived districts received a huge boost. Run passionately yet professionally by amateurs, this flagship project employs reformed addicts, alcoholics or offenders. The project also seeks to lead local citizens and children away from the *pensar mafioso*, the mafia path. It provides a healthy overlap between bourgeois Palermitans, who attend the jazz concerts and art exhibitions, and an alienated underclass who can see the benefits in terms of neighbourhood improvements, greater security, employment and even culture.

Via della Vetreria leads to **Via Alloro**, the city's patrician centre in the Middle Ages, and **Palazzo Abatellis** ⓮, Sicily's most beguiling art collection (open Mon, Wed, Fri–Sun 9am–1.30pm, Tues and Thur 9am–1.30pm, 3–7.30pm). Housed in a Catalan-Gothic mansion, the treasures are matched by a charming setting. Off a Renaissance courtyard lie Byzantine mosaics, Neapolitan Madonnas, and a geometric Moorish door. Other highlights are a serene bust of Eleanor of Aragon and a haunting da Messina *Annunciation*. The masterpiece is the powerful *Triumph of Death*, a frescoed 15th-century *danse macabre* in which a skeletal grim reaper cuts a swathe through the nobles' earthly pleasures.

Piazza Marina ⓯ was a swamp until drained by the Arabs and used as their first citadel. Since then, the square has witnessed the shame and glory of city history. **Palazzo Chiaramonte** ⓰, a Catalan-Gothic fortress, was a feudal stronghold before becoming the seat of the Inquisition in 1598. Carved on the grim prison walls inside is a poignant plea for *pane, pazienza e tempo* (bread, patience and time). Outside, heretics and dissenters were burned. Commonly known as the Steri, the mansion belonged to the Spanish viceroys before falling into the hands of Palermo University, who discourage visitors. As one of the few gentrified squares in the old quarter, Piazza Marina

Map on page 272

TIP

In this area, a collection of historic homes are newly opened to the public, many still lived in by the original families. Request a list of the *"dimore storiche"* from the Palermo tourist office.

BELOW: downtown Palermo.

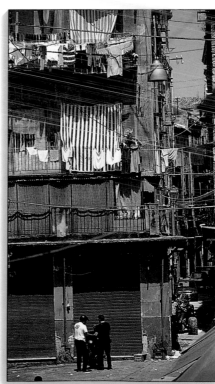

Sample such Palermitan savoury snacks as deep-fried rice balls (*arancini*), chick-pea fritters, or broccoli and artichokes deep-fried in batter, followed by prickly pears, marzipan sweets, water ices or watermelon jelly scented with jasmine. Il Golosone, on Piazza Castelnuovo, is a simple yet good place for Sicilian fast food.

BELOW: Villa Giulia.

is proud of its banyan trees and shady park, around which bric-a-brac traders vie with waiters in their efforts to drum up trade.

In neighbouring Via Merlo is **Palazzo Mirto** ⑰, containing a delightful period museum (open Mon–Fri 9am–6.30pm, Sat–Sun 9am–1pm; entrance fee). The mansion is a testament to the eclectic tastes of Palermitan nobles in the 18th century, with chinoiserie and Empire style clashing with neo-Gothic flourishes. Close by is **San Francesco d'Assisi** (open daily 7am–noon, 4.30–6pm), Palermo's loveliest Gothic church, its austerity softened by a delicate rose window. Opposite is **Antica Focacceria**, a famous Palermitan inn serving rustic snacks from *panini di panelle*, fried chick pea squares to *pani cu' la meusa*, greasy boiled beef spleen.

The **Marina**, Palermo's grand seafront, was, until the *Belle Epoque*, a public parade and a chance for louche encounters. Now known as **Foro Italico** ⑱, the stark waterfront is home to a scruffy funfair overlooked by the newly-restored **Palazzo Butera**, eulogised by Goethe but bombed by the Allies. Beyond is **Villa Giulia**, picturesque formal gardens, and the adjoining **Orto Botánico** ⑲ (Botanical Gardens) (open Mon–Fri, 9am–5pm; entrance fee), dotted with pavilions, sphinx statues and a lily pond.

Vucciria quarter

This dilapidated market district is crammed between La Cala harbour, Corso Vittorio Emanuele and Via Roma. The name is a corruption of the French *boucherie*, thanks to the quantity of flesh on sale in the traditional **Vucciria market** ⑳. The stalls straggle along alleys from Via Roma to **San Domenico** (open daily 9–11am), a vapid baroque church with an impressive facade. Colourful alleys display capers and pine nuts, spices and squirming octopus, skewered giblets and bootleg tapes, and are charming as night falls and the red awnings are illuminated. Sustenance is necessary, since between San Domenico and the port is devastation. However, the ascendancy of Ballarò market means that the Vucciria is truly bustling only on Saturday.

Via Bambinai, a former doll-makers' street, has stayed close to its roots: shops sell votive offerings and Christmas crib figures. The street has a baroque jewel in **Oratorio del Rosario di San Domenico** ㉑ (open Mon–Fri, 9am–1pm, 3–5.30pm, Sat 9am–1pm), a theatrical Serpotta chapel, where *putti* play cellos amid sea-shells, eagles and allegorical exotica. Just around the corner, on Via Valverde, lies an equally celebrated oratory, **Oratorio di Santa Zita** ㉒ (open Tues–Fri 9am-1pm, 3-6pm, Sat 9am–1pm), reached through lush gardens. The noble oratories were used as social clubs and centres for charitable works, as well as for displays of status. Here, Serpotta's ravishing stucco-work depicts the intercession of the Virgin in the *Battle of Lepanto*, with all boats exquisitely differentiated.

Beyond the chapel to the south is **La Cala** ㉓, the scruffy portside. Fishing boats bob against a backdrop of bombed *palazzi* whose cellars house immigrant families. However, regeneration is gradually seeping into this semi-derelict quarter, with the restoration of bomb-damaged churches such as **Santa Maria della Catena** (open Mon–Fri, 9am–1pm), a

Catalan-Gothic church, named after the medieval chain that once shut off the port. The new maritime museum is an attempt to reconnect this inward-looking city with the sea. **Museo del Mare ㉔** (open daily, 9.30am–noon; entrance fee), set in the former arsenal on Via Cristoforo Colombo, is a maritime showcase with a terrace and sea views.

From the port, retrace your steps to Via Roma and take Via Bara to Piazza Olivella, part of a charming artisans' quarter of puppet-makers, *pasticcerie* and *trattorie*. The baroque **Olivella** church adjoins the **Museo Archeologico ㉕** (open Mon–Fri 9am–1pm, 3–7pm; Sat 9am–1pm; entrance fee), the essence of classical Sicily encased in a late-Renaissance monastery. The inner courtyard has a tangle of lush vegetation and a lily pond, a showcase for inscrutable Egyptian and Greek statuary or Phoenician sarcophagi. The superb **Sala di Selinunte** displays one of the main friezes from the classical site of Selinunte *(see page 285)*. In stylised friezes, Athena protects Perseus as he battles with Medusa, Hercules slays dwarves and Zeus marries a frosty Hera.

Belle Epoque and modern quarter

After the labyrinthine alleys of old Palermo, the grid system of the modern city comes as a shock. From the Museo Archeologico, Via Orologio leads to the well-restored **Teatro Massimo ㉖** (guided visits 9am–1pm; tel: 091-334246), the city opera house. Designed by the Palermitan Basile in 1864, this is one of the largest opera houses in Europe. The monumental building was designed in eclectic rather than neoclassical style: the portico, graced by Corinthian columns, is of clear Greek inspiration while the cylindrical shape of the building and the cupola itself owe more to Roman designs. The interior is equally eclectic, with

Map on page 272

Consider a drink in the faded grandeur of Hotel des Palmes on Via Roma. Wagner composed part of Parsifal in a gilded salon here in 1882, while the wartime Mafia boss Lucky Luciano held court in the dining room.

BELOW: Teatro Massimo, the city opera house.

Viale della Libertà district is often thought to be for rich residents only, but like all other areas it is socially mixed. Noble families retain their city palazzi and live cheek by jowl with all classes.

a grandiose baroque staircase contrasting with floral, decidedly Art Nouveau decor. During its recent lengthy closure, the opera house re-opened only briefly, for the shooting of the climactic scene in Coppola's *The Godfather, Part III*.

North of Via Cavour lies the bland Viale della Libertà and chic hotels, a neo-classical district containing remnants of Palermo's late flowering *Belle Epoque*. The smart shopping street of **Via della Libertà ㉗** was once studded with Art Nouveau villas, but most have been demolished or disappeared in fires linked to fraudulent insurance claims. The northern end leads to attractive gardens but fashionable bars and the sophistication of the evening *passeggiata* cannot conceal the fact that style has deserted the quarter. Even so, the landscaped **Giardino Inglese** is a good place for a romantic stroll while **Piazza Castelnuovo**, at the southern end, is the frenetic early evening meeting-place for Palermitan youth. Further afield, Palermo offers an eclectic mixture of vibrant seaside suburbs, citrus groves and macabre catacombs *(see panel below).*

The Moorish palace

In Norman times, palaces encircled the city "like gold coins around the neck of a bosomy girl". The vivid description given by the Arab poet, Ibn Jubayr, conjures up the pleasure dome of **La Ziza ㉘**, one of the most impressive legacies of Moorish Palermo. An Arab arch leads to a palace (open Mon–Sat, 9am–6.30pm, Sun 9am–1pm; entrance fee) built on the site of a Roman villa, to exploit the existing aqueduct. Fed by canals, the lake was paved with marine-inspired mosaics. La Ziza's most charming spot is the vestibule, adorned by honeycomb vaults, a Saracenic fountain and a glorious mosaic frieze of peacocks and huntsmen. In this breezy chamber, the emir and his court listened to

BELOW: resident of the catacombs.

THE UNDERGROUND CITY

For the ghoulish, the grim catacombs of Palermo represent an unnerving vision of the city. **The Convento dei Cappuccini** (open daily, 9am–noon, 3–5pm) lies on Via Cappuccini, midway between La Cuba and La Ziza (*see above*). In macabre Sicilian style, superior corpses were mummified here from the 16th century until 1920. In death, the clergy, nobles and bourgeoisie opted for posterity rather than the communal trench: the corpses were displayed according to their sex, status and profession, all dressed in their Sunday best. In these galleries, embalmers have stored more than 8,000 moth-eaten mummies. Fascinating, but not for the faint-hearted.

For a bizarre visit to underground Palermo and the 10th-century **water channels** created by the Arabs, non-claustrophobic visitors should go on a morning trip with expert pot-holers, organised by the Sotto-Sopra group (tel: 091-6523919). No experience is necessary and all equipment is provided, but take a change of clothes. Visitors are lowered down a deep well-shaft into a waist-high water channel, and follow the guides in wading through the winding channels that once provided irrigation for Arab palaces and farmsteads.

the lapping of water. The interior, now a museum of Arab culture, is a mixed success. Critics claim that clumsy restoration has ruined the Arab lines and replaced filigree windows with heavy-framed versions.

Cantieri Culturali alla Ziza (Via P. Gili, adjoining Palazzo La Ziza) is Palermo's main cultural complex in the north of the city. Now a trendy venue for concerts and exhibitions, this former industrial site began life as Art Nouveau furniture workshops before being converted into a munitions factory.

On Corso Calatafimi not far from La Ziza is **La Cuba** ㉙ (open Mon–Fri, 9am–1pm, 3–6.30pm), the final piece of the Moorish jigsaw. Once an Arab pleasure pavilion, it is now a roofless ruin marooned in an army barracks. In Arab times, this quaint pavilion was set on a lovely artificial lake within the luxuriant grounds of La Ziza. For those with no taste for the macabre, the return to Palermo is via Porta Nuova, a Spanish gateway decorated with turbaned Moorish giants. For the ghoulish, the grim catacombs represent an unnerving vision of the city (*see panel on facing page*).

Paddling and the Patron Saint

Palermo's main beach lies to the north of the city at **Mondello**. The sandy seaside here was appreciated by the Bourbons but the pier is a northern European confection, an Art-Nouveau pleasure palace created by a Belgian entrepreneur.

The patron saint of Palermo is enshrined in the **Santuaria di Santa Rosalia** in a mountain grotto above the city on San Pellegrino *(see page 288)*. It was built in 1624 after a dreamer had been instructed to find her relics and wave them three times around the city to rid Palermo of the plague. Her saint's day, in July, is a six-day extravaganza, when Palermo barely sleeps. ❑

"The city awaits us... early persimmons glowing orange amidst pyramids of bright green cauliflowers, smoking tripods of chestnuts roasting at the curbstones, bloodshed and decaying beauty."
– FROM *IN PERSPHONE'S ISLAND* BY MARY SIMETI

BELOW: meeting on the theatre steps.

WEST AND CENTRAL SICILY

*Monreale is the Arab-Norman achievement,
Selinunte and Agrigento are the splendours of Greece,
while inland Corleone is associated with the Mafia*

Map
on page
268

Western Sicily is the most seafaring and African part of the island. Poignant Mozia is Sicily's greatest Punic site while the colourful fishing port of Mazara del Vallo could be in Tunisia. Trapani province, in particular, feels tangibly Phoenician and African yet, paradoxically, produces alcoholic Marsala in the heart of Muslim Sicily. The cultural cavalcade is matched by a natural landscape of salt pans, vineyards, woods and coastal nature reserves. Despite such resources, the region suffers from degradation, pervasive criminal undercurrents, and a torpor conditioned by centuries of failure. This malaise is most clear in the hinterland, exacerbated by earthquake damage in the centre of the region and the economic collapse of the sulphur-mining industry in the south. The western hinterland is far less promising than the glittering coast.

Easily reached from **Palermo ❶** along the Palermo-Trapani motorway, **Segesta ❷** (open daily, 9am–7pm; entrance fee) lies in rolling countryside and is one of the most romantic classical sites. Founded by the Elymians, whose language has yet to be transcribed, the settlers claimed to be refugees who escaped the Fall of Troy in Asia Minor and the Trojan link would explain their hatred of the Greeks, an enmity which led to their role in the razing of nearby Selinunte. Segesta was sacked by Siracusa in 307 BC. Crowning a low hill is the roofless Doric temple. Linked by a minibus service, the Greek theatre on the facing hill has an air of poetic desolation and stages Greek tragedies in summer.

LEFT: the romantic site of Segesta.
BELOW: steep street in Castellammare del Golfo.

The coast to San Vito Lo Capo

The coastal road from Palermo, runs west to **Castellammare del Golfo ❸**, an overgrown fishing village which has panoramic views across the gulf. From the port, a boat ferries visitors to the scenic **Lo Zingaro nature reserve** *(see page 284)*. On the headland lies **San Vito lo Capo**, a burgeoning resort noted for its fine coast, its sandy beaches and lively fish restaurants.

Trapani ❹, the provincial capital, remains an important port and an embarkation point for the Egadi Islands and Pantelleria *(see pages 316–19)*. Apparently Cronos, one of the Titans, castrated his father Uranus with a sickle and threw his genitals into the sea at Cape Drepanum. The result is modern-day Trapani. The Arab influence is felt in architecture, attitudes and cuisine.

Trapani's traditional industries of coral, tuna fishing and salt linger on. Apart from a fish and fruit market on Piazza Mercato del Pesce, Trapani offers a graceful Gothic church, a fine arts-and-crafts collection, and a cluster of dilapidated baroque *palazzi*. About 3 km (2 miles) north of the old town is Santuario dell'Annunziata (open daily 7.30am–noon, 4–7pm; entrance fee), Trapani's main monument. Museo

Fishermen's house in the provincial capital of Trapani.

Nazionale Pepoli (open daily 9am–2pm; entrance fee), the city's eclectic museum, is in the adjoining convent.

Erice ❺, a medieval walled town just north, makes a much more enticing base than Trapani for exploring the African coast. In spring, the winding road climbs past views of acacia, wild gladioli and waxy lemon blossom to the legendary Mount Eryx. This mystical city was founded by the Elymni, mysterious settlers of Segesta who worshipped the fertility goddess known as Astarte to the Phoenicians, Aphrodite to the Greeks, and Venus to the Romans. Each spring, she flew off with an escort of doves to her shrine in Sicca Veneria, modern El Kef in Tunisia. Her return signalled the reawakening of nature. In Erice's temple, Romans followed earlier customs of worship, including the cult of sacred prostitution. The battered marble remains of the temple to Venus lie beside a well in the Norman castle (open daily, 8am–2pm, 3–6pm; entrance fee) on a rocky outcrop overlooking Torretta Pepoli, a Gothic fantasy created by Count Pepoli. Below stretch ragged turrets, wooded groves and vineyards; a tapestry of salt pans and sea slip all the way to the Egadi Islands and to Cap Bon in Tunisia. Porta Trapani, a medieval gate, leads to a winding cobbled street lined with medieval *palazzi*. Carthaginian walls survive, with Punic symbols.

The salty "African coast"

South of Trapani is the "African coast", closer to Tunisia than to mainland Italy. It is known for its salt pans, a reminder of an industry that has flourished since Phoenician and Roman times. **Marsala ❻** occupies the next cape, which takes its name from the Arabic Mars-al-Allah, meaning "harbour of God". As Carthaginian Lilybaeum, it was the best-defended Punic naval base in Sicily, the

BELOW: Lo Zingaro Nature Reserve.

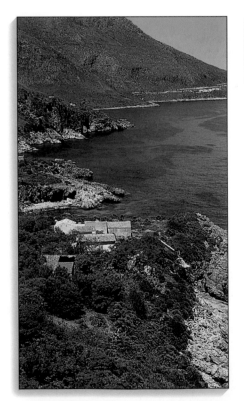

LO ZINGARO NATURE RESERVE

Lo Zingaro is set on a rocky headland pierced with coves and bays and dotted with clearly marked paths but containing no official roads. Scopello di Sopra, 10 km (6 miles) before Castellammare, marks the southern entrance to the reserve and is a fishing village based around a *baglio*, an imposing medieval farmstead. Apart from a rustic *trattoria* and a chance to buy farm-fresh cheese, the only site of note is the Tonnara, the finest tunnery on the coast, which overlooks the bay and a shingle beach, one of five, which is popular with swimmers. Above are a couple of rugged Saracen towers, built to combat raids by pirates. The northern entrance to Lo Zingaro lies 11 km (7 miles) southeast of San Vito lo Capo, just before the ruins of Torre dell'Impiso. The reserve is a glorious home to buzzards and peregrine falcons as well as palms, carobs and euphorbia. The continuing success of the reserve, with a natural history museum, marine laboratory and visitor centre, causes cynical Sicilians to dismiss it as a fabricated Disneyworld, but this comparison bemuses foreigners, who are only too delighted to find a semblance of order in any Sicilian site. The ever-changing coastline can be appreciated by boat, on horseback or on foot.

Map on page 268

only city to resist Greek expansion westwards. The site now houses the Museo Marsala (open daily 9am–1pm; entrance fee), with a reconstructed Punic ship that was sunk off the Egadi Islands. It was manned by 68 oarsmen and has iron nails that have not rusted. In the adjoining Capo Boeo archaeological zone (open daily 9am–1pm, 4pm–1 hour before sunset; entrance fee) are Roman mosaics of a chained dog and a Medusa. The cathedral is dedicated to St Thomas of Canterbury and pillars destined for Canterbury grace the nave. The Stabilimento Florio (tel: 0923-781111) is a typical Marsala distillery, most of which are set in *bagli*, traditional walled estates with elegant courtyards.

From Cape Boeo, the coastal road passes salt pans or marshes south to **Mazara del Vallo ❼**, a place of moods rather than specific sights. The fishing port flourished under Arab rule and it still feels like a North African town. A ragged Norman castle overlooks the seafront, while the Norman cathedral has a baroque veneer and contains two dramatic Roman sarcophagi. However, the best church, the crenellated Norman-Byzantine San Nicolò Regale, is at Porta Palermo in the heart of the fishing quarter. One of Italy's largest fishing fleets operates here and the Mazaro river is packed with trawlers. Behind lies the Kasbah, the Tunisian quarter, where North Africans smoke hubble-bubbles.

Selinunte ❽, 30 km (20 miles) east of Mazara, is a pocket of Greece in African Sicily. It was founded in 628 BC by colonists from Megara Hyblaea but, as Segesta's sworn enemy, became embroiled in clashes with the Carthaginians and Athenians. After being sacked by Carthage in 409 BC, the city never fully recovered and was destroyed in 250 BC. However, an aerial view of the collapsed columns reveals that they fell like dominoes, evidently the result of an earthquake. A lengthy visit to the sprawling site can be followed by a swim off the sandy coast. Framed by temples, the beach at Marinella consists of a dune-fringed shore, with the seafront lined by lively restaurants.

Overlooking the countryside and the sea, the beguiling archaeological site (open daily 9am–7pm; entrance fee) is hemmed in by two silted-up rivers and ports. Selinunte is a hauntingly lovely spot. There are half a dozen temples, and within a walled enclosure, the acropolis retains some original fortifications, communication trenches and gates. North of the acropolis is the ancient Greek city and, on either side of it, lie necropoli, quarters that have yet to be excavated. Just 4 km (2 miles) south of Campobello are the **Cave di Cusa**, the Classical quarries that provided the stone for Selinunte, now overrun with goats and wild flowers.

The region has also been subject to natural disasters, notably in the inland earthquake zone centred on Calatafimi, Salemi and Gibellina. In 1968 a major earthquake here left more than 50,000 people homeless. From Selinunte, an unspoilt coastal route leads eastwards to Agrigento, taking in the classical site of Eraclea Minoa. Midway between Selinunte and Eraclea is **Sciacca ❾**, a forthright fishing port noted for its sandy beaches and spa waters. This ancient spa town was praised by Pliny and prospered in Arab times. The modern revival of the port and spa has been aided by an injection of Mafia funds and close links with North Africa. It is a split-level town; the

Erice has a tradition of "dolci ericini", excessively sweet cakes once made by novice nuns. Maria Grammatico's Pasticceria in Via Vittorio Emanuele is one of the best in Sicily, selling "pasta reale" (marzipan), "sospiri" (sighs) and "belli e brutti" (beauties and the beasts).

BELOW: "Temple A" in the acropolis at Selinunte.

Santa Maria dei Greci in Agrigento, built over a Greek temple.

port is overlooked by the natural balcony of the old town. The Moorish quarter is on the highest level, a raggedy mass of alleys, arches, courtyards and wary, illegal immigrants. Sciacca lacks spectacular architecture but exhilarating sea views and an engaging ensemble of tawny, weather-beaten buildings justify a visit. On summer evenings the Piazza Scandaliato belongs to Tunisian hawkers flogging exotic clothes or Sciacca ceramics. By contrast, the Terme Selinuntine, an aloof, Art-Nouveau establishment, attracts wealthy Italians to its mud baths.

From Sciacca, a winding road climbs inland past farmhouses and deep gorges to **Caltabellotta**, the loveliest village in Agrigento province, with a cluster of towers and churches framed by spring blossom. Alternatively, from Sciacca the coastal road skirts countryside to the classical site of **Eraclea Minoa** ❿ (open daily 9am–one hour before sunset; entrance fee). A satellite of Selinunte, it suffered at the hands of the Carthaginians. Eraclea overlooks white cliffs, a crescent of golden sands and a pine grove. Excavations have so far revealed city walls, a Hellenistic theatre, a necropolis, and ruined villas.

Agrigento, home of Greek Luxury

The classical splendour of the Valley of the Temples triumphs over the mishmash that is the "modern" city of **Agrigento** ⓫. Siracusa may have been the most powerful city in Greek Sicily but Agrigento (Akragas) was the most luxurious. Akragas was settled by colonists from Gela in 580 BC, attracted by the abundance of springs and a dreamy, well-fortified site. This most sybaritic of Sicilian cities was run by tyrants and sacked by the Carthaginians in 406 BC. The city flourished again under the Romans but in AD 535 the Byzantines destroyed all but one of the pagan temples. The medieval city abandoned,

BELOW: pride of the province, Caltabellotta.

Akragas and the classical site was ignored until popularised by Goethe and the 19th-century German Romantics. The city rivalled Athens in the splendour of its temples, but in its hedonistic lifestyle Akragas was the Los Angeles of the ancient world.

The deprived modern city, resting on an economy beholden to the Mafia, relies on a surface gloss of chic bars and jewellery shops. Charmless middle-class apartments gaze across at the temples, often from within the park confines. The "modern" city is not without interest, but if only in the area for a day, head straight for the Valley of the Temples, and restrict a city visit to dinner and an evening stroll. Above Via Atenea, the main street, stands Santo Spirito, a fine Cistercian abbey founded in 1290. Agrigento's commercial spirit triumphs in the form of sweet *dolci di mandorla*, almond and pistachio pastries sold by the resident Cistercian nuns.

Dominating neighbouring Piazza Purgatorio is the baroque church of San Lorenzo, which marks the entrance to the Greek *hypogeum*, the ancient underground water and drainage system. Set among Moorish alleyways further west is Santa Maria dei Greci, a Norman church built over a Greek temple. The cathedral, which surmounts a ridge in the west of the city where the Greeks had their acropolis, is designed in eclectic style with Arab-Norman, Catalan-Gothic and baroque elements.

The Valley of the Temples

The **Valle dei Templi** (Valley of the Temples) ⑫ forms a natural amphitheatre, with a string of Doric temples straddling a ridge south of the city. This is still a valley of wild thyme, fennel, silvery olive groves and almond blossom. This crest of temples was designed to be visible from the sea, both as a beacon for sailors and to show that the Gods guarded the sacred city from mortal danger. From the valley, views of the town may offend purists but olive and almond groves mask the modernity. The park falls into two sections: the open Eastern Zone, best viewed in the early morning, at sunset, or even from afar, when floodlit at night, and the enclosed Western Zone (open daily 8.30am–7pm).

Map on page 268

In the Eastern Zone the first treasure visible is the Temple of Hercules, dating from 5 BC. Agrigento's oldest temple had similar proportions to the Parthenon in Athens. Villa Aurea, set in olive and almond groves beside the former Golden Gate, belonged to Hardcastle, the Englishman who in the 19th century devotedly excavated the site. A path leads to the well-lit catacombs, which emerge in a necropolis nearby. At the end of Via Sacra lies the Temple of Concord, which, after the Theseion in Athens, is the best preserved Greek temple in the world. Many scholars argue that this temple was in fact dedicated to Demeter, goddess of fertility and peace. The tawny temple slopes into the valley below, a pastoral scene at odds with its bloody history; on this bulwark thousands were slain in battle against Carthage. Dating from 430 BC, the temple was saved from ruin in the 6th century by being converted into a church, which it remained until 1748, when it was restored to its classical simplicity.

A sandstone giant, like the ones from the Temple of the Olympian Zeus.

The Temple of Hera surmounts a rocky ridge which formed the city ramparts. Known as Juno to the Romans, she was protectress of married couples. Fittingly, Hera is held to be the most romantic of temples, set "high on the hill like an offering to the goddess". Part of the *cella* and 25 columns remain intact; the rest fell over the hill during a landslide. The valley views reflect Pindar's praise of Agrigento as "loveliest of mortal cities".

BELOW: old stones in Agrigento.

The main entrance to the temples in the Western Zone (open daily, 8.30am–7pm; entrance fee) faces the Temple of Olympian Zeus. The size of a football pitch, it is the largest Doric temple ever known. The facade was supported by 38 *telamones* (giant figures) thereby distributing the weight of the pediment between the columns of the peristyle and the giants. A sandstone copy of a *telamone* stretches dreamily on the ground, while originals lie in the archaeological museum. West of this temple is a confusing quarter, dotted with shrines dating from pre-Greek times.

The sandy Via Sacra leads to the Temple of Castor and Pollux (or the Dioscuri), named after the twin sons of Zeus. Although it has become the city symbol, the result is theatrical pastiche, erected in 1836 from several temples. Known as the Sanctuary of the Chthonic Divinities, the general quarter conceals sacrificial altars and ditches, a shrine to fertility, immortality and eternal youth. Pale-coloured beasts were offered to the heavens but black animals were sacrificed to gods of the Underworld. Outside the ancient walls, and half-hidden in an almond grove, is the isolated Temple of Asclepius, dedicated to the god of healing.

Via dei Templi leads past olive groves to the archaeological museum, the Hellenistic-Roman quarter and several pagan shrines. San Nicola, on Via Petrarca, is a Romanesque church built from recycled Greek stone. Next-door is the fine Archaeological Museum (open Mon, Tues and Sun 9am–1pm, Wed and Sat 9am–1pm, 2–5.30pm; entrance fee) incorporating a church, courtyard and temple foundations. The Graeco-Roman section is the centrepiece, featuring a telamone in all its massive glory. The Hellenistic-Roman Quarter (open daily, 9am–1 hour before sunset) lies opposite, an ancient commercial and residential area laid out on a grid system. The remains of aqueducts, terracotta and stone water channels are visible, as well as vestiges of shops, taverns and patrician villas. Seen in spring, against a backdrop of almond blossom, the view is magical.

The softness of the people of ancient Agrigento was notorious. At the prospect of war with Carthage, soldiers on watch were under orders to make do with no more than two mattresses, two pillows and a blanket each.

The north coast and Monreale

On the northern side of the island, the centuries unfurl in a clannish yet sparsely populated countryside stretching from Palermo towards Enna, the centre of Sicily. Curled into the fold between coast and mountains is Palermo's **Conca d'Oro**, the city's summer gardens and citrus groves in times gone by. By rights, the city outskirts should be carpeted with marigolds and lemon trees, but land speculation and Mafia funding have ensured that Palermo's countryside is being encased in concrete.

In a mountain grotto at the top of Monte Pellegrino is the **Santuario di Santa Rosalia** (tel 091-540326), a kitsch but popular shrine allegedly containing the bones of Palermo's revered patron saint. In the lee of the mountain lies the fashionable resort of **Mondello ⓭**, a resort pioneered by the Bourbons, which began as a tuna-fishing village. The centre of attraction is the striking

BELOW: Temple of Concord, the Valley of the Temples.

striking ochre-and-maroon Art Nouveau pier, created by a Belgian entrepreneur in the 1890s. On the pier is The Charleston, an exclusive seafood restaurant with a spacious summer terrace and a snooty *maître d'hôtel*.

The cathedral of **Monreale** ⑭ (open daily, 8am–8pm; entrance free), which commands views over the Conca d'Oro, is a sumptuous building, the apogee of Arab-Norman art. The cathedral and Benedictine monastery were completed by the time of William II's death in 1189, allegedly inspired by a vision. In truth, his political rivalry with the English Walter of the Mill, the Palermitan archbishop, fuelled his desire to build a cathedral greater than Palermo's. Ultimately, William triumphed: his white marble sarcophagus lies in Monreale, and his shimmering tapestry is unequalled in Europe. His legacy is a vast cycle of mosaics, second in size only to Santa Sofia in Istanbul.

Map on page 268

Flanked by severe belltowers, the cathedral is not instantly awe-inspiring yet the details are exquisite. An arched Romanesque portal, made by a Pisan master, is framed by a greenish bronze door. The portal displays sculpted bands of garlands, figures and beasts alternating with multi-coloured mosaics. To the left, a Gagini portico shelters another Romanesque bronze door, inspired by the delicacy of Byzantine inlaid ivory. The apses are the most opulent in Sicily: a poetic abstraction of interlacing limestone and basalt arches, sculpted as delicately as wood. Monreale drew craftsmen from Persia, Africa, Asia, Greece, Venice, Pisa and Provence. The shimmering gold interior fuses Arab purity of volume with Byzantine majesty. The date of the mosaics is disputed: some scholars believe they were finished by 1100; others maintain that while the Byzantines began before then, the Venetians only completed the work by 1250. The highlight is the Creation series on the upper walls in the right of the nave:

Figurative capitals in the cloister of Monreale Cathedral.

BELOW: Monreale Cathedral.

Dressed up for the visitors in Monreale.

BELOW: the Mafia town of Corleone, home of a UN-backed anti-mafia research centre.

the delicacy of the flowers, fruit trees and birds singles out these scenes from Genesis, and the whole mosaic cycle is a *Biblia pauperum*, a poor man's Bible.

The **cloisters** (open Mon–Fri, 9am–1pm, 3–6.30pm, Sat–Sun, 9am–noon; entrance fee) express William's love of Islamic art and are the world's most sumptuous Romanesque example. Every second pair of white marble columns has a vivid zigzag mosaic pattern spiralling up the shaft. The sophistication of these columns suggests a Provençal influence while the Moorish mood, evoked by mosaic inlays or arabesque carvings, conjures up the Alhambra in Spain.

While Monreale is an anticlimax after the mosaics, a horse-and-cart ride or stroll from the Duomo brings a chance to savour the town's pedestrianised centre of crumbling, baroque churches and shops selling ceramics and ices. As a Mafia-controlled town, it is supremely safe for visitors. It was here that Toto Riina, the former Mafia boss, chose to live quite openly until his arrest in 1993. Local *trattorie* offer *pasta con le sarde*, a sardine speciality, or dry *biscotti di Monreale*. **Madonna delle Croci**, set on a hill, offers a lingering view from the cathedral to the coast.

Bandit country

From Monreale south into the interior unfolds a brooding Mafia heartland of gulleys and mountain lairs. Nurtured by the mythology of banditry, the hinterland falls back on ancient suspicion and insularity. As such, the villages south to Corleone are places of subtle mood shifts rather than specific sights or scenery. However, **Piana degli Albanesi** ⓯, reached along the SS624, is both an ethnic oddity and representative of this diverse province. The village, which appears suspended above a lake, is home to 15th-century Greek-speaking Albanian

immigrants, and encircled by lush pastures and hills. Traditional Byzantine ceremonies include services celebrated in both Albanian and Greek. Local cuisine is a cultural stew such as *dash*, castrated ram, Albanian-Greek style.

Map on page 268

Corleone ⓰, perched along the rural SS118, is enfolded in desolate, scorched hills and high verdant plains. The town lies clamped between two rocks, below a weather-beaten escarpment. In the centre looms the Castello, a rocky outcrop topped by a Saracen tower. It was a prison until 1976 but is now home to Franciscan friars who take their vow of poverty seriously. Below, the rooftops are stacked in a chromatic range of greys. At first sight, Corleone fails to live up to its infamous reputation but, on closer inspection, an air of watchfulness hangs over the town. Nonetheless, it has a reputation for producing great minds, whether priests, scholars or criminals.

Unlike neighbouring towns, Corleone's shops and businesses pay no *pizzo* (protection money) because the town is the stronghold of a powerful Mafia clan. But the arrest in 1993 of Totò Riina, the Corleonese *capo di tutti capi*, has created the glimmerings of a new openness, particularly among the young, with public-spirited citizens ready to guide visitors around town (tel: 091-8463655).

The road to Cefalù

The coast road from Palermo curves east past fishing villages and coves to Cefalù ⓱, one of Sicily's most engaging resorts, and to visit the province's great counterpoint to Monreale Cathedral. Sitting snugly below a headland, Cefalù is Taormina's north-coast rival. The consensus is that Taormina has better hotels, nightlife and atmosphere, but that Cefalù is more compact, peaceful and family-oriented. Out of season, Piazza del Duomo, the town centre, is a

BELOW: old town and beach, Cefalù.

Pistachio nuts ripening, to eat and to flavour ice-cream.

delightful sun trap, with a view of the cathedral at the foot of steep cliffs and looming fortifications. The square is also framed by the Corso, a Renaissance seminary and a porticoed *palazzo*. Here, the chic Caffè Duomo is the place for an atmospheric *aperitivo al fresco*. In summer the town is a delightful tourist trap with quaint craft boutiques selling ceramics and gold jewellery, matched by sophisticated restaurants catering to fastidious French palates. In the evening, the seafront, bastion and Corso become a cavalcade for *passeggiate* and *gelati*.

The cathedral (open daily, 8.30am–noon, 3.30–6pm) built in 1130 by Roger II, has a bold twin-towered facade and a triple apse with blind arcading. Roger used the see of Cefalù as a counterweight to Monreale and favoured Cefalù as the official mouthpiece of the state church. Inside, a severe nave is flanked by Roman columns surmounted by Romanesque arches, a reminder that a temple lies below. A sense of space and majesty is created by the concentration of other-worldly mosaics in the distant dome. These luminous Byzantine mosaics are among the earliest Norman creations and the purest extant depiction of Christ. The rest of the interior is imbued with majesty: the raised choir represents an Oriental element whereas the gold firmament behind Christ is Byzantine.

A warren of alleys leads west from Corso Ruggero, the main street, and reveals Renaissance facades, Gothic parapets and mullioned windows overlooking tiny courtyards. The old port, tangibly Moorish and home to Tunisian fishermen, has been a backdrop in countless films, including *Cinema Paradiso*. An underground spring bubbles up in the arcaded Arab baths, sited at the bottom of curved steps, beside a lively bar. Via Porto Salvo passes battered churches and flourishing craft shops. From Piazza Duomo, a steepish hill leads down to Museo Mandralisca (open daily, 9am–1.30pm, 3.30–7.30pm; entrance fee) containing Antonello da Messina's *Portrait of an Unknown Man*. A jagged outcrop overhangs the medieval town and is the site of the Citadel, the original Arab settlement. Marked walks climb through pine groves to the rocky cliffs and views over rust-coloured roofs and an azure sea studded with inlets and sandy beaches.

After Cefalù, coastal olive groves give way to pine woods and rugged valleys. A superior feudal castle towers over **Castelbuono** ⑱, 12 km (8 miles) just inland, a civilised, prosperous, well-kept place that could be mistaken for somewhere in Tuscany. Weekend visitors are drawn to the lively atmosphere, well-restored churches and welcoming restaurants. In the centre awaits one of finest gastronomic experiences in Sicily: Nangalarruni (tel: 0921-671428), celebrated for its mushroom dishes, roast meats and grilled vegetables. Nearby is the Caffè Fratelli Franconari, run by three brothers, which produces some of Italy's finest artisanal *panettone*, exported all over the world.

The rural route follows the SS286 22 km (14 miles) south to **Geraci** and then winds up to **Gangi**, a tortoise-shaped town with a crumbling watchtower and and, beyond, the grey-green slopes of the Madonie rising to the snow-capped Madonna dell'Alto, at 826 metres (2,707 ft) the highest peak. From here, one can either continue east to Nicosia or complete a circuit back to Cefalù via Petralia and Polizzi. West of Gangi,

Map on page 268

the ss1 reveals the jagged skyline of **Petralia Soprana** ⑲. Half-hidden in its alleys are striking mansions with baroque or rococo balconies as well as two watchtowers. Now a mountain resort, this former Norman citadel has a trio of Romanesque, Gothic and baroque churches. The Chiesa Matrice is perched on a belvedere and swathed in mist; inside is a precious Arabian altarpiece.

The road west to **Polizzi Generosa** passes *masserie*, feudal farmsteads that were as self-sufficient as most villages. Polizzi is a trekking centre which sustains walkers with *pasta* and asparagus (*pasta cu l'asparaci*). From here, the fast A19 returns to the coast, as does the winding route via the ski resort of Piano Battaglia.

The navel of Sicily

East of Gangi, Palermo province merges into Enna, the desolate, sun-parched centre of the island. This lofty inland province remains resolutely agricultural, producing corn, olives, cheese, nuts and wine, a fitting destiny for a place connected with Greek fertility rites. The province suffers from emigration and has pinned its hopes on tourism. The signs are promising; Enna possesses Sicily's greatest Roman villa and a succession of strategic castles and classical sites.

To the north of the provincial capital lies **Sperlinga** ⑳ (open daily, 9am–1pm, 2pm–sunset; entrance fee), an intriguing castle with battlemented towers and bastions that stretch to the bottom of the cliff. Below the castle, the rock is riddled with chambers, a secret underground city. Dating from 1082, the Norman castle passed from the Chiaramonte into the hands of the Natali, Princes of Sperlinga. The castle became the Angevins' last stand 200 years later after the bloody Sicilian Vespers in 1282. The French forces held out for more than a year, aided

TIP

Farm stays *(agriturismo)* make an appealing way of exploring The Madonie Mountains. Gangi Vecchio, on the outskirts of Gangi, is a charming Madonie haunt for a farm stay (tel: 0921-689191). It also sells wine, oil, cheeses and salami.

BELOW: countryside around Enna.

Flag waver in the annual Palio in Adrano.

BELOW: catching up with news, Enna.

by trap doors that deposited invaders in underground pits. From the crenellations stretch sweeping views over oak woods, olive groves and pasture. **Nicosia** ㉑, 8 km (5 miles) southeast of Sperlinga, is set on four hills and ringed by rocky spurs. In the Middle Ages, it was riven by religious rivalry between Roman Catholic newcomers and the indigenous Eastern Orthodox population. After pitched battles, the matter was settled in favour of the natives: the 14th-century San Nicolò triumphed as the city cathedral, with a lacey Catalan-Gothic campanile rooted in a gracious Moorish tower. Leading off Piazza Garibaldi, a square dotted with dingy bars and working-men's clubs, are myriad crooked alleys climbing Nicosia's hills.

Further south is **Leonforte**, a 17th-century Branciforte fiefdom best known for the Granfonte, a magnificent arched fountain on the edge of town. This act of feudal largesse is still appreciated by thirsty donkeys.

Balcony over Sicily

Enna ㉒, a lofty city in the clouds, feels aloof from its rural hinterland and the rest of Sicily. To Ovid, Enna was "where Nature decks herself in all her varied hues, where the ground is beauteous, carpeted with flowers of many tints", a city in thrall to the cult of Demeter and the myth of Persephone. Enna is still strewn with narcissi in spring but always feels cloaked in winter, shrouded in mist or blown by wintry gusts. Under the Greeks, Enna was prosperous and relatively independent. Under Roman rule, the old fertility goddesses were worshipped under the new names of Ceres and Proserpine. The vassal city became the breadbasket of Rome, despite several great slave revolts. The Arabs also cultivated the region, planting cotton, cane and pistachio nuts, while the Normans focused on reinforcing the city's formidable castle. The Bourbon regime of "hangings and holidays" confirmed Enna's rebellious reputation.

Tradition has it that the cathedral (open daily, 9am–1pm, 4–7pm) was begun by Eleanor of Aragon but a fire in 1446 swept away most of the treasures. Yet the cathedral is a fascinating romp through Enna's mystical past. The elaborately carved white pulpit is encrusted with cherubs and rests on a Graeco-Roman base removed from a temple to Demeter, as does the marble stoup nearby, and the wrought-iron sacristy gate once graced a Moorish harem in the Castello di Lombardia.

Along bustling Via Roma are a string of dignified mansions and churches, such as the Catalan-Gothic Palazzo Pollicarini and the baroque Chiesa San Benedetto. Via Roma is pedestrianised for the evening *passeggiata* and contains a good *pasticceria* as well as some cosy restaurants. At the bottom are sweeping views from the belvedere and Torre di Federico II, a tumbledown octagonal tower linked by secret passageways to Castello di Lombardia (open daily, 9am–1pm, 3–5pm; entrance fee) on the hill at the far end of Via Roma. One of the largest medieval castles in Sicily, it began as a Byzantine keep but acquired towers with each wave of invaders. Courtyards lead to the majestic eyrie of Torre Pisano, the tallest of six surviving towers, which commands views over the whole of Sicily.

Imperial glory

Further south is **Piazza Armerina** and the nearby villa that is Sicily's greatest wonder of the Roman world. The **Roman Villa ㉓** (Villa Imperiale) lies 5 km (3 miles) southwest, at **Casale**, where the splendid mosaics triumph as "the last pagan achievement in Sicily executed under the old dispensation". The villa probably first belonged to Diocletian's co-Emperor Maximinian between AD 286 and 305. It was occupied during the Arab period but destroyed by King William in 1160. These fluid, impressionistic mosaics may have inspired the Normans in their designs for Palermo's Palazzo dei Normanni. Whether hunting lodge or country mansion, the villa disappeared under a landslide for 700 years. The vaulting may be lost and the frescoes faded but the villa's magic lies in the 50 rooms covered in Roman-African mosaics. Their vitality, expressive power and free-ranging content set them apart. All the scenes excluded from Christian art lie here. The villa highlights intimate pleasures such as child's play and youthful dancing, massage and love-making.

The Museo Archeologico (open daily, 9am–1.30pm, 3–7.30pm; entrance fee), set in a 17th-century monastery in the village of **Aidone ㉔**, 10 km (6 miles) north of Piazza Armerina, is an introduction to the site of Morgantina, perhaps the most "legible" site in antiquity. **Morgantina ㉕** 5 km (3 miles) east, occupies a rural paradise worthy of Persephone, its slopes covered in calendula, pines or olives and framed by grey-blue hills. Its sanctuaries to the Chthonic gods shows that the city's focal point was a devotion to the cult of Demeter and Persephone. This is a reminder that mystical Enna marked the crossroads of Trinacria, ancient Sicily's three provinces. According to one historian, Enna is the hub of a giant geomantic chart, lying on ley lines spanning the island. ❑

Map on page 268

In Piazza Armerina, Aidone, Sperlinga and Nicosia, the older inhabitants speak in "gallo-italico", a Lombard dialect stemming from northern settlers. They may well be talking about emigration since half the adult population emigrated between 1950 and 1970.

BELOW: Enna, the high point of Sicily.

EASTERN SICILY

*Here is baroque Catania, chic and timeless Taormina,
the dramatic hinterland of Mount Etna and Siracusa,
the most civilised town on the island*

Map
on page
268

Palermo

astern Sicily has coasts on three seas: the Tyrrhenian in the north, the Ionian in the east, facing mainland Italy, and the Mediterranean in the south. It is the main entry point to the island and its historic sites at Taormina, Catania and Siracusa attract most visitors, who also come to see the sleeping giant of Mt Etna. More than 20 percent of Sicilians live on the flanks of the volcano. Farmers are drawn by the fertile soil since, within 20 years, volcanic ash is ideal for producing sun-drenched fruit, wine and aubergines. Likewise, wealthy city residents have constructed villas for the views, cool summer climate, and for winter skiing on the slopes.

Coastal **Catania** ㉖ turns away from the volcanic hinterland, with its atavistic spirit and peasant culture. This is commercial Sicily, profiting from its entrepreneurial roots as a Greek trading colony, founded by settlers from Naxos in 729 BC. It has budding resorts and exercises strict control over the Etna national park. Yet despite its forward-looking air, the city remains in thrall to the powers of its patron saint, Sant'Agata, and to Mt Etna's whims. The 1669 eruption struck the city centre while the 1693 earthquake killed two-thirds of the population. However, the subsequent rebuilding transformed the city with a series of trail-blazing baroque palaces, spacious streets and sinuous churches. Visually, Catania is the most homogeneous Sicilian city, stamped with the vision of Vaccarini, an architect influenced by grand Roman baroque. The colour of the volcanic stone seems oppressive at first, but the chiaroscuro effects accentuate the billowing balconies and sweeping S-curves.

Piazza del Duomo, the baroque centrepiece, is a dignified composition on a grand scale. In the centre is the city symbol, Fontane dell'Elefante, Vaccarini's fountain: an ancient black volcanic elephant surmounted by an Egyptian obelisk taken from the Roman circus. The newly-restored cathedral was begun by Count Roger in 1092 but rebuilt after the earthquake. The interior conceals vaulted Roman baths; a Romanesque basilica lies under the nave; while Roman and Byzantine and Roman columns line the transepts. Via Crociferi, just west of the Duomo, is Catania's most characteristic street, with its succession of baroque churches and noble *palazzi*. Further north stands Chiesa San Giuliano, distinguished by its graceful *loggia*. The steep, student-infested Via Sangiuliano ends at San Nicolo all'Arena, which resembles a grim religious factory rather than a church. As the largest in Sicily, this unfinished, desolate 16th-century work has an eerie, amputated look.

The grandiose **Via Etnea**, the main city thoroughfare, runs parallel to Via Crociferi and climaxes in a stunning view of Mt Etna. The sweeping street passes

LEFT: performers in
the Greek theatre
in Siracusa.
BELOW: Taormina's
Greek theatre.

Fishing at Catania.

the university, baroque churches and a Roman amphitheatre. The street is particularly popular during the evening *passeggiata*, when the locals parade past chic shops selling jewellery, shoes, fruit sorbets and nougat ice cream. Directly south of Via Etnea is Castello Ursino (open Tues–Sun, 9am–6pm; entrance fee), a Swabian castle built on a steep bastion that commands a view of what was once the harbour.

The main **Classical theatres** tend to be in dilapidated areas, where every second turning reveals the odd Roman column or *hypocaust*. Teatro Greco-Romano, off 266 Via Vittorio Emanuele, (open daily 8am–1 hour before sunset; entrance fee) was built over a Greek theatre but retains its Roman underground passages. Next door is the semi-circular Odeon, designed for oratory. The intimate site is still hemmed in by a medieval and baroque quarter. In Piazza Stesicoro, off Via Etnea, lies the Anfiteatro Romano (closed but visible), the battered remains of the largest amphitheatre in Sicily, the place where St Agata supposedly met her doom and where earthquake ruins were dumped in 1693.

Just south of the Duomo, sandwiched between the cathedral quarter and the port, is **La Pescheria**, the popular morning fish market which makes a fitting farewell to the city. Spread-eagled on slabs of marble lie sea bream and swordfish, mussels and sea urchins, squirming eels and lobsters.

Cyclops Riviera

Heading north from Catania is a welcome release: sea breezes sweep away images of Catania's scruffy outskirts. The **Coast of Cyclops**, named after the Homeric myth, presents a spectacular seascape of jagged basalt rocks off **Aci Trezza**. Legend has it that these rocks were flung at the fleeing Odysseus by an

enraged, blinded Cyclops. In summer, the restaurants are full, and flotillas of fishing craft act as pleasure boats, but essentially these fishing villages remain simple places to sample catches of anchovies and sardines.

Acireale **㉗** stands aloof, both from the over-commercialised resorts and the rural hinterland. As Akis, the Greek settlement fared badly in the face of eruptions and earthquakes. However, thanks to the ravages of Etna and the talent of local craftsmen, Acireale is predominantly baroque, an untouristy town admired for its quality of life, sulphur spas and exuberant carnival. The tiny, dark alleys yield rewards in the form of pastry shops and ice-cream parlours. Acireale is credited with inventing sorbets, aided by a profitable monopoly on snow held by the local archbishop until modern times. Castorino, a café in Corso Savoia, is famed for its ice cream, pastries and *pasta reale*, decorated marzipan concoctions. **Santa Venera**, a spa to the south of town, exploits the healing properties of Etna's radioactive waters. Sulphurous lava mud baths have been beneficial for rheumatism and skin conditions since Roman times.

Map on page 268

Routes around Etna

The circular journey around the volcano is a game of light and shade, with dark volcanic villages and Norman castles contrasted with the glistening citrus and olive groves, orchards and nut plantations. To appreciate Etna's grandeur, drive around the base or follow a similar route on the Circumetnea single-track railway from Catania or **Giarre-Riposto**, a strange trail which passes lush almond and hazel groves, interspersed with a black lava-stone moonscape.

Castiglione di Sicilia, 17 km (10 miles) north, is a stop on the scenic railway. Perched on a crag, this ancient bastion possesses Greek ramparts but is

BELOW: Castiglione de Sicilia.

Eruptions most commonly occur in Etna's side vents which, in turn, create smaller, secondary cones. The south-eastern crater in particular has been responsible for virtually all the eruptions since 1997. Today the volcano has virtually guaranteed a regular nightly spectacle of molten bombs shooting from its cones.

BELOW: climbing Etna's lava slopes.

better known as a Norman fiefdom. **Francavilla di Sicilia**, just north, is set in a fertile valley of citrus plantations and prickly pears. Founded by King Roger, his ruined castle occupies a lone mound in the valley and once guarded the route to Randazzo. From here, a lovely foray leads to the **Gole dell'Alcantara**, a delightful gorge along the Francavilla–Taormina road.

Continue the anti-clockwise drive around Etna to **Randazzo** ㉘, the most atmospheric medieval town on the northern slopes. First settled by Greeks fleeing from Naxos, Randazzo became a summer retreat from the heat of Messina. It remains a self-contained market town, with crenellated churches and medieval walls. For a town in the jaws of Etna, Randazzo has survived magnificently, despite the 1981 eruption which engulfed vineyards, roads and railway lines, leaving the lava flow visible today.

Between Randazzo and Bronte extends a wooded, volcanic landscape south to **Maletto**, noted for its wine and strawberries. Maletto marks the highest point on the Circumetnea line and offers views of recent lava flows. Around **Bronte**, the slopes are covered with small nut trees, a reminder that 80 percent of Italy's pistachio crop comes from these well-tended terraces. **Paterno** ㉙, halfway between Biancavilla and Catania, is famous for cultivating the juiciest oranges in Sicily. This baroque market town also has a fine Norman castle which was used as a Nazi observation post until it drew heavy Allied fire, resulting in the death of 4,000 people. The castle quarter is now the focus for concerts and feasts of stuffed aubergines. East of Paternò is **Nicolosi** ㉚, a charmless ski resort. Nicolosi is the southern gateway to Etna's wine and walking country, offering bracing treks to extinct cones and prehistoric craters. Just east, along the road to **Trecastagni**, the lava beds of 1886 and 1910 are visible.

ASCENDING ETNA

Circling the volcano is intriguing and safe but an ascent requires caution. The sensible way of tackling Etna is to purchase a cable-car ticket at Rifugio Sapienza that also includes a drive and guided walk to the summit. If driving in the volcanic foothills, follow signs for Etna Sud, the main southern access point, reached via Zafferana Etnea. From here, a road leads to the Sapienza base camp at 1,800 metres (5,900 ft) and a cable car which leads to the top. Here minibuses deliver passengers to the correct departure point of an ever-changing volcanic route. For sheer adventure, go with a private alpine guide. Without a guide, suitably-clad explorers can clamber up to 3,000 metres (9,800 ft) at their own risk.

The sights will depend on volcanic activity and weather conditions, particularly the prevailing winds: it is vital to avoid the gases and volcanic matter emitted from active craters. Blue smoke indicates the presence of magma while a halo of sulphurous vapour is a rare event. At most, you may see an active crater belching out sulphurous fumes or molten "bombs", or the bottom of the misty cone bubbling with incandescent lava. In periods of intense seismic activity, the volcano spits out molten rock or fireballs, a dramatic sight at night.

Sicily's most dramatic resort

Taormina ㉛ is Sicily's most dramatic resort, a stirring place celebrated by poets from Classical times onwards. Citrus groves carpet the slopes while the cliff face is a tangle of cacti and orchids. Below stretches a craggy coastline and the romantic islet of Isola Bella. The mood may be heightened by sightings of a smouldering volcano or snow-capped peak. May, September and October are the loveliest months in Taormina, with the city enjoying a semblance of solitude.

Taormina was an outpost of Naxos until the Greeks fled the first colony for Tauromenion in 403 BC. Under the Romans, the city acquired a garrison and the new name of Tauromenium, and later became the capital of Byzantine Sicily in the 9th century. Aristocratic leanings later drew Taormina into the Spanish camp, with the Catalan legacy refle`cted in Taormina's array of richly decorated palazzi. In Edwardian times, the terraced resort was a wintering place for frustrated northerners and gay exiles. Today, this haven appeals to romantic couples of both sexes, sedate shoppers and the cultured middle classes. Yet despite designer glamour and the hordes of *blasé* cruise liner passengers, the site's majesty is not manufactured. Nor is the heady decadence and timeless charm. Taormina may now have an Internet café, but the locals prefer to pass the time of day chatting from an ancient balcony overlooking the sea. At night, Etna's fiery cone glitters before dissolving into the sea, stars and smoky peaks.

Taormina's *raison d'être* is the **Teatro Greco** (open daily 9am–5.30pm; entrance fee), a setting that is pure drama, hewn out of the hillside. In Greek theatres, sea and sky were the natural backdrop; the Romans preferred proscenium arches. Where the Greeks worshipped nature, the Romans tried to improve on it. The Hellenistic theatre was built under Hieron in the 3rd century BC and

Map on page 268

"Taormina is the dawn-coast of Europe."
– D.H.LAWRENCE

BELOW: the Greco-Roman amphitheatre in Taormina.

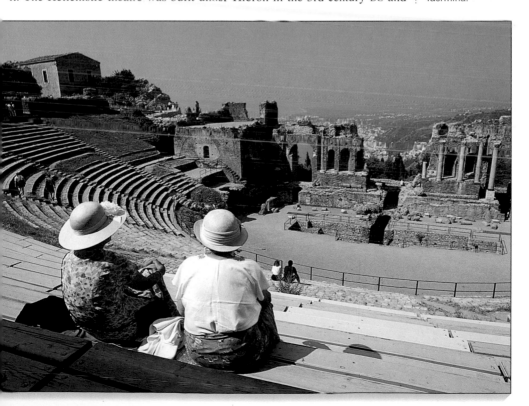

Taormina Arte is a season of drama, cinema, ballet and music put on every July and August in the Greco-Roman theatre. Tickets and information from the tourist office (tel: 0942 23243).

enlarged by the Romans in AD 2. Like Tindari's Greek theatre, Taormina's was turned into an arena for gladiatorial combat. Piazza Emanuele lies beyond, a noisy market square built over the Roman forum. Bordering the *piazza* is a crenellated Catalan-Gothic palace, a medieval gate, and the charming church of Santa Caterina. **Corso Umberto**, the pedestrianised main street, is a feast for shopaholics. The 15th-century *palazzi* are converted into bars, craft shops and boutiques displaying candied fruit, marzipan animals and fresh kumquats, as well as majolica tiles, leather goods and traditional puppets. Just off the Corso lie the arched buttresses of the Naumachia, a hybrid construction which evolved into a Roman gymnasium. For lunch, the restaurant terraces of the adjoining Via Naumachia beckon, with Gambero Rosso arguably the best.

Halfway down the Corso, **Piazza Aprile** offers glittering views of Etna and close-ups of preening poseurs at chic cafés. Further along, the baroque fountain on Piazza del Duomo marks the central meeting place. At sunset, or at the first sign of spring sun, kids fetch their footballs, the *jeunesse dorée* pose, and the town's perma-tanned lounge lizards search for foreign prey. From Taormina, a winding road climbs to Castelmola, a quaint hamlet perched on a limestone peak. Below Taormina, sheer cliffs drop to the islet of **Isola Bella** while, from Via Pirandello, a cable car links the city to the pebbled beach at **Mazzaro**.

The Ionian coast

BELOW: Taormina, with snow-capped Etna behind.

Neighbouring **Giardini-Naxos** is Sicily's fastest-growing resort, and is considered a poor man's Taormina. It was founded on an ancient lava flow by Euboans in 735 BC and became a springboard for the colonisation of Catania and the east coast. The archaeological site (open daily 9am–sunset; entrance fee)

which occupies the promontory of Capo Schiso, has revealed Greek lava-stone city walls but is still being excavated. **Mazzaro**, linked to Taormina by a cable car, is convenient for families. **Letojanni**, a humble fishing village until the 1960s, is now a bustling resort with facilities for riding and water sports.

From Taormina, the motorway hugs the shore north to Messina. Leave the coastal crowds at **Santa Teresa di Riva** for a slice of timeless Sicily, marked by scorched peaks and brooding ravines. Just inland is the battered mountain village of **Savoca** ㉜, best-known for its mummies. The catacombs of the Cappuccino Convento (open daily 9am–1pm, 4–7pm; entrance fee) contain 32 ghoulish mummified corpses dating from the 17th century. After this macabre scene, leave the monastery for the evocative medieval village whose roads were repaved with the proceeds of *The Godfather*, filmed on location here.

Map on page 268

City of swordfish

The road hugs the coast to **Messina** ㉝, the ferry port to Reggio on the mainland side of the Straits of Messina. A Phoenician colony settled by the Greeks, Messina thrived for centuries as a seafaring power but was devastated by the calamitous 1908 earthquake which killed 84,000 people in 30 seconds. The shore sank by half a metre and the reverberations were felt in Malta a day later. In 1943, Messina represented the Nazis' last stand, leading to the death of 5,000 people during Allied bombing. Such disasters have engendered a salvage mentality: every recoverable stone has been re-used or re-created. Even so, the wide boulevards, grid system and matter-of-factness make Messina the most American-looking Sicilian city. Although tourism is important, the city's prosperity depends on better communications. But a suspension bridge over the Straits is

BELOW: approaching Messina.

still only a gleam in the regional government's eye. As a touring base, however, Taormina or a Tyrrhenian coastal resort are infinitely preferable.

The harbour welcomes grey Nato warships and long-prowed *feluccas* in pursuit of swordfish. These creatures, which weigh up to 300 kg (660 lb), are the local delicacy par excellence. Despite lively cafés and sweeping sea views, mercantile Messina only looks romantic at night, its lights glittering along the harbour front. The Duomo symbolises the stubbornness of the natives. This Norman cathedral has survived medieval fires, earthquakes and wartime American firebombing. The restored Renaissance fountain outside the cathedral is a masterpiece by a pupil of Michelangelo, overshadowed by an incongruous free-standing Flemish belfry. Although several other churches survived the earthquake, the artworks salvaged from the disaster are more significant, and are housed in the **Museo Regionale** (open daily 9am–2pm; entrance fee), on Via della Libertá. This museum is noted for works by two honorary citizens, Antonello da Messina, Southern Italy's greatest Renaissance artist, and Caravaggio, a city resident whose theatricality imbues Sicilian art.

The Tyrrhenian Coast

This stretch of coast is devoted to popular summer tourism and swordfishing. As a result, the air is heavy with a peculiar combination of petrol fumes and grilled fish. From Messina, tunnels thread through pine and olive groves to **Milazzo** ㉞. The vision of this verdant peninsula is slightly marred by the presence of an oil refinery. Compensations lie in the welcoming breezes and dramatic castle, with views of the jagged green spit stretching towards the Aeolian Islands *(see page 313)*. This is the place to while away the time waiting for a ferry by sampling swordfish or *bottarga* (mullet roe).

BELOW: St Martino in Ortygia, Siracusa.

Following the SS113 westwards leads to **Oliveri** ㉟ and the chance to exchange churches for seafood and excellent beaches. Between here and Cefalù is one of the cleanest stretches of coastline on the island. Oliveri itself is a standard Sicilian resort with a Norman-Arab feudal castle and sandy beaches. On the seafront is a converted *tonnara*, the traditional tuna-processing plant, a reminder of life before tourism. Yet the tuna, aubergine and pasta dishes show that life still retains something of its original flavour. Oliveri is on the Golfo di Patti, its bays framed by the moody Nebrodi mountains.

Dominating the headland is **Tindari** ㊱, christened Tyndaris, one of the last Greek colonies in Sicily. The archaeological park (open daily 9am–two hours before sunset; entrance fee), overrun by goats, is pleasingly wild since Italian visitors are more impressed by the sacred Black Madonna housed in the sanctuary bordering the park. **Patti** ㊲ is a historic hill-town ringed by new development. The medieval quarter by the cathedral has a quiet charm and several art-filled churches. Patti's greatest attraction is the Roman villa (open daily 9am–1 hour before sunset; entrance fee) at Marina di Patti, a late Imperial villa revealed in 1973. From Patti to **Capo d'Orlando** are a cluster of bland resorts fighting a battle against coastal ribbon development and the Mafia, currently losing the former but winning the latter.

Map on page 268

Siracusa, a cultured province

South of Catania lies Siracusa, a supremely cultured province, with an ancient savoir-faire that Mafia money cannot mimic or buy. While not beyond the Mafia's reptilian gaze, this southeastern corner of Sicily also has an elegance and grace unmatched by other provinces. The Greeks colonised the province two centuries after settling the rest of eastern Sicily. Since then, Siracusa has rested on its laurels, parading its Hellenistic heart and Levantine soul with the effortless superiority of a born aristocrat. Yet economically, the province has fallen behind Ragusa and other more entrepreneurial neighbours, and also shortsightedly destroyed a sizeable stretch of coast in the 1950s in the rush for petrochemical riches. Still, most visitors can turn a blind eye to the bubbling crisis and simply relish the province's traditional sense of discreet well-being.

In its Hellenistic heyday, the classical city of **Siracusa ㊳** was the supreme Mediterranean power and it has left us a medley of monuments from all eras. Cicero called it the loveliest city in the world but Siracusa has also bequeathed us beauty with a baroque heart: the facades in the district of Ortygia are framed by wrought-iron balconies as free as billowing sails. The city was founded in 733 BC by Corinthian settlers who maintained links with Sparta. Although ruled by a succession of cruel but occasionally benevolent tyrants, Siracusa rose to become the supreme power of its age under Dionysius the Elder, who ruled from 405 BC. After the sun set on ancient Greece, Siracusa became a Roman province and was supposedly evangelised by St Peter and St Paul on their way to Rome. The city catacombs are the finest outside the capital.

The two central areas are the archaeological park of Neapolis and Ortygia, the cultural island at the heart of the ancient city. **Neapolis archaeological**

Dionysius, ruler of the city of Siracusa (405–367 BC), personified Sicilian tyranny. His death is said to have been provoked by a heart attack brought on by delight at receiving a (politically expedient) prize for his poetry at the Olympic Games.

BELOW: the Duomo, Siracusa.

A breadbasket in Siracusa.

park: this ancient quarter is also synonymous with its sprawling park (open daily 9am–1 hour before sunset; entrance fee) containing rough-hewn quarries, grandiose theatres and tombs. A stroll to the Greek theatre passes the rubble of Hieron II's Altar, built in honour of Zeus. Surrounded by trees, the vast Teatro Greco seats 15,000 and is praised as the masterpiece of ancient Greece. The theatrical tradition survives, with the dramas of Sophocles and Euripides played on a stage once viewed by spectators as illustrious as Plato and Archimedes.

Although partially closed, Via dei Sepolcri, the path of tombs, offers glimpses of tombs and carved niches. Further uphill lie the Grotticelli Necropolis, a warren of Hellenistic and Byzantine tombs, including the supposed Tomb of Archimedes *(see page 24)*. The best catacombs lie nearby, with the entrance opposite the tourist office on Via Sebastiano. The **San Giovanni Catacombs** (open Wed–Mon, 9am–1pm, 2–5pm; entrance fee) provide entry to the persecuted world of the early Christians. A reluctant friar shows visitors early Christian sarcophagi, an early drawing of St Peter and a mosaic depicting Original Sin. In the wild garden outside is the shell of San Giovanni Evangelista, Siracusa's first cathedral, dedicated to St Marcian, the city's earliest bishop.

Probably the finest archaeological collection in Sicily lies in the **Museo Archeologico** (open daily 9am–1.30pm, 3.30pm–6.30pm in high season; entrance fee) on the neighbouring Viale Teocrito, built over a quarry and pagan necropolis. It is divided into prehistoric, classical and regional sections.

A stroll across Ponte Nuovo leads past prettily moored boats and pastel-coloured Venetian palazzi to the Darsena, the inner docks, with the atmospheric **Ortygia** on the far side. This seductive island was dedicated to the huntress Artemis. Via Cappodieci is home to **Palazzo Bellomo** (open daily 9am–2pm;

BELOW: trattoria in Ortygia.

entrance fee), a lovely Catalan-Gothic mansion and the city's compact art gallery. Inside, awaits Caravaggio's masterpiece, *The Burial of St Lucy*, and Antonello da Messina's *Annunciation*. From here, a flight of steps leads to the cathedral (open daily 8am–noon, 4–7pm, free admission), a Temple to Athena masquerading as a Christian church. Ortygia has cosy bars and pubs, *pizzerie* and *birrerie* (beer halls). The evening's summer parade of fashion victims is centred on the western shore, especially the strip between Porta Marina and Fontana Aretusa, a pool which signals the start of bracing sea walks. Short cruises around the headland leave from Molo Zanagora, off Largo Porta Marina.

Siracusa's mythical environs

In ancient **Epipolae**, 8 km (5 miles) northwest of Siracusa, you will find **Castello Eurialo** (open daily 9am–one hour before sunset; entrance fee; follow signs to Belvedere). The fort represented the fifth component of the Greek pentapolis and was the most magnificent of Greek military outposts. Inland from Siracusa, the countryside is rocky and parched. This is Sicily with its roots laid bare.

The rocky tableland is home to **Necropoli di Pantalica** ⑳, the foremost prehistoric site, best reached via Sortino, following signs for Pantalica Sud. The drive skirts the bleached white Iblean hills before reaching the Anapo Valley and Necropoli di Pantalica (open daily 9am–sunset; entrance fee), set in lush gorges, studded with citrus trees and wild flowers, acanthus and prickly pears. The Anapo river has carved a path through the cliffs and is invitingly cool for swimmers. As the largest Bronze- and Iron-Age cemetery in Sicily, the necropolis has more than 5,000 tombs carved into the cliffs of a limestone plateau.

Map on page 268

TIP

If Siracusa's central Jolly Hotel (Corso Gelone 45, tel: 0931-461111) is the most welcoming in town, Ortygia's most romantic beds are in the Art Nouveau-style Grand Hotel (Viale Mazzini, tel: 0931-464600), overlooking the waterfront.

BELOW: ice cream in the sun, Siracusa.

BELOW: San Carlo Borromeo, Noto.

South from Siracusa

The journey south provides a fair introduction to gentle farming country, with lemon, olive and almond groves giving way to more rugged views of limestone escarpments and rocky gorges. The SS115 leads to **Noto** ㊶, the finest baroque town in Sicily, both blatantly theatrical and deeply rational. Visitors praise its proportion, symmetry, spaciousness and innate sense of spectacle. Sicilians simply call it "a garden of stone". Yet much is crumbling in the garden and most museums and interiors are closed for eternal "restoration".

Luckily, on this open-air stage, Noto's chief pleasures are on permanent display, charmingly illuminated by antique lamps. After Noto Antica was destroyed in the 1693 earthquake, Giuseppe Lanza, a Sicilian-Spanish architect, was entrusted with the urban design. Noto was composed around three parallel axes running horizontally across the hillside. To create interest, he conceived three squares, each enlivened by a scenic church as a backdrop. The design was clothed in warm, golden limestone and used monumental flights of steps to enchant with tricks of perspective. The realisation of this ambitious plan was the work of Gagliardi and Sinatra, both of whom were gifted local architects who also worked in Ragusa province.

On the lower slopes, three scenic squares unfold in a succession of theatrical perspectives sculpted in burnished stone. The lower part of town was designed as the civic and religious centre whereas the upper town was laid out as a cramped *quartiere popolare*. Paradoxically, the higher the level, the lower the class of the residents. Even so, the two-tiered city looks entirely homogeneous. The Corso sweeps towards Piazza Municipio, Noto's stage set, with the golden grace of the buildings matched by the majestic proportions of the design.

Southeast of Noto lies **Eloro** ㊷, a classical site on the unpolluted coastline that stretches south to Capo Passero. Now in ruins, the Siracusan city of Elorus (open daily 9am–one hour before sunset; entrance fee) was founded at the end of the 6th century BC. Beside this wild site are rocky and sandy beaches which tend to be deserted, but the most appealing beaches await in **Vendicari** ㊸, 6 km (4 miles) south, past citrus and almond groves. As an established nature reserve, the **Vendicari wetlands** are salt marshes popular with nesting and migrating birds, from flamingoes and falcons to herons and storks. Further down the coast lies **Marzamemi**, an appealing fishing village and low-key resort, noted for its tasty seafood. In summer, Sicilians from Catania and Siracusa flock south to **Pachino** and the sandy beaches around Capo Passero.

From here, it is a short drive west to the Ispica canyon. **Cava d'Ispica** ㊹ (open daily 9am– 6.30pm; entrance fee) is a 11-km (7-mile) limestone gorge whose ghostly galleries have been inhabited almost continuously since prehistoric times.

Ragusa province

Ragusa ㊺ is the capital of the self-confident agricultural province southwest of Siracusa. It thrives on wine-growing, cattle-breeding and cheese-making as well as hot-house flowers and genetically modified tomatoes. The town of Ragusa, like Modena and Scicli, is part

Map on page 268

of a cave-dwelling civilisation. Its mines, both underground and opencast, have produced asphalt that has paved the streets of Berlin, Paris, London and Glasgow. However, Ragusa is a hidden treasure in its own right, rivalled only by Siracusa as the capital of serendipity. Like Ortygia, the partly pedestrianised enclave of **Ragusa Ibla** is the place for aimless wandering, leisurely lunches, and sleepy ruminations amidst a crumbling cityscape.

After the 1693 earthquake reduced medieval Ragusa to rubble, the merchants and landed gentry responded by building Ragusa Alta, the new city on the hill. But the aristocracy refused to desert their charred homes so recreated Ragusa Bassa (Ibla) on the original valley site. In the rivalry between the two centres, Ibla is finally beginning to triumph, with the cultural life returning to the historic centre. As a baroque city recreated on a medieval street plan, an old-world intimacy prevails. Gentrification and restoration have reversed the neglect of Ibla in recent years. A number of bars have taken over historic palaces, with tasteful bohemian conversions co-existing with the clubby, patrician side of town. In the evening, in particular, all feudal posturing is banished in favour of food and flirtation.

Santa Maria delle Scale, framed by parched hills, represents the gateway to Ibla. This Gothic church is a balcony over Old Ragusa; 250 steps zigzag down to Ibla, offering a commanding view over isolated farms and the blue-tinged cupola of the cathedral below. The covered passageways, golden mansions and crumbling church make a quaint chiaroscuro introduction to Ibla, part of a picturesque route winding down to the cathedral. After the cosy claustrophobia so far, the spacious Piazza Duomo below comes as a shock. The sloping square is lined with palm trees, baroque mansions and aristocratic clubs but dominated by Gagliardi's San Giorgio, a masterpiece of Sicilian baroque. Giardino Ibleo, an appealing, recently landscaped park, is set on a spur at the eastern end of Ibla. Around the grounds are three ruined churches, victims of the 1693 earthquake: the majolica dome of San Domenico overlooks Gothic San Giacomo, built over a pagan temple, and Chiesa dei Cappuccini, a baroque monastic church.

Ragusa's coast

An intriguing drive past greenhouses of ripening tomatoes leads to two archaeological sites on the coast. Classical **Camarina** ㊻ was founded in 598 BC, a sophisticated piece of urban planning covering three hills at the mouth of the Ippari river. The city of perfect parallel lines was destroyed by the Romans in AD 258. The Antiquarium (open 9am–1 hour before sunset; entrance fee) marks the centre of the site, with an array of city walls, a tower, tombstones and the ruins of Hellenistic villas nearby.

At Punta Secca, the headland just southeast of Camarina, the Roman port of **Kaukana** ㊼ is slowly being excavated. The port, partly preserved by sand, is a lovely but inscrutable puzzle compounded by the discovery of Hellenistic amphora, Roman coins and Jewish candelabra. Leave the shady umbrella pines for a picnic on the sandy beaches below the headland or consider a fish lunch at the modern resort of **Marina di Ragusa**, a bustling summer resort. Discreet well-being is indeed the keynote to this relaxed region. ❑

THE GREAT TUNA HARVEST

"La Mattanza", the annual tuna hunt, is a tradition that dates from the 9th century, and it still has a distinctly Arabic sound

Tuna fishing, along with swordfishing, is rooted in the Sicilian psyche. Nowhere is this more so than in the Egadi island of Favignana, off the west coast of Sicily. It is considered the sea's ultimate challenge to man, as well as the island's traditional livelihood. The fast-swimming tuna hunt off the coast of Norway but spawn in Sicily's warm spring waters. Here they are captured in a system of chambered nets introduced by the Arabs in the 9th century. The season lasts from May to mid-June, and *la mattanza*, the ritual catch, is the fate of a passing shoal. In the past, one day could determine the island's fortune for the rest of the year but numbers are now negligible. The tradition and tourist spectacle survives despite conservationists' concerns and the contravention of conventions on driftnet fishing.

THE MADONNA GOES TOO

Buoys mark out a 100-metre (330-feet) rectangle on the sea; up to 10 km (6 miles) of nets are suspended between the floats. At dawn, or when the winds are right, the black boats set off to check the nets. The helmsman leads the fleet in prayers, aided by an image of the Madonna. The 60-strong crew sings and chants the *cialoma* in guttural Arabic accents. Entreaties are uttered by the *rais*, a Moorish title given to the chief fisherman, who travels in a separate boat and constantly checks the entrance to the *camera della morte*. The eight black boats encircle the nets. As the net is drawn in to the length of a football pitch, the fish circle frantically in the *sarabanda della morte*, the dance of death. The chanting stops and the slaughter begins.

Tuna processing can occupy the following three months. The bulk of the harvest ends up in Japan, but some tuna reaches El Pescador, a restaurant run by Favignana fishermen.

◁ **INVOKING ALLAH**
To the command of "*tira, tira!*" the net is pulled tight. The fishermen's sea shanty chorus of "*aiamola, aiamola*" is derived from *Allah! Che muoia!* (Allah, may it die!).

△ **FATAL ATTACK**
Some tuna are man-sized and their razor-sharp tail fins can kill. Some, however, die of heart attacks or over-oxygenation.

◁ **THE FINAL CHAMBER**
When the *rais* decides that the currents are right, the shoal is steered into the *camera del morte*, the central chamber in 10 km (6 miles) of nets. As the chamber fills with fish, it begins to sag, like a heavy sack. Then the chanting stops and the slaughter begins.

△ **GRUELLING WORK**
The fish are stabbed and caught behind the gills with gaff hooks on long poles. A proverb says: "Tuna fishing shortens your arms and silences your tongue."

A FEW WORDS ON SWORDFISH

Swordfish is the local delicacy par excellence. Compared with the dwindling tuna stocks, this huge fish has fared better, with prized catches weighing up to 300 kg (660 lbs) readily available, the richest fishing grounds being off the shores of Sicily, close to the coast of Messina and the island of Pantelleria. Swordfish are traditionally pursued in tiny, black, fish-shaped boats, but given the profitability of sword-fishing, fast fleets of *feluccas* are gaining ground. These 30-ton monsters are equipped with a look-out post and a platform on the prow for the harpoonist. Once the prey is sighted, a blessing is shouted to St Mark and the harpoon gun fired. If the victim is female, the grief-stricken male often thrashes around in sympathy and charges the boat. This final gesture of love leads to the capture of the male in what Sicilians see as "a sublime and mysterious synthesis of love and death". Fatalism, if not forgotten, is double-edged: it is the sword-fish's fate to end up as juicy *spada alla messinese.*

SICILY'S ISLANDS

The Egadi and Aeolian archipelagos represent the main attractions but divers will be drawn to Ustica and nature-lovers to the remote African outposts of Pantelleria and the Pelagie islands

Map on page 268

The new millennium was welcomed with the brief resurfacing of a long-vanished piece of the British Empire off the coast of Sicily. Graham Island, a submerged volcano first recorded in 10 BC, had not been seen since 1832, but reappeared, amid sulphurous emanations, off the western coast of Sicily. This phantom island, also claimed by Italy and France, last featured in an international dispute in 1987, when a US warplane mistook the tip of the island for a Libyan submarine and dropped depth charges on it. Fortunately, Sicily's remaining "real" islands contain enough explosive drama for such phantoms to pale into insignificance.

Posers can preen on yachts off Panarea, divers can explore underwater wrecks off Ustica, while nature-lovers and ramblers can seek out lush Marettimo or barren Lampedusa, Sicily's wild west. On the Moorish islands of Pantelleria and the Pelagie, the kasbah and the curious white-domed *dammusi* houses evoke a distinct sense of North Africa. Pantelleria, a remote lump of volcanic rock, represents a Tunisian outpost far closer to Africa than mainland Italy; even the excellent wine has an exotic flavour. For adventure-lovers, the Aeolian Islands are the most dramatic in Sicily, shaped by volcanic eruption and wind erosion. The island of Stromboli, in particular, is a byword for wonderful pyrotechnics.

A four hour hydrofoil crossing links Naples and Palermo, or Naples and the Aeolian Islands, with far longer ferry crossings also on offer. Palermo, Milazzo, Trapani and Porto Empedocle are the gateways to island life. Within each archipelago, there are good summer connections but island-hopping between archipelagos is difficult. Some islands accept cars, but transport is generally by boat, bicycle or by three-wheeled vehicles, used to navigate the tiny alleys.

AEOLIAN ISLANDS

The **Aeolian Islands** ❹, known as the **Isole Eolie** in Italian, form a dazzling archipelago of seven volcanic islands, and represent one of Sicily's most compelling attractions. Named after Aeolus, the god of the winds, these elemental islands still exude an other-worldly air and a sense of isolation, despite their growing popularity. The islands also represent an assault on the senses, from sweet-smelling herbs and acrid sulphurous emissions to mustard-tinted radioactive waters and shores buffeted by the choppiest seas in the Tyrrhenian.

Lípari is the largest, best-equipped island and the usual gateway to the archipelago, while **Panarea** is the prettiest, **Salina** the homeliest, and **Filicudi** and **Alicudi** the least developed. For drama, it is difficult to compete with the volcanic activity on **Stromboli**'s seething crater. Other natural wonders include hot

LEFT: trip around the Aeolian Islands.
BELOW: Lipari shopkeepers.

Hydrofoils bring the islands closer to the Messina coast.

springs on Lípari and Panarea, with fumeroles (holes emitting volcanic gases) bubbling underwater on **Vulcano** and Stromboli. Apart from pyrotechnics, the archipelago promises sapphire-coloured seas and a dramatic coastline, as well as distinctive honey-coloured wine and food flavoured with capers and olives. Arrival is by hydrofoil or ferry from Naples, Palermo, Cefalù, Messina or Milazzo, with the fastest services from Milazzo *(see page 304)*.

Lípari , the main island in the archipelago, has a dormant volcano but a bustling holiday mood, at one with the local hot springs and fumeroles. **Lípari town** has an appealing port and alleys lined with chic boutiques and open-air cafés. The upper town is a fortified **citadel** perched on lava rock. Centred on the **Castello**, the Spanish-style bastions incorporate urban traces from medieval and Greek eras. The citadel is also home to a heavily remodelled Norman cathedral and the neighbouring **Museo Eoliano** (open daily 9am–2pm; entrance fee), containing one of the finest Neolithic collections in Europe. **Canneto**, north of the capital, has a sandy beach and lively bars but is better-known as the hollowed-out heart of the pumice-mining industry. Campobianco's quarries are the world's best source of pumice. Glossy black obsidian, once used to fashion tools and knives intended for human sacrifice, is also found.

Vulcano , the mythical home of Vulcan, the Roman god of fire, lies just south of Lípari and is the closest island to the Italian mainland. This volcanic outpost rivals Panarea as the most exclusive and expensive island, and has a lively nightlife, luxurious villas, a fine beach, and the drama of the volcano itself. The main crater last erupted in 1890, but there is plenty of secondary activity. It is enough to dock at the small port to be overwhelmed by sulphurous odours and steaming fumaroles. Close to **Porto di Levante**, the only landing place, are the radioactive mud baths known as *fanghi*, essentially a slimy pool of sulphurous mud favoured by wallowing fitness freaks and sufferers from arthritis or rheumatism. The surreal experience is sealed by a dip in the bubbling, occasionally scalding, sea. The **Gran Cratere**, just south, marks the start of the arduous but rewarding ascent of the eerie main crater, best attempted early in the morning or late in the afternoon. The less intrepid can climb Vulcanello, a smaller crater on the northeastern end of the island.

Salina , the second largest island on the archipelago, lies north of Lípari. This lush island, named after an ancient salt mine, has a plentiful water supply and was the evocative setting for the 1994 movie *Il Postino*. Quieter than Lípari and Vulcano, this welcoming island has a family-oriented feel. **Santa Marina di Salina**, the main port, is pleasant but **Malfa**, in the north, is more picturesque, with a harbour and pebble beach.

Panarea , the island north of Lípari, has an elitist reputation, like a miniature Portofino or Sicilian St Tropez. Since the 1960s, when it was discovered by wealthy northerners, this amber-coloured jewel has been a retreat with a *dolce far niente* reputation. While the fashionable yachting fraternity explores the islets and coves by boat, lesser mortals can enjoy the romantic walks, sophisticated nightlife, and the bronze-hued beaches. Tortuous cliffside paths lead

BELOW: Lípari town.

past flower-bedecked Moorish-style villas owned by Milanese industrialists to a wilder landscape of rosemary, olives or capers. A stroll from **Punta Milazzese**, a basalt-walled promontory inhabited in prehistoric times, leads to the charming cove of **Cala Junco**, a popular place for snorkelling. Another highlight is the dramatic cliffs, beach, fumeroles and small geysers at **Calcara**.

The lighthouse of the Mediterranean

Stromboli ⓕ, the easternmost Aeolean island, is black by day but spectacular fireballs and showers of volcanic debris make it incandescently red by night. The ancients called it "the lighthouse of the Mediterranean" and the presence of an active volcano ensures that it remains the most celebrated island. Stromboli further beguiles visitors with whitewashed houses swathed in bougainvillaea, and vistas over palm trees, olive and lemon groves. It also has the best nightlife in the archipelago, and pays the price in terms of over-popularity. But boat trips around the craggy coast reveal secluded coves and creeks, as well as black sandy beaches and deep waters for divers.

An excursion to the crater is the highpoint of most visits. The ascent of the volcano is best at night, and always accompanied by a guide, with three hours allowed for the ascent and two for the descent. **Strombolicchio**, off the north coast, and surrounded by swirling currents, makes an atmospheric boat trip. From afar, this petrified basalt rock looks like a Gothic cathedral or formidable castle. A steep rock staircase rises to a terrace with sheer slopes to the sea.

Filicudi ⓖ, which you will find midway between Salina and Alicudi, was named after the prodigious ferns that covered the slopes in classical times, but more common today are the dark-green capers, vineyards and olive groves.

Pumice is a porous volcanic rock so light that it floats on water. It is used as a bleaching agent and also in toothpaste and lightbulbs.

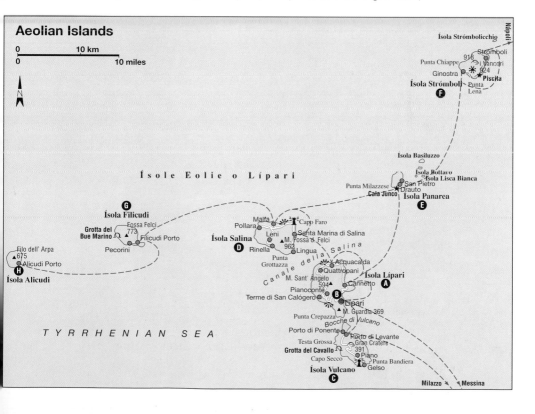

Sun hats on the upper deck.

BELOW: Favignana, Egadi Islands.

The unattractive port is not representative of this undeveloped rural island, dotted with flowering cacti and riddled with mule tracks. The most appealing boat trip is to **Grotta del Bue Marino**, a damp cave that was once inhabited by a colony of seals. **Alicudi** , Filicudi's sister island, is the most westerly in the archipelago, and remains more interested in catching lobsters than in luring hordes of tourists.

USTICA

Lying off the north coast, 60 km (40 miles) from Palermo, **Ustica** ⓭ is by common consent a diver's paradise. The island is connected by hydrofoil and ferry with both Palermo and Naples, and can be visited on a day trip. This volcanic, turtle-shaped island has tolerated Phoenicians, Saracen pirates and a penal colony but has flourished as a well-managed marine reserve and resort since the 1960s. Ustica's waters reveal an explosion of colour, from corals, sea-sponges and anenomes to barracudas, breams, scorpion fish and groupers.

The rugged coastline is riddled with caverns and coves, partly accessible along coastal paths. Landlubbers can visit the fort, lighthouse and aquarium, as well as a marine study centre in a watchtower.

EGADI ISLANDS

The **Egadi Islands** ⓾, a small archipelago off the western coast of Sicily, lie in multicoloured waters teeming with marine life. From the docks of Trapani *(see page 283)*, point of departure for the frequent ferries and hydrofoils, the islands resemble dark humps floating on the not-too-distant horizon. Close-up, however, contrasts emerge. **Lèvanzo** is rugged and friendly, **Favignana** the liveliest,

most developed and family-oriented, while **Maréttimo**, furthest from the mainland, is the loveliest. As the easiest offshore islands to visit, the Egadi cannot avoid the summer crowds; however, these are focused on tourist-oriented Favignana, leaving Lévanzo and Maréttimo relatively undiscovered, the place for boat trips and gentle hiking.

The Egadi have 15,000 years of history and the finest prehistoric cave drawings in Italy. The Egadi were once a land bridge linking Africa to mainland Italy and became the springboard for the Arab conquest of Sicily. Arab culture is evident, from the guttural local accent to the cube-shaped architecture. In 1874, the islands were bought by the Florio family, one of Sicily's most famous dynasties of entrepreneurs, who developed the tuna industry.

Favignana ⑤, the largest and most populous island, shaped like a lopsided butterfly, presents itself as the land of tuna, tufa and tourism. Quarrying has made the island a homage to stone; slopes are dotted with tufa houses and material from the maze-like Cala Rossa built entire Moorish cities. Figs and tomatoes are planted on the floor of abandoned quarries and sheer stone walls, overgrown with thyme and capers, shelter orange and lemon trees from the sweeping sea winds. The chiselled walls and eroded geometry of seaside quarries such as Cala Rossa and Cavallo make them popular picnic and swimming spots.

The still waters of the harbour reflect the tiled roofs and stone smoke-stacks of Tonnare Florio, a tuna fishery converted into a handsome monument to industrial archaeology. On the peak of the island's one hill looms the Arab-Norman **Forte Santa Caterina**, a political prison in Bourbon times and now a forbidden military zone. **Forte San Giacomo**, a Norman castle and Bourbon prison, is a maximum-security prison for Sicily's *mafiosi*.

TIP

Hikers should remember to carry plenty of water, particularly on Maréttimo. On these parched islands, water is more precious than wine.

BELOW: Lévanzo.

Levanzo ⑫, facing Favignana, is a simpler proposition than the main island, with the tiny port of **Cala Dogana** the sole centre of civilisation. From here, a track passes farmhouses and sheep-pens before zigzagging down to the coast. The stony slopes are covered with *macchia mediterranea*, arid, grey-green scrub that blooms in late spring. The **Grotta del Genovese**, a deep cavern overhanging the rocky shoreline, is the main reason for visiting Lévanzo. One can reach the grotto by boat, and sail and swim from a craft hired at Cala Dogana (or book with the custodian of the caves; tel 0923-924032). The grotto walls hold Lévanzo's greatest treasure, Mesolithic rock carvings.

Maréttimo ⑬, the most mysterious, mountainous and greenest of the Egadi, lies to the west, separated from her sister islands by a stretch of sea rich in sunken archaeological treasure. To Sicilian scholars, Maréttimo is a mythical island, nothing less than Odysseus' Ithaca. The little port has no hotel but the fishermen of Maréttimo happily accept guests in their homes.

Dammusi, the traditional cuboid Arab houses with domed roofs, date back to designs created in Neolithic times by Tunisian settlers to the archipelago. They are designed to keep the interior cool.

PANTELLERIA

Lying off the southwestern coast of Sicily, **Pantelleria** ⑭ is closer to Tunisia than to Sicily, and is reached on a five-hour ferry crossing from Trapani, or on a flight from Palermo. Pantelleria's evocative name probably derives from the Arabic "daughter of the winds" after the breezes that buffet this rocky outpost, even in an African August. The landscape is rather bleak, with jagged rocks and coves instead of beaches. Cool, low-domed Moorish *dammusi* houses are surrounded by terraces of capers and grapes; vines are trained low to protect them from being battered by the hot southern winds or cold northern winds.

The volcanic origins of Sicily's biggest island are visible in lavastone, basalt rock, hot springs, and a landscape pitted with "cuddie", small, extinct volcanic craters. A startling scene awaits at **Lago di Venere**, near the hamlet of **Bugeber**: set inside a former crater, the small lake is full of warm, bubbling, sulphurously brown waters, imbued with myriad cures. Steam baths can also be taken in the island grottoes. A rewarding hike from Pantelleria town in the north to the port of **Scauri** on the southern coast allows sightings of traditional *dammusi* houses, terraced vineyards, small settlements and the blackened, lavastone landscape. Drystone walls enclose orange groves and capers, and are often overlooked by hardy donkeys. The route also passes Neolithic dome-shaped funerary monuments, known as *sesi*, perhaps built by early Tunisian settlers. Although modern and rather scruffy, Pantelleria town has a lively air as well as an exoticism encapsulated by white-cubed houses and restaurants serving fish *couscous*. The volcanic soil benefits vine-growing, and the island produces prized fortified wines.

BELOW: cactus on Pantelleria.

PELAGIE ISLANDS

The **Pelagie Islands** ⑮ are a scorching archipelago of three islands lying amid strong currents off the coast of Africa, closer to Tunisia than the Sicilian mainland. Although there are pockets of agriculture, the islands are unnaturally barren due to wanton deforestation and the virtual disappearance of the native olive groves, juniper and carob plantations. Fifty years ago, much of this lunar land-scape was farmland bounded by drystone walls but today, the local economy rests on fishing, from sponge fishing to canning, supplemented by tourism in Lampedusa. However, the islanders have belatedly realised the error of their unecological ways and started small-scale reafforestation programmes on Lampedusa. In terms of cultural heritage, there are no outstanding sites but the waters are translucent, and rich in marine life, while the rugged native charac-ter and cuisine are distinctly Tunisian.

Highlights of a stay include *dammusi* houses, couscous and fish, coastal walks and, except for high summer in Lampedusa, peace and quiet. A curious summer feature is the virtually continuous breezes and chilly nights. These unspoilt islands are reached by ferry from Porto Empedocle near Agrigento (an 8-hour crossing) but direct flights to Lampedusa also operate from Palermo.

Linosa ⑤⑥, the island closest to the shore, can be reached on a day trip from Lampedusa, and represents the tip of a vast submerged volcano. The three vis-ible volcanic cones may now be extinct but the beaches, still strewn with black boulders, can coat the unwary in ash and grit. Even so, in this cauldron of an island, most visitors congregate on the lavic beaches or quickly develop an interest in scuba-diving. On this lump of volcanic rock, there is little to do except rest, roast, swim, trek along dusty paths through vineyards or spot *dammusi*, pastel-coloured cubes with white window-frames.

Lampedusa ⑤⑦ is known as "a gift from Africa to Europe", or, due to its recent popularity with illegal immigrants, "the backdoor to Italy". The island was first settled by the Phoenicians and Greeks but was later owned by the Princes of Lampedusa. Weather-beaten Tunisian fishermen live on the south coast, the only inhabited centre. Lampedusa's recent claim to fame is as an American radar base for bomb-ing Libya in 1986 and as an arrival point for boat-loads of illegal immigrants (and the occasional drug-runner) who land on remote beaches. Sponge fishing represents the mainstay of the island's econ-omy, with a local cannery used to process a wide range of Mediterranean fish. The wonderful marine life is similar to that off the North African coast, with the waters home to shoals of dolphins, monk seals and, in March, witnessing the sperm whale migration. Parrot fish and seals abound in the limpid waters, while turtles lay their eggs on **Isola dei Conigli**, an offshore nature reserve named after its rabbit colony.

Lampedusa port has a rabbit warren of a *kasbah* which reeks of spices, sardines, anchovies and goats. Indeed, the port is the best place for sampling such dishes as pasta with sardines, sweet and sour rabbit, or Sicilian candied fruit and spicy desserts. Buses from the port are infrequent and, despite the rocky roads, bicycles and mopeds are a popular way of exploring the interior. A boat trip is the best way of appreciating Lampedusa's secluded grottoes, craggy inlets and sheer limestone cliffs. Lampione, an uninhabited reef, is scorched dry due to man's negligence. Its drama lies underwater: the translucent sea is clean and rich in marine life, from sponge beds to hungry sharks. Sicil-ian pleasures are notoriously double-edged. ❑

Map on page 268

Despite, or because of its isolation, Pantelleria is popular with privacy-seeking celebrities from Madonna to Giorgio Armani, who has a villa on the island.

BELOW: Lago di Venere, Pantelleria.

INSIGHT GUIDES

Travel Tips

CONTENTS

Getting Acquainted

The Place

Area: Italy: 301,308 sq km/ 116,335 sq miles
Capital: Rome
Population: Italy 57 million; Naples 1,400,000; Bari 353,000; Catania 333,000; Palermo 700,000; Reggio Calabria 180,000
Language: Italian
Religion: Roman Catholic
Time Zone: Central European Time (GMT plus 1 hour, EST plus 6hrs)
Currency: The euro (€).
Weights and Measures: Metric
Electricity: 220 volts. Take an adaptor to operate British three-pin appliances and a transformer to use 100–120 volt appliances
International Dialling Code: 39

Geography

While Southern Italy may appear to be simply the lower portion of the famous boot (and Sicily the triangular-shaped football it is about to kick), the geography of this portion of the peninsula consists of a series of mountain ranges (the

Climate

Southern Italy's typically Mediterranean climate leaves it dependably sunnier than Northern Italy. July and August can be unpleasantly hot and humid in all but coastal areas and the mountainous and forested portions of the interior. As with the rest of Italy, late spring and early autumn are the best times to visit, with the weather at its mildest and the crowds at their nadir.

southern portion of the Appenines, the Pollino massif that covers much of Calabria) and the volcanic terrain of Campania and the plains of Apulia. Well-known volcanoes form the landscapes of Naples (Vesuvius), Eastern Sicily (Etna), and the entire island of Stromboli.

Government

Italy's president is elected for a term of seven years by Parliament, which is composed of two houses: the Senate (with 315 members) and the Chamber of Deputies (630 members). The president (currently Carlo Ciampi elected in 1999) nominates the prime minister and, on the latter's recommendations, the Cabinet.

After a period of constitutional corruption in the early 1990s, Italy reduced its dependence on proportional representation and moved towards a "first-past-the-post" system, under which the country elected its first left-wing government, a loose centre-left coalition, in 1996. In 2001 the pendulum swung back with the election of Berlusconi's right-wing Casa della Libertà coalition. As in the US, elected mayors wield considerable power.

The regions tend to have strong political affiliations, and special autonomous status has been granted to five of them. Northern Italy is influenced by federalist tendencies. A separatist party, the Northern League, campaigns for an independent Northern Italy, which it has named Padania. It polls about 10 percent of the vote.

The politics of Southern Italy is marked by its historic contrast with the North: it is less developed economically and stigmatised by high unemployment and corruption.

Sicily has the special status of 'autonomous region', with its own parliament and institutions that are organised separately from the Italian state.

Economy

Southern Italy is notoriously economically underdeveloped, with

high unemployment and a long history of corruption, despite decades of failed subsidies and promises from revolving governments to solve the southern problem once and for all. Great strides have been made, and progress continues, albeit slower than anyone wants.

Distance from European markets, poor rail and postal services, a lack of a skilled and educated work force all help explain the low productivity statistics for Southern Italy. But the poverty should not be exaggerated. The black economy ensures that major cities meet the national average for consumer spending.

Recent subsidies from the European Union have led to increased manufacturing, but such development has often come at great cost to the natural environment. One industry that continues to grow is tourism.

Public Holidays

- **January** New Year's Day (1), Epiphany (6)
- **March/April** Good Friday, Easter Monday
- **April** Liberation Day – *Anniversario della Liberazione* (25)
- **May** Labour Day – *Festa del Lavoro* (1)
- **August** Assumption of the Blessed Virgin Mary – *Ferragosto* (15)
- **November** All Saints – *Ognissanti* (1)
- **December** Immaculate Conception of the Blessed Virgin Mary – *Immacolata Concezione* (8), Christmas Day (25), St Stephen's Day (26)

In addition to these national holidays, almost all cities have a holiday to celebrate their own patron saint. Check with the local tourist office for details. Here are a few examples:

- **Festa di San Gennaro in Naples** (1st Sun in May, Sep 19, Dec 16)
- **Sant'Andrea in Amalfi** (June 27)
- **San Nicola in Bari** (1st weekend in May)
- **Santa Rosalia in Palermo** (July 15)

Planning the Trip

Visas and Passports

EU citizens do not need a visa to enter Italy, just a passport or an identification card valid for foreign travel. Visitors from the following countries need a passport but not a visa providing they do not stay for more than three months: Australia, Austria, Barbados, Canada, Iceland, Jamaica, Japan, Kenya, South Korea, Kuwait, Malaysia, Maldives, Malta, Mexico, Monaco, New Zealand, Niger, Norway, Paraguay, Poland (for a stay up to 30 days), Singapore, Switzerland, Trinidad and Tobago, United States, Uruguay, Venezuela (up to 60 days). Other nationalities should contact their nearest Italian consulate.

You are supposed to register with the police within three days of arriving in Italy. In fact, this procedure will be taken care of by your hotel, whatever the level of accommodation. If you are not staying in a hotel, contact the local police station.

Money Matters

The euro (€) replaced the Italian lira in February 2002. The currency is available in 500, 200, 100, 50, 20, 10 and 5 euro notes, and 2-euro, 1-euro, 50-cent, 20-cent, 10-cent, 5-cent, 2-cent and 1-cent coins. There are 100 cents to one euro. Most shopkeepers and restaurateurs will not change money, so it is best to change a limited amount at the airport when you arrive, especially if it is the weekend, when banks are closed. Try to avoid changing money in hotels, where the commission tends to be higher than in banks.

Banks: Generally open from 8 or 8.30am–1.30pm and for 1½ hours in the afternoon (usually 2.30–4pm).

You will find current exchange rates are published in the press and posted in banks. Rates fluctuate considerably.

Cash machines: The most convenient way to get money in Italy is to use the ATM machines, which are easily found in all but the most remote towns, accessible 24 hours a day and providing the best exchange rates.

Credit cards: In cities, many restaurants, hotels, shops and stores will take major credit cards (Visa, American Express, Diner's Club, MasterCard and Carte Blanche) but most petrol stations require cash. Don't rely on being able to use credit cards in rural areas.

What to Wear

The Italians are known for their sense of style. This does not mean that one has to dress formally, but you may be barred from entering some churches if dressed in shorts (or short skirts in the case of women) or if you have uncovered shoulders.

Unless you are going to visit mountain areas, the moderate climate makes heavy clothing unnecessary in summer. A light jacket will be adequate for summer evenings. In winter (November–March), the climate can be cold and wet in Southern Italy, so bring the appropriate clothing.

Customs Regulations

Used personal effects may be imported and exported without formality. The import of narcotics, weapons and pirated materials is forbidden.

Alcoholic drinks, tobacco and perfume can be imported in limited quantities, depending on your nationality.

Duty-free shopping for EU citizens within Europe ended on 1 July 1999. Goods on which duty has already been paid in another

Animal Quarantine

Pets must be vaccinated against rabies and you should obtain an officially stamped document stating that your animal is healthy. This should be done no more than a month before you arrive in Italy.

Tourist Offices

Australia: Italian Government Travel Office (ENIT), 123 Clarence Street, Sydney, tel: 02 9299 4574.
Canada: Italian Government Travel Office (ENIT), Montréal, Québec H3B 2C3 1, Place Ville Marie, Suite 1914, tel: 514-8667667, fax: 514-3921429.
UK: Italian State Tourist Board (ENIT), 1 Princes Street, London W1R 8AY, tel: 020-7408 1254, fax: 020-7493 6695.
US: Italian Government Travel Office (ENIT), Suite 1565, 630 Fifth Avenue, New York, NY 10111, tel: 212-245 4822, fax: 212-5869249 and Suite 2240, 500 North Michigan Avenue, Chicago 1 – Illinois 60611, tel: 312-6440996, fax: 312-6443019. ENIT, Suite 550, 12400 Wilshire Blvd, Los Angeles, CA 90025-12400, tel: 310-8201898, fax: 310-8206357.

Getting There

By Air

In addition to the national airline, Alitalia, most airlines run direct flights to Italy, including many

EU country may be freely imported, provided the amount falls within what might be reasonably described as "for personal use".

For US citizens, the duty-free allowance is: 200 cigarettes, 50 cigars or 3 lb tobacco; 1 US quart of alcoholic beverages and duty-free gifts worth up to $100.

The airports at Naples, Bari, Reggio Calabria, Catania and Palermo have duty free shops.

charter flights with budget fares. There has been an explosion in the variety of low-price tickets available since the late 1990s, owing to the expansion of low-cost airlines such as Easyjet, Ryanair and Buzz. These airlines fly to numerous airports across Italy, including Naples. The following are the main airports in Southern Italy:

Bari: Aeroporto di Bari (10 km/ 6 miles north of Bari), tel: 080-5316182. Shuttle bus to the centre of town every half hour.

Catania: Aeroporto Fontanarossa (7 km/4½ miles south of Catania), tel: 095-7306266. Bus to central train station about every half hour.

Naples: Aeroporto Capodichino (7 km/4½ miles north of Naples), tel: 081-7896111. Frequent buses to Piazza Garibaldi (taking 20 minutes).

Palermo: Aeroporto Punto Raisi (32 km/20 miles west of Palermo), tel: 091-591698; flight information 091-7020486; buses every half-hour for most of the day (50 minutes).

Reggio Calabria–Messina: (5 km/ 3 miles from Reggio Calabria), tel: 0965-643291. Buses roughly every hour (20 minutes into town).

Trapani Airport (Birgi): (20 km/ 12 miles south of Trapani), tel: 0923-842502. Flights to Rome and Pantelleria weekdays.

By Car

When calculating the cost of travelling to Italy by car, allow for motorway tolls as well as accommodation en route and petrol. Motorists driving through Switzerland will need to purchase a *vignette*, an annual road pass which costs around €30 and can be bought either at the border or at any national tourist office. If you want to travel by toll-free roads in Italy, get hold of the Italian State Tourist Office's *Traveller's Handbook*, which lists them.

The usual route from France to Italy is via the Mont Blanc Tunnel (between Chamonix and Courmayeur) or from Switzerland through the Gran San Bernardo Tunnel (between Bourg St Pierre and Aosta). Some of the many alpine passes are seasonal, so it is best to check the

viability of your route with the tourist board or a motoring organisation before setting off. Alternatively, motorists can head down the French autoroute to Nice and cross the border at Ventimiglia on the Riviera.

To take your car into Italy, you will need your current driving licence (with an Italian translation unless it is the standard EU licence), your vezhicle registration document (which must be in the driver's name or supported by the owner's written permission for the driver to use the vehicle) and Green Card insurance. You must also carry a warning triangle in case of breakdown.

Car Trains

The Italian railway 'auto al seguito' service can save you the effort of driving and the expense of petrol and toll roads. Vehicles should be no larger than 1.58 metres (5 ft 2 ins) in height, 1.8 metres (5 ft 10 ins) in width, and 7 metres (22 ft 11 ins) in length. A car must be accompanied by at least one passenger on the train. The cost varies with the season, number of travellers (above age 4), and the route (cheaper to buy round trip than two one-way tickets). For example, a Milan–Palermo one-way costs between around €90 and €210.

There are 36 other official routes between the main train stations in Northern Italy (Milan, Turin, Venice, Genoa, Calalzo, Bologna, Florence) and Rome, Naples, Bari, Crotone, Lamezia Terme, Villa San Giovanni, Milazzo, Catania and Palermo. But note that the 'auto al seguito' service along these routes only operates on particular periods/ days during the year. Reservations are obligatory, and can be made two months in advance right until the day before departure. Travellers would be wise to check on their insurance coverage and mind valuables, as theft from vehicles carried on this service are not unheard of.

By Coach

The cost of travelling to Italy from Great Britain by scheduled coach is not much cheaper than travelling by air. National Express Eurolines runs coaches from London Victoria, via Paris and Mont Blanc, to Aosta, Turin, Genoa, Milan, Venice and Bologna. To book from London, contact: National Express Eurolines, Victoria Coach Station, Buckingham Palace Road, London SW1, tel: 0990-808080.

By Rail

Rail travel is not a particularly cheap option unless you are visiting different places in Italy as part of the Inter-Rail or Eurail schemes. These provide a month's unlimited train travel in Europe for anyone under the age of 26 at a very reasonable price. They can be an attractive option, especially if you are planning to stop off en route.

For details of rail travel contact:
Australia: CIT, 123 Clarence Street, Sydney, tel: 02 9299 4574.
UK: European Rail Ltd
tel: 020-7387 0444.
Italian State Railway, Marco Polo House, 3–5 Landsdowne Road, Croydon, Surrey, tel: 020-8686 0677.
USA: CIT Tours, 342 Madison Avenue, Suite 207, New York, NY 190173, tel: 1-800 223 7987/212 697 1482.

When travelling from Britain via Paris, it is necessary to change in Paris (from Gare du Nord to Gare de Lyon). EC (Eurocity) and TEE (Trans Europe Express) trains are luxury first-class only trains running between the main European cities. A special supplement is charged and seat reservation is obligatory. Keep in mind that the travel time by train to the south once you cross the border is as follows:
Turin–Naples: 9 hrs
Turin–Bari: 10 hrs
Milan–Bari: 8½ hrs
Milan–Naples: 9 hrs
Naples–Reggio Calabria/Catania: 5 hrs
Reggio Calabria/Catania–Palermo: 6 hrs

For train information, call the same number from anywhere in

Italy: 147 888 088. Alternatively, check routes on the official railway website: www.fs-on-line.com.

Package Tours

From the UK, Ireland, or the US, this is usually the easiest and most economical way to visit historic centres. It can be an advantage to travel with a company that has good local representation. Current brochures are generally available from your travel agent.

Specialist Tours

Andante Travels
The Old Barn, Old Road, Alderbury, Salisbury SP5 3AR, tel: 01722-713800; fax: 01722-711966,
www.andantetravels.co.uk
Specialises in archaeological tours
ATG Oxford
69–71 Banbury Road, Oxford OX2 6PE, tel: 01865 315678, fax: 01865-315697/8/9, www.atg–oxford.co.uk.
Walking holidays which involve exploring the countryside while enjoying excellent Italian food and hospitality.
Citalia
8 Lansdowne Rd, Croydon CR9 1LL, tel: 020-8686 5533, fax: 020 8686 0328,
www.citalia.co.uk.
Covering all kinds of holidays, for a variety of budgets.
Long Travel
The Steps, All Stretton, Shropshire SY6 6HG, tel: 01694-722193, fax: 01694-724291, www.long–travel.co.uk
Travel firm dealing uniquely with Southern Italy. Specialise in agritourism (staying in working farms, albeit in great comfort).
Magic of Italy
Magic Travel Group, Kings House, 12–42 Wood Street, Kingston-upon-Thames KT1 1JF, tel: 08700 270500, fax: 020 8939 2286, www. magictravelgroup.co.uk.
Holidays in Southern Italy, taking you off the beaten track.

Practical Tips

Business Hours

Shops are open for business 9am–12.30pm and 3.30 or 4pm–7.30 or 8pm. In areas serving tourists, hours are generally longer than these. Many shops close for one morning or afternoon during the week. Some close on Saturday. Almost everything closes on Sunday.

Tipping

Unless otherwise indicated on the menu, service is included. Therefore it is not necessary to tip your waiter. A modest amount of change left on the table is sufficient to express appreciation for good service. Although *pane e coperto*, an outdated cover and bread charge, has been officially eliminated in most cities, some restaurants have been slow in phasing it out. Only in the finest hotels, and for lengthy stays, is a tip for the maids/head walters necessary.

Media

The Italian press is concentrated in Milan and Rome. The biggest papers are *La Repubblica* and *Il Corriere della Sera,* which publish regional editions. The main regional newspapers for the south are *Il Mezzogiorno* and *Il Gazetto del Sud* for the whole south (based in Reggio Calabria), *Il Giornale di Sicilia* (based in Palermo) and *La Sicilia* (based in Catania) for all of Sicily, *Barisera* for Bari, and *Il Quotidiano* for Reggio Calabria.

Most major cities publish weekly listings magazines which are worth getting, even for visitors with little or no Italian. The local tourist office should also have information on current events.

Television stations include RAI (the national network with three channels), the Vatican network, plus seven national and more than 450 local commercial stations.

Postal Services

Post office hours are usually 8am–1.30pm, or 8.30am–2pm but many towns have a main post office which is open throughout the day. Stamps are also available from tobacconists (*tabacchi*).

The Italian postal system is notoriously unreliable. It's certainly worth spending the extra to send letters home using the priority service. Mail sent *posta prioritaria* gets delivered within 24 hours in Italy and 48 hours in Europe, while a letter or postcard sent via ordinary post can take days, sometimes weeks. Note that you must drop your mail in the special '*posta prioritaria*' boxes. *Postacelere*, the Italian mail's courier service, offers better rates than comparable private services.

If you want to register a letter, ask to send it *raccomandata.* You can receive mail addressed to a *Posta Restante,* held at the *Fermo Posta* window of the main post office in every town, picking it up personally with identification.

For detailed information about rates and delivery times you can call toll-free 800-009966 from Italy or consult the website: www.poste.it.

Telecommunications

Public telephones are often found in bars and on squares. Most accept pre-paid phone cards (*carte telefoniche*), available from tobacconists and many bars.

The cost of long-distance calls depends on the distance and the time of day. Within Italy, the cheapest time to call is 6.30pm–8am, after 1pm on Saturday or all day Sunday.

If you are telephoning to outside Italy, you will be charged the least if you call between 10pm–8am and all day Sunday. Off-peak rates are affected by whether you call in the peak or off-peak period of the country you are calling.

Calling Home

Using a payphone with a pre-paid phone card (*carta telefonica*) is almost always the cheapest and most convenient way to call abroad from Italy. To make an international call, dial 00, followed by:

Australia 61
Canada 1
Ireland 353
New Zealand 64
UK 44
USA 1

Then dial the subscriber number, omitting the initial 0 if there is one.

- European Directory Enquiries: 176
- European operator assistance: 15
- Intercontinental operator assistance: 170
- Telegrams and cables: 186

Area Codes in Italy

Remember that for all calls within Italy (even local calls), you must first dial the appropriate area code, which you can obtain free from Information (tel: 12). The area codes of the main cities in this guide are:

Bari, tel: 080
Catania, tel: 095
Lecce, tel: 0832
Naples, tel: 081
Palermo, tel: 091
Reggio Calabria, tel: 0965
Rome, tel: 06
Taormina, tel: 0942

Local Tourist Offices

Every major town has an **Azienda di Promozione Turistica** (APT) or **Informazione e Accoglienza Turistica** (IAT). For addresses and phone numbers, check the directory or the *Yellow Pages* under ENIT (Ente Nazionale per il Turismo – the Italian state tourist board). The Yellow Pages website is www.paginegialle.it.

Together with helpful information, main APT offices offer a free city map, a list of hotels, and museum hours and addresses. APT offices in the main areas are listed below. A full list of Italian Tourist Board offices can also be found on the Italian tourist web guide: www.itwb.com. For general information, the Italian tourist board web address is www.enit.it

Most towns in Italy have a **Touring Club Italiano** (TCI) office, which provides free information about areas of interest. Phone numbers are listed in the local telephone book.

CAMPANIA

Amalfi
Corso Roma 19, tel: 089-871107. Open Mon–Fri 8am–2pm and 3–6pm, Sat 8am–noon.

Capri
Marina Grande, tel: 081-8370634. Open Mon–Sat 9.30am–5.15pm. Piazza Umberto, tel: 081-8370686. Open 9am–1pm and 3.30–6.45pm. Via Orlandi (Anacapri), tel: 081-8371524. Open Mon–Sat 9.30am–5.15pm.

Ischia
Ischia Porto, tel: 081-991146. Open Mon–Sat 9am–noon and 2–5pm (shorter hours in winter).

Naples
Azienda Autonoma di Soggiorno, Piazza Plebiscito, tel: 081-2525726 or 9. Open Mon–Fri 8.30–3.30pm. Piazza del Gesù, tel: 081-5523238. Open Mon–Sat 9am–8pm, Sun 9am–2pm. Mergellina Funicular Station, tel: 081-761202. Open Mon–Sat 9am–8pm, Sun 9am–2pm. Palazzo Reale, tel: 081-5808216. Open Mon–Sat 9am–8pm, Sun 9am–2pm. Piazza Plebiscito, tel: 081-2471123. Open Mon–Sat 9am–8pm, Sun 9am–2pm. Via Partenope 10, tel: 081-405311. Open Mon–Fri 8.30am–3.30pm. Stazione Centrale, tel: 081-268779. Open Mon–Sat 9am–4pm, Sun 9am–1pm.

Paestum
Archaeological site, tel: 0828-811016. Open Mon–Sat 8am–2pm.

Pompeii
Via Sacra 1, tel: 081-8575280. Open Mon–Sat 8am–2pm (longer hours in summer).

Procida
Tourist Office, Ferry Building, tel: 081-8101968. Open Mon–Sat 9.30am–1pm and 4–6.30pm.

Positano
Via del Saracino 4, tel: 089-875067. Open Mon–Sat 8am–2pm, Sat 8am–noon.

Salerno
Stazione, tel: 089-231432 or toll-free in Italy 800-213289. Open Mon–Sat 9am–2pm and 3–8pm.

Sorrento
Via de Maio 35, tel: 081-8074033. Open Mon–Sat 9am–2.30pm and 3.30–6.30pm.

APULIA

Bari
Piazza Aldo Moro 32a, tel: 080-5242244. Open Mon–Sat 9am–1pm.
Stop Over in Bari, Via Nicolei 47, tel: 080-5232716. Open Mon–Fri 9am–8pm, Sat 9am–2pm and 3–8pm.

Brindisi
Piazza Dionisio (near Lungomare Regina Margherita), tel: 0831-423072. Open Mon–Fri 9am–2pm.

Foggia
Via Emilio Perrone 17, tel: 0881-723650. Open Mon–Fri 9am–noon.

Lecce
Via Vittorio Emanuele II 24, tel: 0832-284092. Open Mon–Fri 9am–1pm and 3–6pm.

Manfredonia (Gargano Peninsula)
Corso Manfredi 26, tel: 0884-581998. Open Mon–Sat 9am–1pm.

Taranto
Corso Umberto 113, tel: 099-4532392. Open Mon–Sat 9am–2pm.

BASILICATA

Maratea
Piazza del Gesù, tel: 0973-876908. Open Mon–Fri 9am–1pm.

Matera
Via De Viti De Marco 9, tel: 0835-331983. Open Mon–Sat 9am–1pm, Mon & Tues also 3.30–6.30pm.

Potenza
Via Alianelli 4 (Piazza Prefettura), tel: 0971-21812. Mon–Fri 9am–1pm and 4–6.30pm; Sat 9am–12.30pm.

CALABRIA

Catanzaro
Piazza Prefettura, tel: 0961-741764. Open Mon–Fri 8.30am–1pm; also Mon and Wed 3–4.30pm.

Crotone
Via Torino 148, tel: 0962-23185. Open Mon–Fri 8am–1pm; also Mon and Wed 2–5pm.

Cosenza
Corso Mazzini 92, tel: 0984-27271. Open Mon–Fri 7.30am–1.30pm; also Mon and Wed 2.30–5pm.

Reggio Calabria
Stazione Centrale, tel: 0965-27120. Mon–Sat 8am–8pm.
Aeroporto, tel: 0965-643291. Mon–Sat 8am–8pm.
Corso Garibaldi 329, tel: 0965-892012. Mon–Sat 8am–8pm.

Tropea
Piazza Ercole, tel: 0963-61475. Open Mon–Sat 9.30am–12.30pm and 4.30–9.30pm; also Sun 4.30–9.30pm; longer hours in the summer.

SICILY

Aeolian Islands (Lipari)
Corso Vittorio Emanuele 202, tel: 090-9880095. Open Mon–Fri 8am–2pm and 4.30–6.30pm (longer hours in summer).

Agrigento
Via Cesare Battisti 15, tel: 0922-20454. Open Mon–Sat 8.30am–1.30pm; also Wed 4–7pm; longer hours in the summer.

Catania
Via Cimorosa 10 (off Via Etnea), tel: 095-531802. Open 9am–7pm (shorter hours in winter).
Stazione Centrale, tel: 095-7306255. Open 9am–7pm (shorter hours in winter).
Catania Airport, tel: 095-7306266. Open 8am–10pm (shorter hours in winter).

Cefalù
Corso Ruggero 7, tel: 0921-421050. Open Mon–Fri 8am–2pm and 4–7pm, Sat 8am–2pm.

Etna (Linguaglossa)
Piazza Annunziata, tel: 095-643004. Open Mon–Sat 9am–1pm and 4–8pm.

Etna (Nicolosi)
Piazza Vittorio Emanuele 33, tel: 095-914488. Mon–Sat 9am–1pm and 4–8pm.

Marsala
Via XXIV Maggio 100, tel: 0923-714097. Open Mon–Sat 8am–2pm.

Messina
Piazza Cairoli 45, tel: 090-2936294; Open Mon–Sat 8.30am–2pm and 3–6pm.

Noto
Piazza 16 Maggio, tel: 0931-836744. Open Mon–Sat 8am–2pm and 3.30–6.30pm, Sun 8.30am–1.30pm.

Regional Websites

Apart from the general Italian State Tourist board site (www.enit. it), each region has its own official site:
Apulia www.puglia.org
Basilicata www.basilicata.com
Calabria www.regione.calabria.it
Campania www.campaniafelix.it
Sicily www.sicily.infocom.it

Palermo
Aeroporto Punta Raisi, tel: 091-591698. Open Mon–Fri 8am–midnight, Saturday–Sunday 8am–8pm, closed holidays.
Piazza Castelnuovo 34, tel: 091-6058351. Open Mon–Sat 8am–6pm.
Stazione Centrale, tel: 091-6165914. Open Mon–Sat 8am–6pm.

Ragusa
Via Capitani 33, (Ragusa Ibla), tel: 0932-621421. Open 9am–2pm and 3–7pm.

Siracusa
Via Maestranza 33 (Ortygia), tel: 0931-65201. Open Mon–Sat 9am–2pm and 4–7pm.

Taormina
Palazzo Corvaja, off Piazza Vittorio Emanuele, tel: 0942-23243. Open Mon–Fri 8am–2pm and 4–7pm, Sat 9am–1pm and 4–7pm.

Trapani (and the Egadi islands)
Piazzetta Saturno, tel: 0923 29000. Open Mon–Sat 8am–8pm, Sun 9am–noon and 3–6pm.

Medical Services

In cases of real need, such as medical aid or ambulances, call the Public Emergency Assistance number, **113**. This service operates on a 24-hour basis, and, in the principal cities, response will be in the main foreign languages. Dial **112** for the Carabinieri immediate action service. Certain tourist cities offer medical interpreting services.

To receive free treatment in cases of illness or accidents, EU citizens (and citizens of countries with other ties to Italy, such as Brazil, Monaco, and the former Yugoslavia), must obtain (in their country of residence before arriving in Italy) the E-111 form. This form is to state that the bearers are registered with their national health service and therefore have the right to the same assistance offered to Italian citizens. (Note: it won't provide repatriation, which you may require in the case of serious illness.) Citizens of non-EU countries must pay for medical assistance and medicine. Health insurance is recommended for travelling in Italy. Keep receipts for medical expenses if you want to claim.

Most hospitals have a 24-hour emergency department called *Pronto Soccorso*, but a stay in an Italian hospital can be a grim experience. For more minor complaints, seek out a *farmacia*, identified by a sign displaying a red cross within a white circle. Trained pharmacists give advice and suggest over-the-counter drugs, including antibiotics. Normal opening hours are 9am–1pm and 4–7.30 or 8pm, but outside these hours the address of the nearest *farmacia* on duty is posted in the window.

Security and Crime

The vast majority of tourists have pleasant, trouble-free holidays in Southern Italy. Although the Mafia has a strong hold in the region, it is highly unlikely that the average tourist will knowingly come into contact with them.

The main problem for tourists is petty crime: pick-pocketing and bag-snatching (by young criminals

Consulates

There is the following limited local consular representation in Southern Italy:

Naples
Canada Via Carducci 29,
tel: 081-401338
UK Francesco Crispi 132,
tel: 081-663511
USA Piazza della Repubblica,
tel: 081-5838111

Bari
UK Via Dalmezia 127,
tel: 080-5543668

Palermo
UK Via Cavour 117,
tel: 091-326412
(F. Tagliavia and Co.)

known as *scippatori* or *scippi*) together with theft from cars. Theft of all sorts is more likely in the tourist areas of Rome, Naples, Palermo, Catania and Siracusa. You can greatly reduce the possibility of theft by taking some elementary precautions (*see below*). Remember, too, that very little violent theft occurs: the chances of being mugged are very much higher in London or New York.

Expect the police to have a casual attitude to petty crime and a slightly suspect attitude to a woman on her own. Expect, also, to have to prove who you are and where you are staying before even beginning to embark on your tale of woe. In the event of a serious crime, contact your country's consulate or embassy as well as the *Carabinieri*.

Anti-theft Precautions

Avoid looking like a tourist and do not wear your wealth ostentatiously: carry your camera out of sight, and do not wave money or wallets. If carrying a handbag, keep it on the side away from the road (one speciality is the motorbike snatch-and-drive). It is best to leave money and valuables in the hotel safe. It hardly needs saying that a wallet poking out of a back pocket is an easy target. You should keep a separate record of credit card and cheque numbers, just in case.

Reporting a Crime

If you are robbed, report it as soon as possible to the local police. You will need a copy of the declaration in order to claim on your insurance. Even more importantly, it is highly likely that part of your property will be returned, often very rapidly. There is apparently an unspoken agreement between police and thieves: provided documents and credit cards are returned and no violence is used, the police apply minimum effort to arresting those responsible. So although your camera, unused film, cash and traveller's cheques have gone for

Personal Security

- Don't linger in non-commercial areas after dark
- Don't carry all your cash
- Use travellers' cheques or Eurocheques rather than large quantities of cash
- Never leave your luggage unattended
- Keep valuables in the hotel safe (most hotels provide a storage service)
- Deposit your room key at the desk before going out

good, the thieves may call the police within hours to report the whereabouts of your passport, credit cards, exposed film and possibly even your empty wallet.

Car Crime

Never leave luggage or valuables visible in a car; in fact, if possible leave nothing visible in a car. Cars are best parked off the street (e.g. in a hotel car park, of which there are sadly very few). You must have all the car documents with you when driving, but carry them with you when you park: if you should be unlucky enough to have the car stolen, they will help you record the theft.

Women Travellers

The difficulties encountered by women travelling alone in Italy are often overstated. Women have to put up with much male attention, but it is rarely dangerous. Ignoring whistles and questions is the best way to get rid of unwanted attention.

Getting Around

Public Transport

BY AIR

Travelling across Southern Italy and Sicily by air is quite feasible, although relatively expensive. Discount flights are often available if you are prepared to arrive and return on certain days, but such fares must be booked in Italy Alitalia (tel: 1478-65643; www.alitalia.com) and several smaller national carriers (Med, Meridiana, Air Sicilia and Air One and Air Industria) offer frequent services between Naples, Bari, Brindisi, Lamezia Terme (in Calabria), Catania, Palermo, Trapani, Lampedusa and Pantelleria.

BY RAIL

For the most part, the cheapest, fastest and most convenient way to travel through Southern Italy is by train, with frequent services connecting most destinations. Noteworthy exceptions are the interior of Calabria and Basilicata, where it's best to travel by car.

Train information is available from the *Uffici Informazioni* at most major stations, listed in the telephone directory under *Ferrovie dello Stato*. You can also telephone 147 888 088 (a local call from anywhere in Italy), which operates daily 8am–9pm with English-speaking operators, or visit the official Italian state railway website: www.fs-on line.it

Local trains are called *Locale, Diretto, Interregionale* and *Espresso*. When travelling considerable distances or along major lines, the faster *InterCity, EuroCity* and *Eurostar* services are the best bet – the supplementary charge being well worth the time saved and the extra comfort. The *Pendolino* is the fastest, most comfortable train,

and requires a supplement and reservation. It is a good idea to buy tickets and make reservations for the *IC/EC/ES* and *Pendolino* in advance, and this can be done at any travel agency as well as at the station.

If you are planning to make a number of train journeys, consider buying the inexpensive official train timetable book from any station kiosk. If travelling a fair distance, it is worth reserving a seat as trains tend to be crowded.

Good fare reductions and special offers are available for groups and young travellers, and it is worth making enquiries about these when you arrive in Italy. Train tickets are valid for two months. Passengers must stamp their tickets in the validating machines in the station before boarding. If for some reason that is not possible, you must find the conductor before he finds you.

BY COACH

Each province in Italy has its own inter-city bus company, and each company has its own lines. It is

Ferries and Hydrofoils

A number of private companies run ferry (*traghetto*) and hydrofoil (*aliscafo*) services between the islands of Southern Italy and the mainland, and also between several cities. Keep in mind that hydrofoils are faster, but more expensive and subject to choppy seas and high winds (which force them to proceed at ferry speed). Tickets are available from travel agencies and ticket offices at the port, but it's best to book in advance if you can. For up-to-date information on times and prices, visit www.gruppotirrenia.it – the shipping group owns Tirrenia, Caremar, Saremar and Siremar.

Campania
From Naples
To Capri, tel: (Caremar) 081-5513882. To Palermo, tel: (Tirrenia) 1991-23199.

To Ischia, by hydrofoil (35 mins); by ferry (80 mins), tel: (Caremar) 081-5513882 and (Lauro) 081-5522838. To Lipari, tel: (Tirrenia) 1991-23199. Naples also has ferry and hydrofoil links to Sorrento and the island of Procida.

From Sorrento
To Ischia (30 mins).
tel: (Partenopee) 081-991888.
To Capri (15 mins), tel: (Alilauro) 081-8073024; by ferry (20 mins), tel: (Caremar) 081-8073077.
There are also regular services to Naples (40 mins) and services to Positano during peak season.

Apulia
From the Tremiti Islands
To Termoli, by hydrofoil (50 mins), tel: (Navigazione Libera 0875-703937); by ferry (1 hr 50 mins), tel: (Adriatica) 0875-705343.
To Termoli, Vieste (1 hr) and

Manfredonia (2 hrs), by hydrofoil, tel: (Adriatica) 0875-705343.

Sicily
From Milazzo
To the Lipari Islands, by ferry (1½–3 hrs), tel: (Siremar) 090-9283242; by hydrofoil (45–60 mins), tel: (SNAV) 090-9284509 and (Siremar) 090-9283242.
From Palermo
To Ustica, by hydrofoil (1 hr), ferry (3 hrs), tel (Siremar): 091-582403.
To the Aeolian Islands, by hydrofoil (3 hrs), tel: (SNAV): 091-333333.
From Porto Empedocle
To Lampedusa/Linosa, by ferry (6/8 hrs), tel: (Siremar) 0922-636683.
Trapani
To Favignana, by hydrofoil (25 mins), tel (Siremar): 0923-545455. To Pantelleria, ferry (6 hrs), tel (Ustica): 0923-22200.

worth taking buses, especially when you are going to the mountainous interior, where they are generally faster than the trains. One advantage of buses is that they usually stop in the centre of town, whereas the train stations in rural towns are often quite a distance from the main piazza. Unfortunately, few of these companies have English-speaking operators, and their information services are limited. Tickets can usually be purchased from tobacconists, who are often well informed on the latest schedules. Check with the tourist office (see page 326) for the latest schedule information.

TAXIS

Taxis in Italy are relatively expensive; they are found at taxi ranks or paged by telephone rather than hailed in the street. If you call up a taxi, you will be charged for the trip the driver makes to reach you.

There is a fixed starting charge and then a charge for every kilometre (and a standing charge for traffic jams). Taxi drivers are obliged to show, if asked, the current list of additional charges. Extra charges are added for night rides (10pm–7am), luggage, journeys outside town and journeys on Sundays and public holidays. It is a general rule to leave a small tip rounding off the fare to the nearest euro.

Private Transport

BY CAR

In Italy, you must drive on the right. The motorways (autostrade) are fast and uncrowded (except in summer), but Italians frequently exceed the speed limit. Nearly all autostrade charge tolls; you must take a ticket as you enter the motorway and pay as you exit.

It is compulsory to wear seat-belts at all times and infants up to nine months must occupy a baby seat. Children between nine months and four years must sit on

Driving Speeds

The following speed limits apply to cars in Italy:
Urban areas: 50 km/h (30 mph)
Roads outside urban areas: 90 km/h (55 mph)
Dual carriageways outside urban areas: 110 km/h (70 mph)
Motorways (autostrade): 130 km/h (80 mph); for cars less than 1,100cc: 110 km/h (70 mph)

the back seat.

Pay attention to street signs advising no parking because police are strict on illegal parking and will remove vehicles found in no parking areas. You'll need plenty of cash to reclaim your car. Try to park in a garage for the night: it will be expensive, but much safer.

Hitchhiking is forbidden on the autostrade and is not advised for women travelling alone.

Car Rentals

Hiring a car is expensive in Italy, as is petrol. Major car rental firms such as Avis, Hertz and Europcar are represented in most cities and at all airports, though local firms often offer better rates. Agencies are listed in the Yellow Pages under Autonoleggio. Collision damage waiver and recovery in case of breakdown are usually included in the price of hiring a vehicle, but be sure to check exclusions carefully. Additional insurance cover is usually available at fixed rates. Also, make sure that the price you are quoted includes VAT (IVA), which is levied at 19 percent.

To hire a car, you must be over 21 and be in possession of a valid driver's licence (an EU licence, an international driving licence or a national driving licence with Italian translation). A deposit equal to the cost of hiring the vehicle is usually required, or a credit card imprint.

Where to Stay

Choosing a Hotel

Several of the international hotel chains (Hilton, Jolly) are represented in the few major cities in the South, but the the likelihood is that you will be staying in privately run establishments. Some of these have banded together with hotels of similar atmosphere, quality and cost into local and national associations. Bear in mind that the number of stars a hotel has been awarded refers only to the facilities and services offered and not their quality.

Although there is a wide variety of hotels to choose from, it is always a good idea to book in advance and get information and confirmation in writing, and stay clear of "representatives" who offer accommodation to tourists coming off the ferry or train.

The following listings offer a selection of hotels at all levels. Your travel agent or the local tourist offices in Italy (see page 326) can give you more information on these and other hotels.

Naples

Hotels in Naples are concentrated along the Lungomare (by the port), in the city centre and up on the hills surrounding the city (many offering panoramic views of the Bay of Naples). Less desirable is the area around the railway station and anything outside the centre of town.
Executive
Via del Carriglio 10
Tel: 081-5520611
Fax: 081-5520611
Centrally located between Spaccanapoli and Castel Nuovo, with modern comforts (gym and

INSIGHT GUIDES

The classic series that puts you in the picture

👁 INSIGHT GUIDES

The world's largest collection of visual travel guides & maps

sauna) in the restored walls of an ex-convent. **$$–$$$**

Miramare
Via Nazario Sauro 24
Tel: 081-7647589
Fax: 081-7640775
Family-run Art Deco villa with views of the Bay from the waterfront of the Borgo Marinari. **$$$$**

Residenza Villa Medici
Via Nuova Bagnoli 550
Tel: 081-7623040
Fax: 081-7624030
Choose between standard hotel rooms and mini-apartments. About 5 km west of Naples on the Bay of Pozzuoli. Thermal baths nearby. **$$**

Rex
Via Palepoli 12
Tel: 081-7649389
Fax: 081-7649227
Best budget choice among the better hotels along the Borgo Marinari. Art Deco decor with period furniture in all the rooms, some of which have a view. **$$**

Santa Lucia
Via Partenope 46
Tel: 081-7640666
Fax: 081-7648580
Facing Castel dell'Ovo, this refined and elegant hotel has spacious rooms, many with hot tubs. **$$$$**

Splendid
Via Manzoni 96
Tel: 081-7141955
Fax: 081-7146431
In the residential quarter of Posillipo, with views of the Bay. Many rooms have private terraces. Very convenient for the funicular, which descends to the Lungomare. **$$**

The Islands

Capri
Bellavista
Via G. Orlandoi 10 (Anacapri)
Tel: 081-8371463
A simple place to stay in Anacapri, this 24-room hotel was once a private villa. **$**

Hotel La Canasta
Via Campo di Teste 6
Tel: 081-8370561
A garden and view from the terrace with comfortable rooms. **$$$**

Luna
Via Matteotti 3
Tel: 081-8370433
Fax: 081-8377459
Fantastic 360 degree views, a swimming pool and peace and quiet are all part of this hotel hidden in the lush vegetation just at the edge of town. **$$$**

Pensione Belsito
Via Matermania 11
Tel: 081-8370969
An old-fashioned inn with pleasant surroundings. **$**

Quisisana
Via Camerelle 2
Tel: 081-8370788
Fax: 081-8376080
One of Italy's most famous hotels – the height of luxury on the one of the world's most luxurious islands. A serious splurge. **$$$$**

Villa Krupp
Via Mattcotti 12
Tel: 081-8370362
Near the gardens of Augustus, the terrace of this pleasant hotel, former home of Russian author Maxim Gorky. Views of the Bay. **$$**

Ischia
Il Monastero
Castello Aragonese, Ischia Ponte (2 km west of the port)
Tel: 081-992435
Friendly *pensione* with romantic location high up in the castle precincts. Views over the bay. **$–$$**

Procida
L'Oasi
Via Elleri 16

Agritourism

Agriturismo is a wonderful way to experience the countryside in Southern Italy. You stay either in private guest rooms or apartments on a working farm or vineyard, often with an opportunity to enjoy home cooking on the premises. Prices average €25 per person per day, with Calabria and Apulia offering the best deals at around €15 per person per day. Ask at the local tourist office for details (*see page 326*).

Price Guide

The price categories are based on a double room in high season with breakfast.
$ = under €75
$$ = €75–125
$$$ = €125–250
$$$$ = more than €250

Tel: 081-8967499
Quiet mid-range villa-hotel with restaurant and garden. This is the only hotel open all year, but check with the tourist office for rooms in private homes. **$$**

Sorrento

Bellevue Syrene
Piazza della Vittoria 5
Tel: 081-8781024
Fax: 081-8783963
Luxurious, elegant seafront hotel. Handsome, balconied rooms with wrought iron beds and views onto the Bay or the hotel garden. Beach access from garden. **$$$**

Excelsior Vittoria
Piazza Tasso 34
Tel: 081-8071044
Fax: 081-8771206
Atmospheric hotel-restaurant in Art Nouveau style. Bathrooms in marble. Fantastic views of the Bay. Pool. **$$$$**

Imperial Tramontano
Via Veneto 1
Tel: 081-8781940
Fax: 081-8072344
Elegant hotel perched on the cliff edge with wonderful views across the bay. Restaurant with very friendly staff. Pool and lift to sea level. **$$$**

Rivage
Via del Capo 11
Tel: 081-8781873
Fax: 081-8071253
A great budget alternative on the western edge of town, most rooms with small terraces facing the water. Pleasant restaurant. **$$**

The Amalfi Coast

Amalfi
Hotel Cappuccini Convento
Via Annunziatella 46

Tel: 089-871877
Fax: 089-871886
Another ex-monastery, with the monastic cells converted into comfortable guestrooms featuring period furniture, with garden, Arab-Norman cloister and fine views. **$$**

Hotel Luna Convento
Via Pantaleone Comite 33
Tel: 089-871002
Fax: 089-871050
A converted 13th century monastery built on the rocks at the water's edge. Breakfast is served in a Byzantine cloister. Good-sized rooms decorated with antiques and local crafts, most with view. Swimming pool. **$$–$$$**

Positano
Hotel Le Agavi
Localita' Belvedere Fornillo,
Via Marconi 127
Tel/fax: 089-875733
Well located just outside Positano and its tourist hubbub, with all the amenities, including a swimming pool, lift to a private beach and, of course, fantastic views. **$$$**

Le Sirenuse
Via C. Colombo 30
Tel: 089-875066
Fax: 089-811798
Once the villa of a powerful Neapolitan family in the centre of town with panoramic views, now a luxurious hotel and arguably the best restaurant on the Amalfi coast. Pool and gymnasium. **$$$**

Villa Franca
Via Pasitea 318
Tel: 089-875655
Fax: 089-875735
First-rate, family-run hotel with 28 well-decorated and comfortable rooms, most with tiled floors and arched windows that look out onto the sea. Pool. **$$$**

Ravello
Marmorata
Via Bizantina 3
(Localita' Marmorata; 7 km/
4½ miles south of Ravello)
Tel: 089-877777
Fax: 089-851189
Quiet and well cared for hotel a short car ride from Ravello. Rooms are decorated with a marine theme,

and most have views. Pool and private beach. **$$$**

Southern Campania

Castellabate
Giacaranda
Contrada Cenito
(localita' San Marco)
Tel: 0974-966130
Fax: 0974-966130
Fourteen-rooms and four apartments in this lovely, well-maintained inn. Excellent restaurant. Tennis court. **$$**

Hermitage
Via Catarozza (localita' San Marco)
Tel: 0974-966618
Fax: 0974-966619
Tasteful hotel with modern amenities and beautiful views of the Gulf of Salerno. Shuttle to the beach. **$$$**

Palinuro
King's Residence Hotel
Baia del Buondormire
Tel: 0974-931324
Fax: 0974-931418
Closed: Mid-Nov to mid-Jan
All the rooms of this comfortable hotel overlook the sea. Guests have free access to a private corner of the panoramic Buondormire beach. Facilities include a garden, swimming pool, sauna and beauty centre. **$$$–$$$$**

San Paolo
Via San Paolo
Tel: 0974-938304
Fax: 0974-931214
Quiet spot at the edge of town and surrounded by green, with panoramic restaurant and piano bar. **$$**

Paestum
Hotel Ariston
C. da Laura 13
Tel: 0828-851333
A couple of miles from the excavations, this modern, full-service hotel (gym, heated indoor pool and sauna) is a bargain. **$**

Vallo della Lucania
Mimì
Via de Marsilio 1
Tel: 0974-4302

Fax: 0974-2663
A good address with a restaurant and a garden on the western side of the Cilento national park, this small, family-run hotel even has three suites. **$–$$**

Apulia

FOGGIA PROVINCE

Foggia
Cicolella
Viale XXIV Maggio 60
Tel: 0881-688890
Fax: 0881-678984
Centrally located near the train station; comfortable and modern, with marble bathrooms. **$$$**

President
Viale degli Aviatori 130
Tel: 0881-618010
Fax: 0881-617930
Outside the centre of town, surrounded by a peaceful park. Good sized, comfortable rooms. **$$**

Manfredonia
Gargano
Viale Beccarini 2
Tel: 0884-587621
Fax: 0884-586021
In the centre of town but rooms all have views onto the Adriatic. Swimming pool and good restaurant. **$$**

Vieste
Pizzomunno Palace Hotel
Lungomare Enrico Mattei (by the beach about 1 km from town centre)
Tel: 0884-708741
Fax:0884-707325
The most luxurious place to stay in the Gargano. Five-star amenities include modern, spacious rooms, swimming pool, tennis court and gymnasium. **$$$$**

BARI PROVINCE

Bari
Palace Hotel
Via Lombardi 13
Tel: 080-5216551
Fax: 080-5211499
Great location, right between the

borgo antico and the modern town. The rooms are tastefully decorated with antiques, and double glazing keeps out the noise. **$$$**

Pensione Giulia
Via Crisanzio 12
Tel: 080-5216630
Fax: 080-5218271
Near the train station, this is a safe and clean budget option. Not all rooms have bathrooms. **$–$$**

Sheraton Nicolaus
Via Cardinale Ciasca 9
Tel: 080-5042626
Fax: 080-5042058
Just outside of town, this is certainly the only modern, high-rise hotel in Southern Italy. All the four-star amenities you would expect from the Sheraton chain, including a swimming pool. **$$$$**

Villa Carducci
Via Capruzzi 326
Tel: 080-5427400
Fax: 080-5560297
Modern hotel in a lovely park. **$$$**

Alberobello
Dei Trulli
Via Cadore 32
Tel: 080-4323555
Fax: 080-4323560
Trulli are circular houses made of whitewashed stone, with conical roofs; in this village you can stay in one of the many *trulli* which have been converted into apartments. **$$**

Trani
Royal
Via de Robertis 29
Tel: 0883-588777
Fax: 0883-582224
Great value four-star hotel in the centre of town, not far from the station. Art Nouveau-style decor. **$$**

BRINDISI PROVINCE

Brindisi
Barsotti
Via Cavour 1
Tel: 0831-560877
Fax: 0831-563851
Conveniently located in the centre of town. Good-sized rooms. **$$**

Ostuni
Masseria San Domenico
Localita' Savelletri
Tel: 080-9557990
Fax: 080-9557978
Surrounded by olive groves, this superb five-star hotel has luxurious rooms set in beautifully restored buildings just one kilometre (about half a mile) off the coastal road. Fantastic sea-water swimming pool with waterfall. Tennis courts, horseriding, gym. **$$$$**

Price Guide

The price categories are based on a double room in high season with breakfast.
$ = under €75
$$ = €75–125
$$$ = €125–250
$$$$ = more than €250

LECCE PROVINCE

Lecce
President
Via Salandra 6
Tel: 0832-311881
Fax: 0832-372283
Four-star modern building and interior in the newer part of town. Basic drab decor, but serviceable rooms. **$$–$$$**

Risorgimento
Via Augusto Imperatore 19
Tel: 0832-242125
Fax: 0832-245571
All the sites in Lecce are within short walking distance of this perfectly situated hotel in the heart of the historic centre. Modern, comfortable and tastefully decorated. Some rooms have terraces overlooking the town. **$$–$$$**

TARANTO PROVINCE

Taranto
Grand Hotel Delfino
Viale Virgilio 66
Tel: 099-7323232
Fax: 099 7304654
On the waterfront, about 2 km

(1 mile) from the old city (Citta' Vecchia). Most rooms with view of the water. **$$–$$$**

Basilicata

Matera
Del Campo
Via Lucrezio 1
Tel: 0835-388844
Fax: 0835-3888757
The nicest place to stay in Matera, this well-run hotel, about 1 km (about half a mile) from the *Sassi* zone, was once the country home of Domenico Ridola, founder of the national museum in Matera. Antique furnishings and good service. **$$$$**

Italia
Via Ridola 5
Tel: 0835-333561
Fax: 0835-330087
The best hotel right in the heart of the old town, the Italia has a great old-world atmosphere. Some rooms look out over the nearby *Sassi* zone. **$$**

Il Piccolo Albergo
Via De Sariis 11
Tel: 0835-330201
Fax: 0835-330201
Centrally located hotel with basic rooms and modern furnishings. **$**

Hotel I Sassi
Via San Giovanni Vecchio 89
Tel: 0835-331009
Fax: 0835-333733
Your chance to stay in *sassi*-style comfort, as the rooms here have been carved straight out of the rock. Great views from the balcony in each room. **$$**

Potenza
Grande Albergo
Corso XVIII Agosto 46
Tel: 0971-410220
Fax: 0971-410220
Modern hotel with spacious rooms and impressive views of the valley. **$$**

Tourist
Via Vescovado 4
Tel: 0971-21437
Fax: 0971-21437
Centrally located, rustic style decor. Rooms at he back have views of the valley below. **$$**

Melfi
Hotel Due Pini
Piazzale Stazione
Tel: 0972-216031
Fax: 0972-21608
Unremarkable and basic but fairly priced hotel opposite the train station. **$–$$**

Maratea
Locanda delle Donne Monache
Via Mazzei 4
Tel: 0973-877487
Fax: 0973-877867
A beautifully renovated 18th-century building which originally served as a convent. Spacious rooms are tastefully decorated with period furniture. Bathrooms have been carved out from the natural stone. Swimming pool. **$$$**

Price Guide

The price categories are based on a double room in high season with breakfast.
$ = under €75
$$ = €75–125
$$$ = €125–250
$$$$ = more than €250

Calabria

Reggio Calabria
Azienda Agrituristica Il Bergamotto
Condofuri Marina (Reggio Calabria)
Tel: 0965-727213
A hospitable farmhouse with a handful of simple rooms with tiny bathrooms (some also have a mini-kitchen) in the old stables. Delicious Calabrian food is served to guests in summertime: all produce is home-grown, including the wheat for the bread. Owner Ugo Sergi organises donkey trekking in the Aspromonte national park. **$**
Excelsior
Via Vittorio Veneto 66
Tel: 0965-812211
Fax: 0965-893084
Comfortable, air-conditioned hotel in the centre of town, near the Museo Nazionale. Some bathrooms with hydromassage. **$$$**
Famiglia Franco
Via XXIV Maggio 51, Bivongi

(Reggio Calabria)
Tel: 0964-731129
This is not a real hotel but the upper floor of a private house. The rooms (all with brand-new private bathrooms) are surprisingly large and comfortable, though, with lots of luggage space and firm beds. You can come and go at your convenience, as keys are provided, and privacy is not an issue. **$**
Lido
Via Tre Settembre 1943
Tel: 0965-25001
Fax: 0965-899393
A basic budget hotel, about one kilometre (half a mile) from the centre of town and two blocks from the water. **$–$$**

Crotone
Costa Tiziana
Via per Capocolonna
Tel: 0962-25601
Fax: 0962-21427
Resort by the sea a few kilometres south of Crotone. Windsurfing and sailing lessons. Mandatory full board in summer. **$$–$$$**

Catanzaro
Grand Hotel
Piazza Matteotti
Tel: 0961-701256
Fax: 0961-741621
Modern and serviceable, one of the few hotels in town. **$$–$$$**

Cosenza
Il Castello di Altomonte
Piazza Castello 6
Altomonte (Cosenza)
Tel: 0981-948933
Fax: 0981-948937
A 12th-century Norman castle with a view, this is arguably the fanciest option in the Pollino area. Guest rooms are decorated with wrought iron, while the common areas are decorated with period pieces and armoury. You can sip wine by the glass in the warm cellar. **$$$**
Excelsior
Piazza Matteotti 14
Tel: 0984-74383
Fax: 0984-74384
Simple but serviceable hotel on a

main piazza, near the train station. Recently renovated. Not all rooms with bathroom. **$–$$**
La Locanda del Parco
Contrada Mazzicanino
Morano Calabro (Cosenza)
Tel/fax: 0981-31304
With a *mamma* shaping pasta dough in a strictly local fashion and fireplaces in the common areas, the 'Park's Inn' makes a very homely place to return to after spending your day hiking in the park. Guided tours on horseback are available all year round. **$$**
Palazzo del Capo
Cittadella del Capo (Cosenza; A3 motorway exits: Lagonegro from Salerno, Falerna from Reggio Calabria)
Tel: 0982-95674
Fax: 0982-95676
An appealing blend of old charm and modern comforts, including a restaurant and a pool with bar service, this small hotel is housed in the former mansion of a local aristocratic family. The panoramic view spans the Tyrrhenian coast just north of Paola to the Sila mountains. **$$$**
Hotel Lo Sciatore
Via Roma 128
Camigliatello Silano (Cosenza)
Tel: 0984-578105
Fax: 0984-579281
Located in the main town of the Sila region just outside the western border of the national park, the Sciatore gets crowded with Italian skiers in the winter months. Its cosy rooms are kept warm with huge, cast-iron heaters, and furnished with tasteful early 20th century pieces. The restaurant downstairs offers unpretentious Italian fare. **$$**

Tropea
Le Roccette Mare
Via Mare Piccolo
Tel: 0963-61358
Fax: 0963-61450
Closed: November–March
Beachfront accommodation, clean and comfortable. Half-board required. Surcharge in August. **$–$$**

Sicily

PALERMO PROVINCE

Visitors need to choose between staying in the bustling centre of Palermo (ideal for seeing the historic sites) or in the select resort of Mondello, just outside town.

In Palermo city, accommodation is reasonably priced and easier to find than in most parts of the island. It is, however, advisable to choose a higher grade hotel in Palermo than you might elsewhere. For safety's sake, choose a hotel on a main street.

There is a large concentration of hotels at the southern ends of Via Roma and Via Maqueda, between the station and Corso Vittorio Emanuele. Further along the Corso, the hotels are more expensive. The modern Viale della Libertà quarter, within walking distance of the historic centre, is a good choice from many points of view, offering safety, convenience and fashionable neighbourhood bars. There are a few very inexpensive places around La Kalsa, but this area is best avoided.

Palermo

Cristal Palace
Via Roma 477
Tel: 091-6112580
Fax: 091-6112589
Modern, centrally located hotel within walking distance of the historic centre of town and the beautiful Via della Libertá. **$$$**

Excelsior Palace
Via Marchese Ugo 3
Tel: 091-6256176
Fax: 091-342139
Extremely comfortable four-star hotel, refurbished in the original 19th-century style, with Venetian glass fixtures. Centrally located for sightseeing in town. Note that while comfortable, the rooms vary considerably in size, and those on the top floor have mansard ceilings. Good restaurant. **$$$$**

Forte Agip Palermo
Viale Regione Siciliana 2620
Tel: 091-552033
Fax: 091-408198

Large four-star hotel with modern decor and all the amenities, several kilometres outside Palermo. Good buffet breakfast. **$$$–$$$$**

Grand Hotel et des Palmes
Via Roma 398
Tel: 091-583933
Fax: 091-331545
One of the oldest hotels in the city, but well maintained for Palermo. Via Roma was probably a lot less congested when Wagner completed *Parsifal* here in 1882, but double-glazed windows keep the noise out. Swimming pool **$$$**

Jolly Palermo
Foro Italico 22
Viale Principe di Scalea (Mondello)
Tel: 091-6165090
Fax: 091-6161441
Large, modern four-star hotel with a garden (where breakfast is served in summer) and swimming pool. On the edge of the Kalsa quarter, but with a shuttle that runs to the main sites in the historic centre. Swimming pool. **$$$**

Letizia
Via Bottai 30
Tel: 091-589110
Fax:091-589110
Near the busy Piazza Marina, with a remarkable garden. Modest rooms. Breakfast not included. **$**

Moderno
Via Roma 276
Tel: 091-588683
Fax: 091 588683
Good value. Centrally located, clean two-star hotel. Breakfast not included. **$$**

Mondello Palace
Viale Principe di Scalea (Mondello)
Tel: 091-450001
Fax: 091-450657
Modern, luxurious four-star seafront hotel surrounded by a garden. Private beach, swimming pool, restaurant and bar. Comfortable good-sized rooms; most offer sea views. **$$$**

Orientale
Via Maqueda 26
Tel: 091-6165727
Plenty of atmosphere in this basic one-star hotel set on the first floor of a beautiful old *palazzo* with marble courtyard. Rooms are basic and rather small. **$**

Politeama Palace Hotel
Via Piazza Ruggero Settimo 15
Tel: 091-322777
Fax: 091-6111589
First-class luxury hotel on Palermo's most attractive grand piazza. Top-floor rooms have a view of the city. **$$$$**

Villa Igeia Grand Hotel
Via Salita Belmonte 43
Tel: 091-543744
Fax: 091-547654
The most stunning place to stay in Palermo. Built as the palatial residence of the Florio family in 1908, this five-star hotel has been restored to its early 20th-century Art Nouveau splendour. Set on a cliff with fantastic views of the city and the bay. Rooms are richly decorated with period furniture and modern amenities. **$$$$**

Cefalù

Cefalù vies with Taormina as Sicily's most appealing resort. Safety, convenience and good infrastructure make it an ideal choice for families or elderly people. The beaches are closer and far better than at Taormina. Like Taormina, the resort feels perfectly safe and free from petty crime. There is a wide range of accommodation to suit all pockets. Visitors out of season would do well to avoid hotels located on the beach since the beaches tend not to be very clean in the low season.

Baia del Capitano
Contrada Mazzaforno
Tel: 0921-20003
Fax: 0921-20163
The best place to stay in the area, this modern three star hotel is set in an olive grove about 5 km (3 miles) west of town. Each small but well kept room has a terrace with great views. Pool, tennis courts and a private beach. **$$$**

Kalura
Via Cavallaro 13 (Localita' Cladura)
Tel: 0921-21354
Fax: 0921-231122
Ten kilometres (6 miles) west of town, ensconced in Mediterranean foliage, the Kalura offers clean,

spacious rooms, each with a terrace. Swimming pool. **$$$**

Ustica
This lovely island off Palermo is extremely popular with swimmers and nature-lovers. It attracts a large number of German, Scandinavian and Sicilian visitors. Hotels tend to fill up fast but there are many opportunities to rent rooms: call in at the Pro Loco tourist office (Vito Longo), tel: 091-8449456, open June–September only, if the fishermen at the port haven't already made you an offer. The Palermo Tourist Office will have information on hotels and rooms to rent.

Pensione Clelia
Via Magazzino 7
Tel: 091-8449039
Located on the main square, the Clelia is the oldest *pensione* in town. Wonderful fish restaurant. **$**
Stella Marina
Via C.Colombo 33
Tel: 091-8449014
Fax: 091-8449325
Open all year, but in season guests must take half board at the hotel. Basic rooms. **$$**

TRAPANI PROVINCE

Trapani
Astoria Park
Lungomare Dante Alighieri
(San Cusumano)
Tel: 0923-562400
Fax: 0923-567422
Three-star hotel about 4 km (just over 2 miles) out of town, the Astoria Park is the most comfortable place to stay in Trapani. Rooms are spacious and look out to sea. Private beach, tennis courts and swimming pool. **$$$**
Vittoria
Via F. Crispi 246
Tel: 0923-873044
Fax: 0923-29870
Located just off central Piazza Vittorio Emanuele. Rooms have a view of the sea or onto a public garden where summer concerts are held. **$$–$$$**

Egadi
Egadi
Via C. Colombo 17
Tel: 0923-921232
Fax: 0923-921232
Twelve simple, pleasant rooms and the best restaurant in western Sicily right downstairs. Book well ahead, especially May–July. **$$**

Pantelleria
Port Hotel
Lungomare Borgo Italia 6
Tel: 0923-911299
Fax: 0923-912203
Modern three-star hotel with air-conditioned rooms. **$$**

AGRIGENTO PROVINCE

Agrigento
Colleverde Park Hotel
Via dei Templi
Tel: 0922-29555
Fax: 0922-29012
Three-star hotel set at the start of the Strada Panoramica, with great views across the Valley of the Temples. Rooms are basic and clean. **$$–$$$**
Villa Holiday
Via Grabrici 9
Tel: 0922-606332
Two-star budget hotel in the town. Breakfast not included. **$**

ENNA PROVINCE

Enna
Grande Albergo Sicilia
Piazza Colajanni 7
Tel: 0935-500850
Fax: 0935-500488
Centrally located and the best of what little there is to choose from in this un-touristy town. Reasonably comfortable hotel, some rooms with views. **$$–$$$**
Park Hotel Paradiso
Contrada Ramaldo
Tel: 0935-680841
Fax: 0935-683391
Three-star comfort. Breakfast not included. **$$$**

Price Guide

The price categories are based on a double room in high season with breakfast.
$ = under €75
$$ = €75–125
$$$ = €125–250
$$$$ = more than €250

Piazza Armerina
This appealing town makes a good stop for visitors wishing to see its famous Roman Villa.
Villa Romana
Via de Gasperi 18
Tel: 0935-682911
Fax: 0935-682911
Three-star. Breakfast not included. **$$**

RAGUSA PROVINCE

Ragusa
Eremo della Giubiliana
Contrada Giubiliana (9 km/6 miles toward Marina di Ragusa)
Tel: 0932-669119
Fax: 0932-623891
A fortified medieval hermitage that has been converted into one of Sicily's most delightful hotels. **$$$$**
Montreal
Via San Giuseppe 8
Tel: 0932-621133
Fax: 0932-621133
Centrally located three-star hotel with modern rooms. The best option in Ragusa Alta. **$$**

SIRACUSA PROVINCE

Siracusa
Domus Mariae
Via Vittoria Veneto 76
Tel: 0931-24854
Fax: 0931-24858
A three-star hotel with good views; the best value on Ortygia. Run by friendly nuns. **$$$**
Grand Hotel
Via Mazzini 12
Tel: 0931-464600
Fax: 0931-464611
Fully restored Art Nouveau-style hotel and the most atmospheric

place to stay in town. On Ortygia, with panoramic views, overlooking the Porto Grande. Private beach. **$$$$**

Hotel Como
Piazza Stazione 10
Tel: 0931-464055
Fax: 0931-464056
An inexpensive, basic three-star hotel located by the train station, between the archaeological park and Ortygia. Good restaurant. **$$**

Jolly Hotel
Corso Gelone 45
Tel: 0931-461111
Fax: 0931-461126
Four-star hotel with modern rooms typical of the chain. Located in the modern part of town. **$$$–$$$$**

CATANIA PROVINCE

Catania
Excelsior Grand Hotel
Piazza Verga 39
Tel: 095-537071
Fax: 095-537015
Expensive but comfortable four-star Art Deco hotel and restaurant. Centrally located. **$$$$**

Camping

Campsites (*campeggi*) can be found in most areas of Southern Italy, and can be a good option when summer resorts are full. Italy is not a place to set up your own impromptu campsite – both for safety reasons and because of heavy fines.

Campsites charge about €20 for two people with car and tent. Most of them are well equipped with a service area for motorhomes, hot showers and shops selling food and basic necessities; in high season, many offer a shuttle bus service to the nearest beach and/or town. Facilities like playgrounds, pools, tennis courts, discos, restaurants and pizzerias are often found in the larger campsites, often called

Nettuno
Tel: 095-7125252
Fax: 095-498066
Three-star hotel with pool and restaurant located just north of the town centre. Sea views. **$$$**

Etna (Nicolosi)
Biancaneve
Via Etnea 163
Tel: 095-911176
Fax: 095-911194
Three-star hotel with pool and tennis courts. **$$$**

Taormina
Excelsior Palace
Via Toselli 8
Tel: 0942-23975
Fax: 0942-23978
Four-star hotel on a promontory with lovely grounds and a spectacularly sited pool. Off season reduction. Rooms face the sea or look on to a lovely garden. Modern rooms with amenities. **$$$–$$$$**

San Domenico Palace
Piazza San Domenico 5
Tel: 0942-23701
Fax: 0942-625506
Once a monastery, the San Domenico is one of the finest hotels in Southern Italy. Magnificent views toward Etna or the sea. Luxurious

'*villaggi turistici*' rather than '*campeggi*', because they also rent out bungalows and/or small apartments. Note that some places require a minimum stay of three or more nights, and that most *campeggi* are closed between November and Easter.

Camping Guidebooks
Good guides to campsites include the multilingual *Guida Camping d'Italia* (Guide to Camping in Italy) from Touring Club Italiano (TCI), *Eurocamping Italia-Corsica*, which also includes a detailed map of Italy, and *Guida ai Campeggi in Italia* (Demetra), which has colour pictures of the most popular resorts. Both are in Italian, with international symbols.

rooms decorated with fine antiques. Excellent restaurant. **$$$$**

Svizzera
Via Pirandello 26
Tel: 0942-23790
Fax: 0942-625906
On the outskirts of town, a well-run one-star hotel with a garden. **$$**

Villa Schuler
Piazetta Bastione 16
Tel: 0942-23481
Fax: 0942-23522
Charming two-star budget hotel. Family run. Most rooms have terraces and views. **$$**

MESSINA PROVINCE

Messina
Excelsior
Via Maddalena 32
Tel: 090-2938721
Fax: 090-2938721
Budget three-star hotel near the train station with very modest rooms. Breakfast not included. **$$**

Jolly dello Stretto
Via Garibaldi 126
Tel: 090-363860
Fax: 090-5902526
Centrally located just opposite the port. Many rooms with panoramic view of the Strait of Messina. Air-conditioning and private beach. **$$$$**

Aeolian Islands (Stromboli)
La Locanda del Barbablu
Via Vittorio Emanuele 19
Tel: 090-986118
Fax: 090-986318
Small (5 rooms) and intimate, offering basic bed and breakfast. Excellent home-made food served on an enchanting terrace. **$$$**

Where to Eat

Introduction

Eating Habits

The gentle lifestyle of Italy is partly a product of its civilised eating habits: eating and drinking in tranquillity at least twice a day are the norm here.

Italian breakfast (*colazione*) is usually light and consists of *cappuccino* (espresso and frothy steamed milk) and a *brioche* (pastry), or simply *caffè* (black and strong espresso coffee).

Except in the industrialised cities, *pranzo* (lunch) is the big meal of the day. It consists of *antipasto* (hors d'oeuvre), a *primo* (pasta, rice or soup) and a *secondo* (meat or fish with a vegetable – *contorno* – or salad). To follow comes cheese and/or fruit. Italians usually drink coffee (*espresso*) after lunch and/or a liqueur, such as *grappa, amaro* or *sambuca*.

Traditionally, dinner is similar to lunch, but lighter. However, in the cities people are tending to eat less at lunchtime and making dinner the major meal of the day.

Local Specialities

Every region in Italy has its own typical dishes *(see page 357)*: Naples is the birthplace of pizza and pasta, and the nearby *pianura campana* produces the region's famous *mozzarella di bufala*. South from Campania is the region of Calabria, with its long coastline stretching around the tip of the boot. Expect seafood on the menu and hot pepper in sauces. Apulia is a region rich with local cuisine, including *purè di fave e cicoria* (fava bean spread and chicory), and *orecchiette* (little ear-shaped pasta) with greens, and the creamy *burrata* cheese. Between the two is

Basilicata, a long-forgotten region with its own specialities, among which pork and lamb dishes stand out.

The cuisine of Sicily cannot be captured in a sentence. The Greeks, Normans, Arabs, Spanish and French imported all sorts of ingredients and cooking techniques which blended into Italy's most sumptuous, brilliant and varied food scene. Sicily's sweet desserts made with ricotta cheese such as *cassata siciliana* and *cannoli* are heavenly. Don't miss fish *cuscus* (cous-cous) in the western towns and islands, particularly in Trapani and Favignana; swordfish in Palermo and Messina; *caponata* (fried aubergine in a tasty tomato-olive-caper sauce) and *pasta alla norma* (with aubergine and hard ricotta cheese).

Listings

Italy has thousands of restaurants, *trattorie* and *osterie*. If you do not want to have a complete meal, you can have a snack at the bar or at *tavole calde* and *rosticcerie* (grills).

If you go to a restaurant, don't order just a salad: the waiters may look down on you and treat you with disdain. If you think a complete meal is too big, forego the *antipasto*, but take a *primo* and a *secondo* at least.

The restaurants listed below have been recommended by Italian food writers and/or the authors of this guide. It is difficult to generalise about prices since much depends on the choice of wine and menu selection. Even noted chefs may offer a less expensive, but restricted, menu in conjunction with the main menu.

Naples

Cantina di Triunfo
Riviera di Chiaia 64 (Chiaia)
Tel: 081-668101
Closed: Sunday and August
This old-style *cantina* run with enthusiasm for great food is a great place for a glass of wine and a light meal. A brief menu (two first courses, two second courses and a few side dishes) is based on what

Price Guide

The price of a three-course meal for one, without wine, is:
$ = below €15
$$ = €15–30
$$$ = €30–45
$$$$ = over €45

the owners found at the market that day. **$$**

La Chiacchierata
Piazza M. Serao, 37 (Galleria Umberto/San Carlo Theatre)
Tel: 081-411465
Closed: Sunday, open only for lunch.
Join the locals for excellent Neapolitan dishes like rigatoni with ricotta and meat sauce in this conveniently located family-run trattoria. **$$**

Ciro a Santa Brigida
Via Santa Brigida 71 (Galleria Umberto/Toledo)
Tel: 081-5524072
Closed: Sunday and 2 weeks in August.
Full-service restaurant with cut-above service and surroundings, this is also considered to be one of the better places in town to sample authentic Neapolitan pizza. **$**

Cafés and *Gelaterie*

Naples is known throughout Italy as the city with the best coffee (thought to have to do with the water), so a good cup of espresso or cappuccino should always be close at hand. Try along the waterfront, particularly out towards Mergellina, where **Ciro** is thought to be one of the best cafés. Alternatively, try **Gambrinus** (Piazza Trieste e Trento, tel: 081-417 582) overlooking the Teatro San Carlo, an elegant 19th-century *gran caffè*; not cheap, but worth it for its old-world atmosphere.

For great ice cream, try **Gelateria della Scimmia** (Piazza Carità 4, tel: 081-552 0272), which also sells delicious pastries. Also recommended is **Remy Gelo** in Mergellino.

La Mattonella
Via Nicotera 13 (Chiaia)
Tel: 081-416541
Closed: Sunday evenings and two
weeks in August
Traditional *osteria* with benches,
long tables and a charming marble
bar. Try the fried salt cod (*baccala'
fritto*) and the Neapolitan version of
meatballs (*polpettone*), and wash it
all down with a bottle of local wine.
$–$$

Mimi' alla Ferrovia
Via Alfonso d'Aragona 21
(near the railway station)
Tel: 081-5538525
Closed: Sunday
Arguably the most famous
'Neapolitan' restaurant in Naples
and long associated with its famous
clientele, Mimi' is still worth the
effort for classic dishes like linguini
with seafood and fried anchovies
and baby cuttlefish. **$$$**

Da Tonino
Via Santa Teresa a Chaia 47
Tel: 081-421533
Closed: Sunday and August; Open
for lunch, plus Friday and Saturday
dinner between October and May.
Run by the same family for more
than a century, Da Tonino is a
relic of the traditional *osteria*,
where the common Neapolitans
came to drink a glass of wine out
for the barrel and have a bite of
whatever was on the fire. You are
likely to find a simple, inexpensive
pasta e ceci (soup of pasta and
chickpeas) or *baooala'* (stewed
salt cod). **$$**

Pizzas and street food
Pizza is a must in Naples – the
reputed birthplace of one of the
world's most beloved foods. You
can find pizzas and other snacks
throughout the city, but the
following are among the most
reliable places to try:

Friggitoria Vomero
Via Cimarosa 44 (Vomero)
Tel: 081-5783130
Closed: Sunday and August
A first-rate Neapolitan fry house
(potatoes, bread dough, polenta,
aubergine balls, etc) where they
charge by the piece and serve in
paper bags. **$**

Cake Shops in Naples

Scaturchio
Piazza San Domenico Maggiore
Tel: 081-5516944
This long-established cake shop
is one of the best in town for
local favourites like almond milk,
babà, *sfogliatelle*, *cassate*, and
chocolate *ministeriale*.

Pasquale Pintauro
275, Via Toledo
Here you will find delicious
sfogliatella, the inimitable
Neapolitan pastry with a wavy,
crisp shell which looks like a tiny
golden fan wrapped around a
filling of ricotta and semolina.

Tripperia Fiorenzano
Via Pignasecca 14 (centre)
Closed: Sunday and mid-August
Not for the faint-hearted, this tiny
place fills with the aroma of stewed
lamb's head, pig's feet, tripe and
other parts of animals that don't
make it to most restaurant tables.
$

Da Michele
Via Sersale 1
Tel: 081-5539204
Closed: Sunday and in August
Century-old restaurant. Open late. **$**

Brandi
Salita S. Anna di Palazzo 2
Tel: 081-416928
Famous for (reputedly) inventing the
margherita (a pizza in honour of the
Queen of Italy, made up of
ingredients representing the three
colours of the Italian flag: red
(tomato sauce), white (cheese) and
green (basil). **$**

Gorizia
Via Bernini 29
Tel: 081-5782248
Closed: Wednesday and August. **$**

Lombardi
Via Lucillio 11
Tel: 081-7646882
Closed: Sunday night and August. **$**

Trianon
Via del Parco Margherita 27
Tel: 081-414678
Closed: Sunday. **$**

Trianon da Ciro
Via Coletta 42
Tel: 081-5539426 **$**

Around the Volcano

Pompeii
President
Piazza Schettini 12
Tel: 081-8507245
Closed: Sunday dinner and Monday;
August
A menu full of good seafood dishes,
a comfortable atmosphere and
excellent service; a welcome
change from the many standard
trattorias and tourist menus that
catch the tourist flow from the
ruins. **$$$**

Herculaneum
Casa Rossa al Vesuvio
Via Vesuvio 30 (About 10 km/
6 miles south of Naples on the
road to Herculaneum)
Tel: 081-7779763
Closed: Tuesday
A great stop for lunch before or
after the ruins; pizza is the
speciality here, baked in the
traditional wood-fired oven. At lunch
or dinner the view of Naples and the
Bay are equally idyllic. **$**

The Islands

Capri
Buca di Bacco da Serafina
Via Longano 35
Tel: 081-8370723
Closed: Wednesdays and November
Beloved local trattoria for fish
dishes and their signature "stuffed"
pizza (with ricotta, prosciutto and
mozzarella cheese). **$$**

Giorgio
Via Roma 34
Tel: 081-8375777
Closed: January–February
Reliable pizzeria with a view of the
sea. Open late. **$**

La Rondinella
(Anacapri)
Via G. Orlandi 245
Tel: 081-8371223
Closed Thursdays; open daily in
summer.
Good value trattoria with appetizing
local specialties like *ravioli alla
caprese* with pesto or tomato
sauce, and a wide assortment of
simple fish dishes. Tables outside.
$–$$

Ischia

Il Focolare
Localita' Casamicciola Terme
Via Cretaio 68
Tel: 081-980604
Closed: Wednesdays (October–May);
three weeks in November.
Located 6 km (4 miles) from the
town of Ischia (2½km or 1½ miles
from the port), Il Focolare is an
ideal place to sample the local
seasonal cuisine. Pasta and bread,
all made in-house, are especially
good. **$$**

Il Melograno
Via Giovanni Mazzela 110
(Forio d'Ischia)
Tel: 081-998450
Closed: Monday and Tuesday
(between October and February).
Simple yet refined cuisine in
an intimate atmosphere, well
worth a trip to the village of Forio
on the west side of the island.
$–$$

Da Peppina
Via Bocca 23 (Forio d'Ischia)
Tel: 081-998312
Closed Wednesday from October to
March; open only for dinner.
This informal and cosy trattoria is
the place to try the island's non-fish
dishes, including rabbit and pasta
in walnut sauce. Great views from
the terrace. **$–$$**

Procida

Crescenzo
Via Marina Chiaolella, 33
Tel: 081-8967255
A family–run restaurant with a
charming view, the spaghetti with
fish sauce is first-rate as is the
coniglio alla cacciatora (rabbit
prepared with tomatoes according
to a local recipe). Pizza is served
only at night. **$$**

Sorrento

Don Alfonso 1890
Corso Sant'Agata 11
(Sant'Agata ai Due Golfi)
Tel: 081-5330226
Closed: Monday and Tuesday; mid
January–mid-February
Widely considered to be the finest
restaurant in Southern Italy.
$$$–$$$$

Caruso
Via Sant'Antonino 12
Tel: 081-8073156
Closed: Monday from
October–March.
Centrally located, classic Sorrentine
food in a refined atmosphere
dedicated to the great Italian tenor.
$$

Antica Trattoria
Via Padre Reginaldo Giuliani 33
Tel: 081-8071082
Closed: Monday and from mid-
January–mid-February.
A reliable local favourite for fresh
fish cooked on the grill or delicately
sautéed with tomatoes and herbs.
$$

Price Guide

The price of a three-course meal
for one, without wine, is:
$ = below €15
$$ = €15–30
$$$ = €30–45
$$$$ = over €45

The Amalfi Coast

Amalfi

Caravella
Via Matteo Camera 12
Tel: 081-871029
Closed: Tuesday and in November.
Refined and exquisite, this is
Amalfi's most celebrated
restaurant, and deservedly so. The
tasting menu is recommended.
$$$

Da Gemma
Via Fra Gerardo Sasso 9
Tel: 081-871345
Closed: Wednesday and in January.
Take a seat at this local trattoria in
front of the Duomo and enjoy a bowl
of fish soup. **$$**

Positano

Donna Rosa
Via Montepertuso 97,
Montepertuso
tel: 089-811806)
Five kilometres (3 miles) north of
Positano, a pleasant restaurant
where you'll find vegetable soups
and fish done in a variety of ways.
$$

'O Capurale
Via Regina Giovanna 12
Tel: 089-811188
Closed: late October and early
February
Wonderful fish at this welcoming
down-to-earth trattoria among the
riches and glamour of Positano. **$–$$**

Il Ritrovo
Via Montepertuso 77
Tel: 089-875453
Closed: Wednesday (October–May);
mid-January–mid-February
Tables outside in the summer and a
roaring fire in the winter, this
homely, family-run trattoria features
many dishes made with vegetables
grown by the proprietors. **$$**

Salerno

La Botte Piccola
Traversa E. da Corbilla
Tel: 089-254101
Open for dinner only.
An intimate, family-run restaurant
where you'll find home-made pasta
dressed with seasonal vegetables
and a good choice of traditional
meat and fish dishes. **$$**

Antica Pizzeria del Vicolo della Neve
Vicolo della Neve 24
Tel: 089-225705
Closed Wednesday and over
Christmas; open only for dinner.
The oldest trattoria in the city and
still worth a stop for excellent
home-style cooking amid a nothing-
fancy ambiance. First-rate pizza and
calzone. **$**

Al Cenacolo
Piazza Alfano I 4
Tel: 089-238818
Closed: Sunday dinner and Monday;
two weeks in August and
Christmas/New Year
Salerno's best restaurant; refined
cuisine in a serene setting in the
centre of town. The food is based
on traditional and age-old recipes,
and the menu changes with the
seasons. The soup of baby squid
should definitely not be missed. **$$**

Southern Campania

Agropoli

Il Ceppo
Via Madonna del Carmine 31
Tel: 0974-843036

Closed: Monday and Christmas to mid-January
Family-run restaurant with adjoining hotel. Fish dishes make up most of the menu, but pizza is also served in the evenings. Don't miss the tasty local cheeses, including a superb *mozzarella di bufala*. **$$–$$$**

Palinuro
Carmelo
Isca, 2 km (about a mile) east of Palinuro on the SS Road 562
Tel: 0974-931138
Closed: Wednesday, November and Christmas; always open in the summer.
In this long-established, family-run restaurant you can sample some of the best local cuisine, based on fish and fresh pasta. Outside dining and one non-smoking room. **$$$**

San Giovanni a Piro
U' Zifaro
Lungomare Marconi 43
Tel: 0974-986397
Closed: Sunday and Monday in winter, December–January.
Tables outside in summer, where you can dine with a view of the port. All fish menu made every which way. Excellent fried fish and fish baked whole in a crust of salt. Save room for dessert, with wonderful fruit ice cream and *cassatine* brought from Sicily. **$$**

Castellabate
La Taverna del Pescatore
Via Lamia
Tel: 0974-968293
Closed: Monday and December–February.
Fantastically well-preserved town. Great *zuppa di pesce* (fish soup) with a wonderful array of local catch. Best wine list in Southern Campania. **$$**

Pisciotta
Perbacco
Contrada Marina Campagna 5
Tel: 0974-973849
Closed: October–June, open weekends Easter to June.
Don't miss this informal *enoteca*, with an interesting selection of wines, and a limited menu that

might include marinated anchovies, pastas dressed in various fish sauces, and even local lamb and pork chargrilled to order. **$$**

Ravello
Palazzo della Marra
Via della Marra 7
Tel: 089-858302
Closed: Tuesday and November.
Welcoming restaurant inside a restored historic *palazzo*. Creative, unusual take on traditional cuisine. Occasional theme dinners (medieval menus on Fridays). **$$**
Cumpa' Cosimo
Via Roma 44
Tel: 089-857156
Closed: Monday and November–February.
Much-loved local trattoria, judging by the dozens of framed pictures on the walls of happy customers over the last decades. **$$-$$$**

Apulia

FOGGIA PROVINCE

Foggia
Trilussa
Via Tenente Lorio 50
Tel: 0881-709253
Closed: Wednesday; open only for dinner.
Worthwhile pizzeria with the best *bruschetta* (toasted bread with various toppings) in Apulia. **$**
Il Ventaglio
Via Postiglione 6
Tel: 0881-661500
Closed: Sunday and Monday dinner.
One of the best restaurants in the region, combining inventive specialities (such as pasta with shrimp, figs and gorgonzola), elegant surroundings and first-rate service. Outside dining. **$$$**

San Giovanni Rotondo
Donna Rosa
Via Berlinguer 12
Tel: 0882-457850
Closed: Tuesday and January
Reliable restaurant at the edge of town, with plenty of fish on the menu. Outside dining. **$$**

Tremiti Islands
Hotel Gabbiano
Piazza Belvedere
Isola San Domino
Tel: 0882-463410
Solid fare at the restaurant of this hotel near the port (tidy serviceable rooms), especially the mixed grill. Outside dining in the garden with a panoramic view.

BARI PROVINCE

Bari
Alberosole ESP/G
Corso Vittorio Emanuele 13
Tel: 080-5235446
Closed: Monday; two weeks in August.
On the main street that divides the ancient and modern parts of the city, this first-rate restaurant is one of Bari's best for Apulian dishes prepared with confidence. Warm, efficient service. **$$–$$$**
Osteria delle Travi
Largo Chiurlia 12
Tel: 0330-840438
Closed: Sunday dinner and Monday; two weeks in August.
No visit to Bari is complete without a walk and a meal in the Borgo Antico. Enjoy the antipasti buffet amid locals, and the local speciality of pasta with horsemeat sauce. **$ $$**
La Taverna Verde
Largo Adua 18
Tel: 080-5540870
Closed: Sunday and two weeks in August.
Simple, much-loved restaurant just off the Lungomare. Excellent *favè e cicoria* (fava bean purée with sautéed chicory). **$$**
Terranima
Via Putignani 213
Tel: 080-5219725
Closed: Sunday dinner and mid-July–mid-August.
Step back in time into this intriguing restaurant, with its 19th-century decor and a brief menu made up of traditional Apulian specialities. **$$**

Alberobello
La Cantina
Via Lippolis 9
Tel: 080-4325593

Closed: Tuesday; two weeks in August.
Among the many tourist restaurants in the town famous for *trulli*, a simple trattoria for a good plate of *orecchiete* pasta, served simply with mushrooms or asparagus, according to the season. **$**

Trani
Torrente Antico ESP/G
Via Fusco 3
Tel: 0883-487911
Closed: Sunday dinner and Monday.
This is an acclaimed restaurant well worth a stop on your way up or down the coast. Not only is the food creative and delicious, but the wine list is one of the best in the region. **$$$**

BRINDISI PROVINCE

Brindisi
Trattoria Pantagruele
Via Salita di Ripalta 1
Tel: 0831-560605
Closed: Sunday dinner and Monday (September–June), Saturday and Sunday (July–August); two weeks in August.
Very handy for the port, this no-nonsense restaurant offers the standard local dishes prepared with care. There is ample choice of grilled meat as well as fish, and the tasty homemade desserts are worth trying. Outside seating too. **$–$$**

Ceglie Massapica
Fornello da Ricci
Ceglie Massapica
(Contrada Montevicoli)
Tel: 0831-377104
Closed: Monday dinner and Tuesday; two weeks in February and three weeks in September.
Difficult to find, this large family restaurant on the outskirts of town has the feel of a country lodge and serves some of the best food in Apulia. Well worth seeking out. **$$**

Ostuni
Osteria del Tempo Perso
Via Vitale 47
Tel: 0831-303320

Closed: Monday and October.
Crowded with locals, this busy rustic trattoria with farm implements and old photos on the walls serves up dependable Apulian standards without fuss. **$$**

LECCE PROVINCE

Lecce
Picton
Via Idomeneo 14
Tel: 0832-332383
Closed: Monday.
Inventive, often wild, combinations in this restaurant make a refreshing change from this otherwise tradition-bound part of the country. **$$$**
Cucina Casereccia
Via Costadura 9
Tel: 0832-245189
Closed: Sunday dinner and Monday; two weeks in September.
The name of this plain trattoria, 'Homemade cuisine', just about says it all. Mamma and good cooking included. **$**

TARANTO PROVINCE

Taranto
Da Mimmo
Via Giovinazzi 18
Tel: 099-4593733
Closed: Wednesday.
Popular local restaurant. Outside dining. **$$**

Martina Franca
Il Ritrovo degli Amici
Corso Massapia 8
Tel: 080-4839249
Closed: Sunday dinner and Monday. (except in summer); February.
This pleasant restaurant is the best place to try this wonderful town's famous salamis and sausages, as well as other local specialities. **$$**

Basilicata

MATERA PROVINCE

Maratea
Taverna Rovita
Via Rovita 13
Tel: 0973-876588

Closed: Tuesday and mid-January–mid-March
Just off the main piazza in Maratea Alta. Eat your spaghetti *alla pecorano* (with tomatoes, ricotta cheese and basil) and other classic local dishes in simple terracotta bowls. **$$–$$$**

Matera
Il Casino del Diavolo
Via La Martella
Tel: 0835-261986
Closed: Monday
A local favourite, this restaurant set in an olive grove on the outskirts of town, features an ample selection of local specialities, many of which are laid out along a long buffet. **$–$$**
La Buca
Via San Pardo 95
Tel: 0835-261984
Closed: Sunday dinner and Monday.
A little off the beaten track (about 1 km or half a mile from the centre of town), this restaurant is for meat lovers. Run by a family that has raised animals and kept a butcher shop for generations. **$$**
Trattoria Lucana
Via Lucania 48
Tel: 0835-336117
Closed: Sunday; August.
A room reserved for non-smokers might be enough to recommend it for some, but the food is good too. Try the wonderful *bruschetta* made with the hearty local bread, and pasta served with seasonal vegetables and sausage. **$$**
Le Botteghe
Piazza San Pietro Barisano 22
Tel: 0835-344072
Fax: 0835-344072
Closed Wednesday and Sunday night.
Traditional cuisine served in a comfortable restaurant carved out of a *sassi* cave. **$$**

Nova Siri
Ai Tre Limoni
Viale Siris 134
Closed: Mondays in winter
Reliable restaurant on the Ionian coast – especially popular for outside dining in the summertime – for fish *antipasti* (marinated salmon, sword fish and anchovies).

Fish soup by reservation a day in advance. **$$–$$$**

POTENZA PROVINCE

Potenza
Antica Osteria Marconi
Viale Marconi 233
Tel: 0971-56900
Closed: Sunday dinner and Monday; August.
Arguably the best restaurant in Basilicata. Don't miss the fresh pasta and the *minestra di fave e cicoria* (broad bean and chicory soup). A temptingly ample wine list features the best of the region's production. **$$**
Due Torri
Via Due Torri 6
Tel: 0971-411661
Closed: Sunday; two weeks in August.
Relaxing restaurant set inside a fortified building in the old part of town. Try the homemade *strascinati* pasta with kid sauce, followed by grilled meat and pecorino cheese. Good service and solid wine list. **$$**

Melfi
Vaddone
Contrada Santa Abruzzese (Melfi)
Tel: 0972-24323
Closed: Sunday dinner and Monday
Rustic family restaurant with wonderful local salami and cheeses. The pasta *maquarnara* (with meat sauce and local pecorino cheese) is a winner. **$–$$**

Rotonda
Da Peppe
Corso Garibaldi 13
Tel: 0973-661251
After working up an appetite exploring the Parco Nazionale del Pollino, you can treat yourself to a hearty dinner here. **$**

Calabria

CATANZARO PROVINCE

Catanzaro
Da Pepe
Vico I – Piazza Roma 6
Closed: Sunday.

One of several places to try *morzello*, the typical dish of Catanzaro: a spicy sauce cooked slowly in an enormous pot, in which veal tripe and innards are stewed. The dish is served in a soft, *pitta* bread and eaten on the spot. **$**

Price Guide

The price of a three-course meal for one, without wine, is:
$ = below €15
$$ = €15–30
$$$ = €30–45
$$$$ = over €45

La Fattoria
Via Magna Grecia 83 (7 km/4½ miles from Catanzaro, in the direction of Catanzaro Lido)
Tel: 0961-782809
Once an olive oil press, this restaurant is a great place to sample different Calabrian dishes from a well prepared and inviting buffet. If you have room, there's also an impressive selection of local cheeses. **$$**

Civita
Agora'
Piazza Municipio 30
Tel: 0981-73410
Closed: Monday.
Simple, family-run, traditional restaurant specializing in the local, Albanian-influenced cuisine. The lamb and kid dishes are wonderful. **$–$$**

COSENZA PROVINCE

Cosenza
Da Giocondo
Via Piave 53
Tel: 0984-29810
Closed: Sunday and August.
Reliable restaurant in the modern part of town. Don't miss the pickled mushrooms, the local cheeses (from the Sila), and the *maccheroni* in kid sauce. **$$**

Castrovillari
La Locanda di Alia
Via Jetticelle 69
Tel: 0981-46370

Closed: Sunday and between Christmas and New Year.
A restaurant renowned for some of the best food in Calabria, its ever-changing menu is sure to be full of dishes that combine traditional recipes with touches of creative fancy. Reservations recommended. **$$$–$$$$**

CROTONE PROVINCE

Crotone
Casa di Rosa
Viale Cristofaro Colombo 117
Tel: 0962-21946
Closed: Sunday and mid-December–mid-January.
Simple, small restaurant above the Porto Vecchio, with a wide selection of fish on the menu. Try the *spaghettoni con cozze e pomodorini al forno* (baked with muscles and cherry tomatoes) and the fried fish. Reservations recommended. **$$$**
Da Ercole
Viale Gramsci 122
Tel: 0962-901425
Closed: Monday.
At the southern end of town, this fish restaurant is the place to enjoy sea urchins and *scrine*, a local mollusc found only here. Outside dining in summer. Reservations recommended. **$$**

Isola di Capo Rizzuto
Da Annibale
Via Duomo 35 (Le Castella)
Tel: 0962-795004
One of the best fish restaurants in the Catanzaro area. Well-attended by locals, Annibale remains affordable. Trust the waiters, who tend to bring you the catch of the day rather than the menu. Ask for a taste of their special pecorino cheese at the end of the meal. **$$**

REGGIO CALABRIA PROVINCE

Reggio Calabria
Taverna degli Ulivi
Via Eremo Botte 32
Tel: 0965-891461
Closed: Sunday

Forget the pizza served here and opt for the *maccarruni I casa* (traditional Calabrian hand-made pasta with meat sauce). Wonderful grilled meat and sausages. **$$**

VIBO VALENTIA PROVINCE

Vibo Valentia
Approdo
Via Roma 22 (Localita' Vibo Marina)
Tel: 0963-572640
Closed: Monday (except in summer).
Acclaimed fish restaurant near Vibo Marina. Try the *fileja* (home-made pasta) with mussels, shrimp and courgettes, and the anchovy and aubergine tart. First-rate service and warm welcome. **$$$–$$$$**

Tropea
Osteria del Pescatore
Via del Monte 7
Tel: 0963-603018
Closed: Wednesday (except in summer).
You'll find this traditional *osteria* set inside a noble *palazzo* behind the Duomo in the centre of Tropea. The short menu features a few pasta choices and a selection of grilled or fried fish. **$$**

Sicily

PALERMO PROVINCE

Palermo
Bye Bye Blues
Via del Garofalo 23 (Mondello)
Tel: 091-6841415
Closed: Tuesdays, open only for dinner.
Well worth the trip from Palermo (or further), this simple and quiet restaurant offers by far the best food in the area. Ever-changing menu based on fresh fish and seasonal vegetables. **$$$–$$$$**
Shanghai
Vicolo dei Mezzani 34
Tel: 091-589702
Crumbling little restaurant on a small terrace above the bustling Vucciria market, from which the food is hauled up in wicker

baskets. A memorable simple meal. No credit cards. **$**
Capricci di Sicilia
Via Istituto Pignatelli 6
(Piazza Sturzo)
Tel: 091-327777
Simple, rustic and informal, this is the best place to stop for lunch after a walk through the Borgo Vecchio and Piazza Politeama; try a delectable bowl of spaghetti dressed with a sea urchin sauce and traditional Sicilian aubergine rolls. **$$**
Osteria Paradiso
Via Serradifalco 23
Closed: Sunday; open only for lunch.
Cosy, family-run restaurant near Piazza Politeama. A local favourite for specialities like *pasta alle sarde* (with sardines). **$$**
Charleston
Piazzale Ungeria 30
Tel: 091-321366
Closed: June–September when the restaurant moves to the Stabilimento Balneare in Mondello. Historic, classy restaurant in Palermo. Where else can you eat champagne risotto? Reservations required, as is elegant dress. **$$$–$$$$**
Hosteria dei Vespri
Piazza Croce dei Vespri 6
Tel: 091-6171631
Closed: Sunday and November.
Great wine selection at this *enoteca,* with a limited but appetizing menu that always includes marinated fish and pasta with swordfish sauce. Outside seating in an attractive piazza. **$$**
Il Ristorantino
Piazza de Gasperi 19
Tel: 091-512861
Closed: Monday and two weeks in August.
Popular restaurant in a residential part of town, where locals enjoy warm, excellent service and good food. Dependably great selection of Sicilian and Italian wines. **$$$**
La Scuderia
Viale del Fante 9
Tel: 091-520323
Closed: Sunday and two weeks in August.
Worth the trip a few miles out of

town to enjoy a view of the city from the terrace and the usual array of reliable Sicilian specialities. **$$$**
Antica Focacceria San Francesco
Via Paternostro 58
Tel: 091-320264
The historic shop to drop into for your fill of Palermitan street food, including *milza* (spleen) sandwiches, fried rice and cheese balls, and chickpea fritters. **$**

Cefalù
La Brace
Via XXV Novembre 10
Tel: 0921-23570
Closed: Monday and mid-December–mid-January.
Pleasant little restaurant near the Duomo. Nice mix of classic Sicilian and more innovative cuisine. Good selection of local wines. **$$**
Hostaria del Duomo
Via del Seminario 5
Tel: 0921-21838
Closed Mondays (except in summer) and December.
Lovely open-air setting overlooking the Duomo. Authentic *caponata* (aubergine ragout) and *carpaccio di pesce* (thinly sliced raw fish, lightly marinated). **$$$**

Ustica
Mamma Lia
Via S. Giacomo 1
Tel: 091-8449594
Closed: December–March.
The island's most popular restaurant with locals and visitors. Try the soup made from local lentils, followed by swordfish croquettes. **$$**
Da Mario
Piazza Umberto I 21
Tel: 091-8449505
Closed: Monday and January.
Local fish dishes in a pleasant, family-run trattoria. Try the spaghetti with sea urchin and shrimps. Outside dining in summer on the town's main piazza. **$$**

TRAPANI PROVINCE

Trapani
Trattoria del Porto
Via Staiti 45
Tel: 0923-547822

Price Guide

The price of a three-course meal for one, without wine, is:
- **$** = below €15
- **$$** = €15–30
- **$$$** = €30–45
- **$$$$** = over €45

Closed: Monday and 2 weeks in December.
The TV blares the latest news and soccer scores from this brightly lit, family run trattoria opposite the hydrofoil to the Egadi islands. Fish couscous and *spaghetti alla trapanese* (with a pesto sauce made of almonds) are local favorites. **$$**

Ai Lumi
Corso Vittorio Emanuele 75
0923-872418
Closed: Sunday.
A thick wooden door on the town's main drag hides this cosy restaurant with wooden tables and memorabilia on the walls, and the best food in town. If you happen to be here during tuna season (May–June), you can try *lattume* (tuna roe). **$$**

Egadi
Egadi
Via Cristoforo Colombo 17
(Favignana)
Tel: 0932-921232
Closed: one month in autumn, open for dinner, reservations necessary.
A must for any visitor to Favignana, the plain dining room of the little Hotel Egadi serves up what is arguable the best food in Western Sicily. Memorable dishes include marinated fish, pasta in lobster broth, fish cous-cous and fresh tuna in season. **$$**

Pantelleria
La Nicchia
Contrada Scauri Basso
Tel: 0923-916342
Closed: October–April
Wonderful informal restaurant with outside dining and a view of the sea. Try the delicious house speciality, spaghetti with shrimps, capers and tomatoes. **$$**

AGRIGENTO PROVINCE

Agrigento
Leon d'Oro
Via Emporium 102 (loc. San Leone)
Tel: 0922-414400
Closed: Monday and November.
Well worth the short drive (about 8 km/5 miles) west of the town centre, this much loved restaurant serves the best food in Agrigento. Outside dining. Excellent spaghetti with swordfish and mint sauce. **$$**

Trattoria dei Templi
Via Panoramica dei Templi 15
Tel: 0922-403110
Closed: Thursday and November.
How refreshing to find a restaurant in the shadows of the Valle dei Templi that is not a tourist trap, with honest food, good service and fair prices. Good *caponata* (aubergine ragout). Outside dining. **$$**

ENNA PROVINCE

Enna
Ariston
Via Roma 353
Tel: 0935-26038
Closed: Sunday and two weeks in August.
Reliable local restaurant for Sicilian standards like *rigatoni alla Norma* (with aubergine and salted ricotta). Good grilled meat and fish. Efficient service. **$$**

SIRACUSA PROVINCE

Siracusa
Il Porticciolo da Piero
Via Trento 22 (Ortigia)
Tel: 0931-61914
Closed: Monday and two weeks in October.
This friendly trattoria is a favourite with shoppers and vendors in the nearby market. Especially busy at lunchtime. Good selection of fish. Outside dining on the veranda. **$$**

Archimede
Via Gemmellaro 8
Tel: 0931-69701
Closed: Sunday dinner and two weeks in July.

Located off the central piazza of the same name, this is the oldest restaurant in the city, and a good place to sample from a changing menu of traditional dishes. **$$**

Jonico
Riviera Dionisio il Grande 194
Tel: 0931-65540
Closed: Tuesday.
Worth a visit for the fabulous Art Deco interior and stunning view from the roof terrace (outside dining in summer). Varied menu of fish and pasta dishes, including spaghetti with wild fennel. Pizza in the evenings. **$$–$$$**

La Siciliana
Via Savoia 17
Tel: 0931-68944
Closed: Monday
A handy pizzeria in the old part of town, a stone's throw from the Tempio di Apollo. Outside dining. **$**

CATANIA PROVINCE

Catania
Il Cantine del Cugno Mezzano
Via Museo Biscari 8
Tel: 095-7158710
Closed: Monday and August; open only for dinner.
Centrally located in one of Catania's grandest baroque *pallazi*, this wine bar/shop (*enoteca*) has a limited menu of delicious and creative dishes such as almond soup with clams. Outside seating and great selection of wines. **$–$$**

Metro'
Via dei Crociferi 76
Tel: 095-322098
Closed: Saturday and Sunday lunch.
Sit outside on a pedestrian street in the shadow of baroque buildings and enjoy food inspired by ancient recipes, such as meatballs flavoured with pomegranate. Home-made desserts worth saving room for. **$$$**

Nicolosi
Etna
Via Etnea 93
Tel: 095-911937
Closed: Monday and mid-February to mid-March.
Traditional Etna cuisine in a post-

modern restaurant and pizzeria. Try the grilled wild boar. **$$**

Taormina
Al Duomo
Vico Ebrei 11
Tel: 0942-625656
Closed: Wednesday (except in summer).
Efficient service, elegant restaurant; delicious pasta with fried courgettes and ricotta. Finest eating in Taormina. **$$$**

La Giara
Vicolo Floresta 1
Tel: 0942-23233
Closed: Monday (except in summer) and November.
Elegant restaurant. Specialities include spaghetti with swordfish roe. **$$$–$$$$**

Granduca
Corso Umberto 172
Tel: 0942-24420
This chic, old-fashioned grand restaurant offers lovely views over the bay. **$$$**

Nautilus
Via San Pancrazio 48
Tel: 0942-625024
Closed: Tuesday.
Creative and delicious food – influenced by the owner's experience working aboard an Oriental cruise liner. Outside dining on a terrace near the church. **$$$**

Trattoria Rosticepi
Via San Pancrazio 10
Tel: 0942 24149
Good value and reliable cooking at the top of Via Pirandello. **$**

MESSINA PROVINCE

Messina
Le Due Sorelle
Piazza Municipio 4
Tel: 090-44720
Closed: Monday and August, weekends open for dinner only.
Traditional Mediterranean cuisine with creative touches from India and North Africa. Great wine list and dining outside on the piazza. **$$**

Nightlife

Clubs go in and out of fashion (or in and out of business) at a fast rate, so it's a good idea to check with the local tourist office and ask around (hotels, local bars, etc) for the latest nightspots. Bear in mind that during the summer months many clubs and discos set up on the beach or by the water.

Naples

Neapolitan nightlife is concentrated in the chaotic but characteristic historic centre, the area stretching towards the sea, and the Pozzuoli district by the port. The Borgo Marinaro area, which used to be patronised by pensioners, is now popular with all ages, although the bars and *trattorie* are just the same as they were 30 years ago.

CLASSIC CAFES, WINE BARS & LIVE MUSIC

As well as classic cafes, such as the legendary Gambrinus, Naples has a decent range of bars, including several atmospheric *vinerie*. Note that most places here close on Monday.

Caffè Gambrinus
Via Chiaia 1–2, Piazza Plebiscito
This is the city's most famous bar, adorned with gilt-and-plaster reliefs. Although it's crowded, the terrace makes a good spot for watching the world go by, sipping an *aperitivo* or coffee. Open from early morning until about 10 or 11pm.

Chiatamon
Via Chiatamone
This informal and fashionable bar overlooks the seafront of Via Caracciolo. DJs most weekends.

City Hall
Corso Vittorio Emanuele
City Hall is a trendy venue, with good jazz, fusion style; the place to rub shoulders with Neapolitan greats including Bennato and De Piscopo.

Frame
Via Paladino
Next-door to the Vineria *(see below)* this is a loud, lively bar that buzzes until five or six in the morning.

Notting Hill
Piazza Dante
As hip as the London district, Notting Hill is the place to go in Naples for live ethnic music. The city's best visiting percussionists are often invited to perform here.

Pinterre
Borgo Marinaro
Tel: 081-7649822
Borgo Marinaro is the tiny bay at the foot of Castel dell'Ovo *(see page 145)*. Here you can find the largest *birreria* in the city, the place for every kind of beer, as well as music and snacks at all hours.

A Ret' A' Palm
Piazza Santa Maria La Nova
Called "Behind the palms" in Neapolitan dialect, this wine bar and inn *(osteria)* is set on a square close to Piazza del Gesu Nuoovo in an unpretentious *palazzo*. It has an excellent wine list and good bar snacks at very reasonable prices. The musician-owner performs live every Wednesday.

Vinarium
Via Cappella Vecchia 7
Tel: 041-7644114
Conveniently located in the city centre, this classic wine bar is particularly popular with trendy professionals over 30. The ambience is smart/casual, with a pleasant, relaxing feel despite the relative formality of the surroundings. From here, it is just a quick stroll to Via Carlo Poerio, which is bursting with small bars, pubs and wine bars.

Vineria
Via Paladino
This atmospheric wine bar set close to Piazza San Domenico Maggiore was once a student haunt, but now attracts a wider cross-section. The atmosphere is "intellectual yet

homely", a mood enhanced by low lighting and wood and marble fixtures and fittings. Closed Monday.

Virgilio Sports Club
Via Tito Lucresio Caro 6
Tel: 081-5755261
The name is a bit misleading, even if there is a sports club here too, since this is in fact now a disco-bar for twenty and thirty-somethings. However, in true Neapolitan style, different sets of people go on different nights, with Thursday a typical night for *per bene* (well-bred) thirty-somethings. There are sea views from the terrace.

Clubs & Disco-Bars

Although the following are among the most stylish or fashionable places for dancing in Naples, note that the city is not known for cutting-edge clubs and avant-garde music. Most venues tend to play a similar mainstream mix of classics from the '70s and '80s right through to rap, house music or the current chart hits. Most places close on Monday.

Chez Moi
Via del Parco Margherita 20
This is similar in approach to **My Way** *(see below)*.

Kiss-Kiss
Via Sgambati 47
Tel: 081-5466566
Located in the Vomero district, this large disco has a restaurant and tends to attract a young crowd of students.

La Mela
Via dei Mille 40b
Tel: 081-413881
This is a smart, trendy place. However, given allegations of Mafia involvement in the club, there are occasional shootings, after which the place is closed for a while. Whatever its dubious associations, many locals miss it when it's gone.

My Way
Via Cappella Vecchia 30c
Tel: 081-7644735
This is another trendy disco-bar, with different nights (unofficially) for different age groups and sets.

The Islands

Capri

Nightlife in Capri is vibrant: clubs, bars and cafés with live music stay open late. If a quiet, romantic walk is more appealing, there's a path from Anacapri to the Belvedere Migliara or you can walk from Capri town to the Belvedere Cannone and the view of the Faraglioni at Tragara.Here are a few suggested night-spots.

La Palma – popular piano bar in the centrally located hotel of the same name. Open late. Via Vittorio Emanuele 39, tel: 081-8370133.

Taverna Guarracino – Neapolitan folk music and sing-a-longs. Via Castello 7, tel: 081-8370514.

Taverna Anema e Core – Live mostly contemporary music. Very popular with the chic crowd. Via Sella Orta 39/e, tel: 081-837646.

Pentothal – Popular disco for the island's younger crowds. Via Vittorio Emanuele 45, tel: 081-8376793.

Number Two – Dancing til' dawn (long after the other clubs have closed). Via Camerelle 1, tel: 081 8377078.

Ischia

Megadisco Jane – The island's biggest dance club, set on the beach, not far from the Port. Ischia Porto, Via Pagoda, tel: 081-993296.

Apulia

Bari

Legends – Pizza, sandwiches and various beers to choose from at this pub with live music and a view of the Adriatic. V. Gentile 53/d, tel: 080-5543532.

Hakuna Matata – African club with typical decor, food and music from the sub-Sahara. Corso Vittorio Emanuele 128, tel: 0348-3405699.

Lecce

Etnie – Great bar with four rooms, each decorated in a style that evokes different cities around the world. Corso Libertini, tel: 0832-307120

Basilicata

Matera

Caffè Schiuma – Sooner or later it seems everybody in town passes through this bar. A good place to see what is going on in town. Via Stigliani 92, tel: 0835-334283.

Potenza

Carpe Diem – The big club in town for live music. Open Friday and Saturday. Via Scalo, tel: 0971-485863.

Calabria

Reggio Calabria

Maharaja – Disco with Indian-style decor, but decidedly Euro-pop music. Via Gallico, tel: 0965-371797.

Catanzaro

Ponte Roi – Trendy bar and live music venue. Via della Stazione 2, tel: 0961-753734. Closed Monday.

Cosenza

Soho Musical – Warehouse-style disco, popular with a wide range of locals. Via R. Montagna, tel: 0984-790199.

Sicily

Palermo

Il Cerchio – Dance club open weekends only. Viale Strasburgo 312, tel: 091-6885421.

Grand Hotel et des Palmes – Classy piano bar in one of the city's historic hotels. Via Roma 398, tel: 091-583933.

Grant's Club – Dance club popular with the very young; experimental music. Via Principe di Paterno' 80, tel: 091-346772.

Mondello Palace – Grand piano bar in chic Mondello hotel. Viale Principe di Scalea 2, tel: 091-450001.

Further Information

For up-to-date information on events and venues, contact the local tourist office *(see page 326)*.

La Passeggiata

The *passeggiata* (evening or Sunday stroll) is an Italian institution that finds favour in Sicily. Mondello is the place to see a nightly parade of Milanese fashion. On summer nights, the offshore islands come alive. In particular, Ustica, the Egadi Islands (especially Lévanzo) and the Aeolian Islands (especially Lípari) are awash with strollers admiring one another.

Villa Boscogrande – Public villa where Visconti filmed scenes for *The Leopard*, used in the summertime as a club venue. Via Tommaso Natale 91 (Mondello), tel: 091-241179.

Catania
Empire – The main disco in town, set in what was once a sulphur plant. Via Solfatai 12, tel: 095-531266 or 375684.
La Cartiera – Once a paper factory, this is now a big live music club popular with the under-30 crowd. Via Sasa del Mutilato 8, tel: 095-532820.

Taormina
La Giara – For decades the preferred disco of the smart set, it hasn't yet fallen from favour. Vicolo La Floresta, tel: 0942-23360
Le Perroquet – Taormina's gay club. Piazza San Domenico 2, tel: 0942-24808.
Tout Va – The younger crowd assembles in the open air at this large dance club with a great view of the sea and occasional live music. Via Pirandello 70, tel: 0942-23824.

Culture

Campania

Naples
The **San Carlo Opera House** in Naples is Italy's largest, and rivals Milan's La Scala for its near-perfect acoustics (tel: 081-7972111). Dress is formal, especially for opening night. The season runs from January to mid-July. Another music venue is the **Teatro delle Palme** (tel: 081-418134, Via Vetriera 12) where a classical music season runs from January to April. Naples' summer season is one of Italy's liveliest: from rock and Italian pop concerts to traditional Neapolitan and classical music. Most events take place under the stars in the **Villa Comunale**, out of town in the **Ville Vesuviane**, and at **Bagnoli** in the grounds of a former industrial complex (bring along a cushion and some mosquito repellent). The cinema **Abadir** (tel: 081-5789447, Via Paisiello 35) screens films *in lingua originale* (almost always English).

Salerno
The **Teatro Giuseppe Verdi** (tel: 089-662141, Via Indipendenza) stages opera, ballet and concerts from October to May.

Ravello
From June to September, the focus of the music scene is **Villa Rufolo's gardens** where concerts are held on a cliff, with the sunset as a dramatic backdrop (tel: 089-858149).

Amalfi
Throughout the summer, Amalfi's **Duomo and Cloister** house international visiting orchestras and artists.

Apulia

Bari
Sadly, Bari's beautiful and famous **Teatro Petruzzelli** was destroyed by fire in 1991, and restoration work is expected to last for many years. Meanwhile, an interesting season of opera and concerts is held at other minor and temporary venues, the most important of which is the **Teatro Team** (tel: 080-5547730, Via Trecciolini, in the suburbs of Bari). Another important venue for classical music is the **Teatro Nicolò Piccinni** on Corso Vittorio Emanuele, which reopened in 1999 (tel: 080-5586906, call mornings).

Lecce
A **Baroque music festival** is held in churches throughout the town in September. Plans are underway to use the restored Roman Amphitheatre in Piazza Sant'Oronzo as a venue for concerts and plays.

The Gargano
In the summer, the Gargano has a vibrant cultural scene: the Italian weekly *Viveur*, available at night spots, cinemas and some bars in the province of Foggia, has a complete schedule of events.

Foggia and San Severo
In Foggia, the **Teatro Giordano** (tel: 0881-774640, Piazza Cesare Battisti 21) runs a winter season of concerts and opera, as does the **Teatro Giuseppe Verdi** in San Severo (tel: 088-2222954, Corso Garibaldi 3).

Calabria

Reggio Calabria
The Conservatorio Cilea (tel: 0965-812223, call mornings, Via Aschenez) provides up-to-date information about music events throughout town. The city's cultural scene livens up in the summer, with performances staged under the stars at the **Villa Comunale** and at the **Lido Comunale**. In July and August, a floating platform is anchored in front of the Lungomare where movies (often dubbed but

Sicilian Puppet Theatre

Traditional plays performed by puppets (*see page 88*) can still be seen in the towns listed.

Palermo
Associazione Figli d'Arte Cuticchio, Via Bara all'Olivella 95, tel: 091 323400. Modern versions of traditional puppet theatre.
Opera dei Pupi, Vicolo Ragusi 6, tel: 091 329294. Two or three shows weekly at 9pm.
Teatro Bradamante, Via Lombardia 25, tel: 091 6259223. A free show at 10pm most Fridays in summer.
Museo delle Marionette, Via Butera 1. Free shows in summer.

Monreale
Munna, Via Kennedy 10. Puppet performances on Sundays in summer.

Acireale
Cooperativa E. Magri, Corso Umberto 113, tel: 095 604521/606272.
Turi Grasso, Via Nazionale 95, tel: 095 7648035.

Siracusa
Opera dei Pupi, Via Nizza 14. In summer there are usually performances on Tuesday, Thursday and Saturday at 9.30pm.

sometimes in the original English) are screened al fresco.

Crotone
Every year in May, Crotone hosts the *Festival dell'Aurora*, a schedule of concerts, conferences, and theatrical pieces focused on Pythagorean themes and those of Magna Graecia.

Altomonte
Altomonte hosts the *Festival Mediterraneo dei Due Mari* (Mediterranean Festival of Two Seas) every year in July and August, focusing on Mediterranean culture and traditions.

Bova
In August, Bova hosts the most important ethnic music festival in the Mediterranean, the *Paleariza*, where you can also buy artisanal products and local gastronomical items (for information contact GAL Area Grecanica tel: 0965-762230, Piazza Roma 2).

Sicily

Palermo
Palermo's **Teatro Massimo** (ticket office tel: 091-6053315, Piazza Giuseppe Verdi, guided tours Mon–Fri 9am–1pm) organises a concerts, operas and ballets all year-round, its summer venue being the **Teatro della Verdura** on Via del Fante.

Catania
The **Teatro Massimo Bellini** (tel: 095-7150921, Piazza Teatro Massimo) is also a widely recognized venue for opera and ballet. Bellini's Norma premiered here in 1890. In the summer, performances are held in the open air at the Giardino Bellini (tickets sold by the agent Primafila tel: 095-314280).

Taormina
In Taormina, the **Teatro Antico** (Greek Theatre) and the nearby **Palazzo dei Congressi** (tel: 0942-23836, Via Timeo 1) are the main venues for the *International Taormina Arts Festival*, embracing classical music, ballet and theatre, and also for the famous *Taormina Film Festival*. Both events take place in July and August (tel: 0942-21142, Corso Umberto 19). If you're visiting in winter, look out for *Natale a Taormina*, a series of free Christmas concerts held in the Duomo and some of the town's other churches in December and January.

Festivals

Special Events

The Italian year is packed with special events, some linked to the Catholic calendar, others to the harvest season. Many involve processions, public performances, religious ceremonies, ceremonial races and competitions, elaborate costumes, singing, dancing and communal meals. (*See page 88.*)

Calendar

February
Early February: Almond Blossom Festival – music and folk dancing (Agrigento).
3–5 February: Festa di Sant'Agata – procession of wooden floats through the city (Catania).
End February: Carnevale – Celebrated with costumes and street festivals in Manfredonia (Apulia), Trapani, Taormina and Caltanissetta.

March
Sunday following 19 March: Festa di San Giuseppe, in Salemi, celebrated with bread sculptures.
March–April: 'Ndrezzata on Ischia (at Buonopane near Barano): on the festival of San Giovanni Battista, on Albis Monday and other religious festivals the frenetic dance known as 'Ndrezzata ('intertwined') takes place. Dancers wear traditional costumes and are armed with rolling pins.

April
Easter Week: Notable celebrations in Naples and Palermo. Dramatic processions and celebrations also in Taranto, Enna, Messina, Ragusa, Marsala, Erice and Prizzi.
In the Albanian town of Laino

Borgo in Calabria, the *Giudaica*, a passion play, is staged in the streets, and has been ever since 1557.

May
Saturday preceding 1st Sunday: Festival of San Gennaro in Naples – liquefaction of the Saint's blood.
1st Sunday: Festa di Santa Lucia in Siracusa.
May 4: Festa di San Francesco da Paola at Paola.
May 15: Festa di San Vito in Positano with fireworks.
Last weekend: Sagra del Taratatà or Festival of the Holy Cross at Casteltermini (30 km/18 miles north of Agrigento): processions and horse-riding in historical costumes; duels too.

June
● La Mattanza, the annual tuna hunt off the coast of Favignana Island *(see page 310)*.
● Plays, films and concerts in Taormina's Greek theatre.
● Classical drama staged in Greek theatres, alternating between Syracuse and Segesta each summer.
Mid-June–mid July: Summer classical music festival in Ravello.
June 27: Festa di San Andrea (patron saint of Amalfi) – processions and street celebrations in Amalfi; Festa dei Gigli in Nola, near Naples; procession of towering floats, recalling the homecoming of a local bishop in the 4th century.
Every four years: Amalfi hosts a dramatic regatta staged in period costume between teams representing what were once the four maritime republics that dominated the Italian peninsula (Pisa, Genoa, Amalfi and Venice). The Regatta will next come to Amalfi in June 2001.

July
● The Marsala Jazz Festival in the heart of the eponymous city; throughout the month.
● Summer Opera and Music Festival, Ravello.
● Teatro di Verdura Villa, Castelnuovo, in Palermo — outdoor performances of ballet and jazz.
Early to mid-July: Renaissance

music festival in Erice.
Early July: Sagra del Pesce Spada (swordfish festival) at Bagnara Calabra to celebrate the end of the local fishing season.
2 July: Festa della Madonna della Bruna in Matera.
12–15 July: Festa of Santa Rosalia, Palermo – procession to the sanctuary on Mount Pellegrino.
Second half July: Taormina International Film Festival.
Late July: Festivale della Valle d'Itria - opera and classical music performances.
26 July: Festa di Sant' Anna, Ischia – a torchlight procession of hundreds of boats, transformed into floats.
Late July/early August: Festival of the Itria Valley, Martina Franca; concerts and opera.

August
Early August: Settimana Pirandelliana, in Agrigento – opera and ballet performances.
13 August: Palio dei Normanni, Piazza Armerina in Sicily – fierce competition among the various neighbourhoods of town.
15 August: Procession of the Varia in Palmi: giant papier mâché models are carried through the streets. Procession of the Grande Vara in Messina: a giant float representing the Assumption is pulled across town.

September
Early September: Traditional Neapolitan music festival at Piedigrotta, with fireworks.
19 September: Festa di San Gennaro, in Naples – the faithful gather to watch the liquefactionof the saint's blood *(see page 137)*.

November
10 November: Festa di San Trifone, Adelfia, Bari – children dressed as angels ride on horseback.

December
8 December: Sausage and polenta festival, San Bartolomeo in Galdo, Benevento.
Christmas: Particularly beautiful public celebrations in Bari and Naples.

Outdoor Activities

National Parks

While there are several national parks in Southern Italy, they are more like protected areas than parks, with organised visitor's centres, campsites, well-marked trails and facilities. See the chapter on Southern Italy's Wild Places *(page 119)* for descriptions.

Parco Nazionale del Pollino
Equally split between Basilicata and Calabria, this is Italy's largest national park and the richest repository of wildlife in Southern Italy.

Sentiero Italia
This is a national trail project running all through the *Mezzogiorno*, beginning in Calabria's Parco Nazionale d'Aspromonte. It runs along the spine of the Appenines with refuges at strategic points along the way where hikers can stay the night. For more information, contact Nuove Frontiere in Reggio Calabria, tel and fax: 0965/898295.

Parco Nazionale della Sila
Relatively small, this national park has an informative Visitors' Centre at Cupone, where you can pick up a map illustrating 10 easy itineraries that can all be done in less than a day. Contact the tourist office in Camigliatello Silano for information.

Parco Nazionale d'Aspromonte
This is the area around the toe of Italy, a wall of ragged peaks looming over the narrow coastal plain. In summer, a good starting point for hikers is Gambarie, with pine forests and views over the straits and Sicily. In winter, Gambarie is Calabria's ski resort.

Promontorio del Gargano

The Gargano Peninsula, the spur of the Italian boot, was declared a national park in 1991, though only the Foresta Umbra can be described as "wild". There are several buses a day from Manfredonia to Monte Sant'Angelo (tel: 0881-773117), and an early morning bus from Monte Sant'Angelo up into the forest.

SICILY

Parco dell'Etna

Founded in 1981, this national park is the most interesting of Sicily's protected areas.

Parco dei Nebrodi

A varied mountainous and coastal landscape, with lakes, marshes and streams where a number of migratory birds overwinter.

Parco delle Madonie.

With 200-million-year-old fossils, the rocks here are the oldest on the island. There is a good network of paths and gravel roads for hikers.

Spectator Sports

Soccer

The national obsession is felt in the South as strongly as in the North. The Serie A (Premiership) championship is played from September to May. At the time of writing, only the teams from Naples, Bari, Lecce and Reggio Calabria are in Serie A. If you would like to go to a match, be sure to call the tourist office for ticket information well in advance of your visit.

Other Sports

Almost all other sport is enjoyed in Southern Italy, including basketball, golf, water polo, cycling, tennis, horse-racing, rugby, rowing and sailing, and skiing. If you are interested in buying tickets for any match or event, buy the pink *Gazzetta dello Sport* newspaper, which lists everything you want to know about sport in Italy.

Shopping

Shopping Areas

NAPLES AND AROUND

You needn't walk too far through central Naples or any touristy part of Campania to find the region's most famous products: coral jewellery from the world's coral capital, Torre del Greco, and leather goods. Most of the leather shoes and bags that make Northern Italy famous are actually manufactured here. Be warned that street sellers are not likely to have authentic merchandise.

Naples also has its share of great antique shops, mostly on Via Santa Maria di Costantinopoli, where at no 102, Mario Raffone (tel: 081 459667) sells artisanal prints of Mount Vesuvius and figures from nativity scenes. Don't miss Via San Gregorio Armeno, which is lined with shops selling hand-carved figures for nativity scenes, a cottage industry in Naples. Look for some of the year's noteworthy figures (athletes, movie stars, politicians), who are often represented. In Naples, the main shopping area is around Piazza dei Martiri, along Via Chiaia, Via Roma and pedestrian-only Via Calabritto. The Galleria Umberto (Via San Carlo) is definitely worth a look, as much for its glorious architecture as the stores inside. Marinella (Riviera di Chiaia 287/a, tel: 081-2451182) sells made-to-measure ties. Adele Improta on Via Carlo Doria 8 (tel: 081-5449753) has a delightful shop that specialises in talismans and amulets to ward off evil spirits.

Torre del Greco (15 km/9 miles east of Naples on the Circumvesuviana train line) teems

with over 60 coral workshops selling cameos, objects and jewellery carved out of not only coral, but also turtle shell, turquoise, jade and other semi-precious stones. Keep an eye out for the wood inlay *(intarsi)* made in nearby Sorrento.

CAPRI

The other shopping centre of Campania is Capri, whose flow of big spending tourists brought all of Italy's most famous boutiques to the island. Between the Piazzetta, Via Vittorio Emanuele and Via Camerelle, you will find the world's most prestigious names in shoes, clothing and jewellery, antique shops, and even an artisanal perfume workshop called Carthusia. In addition, Capri is known for its particular style of hand-made sandals and informal, summery clothing available from small shops all over the island. The town of Capri is small enough to explore on foot, but don't miss the back streets, where the locals shop. There is a *limoncello* factory at Via Roma 79, where you can buy the sweet lemon-flavoured liqueur for which Campania is famous.

AMALFI COAST

The sunny ceramics of the Amalfi Coast – produced in the town of Vietri sul Mare – are famous

Clothing Size Chart

Women's dresses:

Italian	UK	US
38	8	6
40	10	8
42	12	10
44	14	12

Men's shirts:

Italian	UK	US
36	14	14
38	15	15
41	16	16
43	17	17

throughout Italy and well worth a look. Look for a *bottega* (workshop) or shop that sells ceramics of *produzione propria* (their own production), rather than a general gift shop, for the best selection and prices *(see box on p.182 for good addresses)*. In Amalfi, the gift shops clustered around the Duomo sell artisanal paper made by the town's last surviving paper mill.

SOUTH OF NAPLES

Apart from Bari, Catania and Palermo, what the towns south of Naples lack in top-of-the-line designer stores, they occasionally make up for in artisan shops. In big and small places, it usually pays to attend the open-air market (held at least once a week in every town), where interesting items are available at low prices.

Calabria

The craftmanship in Calabria is particularly appealing. In Acri (north of Cosenza on the SS 660), Giovanni Garotto keeps alive the art of building folk guitars and lutes (tel: 0984-953161); for beautiful blankets and table-cloths made from broom, visit To Argalio, Via Pasubio, in Bova Marina (35 km/22 miles east of Reggio Calabria), run by Laura Crisopulli (tel: 0965-761316); in Reggio Calabria, Fabrizio Romeo creates briar pipes for serious collectors (home tel: 0965-57447). Keep an eye open for hand-woven fabric and carpets, whose oriental patterns testify to Calabria's strong Greek, Arabic, Byzantine and Albanian cultural legacies. In Badolato and Tiriolo, in the province of Catanzaro, long and narrow silk shawls with silver and gold embroidery called *vancali* are woven. Tiriolo is also the capital of *pezzare*, attractive fabric mats made from remnants of fabric from industrial production. Longobucco, in the Greek Sila, is known for silk blankets and tapestry; San Giovanni in Fiore, in the Sila Grande, for its Armenian-style carpets; and further south, in Seminara near Palmi, Paolo Condurso makes some of the region's best looking ceramics (Corso Barlam 30, tel: 0966-317123).

Basilicata

In Basilicata, it's worth taking a detour to visit the smaller towns where you can find original hand-made artefacts: the small towns of Avigliano, Forenza, Francavilla sul Sinni, Montalbano Ionico, Nemoli, San Mauro Forte, Terranova di Pollino and Valsinni specialise in wooden handicrafts, while iron work can be found in Lagonegrese, Grassano, Sant'Arcangelo, Trecchina and Tricarico. Grottole, Matera, Melfi and Venosa have a century-old tradition of earthenware production, as does Grottaglie (near Taranto in Apulia), where the prices and huge dimensions of terracotta flower pots and amphorae are hard to beat.

Shopping for Food

Some of the most delicious foods from Southern Italy are made to last and travel well, so they are ideal for bringing home as souvenirs.

Below are some good addresses and more general advice on where to find what, but the list is by no means exhaustive.

Sicily

The world's tastiest almonds and pistachios are used to make several kinds of pastries and sweet treats, called *da riposto* (to conserve in the cupboard): soft macaroons, cookies, *frutta martorana* (marzipan-shaped and decorated like fruit), *pasta reale* (almond paste), and *torrone* (nougat). For almond pastry and *frutta martorana* in Erice there's the famous **Pasticceria Grammatico** (Via Vittorio Emanuele 14 and Via Guarnotte 1, tel: 0923-869390), established by Maria Grammatico who learned her trade while growing up in a local convent.

In Noto, the **Caffè Sicilia** (Corso Vittorio Emanuele 125, tel: 0931-835013), in business since 1892, makes arguably Sicily's best (and at 100,000 lire per kg Italy's most expensive) *torrone*: choose between plain almonds, toasted almonds, pistachios and sesame seeds. Caffè Sicilia also has a selection of rare jams: quince, mulberry, prickly pear and *azzeruoli* (a local variety of wild apple).

Trapani and the Egadi islands offer a variety of tuna products, from various cuts of tuna preseved under olive oil to *ficazza*, a sort of spicy salami.

If you plan on tyring your hand at Sicilian cuisine back home, don't leave without buying a pound or two of capers in salt.

The area around Castelvetrano is known for its excellent extra-virgin olive oil that rivals the best in Italy.

Calabria

A speciality of Calabria is dried figs, which come in all shapes and sizes. Get them plain, strung together, stuffed with orange and almonds or dipped in chocolate and honey at the **Premiata Lavorazione Ficchi Secchi** (Viale Stazione 142, Belmonte Calabro, tel: 0982-47017). Another good address is **Lavorazione Artigianale Fichi Secchi** of Ciccotti Maria Carmela (Via Rupa 15, Paola, tel: 0982-583255).

Top quality dried porcini mushrooms are sold in the Sila and Serre regions.

The Amarelli family has been in the liquorice business for over 250 years. Although their liquorice sweets are available elsewhere in Italy, you'll find more variety than you thought possible on display at their shop, **Liquirizia Amarelli**, in Rossano Calabro (Contrada Amarelli), tel: 0983-511219.

Inexpensive, oven-proof rustic pottery is also produced in Grottaglie.

SICILY

Southern Italy's most sophisticated ceramics come from Sicily. To add lots of character to your dining table, try to create your own unique set of plates and cups by choosing among items sold by the piece rather than buying a full set. The region's most important centres of production are: Collesano (30 km or 19 miles south of Cefalù) for bottles and lamps; Sciacca and Santo Stefano di Camastra (40 km or 25 miles east of Cefalù) for vividly coloured pottery; Caltagirone for tastefully decorated pottery and tiles. G di Blasi in Taormina, Corso Umberto 103, tel: 0942-24671, has them all. Siracusa is famous for hand-made papyrus paper, either plain or painted with Egyptian scenes, but beware of commercially produced items which don't feel silky to the touch – a reliable address is Galleria Bellomo on Via Capodieci 15, tel: 0931-61340.

Palermo

The main shopping area in Palermo is around Piazza Castelnuovo: coming from the railway station, Via Roma and Via Maqueda are lined with boutiques and shops which become increasingly upmarket as you move on to the piazza and nearby Viale della Libertà. The curious should not miss Palermo's outdoor markets – some of the best in Italy – that set up in the Vucciria and Ballarò central neighbourhoods. A flea market is held daily on Via Papireto, near the Cattedrale.

Language

In large cities and tourist centres you will find many people who speak English, French or German. Nevertheless, it is well worth buying a good phrase book or dictionary, but the following will help you get started. Since this glossary is aimed at non-linguists, we have opted for the simplest options rather than the most elegant Italian.

Basic Communication

Yes *Sì*
No *No*
Thank you *Grazie*
Many thanks *Mille grazie/tante grazie/molte grazie*
You're welcome *Prego*
Alright/Okay/That's fine *Va bene*
Please *Per favore* or *per cortesia.*
Excuse me (to get attention) *Scusi* (singular), *Scusate* (plural)
Excuse me (to get through a crowd) *Permesso*
Excuse me (to attract attention, e.g. of a waiter) *Senta!*
Excuse me (sorry) *Mi scusi*
Wait a minute! *Aspetta!*
Could you help me? (formal) *Potrebbe aiutarmi?*
Certainly *Ma certo*
Can I help you? (formal) *Posso aiutarLa?*
Can you show me...? *Può indicarmi...?*
Can you help me? *Può aiutarmi, per cortesia?*
I need ... *Ho bisogno di ...*
I'm lost *Mi sono perso*
I'm sorry *Mi dispiace*
I don't know *Non lo so*
I don't understand *Non capisco*
Do you speak English/French/ German? *Parla inglese/francese/ tedesco?*
Could you speak more slowly, please? *Può parlare piú lentamente, per favore?*
Could you repeat that please? *Può ripetere, per piacere?*
slowly/quietly *piano*
here/there *qui/lá*
What? *Cosa?*
When/why/where? *Quando/perchè/dove?*
Where is the lavatory? *Dov'è il bagno?*

Days and Dates

morning/afternoon/evening *la mattina, il pomeriggio, la sera*
yesterday/today/tomorrow *ieri/oggi/domani*
the day after tomorrow *dopodomani*
now/early/late *adesso/presto/ritardo*
a minute *un minuto*
an hour *un'ora*
half an hour *un mezz'ora*
a day *un giorno*
a week *una settimana*
Monday *lunedì*
Tuesday *martedì*
Wednesday *mercoledì*
Thursday *giovedì*
Friday *venerdì*
Saturday *sabato*
Sunday *domenica*
first *il primo/la prima*
second *il secondo/la seconda*
third *il terzo/la terza*

Greetings

Hello (Good day) *Buon giorno*
Good afternoon/evening *Buona sera*
Good night *Buona notte*
Goodbye *Arrivederci*
Hello/Hi/Goodbye (familiar) *Ciao*
Mr/Mrs/Miss *Signor/Signora/Signorina*
Pleased to meet you (formal) *Piacere di conoscerLa*
I am English/American *Sono inglese/americano*
Irish/Scottish/Welsh *irlandese/scozzese/gallese*
Canadian/Australian *canadese/australiano*
I'm here on holiday *Sono qui in vacanza*
Is it your first trip to Milan/Rome? *É il Suo primo viaggio a Milano/Roma?*
Do you like it here? (formal) *Si trova bene qui?*

Pronunciation and Grammar Tips

Italian speakers claim that pronunciation is straight-forward: you pronounce it as it is written. This is approximately true but there are a couple of important rules for English speakers to bear in mind: *c* before *e* or *i* is pronounced "ch", e.g. *ciao, mi dispiace, la coincidenza. Ch* before *i* or *e* is pronounced as "k", e.g. *la chiesa*. Likewise, *sci* or *sce* are pronounced as in "sheep" or "shed" respectively. *Gn* in Italian is rather like the sound in "onion", while *gl* is softened to resemble the sound in "bullion".

Nouns are either masculine (*il*, plural *i*) or feminine (*la*, plural *le*). Plurals of nouns are most often formed by changing an *o* to an *i* and an *a* to an *e*, e.g. *il panino, i panini; la chiesa, le chiese.*

Words are stressed on the penultimate syllable unless an accent indicates otherwise.

Like many languages, Italian has formal and informal words for "You". In the singular, *Tu* is informal while *Lei* is more polite. Confusingly, in some parts of Italy or in some circumstances, you will also hear *Voi* used as a singular polite form. (In general, *Voi* is reserved for "You" plural, however.) For visitors, it is simplest and most respectful to use the formal form unless invited to do otherwise.

There is, of course, rather more to the language than that, but you can get a surprisingly long way towards making friends by learning how to pronounce a few basic phrases.

How are you (formal/informal)? *Come sta/come stai?*
Fine thanks *Bene, grazie*
See you later *A più tardi*
See you soon *A presto*
Take care *Stia bene*
New acquaintances may ask you:
Do you like Italy/Florence/ Rome/Venice/my city? *Le piace Italia/Firenze/Roma/ Venezia/la mia città?*
I like it a lot (is the correct answer) *Mi piace moltissimo.*
It's wonderful (an alternative answer) *È meravigliosa/favolosa.* (Both responses can be applied to food, beaches, the view, etc.)

Telephone Calls

the area code *il prefisso telefonico*
I'd like to make a reverse charges call *Vorrei fare una telefonata a carico del destinatario*
May I use your telephone, please? *Posso usare il telefono?*
Hello (on the telephone) *Pronto*
My name's *Mi chiamo/Sono*
May I speak to... ? *Posso parlare con...?*
Sorry, he/she isn't in *Mi dispiace, è fuori*
I'll try again later *Riproverò più tardi*
Can I leave a message? *Posso lasciare un messaggio?*
Please tell him I called *Gli dica, per favore, che ho telefonato*
A local call *una telefonata locale*
Can you speak up please? *Può parlare più forte, per favore?*

In the Hotel

Do you have any vacant rooms? *Avete camere libere?*
I have a reservation *Ho fatto una prenotazione*
I'd like... *Vorrei...*
a single/double room (with a double bed) *una camera singola/doppia (con letto matrimoniale)*
a room with twin beds *una camera a due letti*
a room with a bath/shower *una camera con bagno/doccia*
for one night *per una notte*
We have one with a double bed *Ne abbiamo una matrimoniale.*
Could you show me another room please? *Potrebbe mostrarmi un'altra camera?*
How much is it? *Quanto costa?*

Bar Notices

Prezzo al tavolo/in terrazza
Price at a table/terrace (often double what you pay standing at the bar)
Si paga alla cassa **Pay at the cash desk**
Si prende lo scontrino alla cassa **Pay at the cash desk, then take the receipt** (*lo scontrino*) **to the bar to be served.** This is common procedure.
Signori/Uomini **Gentlemen** (lavatories)
Signore/Donne **Ladies** (lavatories)

on the first floor *al primo piano*
Is breakfast included? *É compresa la prima colazione?*
Is everything included? *É tutto compreso?*
half/full board *mezza pensione/ pensione completa*
It's expensive *É caro*
Do you have a room with a balcony/ view of the sea? *C'è una camera con balcone/con vista sul mare?*
Is it a quiet room? *É una stanza tranquilla?*
The room is too hot/cold/ noisy/small *La camera è troppo calda/fredda/rumorosa/piccola*
Can I see the room? *Posso vedere la camera?*
What time does the hotel close? *A che ora chiude l'albergo?*
I'll take it *La prendo*
What time is breakfast? *A che ora è la prima colazione?*
Come in! *Avanti!*
Can I have the bill, please? *Posso avere il conto, per favore.*
Can you call me a taxi please? *Può chiamarmi un taxi, per favore?*
dining room *la sala da pranzo*
key *la chiave*
lift *l'ascensore*
towel *l'asciugamano*
toilet paper *la carta igienica*
pull/push *tirare/spingere*

Eating Out

DRINKS & BAR SNACKS

I'd like... *Vorrei...*
coffee *un caffè* (*espresso*: small,

strong and black)
un cappuccino (with hot, frothy milk)
un caffelatte (like *café au lait*)
un caffè lungo (weak, often served
in a tall glass)
un corretto (laced with alcohol,
usually brandy or grappa)
tea *un tè*
lemon tea *un tè al limone*
herbal tea *una tisana*
hot chocolate *una cioccolata calda*
orange/lemon juice (bottled) *un
succo d'arancia/di limone*
fresh orange/lemon juice *una
spremuta di arancia/di limone*
orangeade *un'aranciata*
water (mineral) *acqua (minerale)*
fizzy/still mineral water *acqua
minerale gasata/naturale*
a glass of mineral water *un
bicchiere di minerale*
with/without ice *con/senza ghiaccio*
red/white wine *vino rosso/bianco*
beer (draught) *una birra (alla spina)*
a gin and tonic *un gin tonic*
a bitter (Vermouth, etc.) *un amaro*
milk *latte*
a (half) litre *un (mezzo) litro*
bottle *una bottiglia*
ice cream *un gelato*
pastry *una pasta*
sandwich *un tramezzino*
roll *un panino*
Anything else? *Desidera
qualcos'altro?*
Cheers *Salute*
Let me pay *Offro io*
That's very kind of you *Grazie,
molto gentile*

Conversion Charts

Metric–Imperial:
1 centimetre = 0.4 inch
1 metre = 3 ft 3 ins
1 kilometre = 0.62 mile
1 gram = 0.04 ounce
1 kilogram = 2.2 pounds
1 litre = 1.76 UK pints
Imperial–Metric:
1 inch = 2.54 centimetres
1 foot = 30 centimetres
1 ounce = 28 grams
1 pound = 0.45 kilogram
1 pint = 0.57 litre
1 UK gallon = 4.55 litres
1 US gallon = 3.78 litres

IN A RESTAURANT

I'd like to book a table *Vorrei
riservare un tavolo*
Have you got a table for... *Avete
un tavolo per ...*
I have a reservation *Ho fatto una
prenotazione*
lunch/supper *il pranzo/la cena*
I'm a vegetarian *Sono
vegetariano/a*
Is there a vegetarian dish? *C'è un
piatto vegetariano?*
May we have the menu? *Ci dà il
menu, per favore?*
wine list *la lista dei vini*
What would you like? *Che cosa
prende?*
What would you recommend? *Che
cosa ci raccomanda?*
home-made *fatto in casa*
**What would you like as a main
course/dessert?** *Che cosa prende
di secondo/di dolce?*
What would you like to drink? *Che
cosa desidera da bere?*
a carafe of red/white wine *una
caraffa di vino rosso/bianco*
fixed price menu *il menu a prezzo
fisso*
the dish of the day *il piatto del giorno*
cover charge *il coperto/pane e
coperto*
That's enough; no more, thanks
Basta (così)
The bill, please *Il conto per favore*
Is service included? *Il servizio è
incluso?*
Where is the lavatory? *Dov'è il bagno?*
Keep the change *Va bene così*
I've enjoyed the meal *Mi è piaciuto
molto*

Menu Decoder

ANTIPASTI
(HORS D'OEUVRES)

antipasto misto **mixed hors d'oeuvres**
(may include cold cuts, cheeses and
roast vegetables – ask, however)
buffet freddo **cold buffet**
caponata **mixed aubergine, olives
and tomatoes**
insalata caprese **tomato and
mozzarella salad**
insalata di mare **seafood salad**
insalata mista/verde **mixed/
green salad**
melanzane alla parmigiana **fried or**

**baked aubergine (with Parmesan
cheese and tomato)**
mortadella/salame **salami**
pancetta **bacon**
peperonata **vegetable stew with
peppers, onions and tomatoes**

PRIMI (FIRST COURSES)

il brodetto **fish soup**
il brodo **consommé**
i crespolini **savoury pancakes**
gli gnocchi **potato dumplings**
la minestra **soup**
il minestrone **thick vegetable soup**
pasta e fagioli **pasta and bean soup**
il prosciutto (cotto/crudo) **ham**
(cooked/cured)
i supplí **rice croquettes**
la zuppa **soup**

SECONDI
(MAIN COURSES)

Typical main courses are fish-,
seafood- or meat-based, with
accompaniments *(contorni)* that
vary greatly from region to region.

La carne (meat)
allo spiedo **on the spit**
arrosto **roast meat**
i ferri **grilled**
al forno **baked**
al girarrosto **spit-roasted**
alla griglia **grilled**
involtini **skewered veal, ham, etc.**
stagionato **hung, well-aged**
stufato **braised, stewed**
ben cotto **well-done** (steak, etc.)
al puntino **medium** (steak, etc.)
al sangue **rare** (steak, etc.)
l'agnello **lamb**
la bresaola **dried salted beef**
la bistecca **steak**
il capriolo/cervo **venison**
il carpaccio **lean beef fillet**
il cinghiale **wild boar**
il coniglio **rabbit**
il controfiletto **sirloin steak**
le cotolette **cutlets**
il fagiano **pheasant**
il fegato **liver**
il filetto **fillet**
la lepre **hare**
il maiale **pork**
il manzo **beef**

l'ossobuco **shin of veal**
la porchetta **roast suckling pig**
il pollo **chicken**
le polpette **meatballs**
il polpettone **meat loaf**
la salsiccia **sausage**
saltimbocca (alla romana) **veal escalopes with ham**
le scaloppine **escalopes**
lo stufato **stew**
il sugo **sauce**
il tacchino **turkey**
il vitello **veal**

Frutti di mare (seafood)

Beware the word "surgelati",
meaning frozen rather than fresh.
affumicato **smoked**
alle brace **charcoal grilled/barbecued**
alla griglia **grilled**
fritto **fried**
ripieno **stuffed**
al vapore **steamed**
le acciughe **anchovies**
l'aragosta **lobster**
il baccalà **dried salted cod**
i bianchetti **whitebait**
il branzino **sea bass**
i calamari **squid**
i calamaretti **baby squid**
la carpa **carp**
i crostacei **shellfish**
le cozze **mussels**
il fritto misto **mixed fried fish**

i gamberi **prawns**
i gamberetti **shrimps**
il granchio **crab**
il merluzzo **cod**
le ostriche **oysters**
il pesce **fish**
il pesce spada **swordfish**
il polipo **octopus**
il risotto di mare **seafood risotto**
le sarde **sardines**
la sogliola **sole**
le seppie **cuttlefish**
la triglia **red mullet**
la trota **trout**
il tonno **tuna**
le vongole **clams**

I legumi/la verdura (vegetables)

a scelta **of your choice**
i contorni **accompaniments**
ripieno **stuffed**
gli asparagi **asparagus**
la bietola **similar to spinach**
il carciofo **artichoke**
le carote **carrots**
i carciofini **artichoke hearts**
il cavolo **cabbage**
la cicoria **chicory**
la cipolla **onion**
i funghi **mushrooms**
i fagioli **beans**
i fagiolini **French (green) beans**
le fave **broad beans**

il finocchio **fennel**
l'indivia **endive/chicory**
l'insalata mista **mixed salad**
l'insalata verde **green salad**
la melanzana **aubergine**
le patate **potatoes**
le patatine fritte **chips/French fries**
i peperoni **peppers**
i piselli **peas**
i pomodori **tomatoes**
le primizie **spring vegetables**
il radicchio **red, slightly bitter lettuce**
la rughetta **rocket**
gli spinaci **spinach**
la verdura **green vegetables**
la zucca **pumpkin/squash**
gli zucchini **courgettes**

I DOLCI (DESSERTS)

al carrello **(desserts) from the trolley**
un semifreddo **semi-frozen dessert (many types)**
la bavarese **mousse**
la cassata **Sicilian ice cream with candied peel**
le frittelle **fritters**
un gelato (di lampone/limone) **(raspberry/lemon) ice cream**
una granita **water ice**
una macedonia di frutta **fruit salad**
il tartufo (nero) **(chocolate) ice cream dessert**

Specialities of Southern Italy

The following is a list of dishes, sauces, drinks and desserts commonly found in Southern Italy:
Alla Puttanesca tomato sauce with garlic, olives, parsley and capers.
Alla Sorrentina tomato sauce with fresh basil and mozzarella.
Bottarga cured fish eggs, grated over spaghetti or salads.
Braciole (brasciole) 'rolls', either meat or aubergine, with various stuffings (not to be confused with the Italian word for 'chops').
Brioche sweet roll sold in bars and gelaterie (ice cream parlours); eaten plain, soaked in iced latte di mandorla (see below) or with an ice-cream filling.
Calzone bread dough filled with vegetables, cheese, sausages, eggs, olives, etc, either al forno

(baked) or fritti (deep-fried). Not to be confused with the folded pizza.
Capocollo spiced cured pork; often cured in red wine and/or smoked.
Caprese tomato salad with mozzarella and basil leaves.
Cavatelli (cavatieddi or cecatelli) tiny wheat dumplings.
Ciambotta (ciambrotta or cianfotta) vegetarian dish prepared in various ways but always featuring peppers, potatoes, aubergines, onion, celery and olives.
Fritto di paranza mixed platter of fried fish and seafood.
Granita home-made ice slush sold in bars and gelaterie; flavours include limone (lemon), caffè, mandorle (almond), fragole (strawberry), gelso (mulberry).
Latte di mandorla almond milk

Minestra maritata "married soup" – made with vegetables and meat,
Pancotto light vegetable soup thickened with stale bread.
Panzanella salad made with stale bread and raw vegetables dressed with olive oil and vinegar; in Campania it's typically made with tomatoes, onion, peppers, garlic, anchovy and olives.
Ragù braised meat; spices and condiments may differ, but the idea is always to use the (meatless) sauce for pasta followed by the meat served as a main course. Not to be confused with Northern Italy's ragù (bolognaise sauce).
Stoccafisso dried cod, prepared in a number of ways, including baked with potatoes and/or other vegetables.

Regional Specialities

Campania

A scapece vegetables or fish prepared *a scapece* are first deep-fried then marinated in vinegar, garlic, herbs and spices.

Babà cake soaked in a light rum syrup served with whipped cream.

Friarielli leafy vegetables of the beet family with a slightly bitter taste.

Impepata di cozze sautéed mussels with parsley, lemon juice and freshly ground black pepper.

Parmigiana di melanzane baked dish made with layers of fried aubergine slices, tomato sauce, mozzarella, basil, parmesan and hard-boiled eggs (optional).

Pesce all'acqua pazza fish poached in 'crazy water' (water flavoured with sautéed onion, white wine and fresh tomatoes).

Sartù thin shell of pilau rice filled with tiny meat balls, sausage, peas, hard-boiled eggs, mozzarella and (optional) chicken liver, baked to a golden crust and served with *ragù*.

Sfogliatella ricotta pastry with a crisp fan-shaped shell filled with ricotta and semolina.

Apulia

Alici arracanate fresh anchovies baked with breadcrumbs, fresh mint and oregano, capers and garlic.

Alici in tortiera as above but with parsley and garlic.

Burrata popular cheese from Andria, like mozzarella with a cream filling.

Carteddate (cartellate) deep-fried, crisp pastry dipped in honey and sprinkled with cinnamon.

Ciceri e tria *tagliatelle* with chickpeas and onion.

Friselle (frisedde, frise) wheat or barley bread topped with fresh tomatoes and basil, or tossed in *panzanella*-style salads.

'Ncapriata (purè di fave e cicoria) dried fava-bean purée served with chicory and a side dish of olive oil.

Orecchiette "little ears"; pasta traditionally served with *cime di rapa* (local name for *friarielli* – see above) and anchovies.

Tiella di riso e cozze baked rice dish with potatoes and mussels.

Basilicata

Gnummerieddi (gnomirelli) baked or grilled lamb (or kid) intestines stuffed with offal, often sprinkled with pecorino cheese.

Lagane e fagioli wide pasta strips with beans, garlic and chilli.

Strascinati (strascenate) Small squares of pasta dressed with tomato sauce and pecorino cheese.

Calabria

Carne 'ncantarata salt-cured pork with tomato sauce and chicory and fennel seeds or honey and spices.

Ferrazzuoli fresh pasta in a meat sauce made with pork, lamb, veal, turkey, onion and tomatoes.

Lagane wide and short eggless *fettuccine* often tossed in bean or chickpea soups, dressed with ricotta and freshly ground black pepper, or boiled in milk and sprinkled with pecorino cheese.

Morseddu (mursiello, suffrittu) pork offal stewed in red wine and tomato sauce, sprinkled with oregano and spread on *pitta (see below)* or bread.

Pesce stocco Calabrian for *stoccafisso (see opposite)*.

Pitta Calabrian for *pizza bianca* (thick plain pizza sprinkled with salt), sold in bakeries.

Pitta 'nchiusa pastry filled with raisins, walnuts, cinnamon and *vino cotto* (reduced wine).

Sagne short for *lasagne; sagne chine* are baked with tiny meat balls, hard-boiled eggs, pecorino cheese, mozzarella, scamorza cheese and, in season, also with artichokes, peas and mushrooms.

Sicily

Arancini deep-fried, crispy balls ('little oranges') of risotto made with meat sauce, cheese and peas.

Cannoli siciliani crisp flaky pastry filled with sweetened ricotta; in Palermo, bits of bitter chocolate and candied fruit are added to the filling.

Caponata fried aubergine slices in a sweet and sour tomato sauce with olives and capers.

Cassata siciliana dessert made with layers of sponge cake, sweet ricotta cream, pieces of bitter chocolate and candied fruit, covered with a pistachio-flavoured almond icing.

Coniglio a 'stimpirata rabbit stew with olives, pine nuts and raisins.

Cuscus(u) Sicilian for couscous, always prepared with fish.

Farsu magru large veal (or beef) roll stuffed with hard-boiled eggs, cheese, *prosciutto* (cured ham), sausage, peas, and pine nuts and raisins (optional), braised in a tomato sauce and served sliced.

Impanata siracusana baked *calzone (see opposite)* stuffed with broccoli, sausage and *primosale* cheese, or with potatoes and onion.

Involtini di pesce spada swordfish rolls filled with breadcrumbs, cheese, capers, olives and parsley, grilled on skewers with onion and bay leaves.

Panelle deep-fried squares of polenta.

Pasta alla Norma short pasta with fried aubergine, tomatoes and a sprinkling of hard ricotta.

Pasta busiata short and thick *macaroni*; in Trapani, it's coated in a pesto made with basil, tomatoes, garlic, olive oil and almonds.

Pasta con le sarde pasta with fresh sardines, wild fennel greens, anchovy paste, capers, onion, pine nuts, raisins and saffron (optional); ground toasted almonds are passed around instead of parmesan.

Pasta 'ncasciata short pasta baked with meat balls, fried aubergine, hard-boiled eggs, peas, salame and *caciocavallo* cheese.

Pesce spada alla ghiotta sword fish steaks poached in a tomato sauce with onion, celery, olives and capers.

Salmoriglio condiment made with olive oil, garlic, lemon juice, parsley and oregano poured on grilled fish.

Sarde a beccafico fresh sardines baked on a bed of bay leaves with breadcrumbs, pine nuts, raisins, anchovies and cinnamon, sprinkled with fresh orange and lemon juice.

Scacciata like *impanata (see above)* but with a basic filling of anchovy and cheese, to which broccoli or other vegetable might be added.

il tiramisù **cold, creamy cheese and coffee liqueur dessert**
la torta **cake/tart**
lo zabaglione **sweet dessert made with eggs and Marsala wine**
la zuppa inglese **trifle**

La frutta (fruit)

le albicocche **apricots**
le arance **oranges**
le banane **bananas**
il cocomero **watermelon**
le ciliegie **cherries**
i fichi **figs**
le fragole **strawberries**
i frutti di bosco **forest fruits**
i lamponi **raspberries**
la mela **apple**
il melone **melon**
la pesca **peach**
la pera **pear**
il pompelmo **grapefruit**
le uve **grapes**

BASIC FOODS

l'aceto **vinegar**
l'aglio **garlic**
il burro **butter**
il formaggio **cheese**
la frittata **omelette**
i grissini **bread sticks**
l'olio **oil**
la marmellata **jam**
il pane **bread**
il parmegiano **parmesan cheese**
il pepe **pepper**
il riso **rice**
il sale **salt**
la senape **mustard**
le uova **eggs**
lo zucchero **sugar**

Sightseeing

aperto/a **open**
chiuso/a **closed**
chiuso per la festa **closed for the festival**
chiuso per ferie **closed for the holidays**
chiuso per restauro **closed for restoration**
Is it possible to see the church? *É possibile visitare la chiesa?*
Entrata/uscita **Entrance/exit**
Where can I find the custodian/sacristan/key? *Dove posso trovare il custode/il sacrestano/la chiave?*

Numbers

1	*Uno*	17	*Diciassette*
2	*Due*	18	*Diciotto*
3	*Tre*	19	*Diciannove*
4	*Quattro*	20	*Venti*
5	*Cinque*	30	*Trenta*
6	*Sei*	40	*Quaranta*
7	*Sette*	50	*Cinquanta*
8	*Otto*	60	*Sessanta*
9	*Nove*	70	*Settanta*
10	*Dieci*	80	*Ottanta*
11	*Undici*	90	*Novanta*
12	*Dodici*	100	*Cento*
13	*Tredici*	200	*Duecento*
14	*Quattordici*	500	*Cinquecento*
15	*Quindici*	1,000	*Mille*
16	*Sedici*	2,000	*Duemila*
		5,000	*Cinquemila*
		50,000	*Cinquantamila*
		1 Million	*Un milione*

At the Shops

What time do you open/close? *A che ora apre/chiude?*
Chiuso per ferie (typical sign)
Closed for the holidays
Tirare/spingere (sign on doors)
Pull/push
Entrance/exit *Entrata/uscita*
Can I help you? *Posso aiutarLa?* (formal)
What would you like? *Che cosa desidera?*
I'm just looking *Sto soltanto guardando*
How much does it cost? *Quant'è, per favore?*
How much is this? *Quanto viene?*
Do you take credit cards? *Accettate carte di credito?*
I'd like... *Vorrei...*
this one/that one *questo/quello*
I'd like that one, please *Vorrei quello lì, per cortesia*
Have you got ...? *Avete ...?*
Can I try it on? *Posso provare?*
the size (for clothes) *la taglia*
What size do you take? *Qual'é a sua taglia?*
the size (for shoes) *il numero*
Is there/do you have ...? *C'è ...?*
Yes, of course *Sì, certo*
No, we don't (there isn't) *Non c'è*
That's too expensive *É troppo caro*
Please write it down for me *Me lo scriva, per favore*

cheap *economico*
Don't you have anything cheaper? *Ha niente che costa di meno?*
It's too small/big *É troppo piccolo/grande*
brown/blue/black *marrone/blu/nero*
green/red/white/yellow *verde/rosso/bianco/giallo*
pink/grey/gold/silver *rosa/grigio/oro/argento*
No thank you, I don't like it *Grazie, ma non è di mio gusto*
I (don't) like it *(Non) mi piace*
I'll take it/I'll leave it *Lo prendo/Lo lascio*
This is faulty. Can I have a replacement/refund? *C'è un difetto. Me lo potrebbe cambiare/rimborsare?*
Anything else? *Altro?*
The cash desk is over there *Si accomodi alla cassa*
Give me some of those *Mi dia alcuni di quelli lì*
a (half) kilo *un (mezzo) chilo*
100 grams *un etto*
200 grams *due etti*
more/less *più/meno*
with/without *con/senza*
a little *un pochino*
That's enough *Basta così*

TYPES OF SHOPS

antique dealer *l'antiquario*
bakery/cake shop *la panetteria/pasticceria*
bank *la banca*
bookshop *la libreria*
boutique/clothes shop *il negozio di moda*
bureau de change *il cambio*
butcher's *la macelleria*
chemist's *la farmacia*
delicatessen *la salumeria*
department store *il grande magazzino*
dry cleaner's *la tintoria*
fishmonger's *la pescheria*
food shop *l'alimentari*
florist *il fioraio*
grocer's *l'alimentari*
greengrocer's *il fruttivendolo*
hairdresser's (women) *il parrucchiere*
ice cream parlour *la gelateria*
jeweller's *il gioielliere*

Tourist Signs

Most regions in Italy have handy signs indicating the key tourist sights in any given area:

Abbazia (Badia) **Abbey**
Basilica **Church**
Belvedere **Viewpoint**
Biblioteca **Library**
Castello **Castle**
Centro storico **Old town/
historic centre**
Chiesa **Church**
Duomo/Cattedrale **Cathedral**
Fiume **River**
Giardino **Garden**

Lago **Lake**
Mercato **Market**
Monastero **Monastery**
Monumenti **Monuments**
Museo **Museum**
Parco **Park**
Pinacoteca **Art gallery**
Ponte **Bridge**
Ruderi **Ruins**
Scavi **Excavations/
archaeological site**
Spiaggia **Beach**
Tempio **Temple**
Torre **Tower**
Ufficio turistico **Tourist office**

leather shop *la pelletteria*
market *il mercato*
newsstand *l'edicola*
post office *l'ufficio postale*
shoe shop *il negozio di scarpe*
stationer's *la cartoleria*
supermarket *il supermercato*
tobacconist *il tabaccaio* (also usually sells travel tickets, stamps, phone cards)
travel agency *l'agenzia di viaggi* (also usually books domestic and international train tickets).

Travelling

airport *l'aeroporto*
arrivals/departures *arrivi/partenze*
boat *la barca*
bus *l'autobus/il pullman*
bus stop *la fermata dell'autobus*
car *la macchina*
connection *la coincidenza*
ferry *il traghetto*
ferry terminal *la stazione marittima*
first/second class *la prima/
seconda classe*
flight *il volo*
left luggage office *il deposito bagagli*
motorway *l'autostrada*
no smoking *vietato fumare*
platform *il binario*
porter *il facchino*
railway station *la stazione dei treni
(ferrovia)*
return ticket *un biglietto di andata
e ritorno*
single ticket *un biglietto di sola
andata*
reservation *prenotazione*

sleeping car *la carrozza letti/
il vagone letto/la cuccetta*
smokers/non-smokers *fumatori/
non-fumatori*
stop *la fermata*
taxi *il taxi*
ticket office *la biglietteria*
train *il treno*

AT THE AIRPORT

I'd like to book a flight to Venice
Vorrei prenotare un volo per Venezia
Are there any seats available? *Ci
sono ancora posti liberi?*
Ha bagagli a mano? **Have you got
any hand luggage?**
I'll take this hand luggage with me
Questo lo tengo come bagaglio a mano
My suitcase has got lost *La mia
valigia è andata persa*
My suitcase has been damaged *La
mia valigia è rovinata*
Il volo è rimandato **The flight has
been delayed**
Il volo è stato cancellato **The flight
has been cancelled**
Posso metterLa sulla lista d'attesa
I can put you on the waiting list

AT THE STATION

Can you help me please? *Mi può
aiutare, per favore?*
Where can I buy tickets? *Dove
posso fare i biglietti?*
at the ticket office/at the counter
alla biglietteria/allo sportello

What time does the train leave?
A che ora parte il treno?
What time does the train arrive?
A che ora arriva il treno?
Can I book a seat? *Posso
prenotare un posto?*
Is this seat free/taken?
É libero/occupato questo posto?
I'm afraid this is my seat *É il mio
posto, mi dispiace*
Deve pagare un supplemento **You'll
have to pay a supplement**
Do I have to change? *Devo
cambiare?*
Where does it stop? *Dove si ferma?*
Bisogna cambiare a Roma **You
need to change in Rome**
**Which platform does the train leave
from?** *Da quale binario parte il treno?*
Il treno parte dal binario uno **The
train leaves from platform one**
**When is the next train/bus/
ferry for Naples?** *Quando parte il
prossimo treno/pullman/
traghetto per Napoli?*
How long does the crossing take?
Quanto dura la traversata?
**What time does the bus leave for
Siena?** *Quando parte l'autobus per
Siena?*
How long will it take to get there?
*Quanto tempo ci vuole per
arrivare?*
Will we arrive on time? *Arriveremo
puntuali?*
Next stop please *La prossima
fermata per favore*

Emergencies

Help! *Aiuto!*
Stop! *Fermate!*
I've had an accident *Ho avuto un
incidente*
Watch out! *Attenzione!*
Call a doctor *Per favore, chiami
un medico*
... an ambulance *... un'ambulanza*
... the police *... la Polizia*
... the fire brigade *... i pompieri*
Where is the telephone? *Dov'è il
telefono?*
Where is the nearest hospital?
Dov'è l'ospedale più vicino?
I would like to report a theft
Vorrei denunciare un furto
**Thank you very much for your
help** *Grazie dell'aiuto*

Road Signs

Accendere le luci in galleria **Lights on in tunnel**	Divieto di passaggio **No entry**	Semaforo **Traffic lights**
Alt **Stop**	Dogana **Customs**	Senso unico **One way street**
Autostrada **Motorway**	Entrata **Entrance**	Sentiero **Footpath**
Attenzione **Caution**	Galleria **Tunnel**	Solo uscita **No entry**
Avanti **Go/walk**	Guasto **Out of order** (e.g. phone box)	Strada interrotta **Road blocked**
Caduta massi **Danger of falling rocks**	Incrocio **Crossroads**	Strada chiusa **Road closed**
Casello **Toll gate**	Limite di velocità **Speed limit**	Strada senza uscita/Vicolo cieco **Dead end**
Dare la precedenza **Give way**	Passaggio a livello **Railway crossing**	Tangenziale **Ring road/bypass**
Deviazione **Diversion**	Parcheggio **Parking**	Traffico di transito **Through traffic**
Divieto di campeggio **No camping allowed**	Pericolo **Danger**	Uscita **Exit**
	Pronto Soccorso **First aid**	Uscita (autocarri) **Exit for lorries**
Divieto di sosta/Sosta vietata **No parking**	Rallentare **Slow down**	Vietato il sorpasso **No overtaking**
	Rimozione forzata **Parked cars will be towed away**	Vietato il transito **No thoroughfare**

Is this the right stop? É la fermata giusta?
Il treno è in ritardo **The train is late**
Can you tell me where to get off? Mi può dire dove devo scendere?

Can you show me where I am on the map? Può indicarmi sulla cartina dove mi trovo?
You're on the wrong road Lei è sulla strada sbagliata

DIRECTIONS

right/left a destra/a sinistra
first left/second right la prima a sinistra/la seconda a destra
Turn to the right/left Gira a destra/sinistra
Go straight on Va sempre diritto
Go straight on until the traffic lights
Va sempre diritto fino al semaforo
Is it far away/nearby? É lontano/vicino?
It's five minutes' walk Cinque minuti a piedi
It's 10 minutes by car Dieci minuti con la macchina
opposite/next to di fronte/accanto a
up/down su/giú
traffic lights il semaforo
junction l'incrocio, il bivio
building il palazzo
Where is ...? Dov'è ...?
Where are ...? Dove sono ...?
Where is the nearest bank/petrol station/bus stop/hotel/garage? Dov'è la banca/la stazione di servizio/la fermata di autobus/l'albergo/ l'officina più vicino/a?
How long does it take to get to ...? Quanto tempo ci vuole per andare a ...?

ON THE ROAD

Where can I rent a car? Dove posso noleggiare una macchina?
Is comprehensive insurance included? É completamente assicurata?
Is it insured for another driver? É assicurata per un altro guidatore?
By what time must I return it? A che ora devo consegnarla?
underground car park il garage sotterraneo
driving licence la patente (di guida)
petrol la benzina
petrol station/garage la stazione di servizio
oil l'olio
Fill it up please Faccia il pieno, per favore
lead free/unleaded/diesel senza piombo/benzina verde/diesel
My car won't start La mia macchina non s'accende
My car has broken down La mia macchina è guasta
How long will it take to repair? Quanto tempo ci vorrà per la riparazione?
Can you check the ...? Può controllare ...?
There's something wrong (with/in the) ... C'è un difetto (nel/nella/nei/nelle) ...

... accelerator l'acceleratore
... brakes i freni
... engine il motore
... exhaust lo scarico/scappamento
... fanbelt la cinghia del ventilatore
... gearbox la scatola del cambio
... headlights le luci
... radiator il radiatore
... spark plugs le candele
... tyre(s) la gomma (le gomme)
... windscreen il parabrezza

Health

Is there a chemist's nearby? C'è una farmacia qui vicino?
Which chemist is open at night? Quale farmacia fa il turno di notte?
I don't feel well Non mi sento bene
I feel ill Sto male/Mi sento male
Where does it hurt? Dove Le fa male?
It hurts here Ho dolore qui
I suffer from ... Soffro di ...
I have a headache Ho mal di testa
I have a sore throat Ho mal di gola
I have a stomach ache Ho mal di pancia
Have you got something for sea sickness? Ha/Avete qualcosa contro il mal di mare?
antiseptic cream la crema antisettica
sunburn scottatura da sole
sunburn cream la crema antisolare
sticking plaster il cerotto
upset stomach pills le pillole per male di stomaco
insect repellent l'insettifugo
mosquitoes le zanzare
wasps le vespe

Further Reading

History and Culture

The Decameron: Giovanni Boccaccio. Some stories are set in Southern Italy. *The Sixth Tale of the Fifth Day* is a raunchy tale set on Ischia.

Easter in Sicily: Antonino Buttitta, Sicilian Tourist Service, Palermo. An introduction to Sicilian festivals.

Thus Spake Bellavista: Luciano da Crescenzo, Picador. Romanticised short tales about Neapolitan life.

Siren Island, Summer Islands, South Wind and **Old Calabria**: Norman Douglas. Atmospheric travel books on Southern Italy.

Grazlella. Alphonse de Lamartine, AC Mclurg, Chicago. The Romantic French poet's affair with a fisherman's daughter on the island of Procida.

History of Sicily: Finley and Mack Smith, Chatto & Windus. The best overall Sicilian history.

The Story of San Michele: Axel Munthe. Story of the Swedish doctor's life and building of his villa on the island.

Christ Stopped at Eboli: Carlo Levi. Story of a year spent in a poverty-stricken community of Southern Italy.

Naples '44: Norman Lewis. Fascinating account of the author's experiences in Naples between 1943–44.

Literature

Volevo i Pantaloni: Lara Cardella, Mondadori. A bizarre account of a young girl's struggles with rural prejudice.

La forma dell'acqua, Il cane di terracotta, Il ladro di merendine, La voce del violino: Andrea Camilleri, Sellerio. These four detective stories written in Sicilian vernacular language have become best-sellers in Italy.

The Last Leopard: A Life of Giuseppe di Lampedusa: David Gilmour, Quartet.

Sicilian Carousel: D.H. Lawrence, Marlowe.

Six Characters in Search of an Author: Luigi Pirandello, Methuen.

The Mask of Apollo: Mary Renault. Sceptre. A novel set in ancient Siracusa.

The Leopard: Giuseppe Tomasi di Lampedusa, Collins.

I Malavoglia (House by the Medlar Tree): Giovanni Verga, Dedalus.

Conversation in Sicily: Elio Vittorini, Quartet.

Kingdom in the South: John Julius Norwich. The Norman period (out of print, available through libraries).

Crime and Society

Men of Honour, the Truth about the Mafia: Giovanni Falcone, Little Brown. Judge Falcone's testament.

Mafia Women: Clare Longrigg, Vintage. A courageous investigation into the changing role of women in Cosa Nostra. Compulsive reading.

Ten Pains of Death: Gavin Maxwell, Alan Sutton. An account of the people the author met while living in Scopello in the 1950s.

Midnight in Sicily: Peter Robb, Panther. Insights on art, food, history, travel and the Mafia.

The Mafia: Clare Sterling, Grafton. Analysis of the Mafia, particularly the "Pizza Connection".

Excellent Cadavers: the Mafia and the death of the first Italian Republic: Alexander Stille, Pantheon Books.

Travel and General

Italian Journey 1786–1788: J.W. Goethe, Penguin. Evocative descriptions of Naples in the 18th century.

Voyage en Sicile: Guy de Maupassant. Edrisi, Palermo.

Journeys to the Underworld: Fiona Pitt-Kethley, Abacus. Bawdy account of the poet's island adventures.

On Persephone's Island: Mary Taylor Simeti, Penguin.

Sicilian Food: Mary Taylor Simeti, Random Century (first published as **Pomp and Sustenance**).

Old Calabria: Norman Douglas, Marlboro Press/Northwestern.

Other Insight Guides

The 550 books and maps published by Insight Guides include comprehensive coverage of Italy.

Insight Guides to *Italy, Florence, Rome, Northern Italy, Tuscany, Venice, Umbria, South Tyrol, Sardinia* and *Sicily*

Thoroughly updated and expanded, the best-selling *Insight Guide: Rome* lifts the lid on Italy's capital.

The new *Insight Guide: Sicily* is packed with up-to-date information, revealing background essays and sumptuous photography.

Recently revamped, with new information and images, *Insight Guide: Tuscany* explores one of Italy's best-loved regions.

Insight Pocket Guides are itinerary-based guides written by on-the-spot authors and accompanied by full-colour pullout maps. Italian titles in the series include *Tuscany, Florence, Milan, Rome, Venice, Sardinia* and *Sicily*.

Insight Pocket Guide: Florence provides tailor-made tours of Italy's art capital. Perfect for a short break. Includes a full-size pull-out map.

Insight Compact Guides are handy on-the-spot reference guides packed with detailed information on sights and museums.

Insight Compact Guide Venice is excellent for practical on-the-spot information.

Also available:
Insight Fleximaps to Florence, Milan, Italian Lakes, Rome, Sicily, Tuscany.
Insight Phrase Book: Italian

ART & PHOTO CREDITS

R. Abbate/Marka 75
AKG London 16/17, 18, 20, 21, 23, 24, 28, 30, 31, 35, 36, 37, 40, 42, 78, 79, 104, 106
V. Arcomano/Marka 233, 242, 260
L. Bota/Marka 95
Yves Breton/Rex Features 112
The Bridgeman Art Library 19, 22, 33, 38, 44, 46, 47, 50, 51, 209T
M. Capovilla/Marka 263
Cephas Picture Library 90, 100, 101, 103
Crabapple Archive 48, 49
M. Cristofori/Marka 86, 96, 110, 144T
D. Donadoni/Marka 94, 176, 253, 261, 284
Nevio Doz/Marka 204
Christer Fredriksson/Bruce Coleman Collection 119
Foto Blitz/Marka 68
Fototeca/Marka 122, 113
Glyn Genin/Apa back cover bottom, 4B, 91, 93, 105, 126/127, 274, 276T, 278, 280, 284T, 285, 286, 286T, 287, 287T, 289, 289T, 290T, 291, 292, 292T, 294T, 297, 298, 298T, 299, 300, 306T, 313, 314, 314T, 316T
F. Giaccone/Marka 114, 123, 276, 279, 301
Herbert Hartmann 1, 8/9, 10/11, 27, 70, 73, 82, 87, 107, 108, 109, 192, 194, 195, 207, 214, 217L/R, 218, 229, 229T, 230, 231, 232T, 235, 251, 270, 271, 272T, 282, 312, 316, 317, 318, 319
John Heseltine back flap bottom, back cover right, 2B, 124/125, 169, 189, 196/197, 198, 200T, 202, 203, 205, 205T, 206, 210, 211, 212L/R, 214T, 215, 219, 220/221, 222, 224T, 225, 226, 228, 236/237, 243, 249, 250R, 252, 254L, 255, 259T
Catherine Karnow 6/7, 52/53, 99, 180L, 182T
Roberto Koch/Rex Features 290
A. Korda/Marka 84, 85

Lyle Lawson 29
G. Mereghetti/Marka 134
Jock Montgomery 34
P. Ongaro/Marka 64, 65, 69, 98, 102
Tony Perrottet 25, 56, 80, 135, 142T, 146, 150, 153, 159, 161, 162, 164, 165, 171, 178, 190T, 213, 320
S. Pitamitz/Marka 143
Press Photo/Rex Features 115
Hans Reinhard/Bruce Coleman Collection 118, 120, 121
Mick Rock/Cephas 101, 100, 103
The Ronald Grant Archive 77
M. Rougemont/Cephas 90
Galen Rowell 39
L. Sechi/Marka 139
Martin Thomas front flap top & bottom, 2/3, 4/5, 14, 57, 58, 59, 60, 61, 81, 92, 97, 111, 130, 144, 166, 170T, 172, 173, 182, 183L, 186, 187, 199, 208, 210T, 227, 258, 259, 296, 302, 307
Topham Picturepoint 41, 43, 45, 66, 67, 76, 117, 156
Bill Wassman 71, 138, 147, 190, 191, 192T, 193, 223, 232, 234, 241, 242T, 244, 245, 246, 250T, 250L, 252T, 254R
Phil Wood/Apa back cover left, back cover centre, spine, 5B, 26, 32, 54/55, 83, 128/129, 140, 141, 141T, 142, 145, 146, 151, 153T, 154, 155, 157, 159T, 160, 160T, 161T, 162T, 163, 167, 168T, 170, 173T, 174, 175, 175T, 177,

178T, 179, 180T, 183R, 184, 201T
Gregory Wrona back flap top, 12/13, 180R, 181, 185, 209, 216, 238, 239, 247, 248, 256, 257, 262, 264/265, 266, 273, 275, 277, 281, 283, 288, 293, 294, 295, 303, 304, 305, 306, 308, 309

Picture Spreads

Pages 62/63: *Top row, left to right:* Glyn Genin/Apa, Bill Wassman, Bill Wassman, Herbert Hartmann. *Centre row:* Marcello d'Ascia, Gregory Wrona. *Bottom row:* Martin Thomas, Magnum, Phil Wood/Apa, Martin Thomas.

Pages 88/89: *Top row, left to right:* Martin Thomas, Martin Thomas, Martin Thomas, Herbert Hartmann. *Centre row:* Martin Thomas, F. Giaccone/Marka. *Bottom row:* D. Donadoni/Marka, P. Ongaro/Marka, Herbert Hartmann, Martin Thomas.

Pages 148/149: *Top row, left to right:* Martin Thomas, Soprintendenza Archeologica di Napoli e Caserta, AKG London, Phil Wood/Apa. *Centre row:* Tony Perrottet, Phil Wood/Apa, Soprintendenza Archeologica di Napoli e Caserta. *Bottom row:* Tony Perrottet, Soprintendenza Archelogica di Napoli e Caserta, Phil Wood/Apa, Martin Thomas.

Pages 310/311: *Top row, left to right:* Ettore Malanca/Rex Features, Letterio Pomara/Rex Features, Ettore Malanca/Rex Features, Glyn Genin/Apa. *Centre row:* Ettore Malanca/Rex Features, Letterio Pomara/Rex Features. *Bottom row:* P. Cipelli/Marka.

INSIGHT GUIDE
SOUTHERN ITALY

Cartographic Editor **Zoë Goodwin**
Production **Linton Donaldson**
Design Consultants
Carlotta Junger, Graham Mitchener
Picture Research **Hilary Genin, Britta Jaschinski, Susannah Stone**

Map Production Phoenix Mapping
© 2002 Apa Publications GmbH & Co.
Verlag KG (Singapore branch)

Index

Numbers in italics refer to photographs

A
B

D
E
F
G
H
I
J
a
b
c
d
e

g
h
i
j
k
l

Insight Guides Website
www.insightguides.com

☀ INSIGHT GUIDES

The world's largest collection of visual travel guides

A range of guides and maps to meet every travel need

Insight Guides

This classic series gives you the complete picture of a destination through expert, well written and informative text and stunning photography. Each book is an ideal background information and travel planner, serves as an on-the-spot companion – and is a superb visual souvenir of a trip. Nearly 200 titles.

Insight Pocket Guides

focus on the best choices for places to see and things to do, picked by our local correspondents. They are ideal for visitors new to a destination. To help readers follow the routes easily, the books contain full-size pull-out maps. 120 titles.

Insight Maps

are designed to complement the guides. They provide full mapping of major cities, regions and countries, and their laminated finish makes them easy to fold and gives them durability. 60 titles.

Insight Compact Guides

are convenient, comprehensive reference books, modestly priced. The text, photographs and maps are all carefully cross-referenced, making the books ideal for on-the-spot use when in a destination. 120 titles.

Different travellers have different needs. Since 1970, Insight Guides has been meeting these needs with a range of practical and stimulating guidebooks and maps